HUMAN RIGHTS
and SOCIAL JUSTICE

*To my mother, for sticking up for me
as a kid. . . . May you rest in peace.*

HUMAN RIGHTS
and SOCIAL JUSTICE

Social Action and Service for the Helping and Health Professions

JOSEPH WRONKA
Springfield College

SAGE Publications

Los Angeles • London • New Delhi • Singapore

For information:

Sage Publications, Inc.
2455 Teller Road
Thousand Oaks, California 91320
E-mail: order@sagepub.com

Sage Publications India Pvt. Ltd.
B 1/I 1 Mohan Cooperative
   Industrial Area
Mathura Road, New Delhi 110 044
India

Sage Publications Ltd.
1 Oliver's Yard
55 City Road
London EC1Y 1SP
United Kingdom

Sage Publications Asia-Pacific
   Pte. Ltd.
33 Pekin Street #02–01
Far East Square
Singapore 048763

Printed in the United States of America

Library of Congress Cataloging-in-Publication Data

Wronka, Joseph, 1948–
Human rights and social justice: Social action and service for the helping and health professions/Joseph Wronka.
   p. cm.
Includes bibliographical references and index.
ISBN 978-1-4129-3872-3 (cloth)
ISBN 978-1-4129-3873-0 (pbk.)
   1. Human services. 2. Human rights. 3. Social justice. I. Title.

HV41.W76 2008
174′.9361—dc22   2007025411

Printed on acid-free paper

08   09   10   11   11   10   9   8   7   6   5   4   3   2   1

Acquiring Editor:	Kassie Graves
Editorial Assistant:	Veronica Novak
Production Editor:	Sarah K. Quesenberry
Copy Editor:	Dorothy Hoffman
Proofreader:	Jenifer Kooiman
Indexer:	Marilyn Augst
Typesetter:	C&M Digitals (P) Ltd.
Cover Designer:	Janet Foulger
Marketing Manager:	Nichole Angress

Contents

List of Tables, Practice Illustrations, and Figures

Tables

Chapter 1

Chapter 2

Chapter 3

Chapter 4

Chapter 5

Figures

Preface

Chapter 1

Chapter 2

Chapter 3

Chapter 4

Chapter 5

Chapter 6

Foreword

*H*uman Rights and Social Justice is an important contribution to social justice theory and practice. Dr. Wronka presents a solid and sound argument that human rights, as proclaimed in 1948 by the United Nations in the Universal Declaration of Human Rights, ought to serve as the foundation for socially just ways of life.

Many crucial notions embedded in the Universal Declaration, such as human dignity, nondiscrimination, meaningful work at living wages, social and economic security throughout all stages of life, and a just global order conducive to the fulfillment of peoples' needs and the actualization of their innate potential, are reminiscent of millennia of teaching in various religious and philosophical traditions that urge us to "love thy neighbor as thyself." Unfortunately, the prevailing global capitalist culture places profits before human needs. People are often treated as mere "factors" of production, working without job security in enterprises whose social utility may be questionable—hardly a situation in which individuals can fully develop. The world's nations seem to disregard many commitments inherent in the Universal Declaration of Human Rights, which is increasingly referred to as "customary international law."

Human rights documents, which ought to be seen in their philosophical and historical contexts as teaching tools, can serve as guiding principles for socially just policies and practices. They can serve as beacons of light urging us to include the rights contained therein in federal and state constitutions, to be implemented through legislative, executive, and judicial mandates. The author's elucidation of core principles of the Universal Declaration of Human Rights and major documents following it, including the International Covenants on Civil and Political and on Economic, Social and Cultural Rights, the Rights of the Child, the Convention on the Elimination of Racial Discrimination, the Convention on the Elimination of Discrimination Against Women, and the Convention Against Torture, is a unique contribution, making such principles more easily accessible.

When discussing social justice-focused initiatives, Wronka stresses the importance of multipronged, interdisciplinary approaches that recognize the interdependency and indivisibility of human rights. One cannot speak of freedoms of expression and assembly without also stressing the importance of economic rights or the right to peace. The pursuit of comprehensive social justice is, inevitably, a long-term project, and one must deal with the ravages of unjust social orders, while simultaneously trying to overcome their roots in the fabric of societies.

The book provides a valuable framework for scholar-activist-practitioners to be conscious of our global interconnectedness, so that efforts to improve the human condition will consistently promote comprehensive human rights for every person, everywhere. Active nonviolence, strength in adversity, and everlasting love are among the ground rules Wronka offers as a basis for implementing multipronged approaches, such as human rights education, public reading of human rights documents, and drafting and implementation of municipal, state, and federal declarations, proclamations, and laws that adhere to human rights principles.

In the tradition of Paulo Freire, the book emphasizes a critical reading of relevant materials. Human rights documents are human creations and, as such, they are not perfect. To view them as simple solutions or "silver bullets" to slay a social order that has taken on destructive aspects is naïve. Rights do have corresponding duties, and issues can become complicated. Governments, too, have duties to provide for just social and international orders conducive to human development.

Aware that only chosen values endure, Wronka places the concept of human rights before his readers, encouraging them to reach their own conclusions, in relation to their own values, hopefully expanding their consciousness beyond narrow parochialisms toward a sense of world citizenship. Only by such reflection and dialogue can people move toward a human rights culture, an awareness of human rights principles on cognitive and feeling levels among growing segments of humankind.

—David G. Gil

Professor of Social Policy
Heller School for Social Policy and Management
Brandeis University

Preface

This book works on the assumption that the idea of human rights is the cornerstone, bedrock if you will, of social justice. This powerful social construct, emerging from the ashes of World War II, can serve as a set of guiding principles to create a human rights culture, a "lived awareness" of human rights principles that can serve as the foundation for a socially just world. Human rights provide the legal mandate to fulfill human need. But such a mandate is fruitless without a general consensus that, indeed, these principles are worth pursuing. Only values that are chosen, not forced, endure. The choice must be not merely intellectual or cognitive, but heart-felt, and the culture will live or die on its own merits.

Humankind has continually tried to implement guiding principles that aspire to infuse virtue and ethics in the world community. The Ten Commandments of Judaism prohibit killing; the Eight Beatitudes of Christianity bless the merciful and those who hunger and thirst for justice; the Five Pillars of Islam emphasize faith, prayer, fasting, pilgrimage, and *zakat*, loosely translated as voluntary charity toward the needy; and the Noble Eightfold Path of Buddhism extols wisdom, ethical conduct, and mental discipline. On a more secular plane, the Humanistic Manifesto laments the inadequacy of the acquisitive profit-motivated system, calling for radical new methods, controls, and motives. From indigenous cultures, the list of Inupiaq Values, drawn up by elders of the Inupiaq Ilitquisiat Movement in the Northwest Arctic, urges humility, responsibility to tribe, and love of children. Or perhaps all we need is the Golden Rule, to "do unto others as you would have done unto you." This book tries not to judge millennia of wisdom, but only to engage in creative dialogue regarding human rights as a means of achieving a socially just world, to which we all aspire.

With the Universal Declaration of Human Rights at its core, and all the values it espouses—human dignity, nondiscrimination, freedom of expression, the right to productive, meaningful, and gainful employment, and duties to our neighbors—human rights ought to help in our struggle for social justice. Although it often reflects millennia of teachings of major spiritual belief systems and philosophical schools of thought, human rights is not the only ethical moral code designed to achieve social justice, but one among many. We need to continually incorporate other value systems, moral codes, spiritual beliefs in creative dialogues about social justice. But in this new millennium, human rights have undoubtedly become an extremely powerful idea that no government would *dare* say it is against. Consequently, in our dialogues we would do well not to relinquish the power of this idea.

Etymological Roots of Social Justice

The word *social* has two plausible Latin roots. *Socius-i* means "friends, allies, partners" and, in another context, "sharing, accompanying, acting together." *Sociare* means "to unite." The word *justice* comes from the Latin *iustus,* meaning "just, equitable, fair, mainly of persons" and, in another context, "what is fitting, what is right." *Social justice,* then, plainly concerns doing right among friends in ways that are equitable and fair and unite us. It is not about helping the poor and defenseless, who need our wonderful knowledge about human rights, social justice, and service!

Ultimately, sharing in the struggle as friends to create a socially just world in which we are all united is our greatest challenge and what this book is about. A person needn't be exclusively an ethicist, doctor of jurisprudence, or a licensed helping or health professional to implement human rights principles. No profession has a monopoly on truth. What is necessary is merely a desire to contribute to the human condition. With my interdisciplinary orientation as a teacher in an advanced generalist practice program in social work, I have written this book primarily for the educated layperson. It appeals to a variety of disciplines, urging interdisciplinary collaboration among areas of study generally concerned with broadly defined helping and health—social work certainly, but also psychology, sociology, anthropology, psychiatry, nursing, medicine, public health, education, law, ethics, religion, philosophy, political science, peace, and indigenous wisdom studies. Concerning Indigenous Peoples, we have much to learn, let alone uncover about their historical global contributions. Often neglected, to say the least, these peoples, with millennia of closeness to the land and nature, may indeed hold the key to our very survival.

Ultimately, this book is phenomenological in that it has a decidedly humanistic flavor and is phenomenon bound, continually seeking to create a socially just world, mindful yet irrespective of our professional point of reference. It is an understatement that the human condition mirrors an inextricable connection not only between mental and physical states, but also with spiritual-existential quests for meaning and within social and environmental contexts. The struggle for social justice constructed on a foundation of human rights therefore requires attunement to such linkages.

Some Personal Experiences

Often, people ask me why I am into human rights. Let me first recount my earliest memory, then describe a few formative experiences. This is to acknowledge the importance of the experiential dimension that gives rise to knowledge in the first place and of socialization processes in value formation. In creating a socially just world, much of our challenge is to transmit values to the children and youth of the world by any nonviolent means necessary. Research consistently demonstrates that once chosen, especially at an early age, values are very difficult to change.

I remember visiting Boston with my family as a child. One of our first tourist sights was Bunker Hill. I walked painstakingly up a hill I didn't much like, with my father walking quickly and vigorously in front of me. When we finally reached the top, I asked him, "Daddy, what is this place?"

Suddenly, this kind person became angry. I did not know why. He said, "This is a place for stupid people." "What do you mean, Daddy?" I asked, a bit taken aback by his unusual, angry tone. He repeated, "This place is for stupid people." Then, pausing and shaking his head a few times, he looked down from the top of the hill and continued: "Imagine that! The Americans were on top of the hill and the English on the bottom. . . . They were sitting ducks. . . . They didn't know anything about the lay of the land and the Americans knew everything about it. . . . They must have taken them by surprise. . . . Imagine that! Killing total strangers: brothers, uncles, sons, fathers, grandfathers, and for what?" He seemed to get really angry then— a person I knew as kind, gentle, and loving—but continued, "And now they have a monument here . . . for what? For killing total strangers!? . . . How could this be? . . . And everyone comes here and thinks how great we as Americans are . . . I don't get it."

To this day, I remember those words well, spoken by a man, who, in World War II, was hospitalized after an unfortunate (or should I say fortunate!) jeep accident, and was unable to fight. Later, his entire platoon died in battle. But most amazing, when I asked my mother my age when we went to Boston, she told me that *I couldn't have been more than 4 years old!* Yet those memories remain with me. There are also other memories, such as my father and uncles of Polish ancestry singing German songs, while I, as a child, struggled to play my accordion. Trying to make sense of my world, I recall asking my father why we sang German songs, if Germany was so mean to Poland during the war. He replied that it was the governments, not the people, who fought against each other and that the German and Polish people loved one another.

And my poor mother! I recall her often being called to school to prevent further antics of perhaps an extremely overactive little boy. Built-in inkwells in large oak desks (I must have been small) in the 1950s and girls' pigtails just didn't mix. Or rather, they mixed very well! They were too tempting for a bored 7-year-old boy, when recess always seemed light-years away. But that may have been the least of my problems. Often shoved to the "crow row," that lineup of poor readers, I recall always scoring low on standardized tests; I could never sit still enough to complete them, especially if distracted by watching a snowfall. Worse, my last name, *Wronka,* in Polish (my father's ethnic heritage) means "crow," and I was taught to think of that bird as special. Only later did I learn I was subtly being socialized to think that black was inferior to white, with the best readers seated in the "dove row." Despite my frustrations and consequent antics, I will never forget the love of my mother in defending me. Yes, she was *my* Human Rights Defender, to whom I dedicate this book.

Then there was my grandfather. I remember well our long walks along the Coney Island beaches in the 1950s. A curious child, I constantly bombarded him with questions, like "Why do they call it a horseshoe crab, Grandpa, when it doesn't look like a horse or a shoe, or even a horseshoe?" Picking up a shell, I would place it to my ear and listen to what I thought were the sounds of the ocean, asking, "Grandpa, can you hear that?" Forcing my shell to his ear, I gave him no choice but to listen. An immigrant from Italy in the 1900s, he died at the age of 97 in the early 1980s. In the middle of my childhood inquisitions, on more than one occasion, he would say in his thick Italian accent, "Giuseppe, because a' you Italian and you're a' skin is more brown than most you always are gonna be getting the shita' work to do. You will always have to put up with the big shots. But keepa' your health . . . you gotta your health, you got everything." As an iceman, he delivered ice for refrigerators and later, he operated elevators in the skyscrapers of New York City at the time of the executions of the socialists Sacco and Vanzetti (now generally considered innocent in the legal community); he often recounted harassment because of his ethnicity. "Hey, wop, so you think they're innocent," he would hear as he ducked snowball after snowball. "*Non capisco l'inglese*" was his response.

As an adolescent in the 1960s, I attended Friday night meetings at the Catholic Worker in Chrystie Street in Manhattan. Those days left a tremendous impression, as if it were only yesterday I heard a roomful of people chanting, "LBJ, LBJ, how many kids can you kill today!" As an adult, in the

1980s, I volunteered as group coordinator for the Fairbanks Chapter of Amnesty International. It was then that I saw the power of human rights as a unifying force. We had adopted a political prisoner, Vladmir Kritsky, arrested for chanting Hare Krishna in Red Square in Moscow. At our town fair, I recall that everyone who read our petition for his release signed it. When we showed a video on torture, the very conservative would engage with the very liberal in extended conversations about the need to eradicate torture worldwide. Whatever it was, this idea of human rights, manifest in various ways from my earliest memory, was a winner, a means of getting us to speak with one another, whatever our orientation, and ultimately create a win-win situation for us all. Human rights are about caring for others, and caring for others is caring for ourselves.

Plan of the Book

Part I: Human Rights as the Bedrock of Social Justice, begins with the basic rationale for this work: Given the horrors of World War II, among other historical atrocities like the transatlantic slave trade and genocide against Indigenous Peoples, no government today dares say it is against human rights. Similarly, the helping and health professions have committed themselves in varying ways to the challenge of incorporating human rights into theory and practice. Chapter 1 provides a basic introduction to the field of human rights, posing fundamental questions about the vulnerability of the human condition, the journey from the mind to the heart, and the reluctance of governments. It also examines core concepts of the Universal Declaration of Human Rights and some of the thornier issues to human rights work, such as the hypocrisy of governments, the sanitization of oppression, and cultural relativity. Despite the complexity of these issues, the chapter concludes that human rights are still a wonderful idea, worth cultivating.

Chapter 2 discusses the human rights triptych, with the Universal Declaration at the center, flanked by its many covenants and declarations (on the right panel) and implementation measures such as human rights reports and world conferences (on the left). Viewing the Universal Declaration as a historical-philosophical compromise among various religious traditions, philosophic schools of thought, and historical epochs, the chapter discusses select writers and documents that appear to be its precursors. Then, it summarizes select core principles of major human rights documents and implementation mechanisms, giving particular attention to human rights reports.

Part II: Building From the Foundation, begins with the introduction in Chapter 3 of practice strategies common to advanced generalist social work and public health practice: the macro (i.e., whole population), mezzo (at-risk), micro (clinical), and research interventions in the helping and health professions that interact in multifaceted ways. It also presents the meta-macro (global) level of intervention and the meta-micro level, which acknowledges the healing power of everyday life. The rest of this chapter concentrates on macro dimensions, emphasizing social justice for every person, everywhere, such as human rights educational exercises, observance of international days, enactment of human rights declarations and bills, promotion of social change through the arts, and other direct nonviolent strategies.

Chapter 4 explores at-risk and clinical interventions in more depth, examining the role human rights documents can play in identifying such groups. It acknowledges that the helping and health professions themselves may be an at-risk group. It also discusses ways to integrate human rights into business activities, administration, social entrepreneurship, and grant writing, activities not uncommon to social justice advocates working at this mezzo level of intervention. In the clinical arena, by way of example, select portions of major documents on the improvement of mental health care and medical ethics are summarized, paying particular attention to the application of human rights principles to the psychotherapeutic relationship, which could have broader implications for other modalities of helping in the health professions.

With emphasis on quantitative and qualitative approaches, Chapter 5 looks at a human rights approach to research-action projects for the helping and health professions. Focusing on the need for a culture of informed consent and attunement to ethics in general, it presents examples in which human rights documents can help define the research problem, expand awareness of human rights violations, and assist in social action and service strategies. Given the importance of writing and speaking in human rights work, the chapter offers helpful suggestions for the aspiring, if not seasoned, human rights defender/social justice advocate.

Chapter 6 largely urges human rights defenders to persist, to always keep smiling, as Charlie Chaplin advised, and to be mindful of the spirit of Crazy Horse, which calls for courage, wisdom, humility, and everlasting love. I distinctly recall my sixth-grade teacher forcing me to redo my book report on a famous person. I had chosen Crazy Horse for my report. Perhaps social justice was in my blood, but for whatever reason, I always felt bad for the Indians in westerns so popular among boys growing up in the 1950s. I remember well the teacher's words: "Who cares about Crazy Horse?" But that spiritual leader's call for the vision and courage of the eagle—a bird notorious for flying into the storm, unafraid of struggle or leaving one's comfort zone—serves very well as a model for social action and service.

At the end of each chapter are Questions for Discussion and Activities/Actions. Please note that these are *my* questions and actions. A major purpose of this book is to elicit questions, expand the dialogue, and broaden the debates by expanding people's consciousness about human rights, not to provide answers. The debates this book stimulates don't have winners and losers; the aim is simply to provide fodder for more thought and action to create a socially just world, where we all can have a decent quality of life. I encourage you, while reading it, to constantly think about your own questions and actions. How do human rights documents compare with major ethical and spiritual belief systems that have inspired you over the years? What would you like to know about and what would you like to do in the name of social justice? Please feel free to share your thoughts, feelings, and ideas for social actions on behalf of social justice with your friends, colleagues, teachers, and, dare I say it, your enemies. As the Dalai Lama said, "My enemy is my teacher."

It goes without saying that as you share your experiences and reflections with friends, colleagues, and classmates, you should always keep in mind what you can do with this information. And when engaging in an action, always reflect on how that action could be improved, what further information you might need to make it more effective. The relationship between thinking and doing is always a strong one.

The back matter includes suggested media resources, a short glossary of terms used throughout this book, and Internet resources. I know it is a bit presumptuous to try to define such terms as *human rights, social justice, social policy,* and *psychotherapy* in one brief glossary. After all, entire encyclopedia entries are devoted to each of these topics. But I risk the criticism, because sometimes things in the final analysis are really that simple. *Social justice,* building on the etymological roots discussed earlier, can easily mean, as the glossary states, "Adherence of a group or society to the principles of the Universal Declaration of Human Rights in theory and in practice." The ideas presented in this book and elsewhere may place this simple understanding in a larger context. The Universal Declaration, for example, has a Eurocentric bias, and the violence that has ravaged Europe for centuries prevents realization of its goals. But some of its crucial notions, such as human dignity, nondiscrimination, and solidarity for all, can be seen as fundamental to social justice.

Life as the Profession

Whereas the book deals mostly with the situation in the United States, readers from other countries may find the material relevant for their own situations. We live in the same world. I discuss gaps between the human rights principles of the Universal Declaration and the U.S. federal and state constitutions, but the book may provide fodder for research-action projects to implement human rights principles in other countries.

This book also uses words like human rights defender, social justice advocate, and social activist interchangeably and at times together (e.g., human rights defender/social justice advocate) to denote anyone who cares about fulfilling human need, thereby improving the human condition. The minutiae concerning any differences in the meanings of these terms is not relevant; the point is that social justice principles constructed from a human rights foundation ought to be implemented. It does not much matter what we call those who do the implementation, as long as it gets done.

Throughout, the book also explores *plausible* etymological roots of words, often from Latin, to open us up to a myriad of basic meanings lost somehow as humanity has supposedly progressed. The etymological roots of the word *profession,* for example, are the Latin words *professio,* meaning in part "acknowledgement, declaration," and *professor,* meaning "authority, expert." Looking more closely, profession may also derive from *fidere,* meaning "to trust." Fully aware of George Bernard Shaw's lament that the professions are a conspiracy against the laity, I perceive professionals as those who have declared themselves authorities in a field and who can be trusted. I use the terms professions and professionals a lot in this book, to bring attention to the trust people tend to place in professionals, etymologically speaking, who have declared themselves authorities. This kind of authority, a perceived expertise, all professionals know should not be abused. Human rights, thus social justice concerns, might assist as guiding principles to enhance the practices of many helping and health professionals indefatigably dedicated to sacrifice and good works. But having a profession is only half of the equation; the other half is that life itself is the profession. The challenge, as the Oracles of Delphi state, is to live a life that adequately responds to these essential questions: who am I; why am I here; where am I going; and how am I going to get there. The struggle for human rights and social justice may move us, however minimally, toward some satisfactory answers.

My hope is that this book will spur social action and service to create a culture in which human rights are lived, not only professionally, but also in our everyday lives, in mind, body, and spirit, to move us toward Martin Luther King, Jr.'s vision of the "Beloved Community". From *communire,* meaning "to fortify, strengthen together," the challenge is to work together, continually encouraging one another in this shared journey toward social justice. Ultimately, what we are asking for is a kind of profound character and cultural transformation allowing human rights to serve as an inspiration. From the Latin *in,* meaning "into," and *spira,* "the base of a column," human rights can be the necessary foundation for asking your own questions, engaging in your own social actions, or as the late Senator Robert Kennedy taught us, not to dream and say why, but to dream and ask why not.

Figure 0.1   Martin Luther King, Jr.'s vision of the Beloved Community and Robert F. Kennedy's Faith in the Power of Our Dreams were a shared belief that a socially just world is possible.

Source: Photograph by Abbie Rowe, National Park Service, in the John F. Kennedy Presidential Library and Museum, Boston.

Acknowledgments

I want to first acknowledge my children, Christopher and Carolyn. Their nearly incessant smiles now turned into occasional concerned glances as teenagers continue to reflect the mystery of life, a kind of spiritual profundity that gives my work the unfathomable significance of improving the quality of life for them and all the world's children. Then there is my sister, Joan, and my brother, John, who continue to be there, providing support as life's losses take their toll. I also want to acknowledge Dr. David G. Gil of Brandeis University's Heller School for Social Policy and Management, formally chair of my doctoral dissertation, but actually my "sounding board," who to this day provides support for my and others' human rights work and continues to respond to my social justice concerns with utmost clarity, thoughtfulness, dedication, wisdom, and the enthusiasm so necessary to persist against the tempests that emerge in the quest for social justice and social change. I always felt that he exemplified the spirit of Crazy Horse, as discussed in this work.

I would also like to acknowledge others committed to social justice who in recent years have provided varied support and opportunities administratively, intellectually, or otherwise. Far be it for me to depart from convention, but as I am often last because my surname begins with "W," and mindful that social justice is a struggle, let me list my acknowledgments in reverse alphabetical order to Dr. Jean Wyld, vice president for Academic Affairs, Springfield College; Ruth Weizenbaum, board member of the Coalition for a Strong United Nations; Xavier Verzat, liaison for the International Fourth World Movement to the United Nations in Geneva; Dr. Francine Vecchiolla, dean of the School of Social Work, Springfield College; Dr. Benjamin Urmston, professor of Peace Studies, Xavier University, Cincinnati; Barrister Majid Tramboo, chair and executive director of the Kashmir Center, Brussels; Rev. Dr. Thomas Tobin, Sacred Heart Church, Tampa, Florida; Dr. Silvia Staub-Bernasconi, director of the Masters in Social Work and Human Rights Program, Center for Postgraduate Studies, Berlin; Thomas Schuyt, Men's Resource Center for Change, Amherst, Massachusetts; Dr. Ann Roy, professor, School of Social Work, Springfield College; Dr. Laura Roskos, board member of the Coalition for a Strong United Nations; Dr. R. K. Nyak, president of the National Institute of Social Work and Social Sciences (NISWASS), Bhubenashwar, Orissa, India; Professor Jennifer Markens, School of Social Work, Springfield College; Dr. Yussef Kly, chair of the International Human Rights Association of American Minorities (IHRAAM), Nanaimo, British Columbia; Lorraine Fortes, administrative secretary, School of Social Work, Springfield College; Professor Ann Drennan (posthumously), School of Social Work, Springfield College; Linda Benoit of Providence Behavioral Health, Springfield, Massachusetts; and Dr. Mulugeta Agonafer, professor, School of Human Services, Springfield College and president of the African and African American Development, Education, Research, and Training Institute (AADERT). I would also like to uniquely thank Noam Chomsky, professor emeritus of MIT, whose time must be at a premium, for his thoughtful responses to my correspondence, an activity I understand he carries on with nearly everyone, a tribute to his continuing commitment.

If, in my weakness, I have failed to recognize you, I ask that you accept my apologies. After all is said and done, we are all plain, simple human beings trying to live the best we can alone and with others. I am no exception.

I also must acknowledge the commitment of so many present and former students, who continue to demonstrate in their own ways a pathological belief in the impossible, so important for human rights and social justice work. Caught in the web of a questionable social order, juggling family, work, schooling, and numerous other responsibilities, they still seem to squeeze out time, however minimal, yet always precious, to make this world a better place for every person, everywhere. Finally, having grown up in a musical family, I am also thankful for "The Beast," my upright piano, a thousand-some-odd pound lovely monstrosity, named by my then very young children. "Nice beast," as I nostalgically remember they would call it as they imaginatively and playfully petted this inanimate object, as children are wont to do. My oasis, my Therapne (read the book!) in struggle, each day it resonates with the music of the Beatles, Beethoven, Bach, Mozart, Liszt, Haydn, Chopin, and others, as if to rubberstamp the concentration camp survivor and philosopher Emmanuel Levinas's notion of the impossibility of death and the possibilities of continuing beauty and spiritual presence of lives well lived, our greatest challenge.

—Joseph Wronka

Amherst, Massachusetts

Publisher's Acknowledgments

Sage Publications gratefully acknowledges the contributions of the following reviewers:

Joel Blau, Stony Brook University
Philip Young P. Hong, Loyola University Chicago
Richard W. Hunter, Portland State University
Francis Powell, Northwestern State University
Marion Wagner, Indiana University

All we ask is that you implement what's on paper.

—Rev. Dr. Martin Luther King, Jr.

PART I

Human Rights as the Bedrock of Social Justice

P art I lays the basic foundation of this book, beginning in Chapter 1 with the rationale for human rights as the bedrock for social justice so that in this millennium no government would dare say it is against human rights. Other sources of human wisdom can also be used to create a socially just world—the Golden Rule, notions of duty to one's neighbor, loving one's enemies, and commitment to nonviolence of major spiritual belief systems. Acknowledging the importance of these perspectives, this book presents only a human rights argument as the foundation for social justice, though indeed, human rights often mirrors much of such wisdom.

Governments' fear of denying the importance of human rights is in large measure an immediate response to the atrocities of World War II, but it also represents a legacy of global repugnance for horrors such as the transatlantic slave trade and genocide against Indigenous Peoples.[1] Chapter 1 focuses on the major document that arose from the ashes of World War II, the Universal Declaration of Human Rights, drafted by a committee chaired by an American—Eleanor Roosevelt. That document, increasingly referred to as customary international law by which all governments must abide, consists of five crucial notions fundamental to social justice concerns: (a) human dignity; (b) nondiscrimination; (c) civil and political freedoms; (d) economic, social, and cultural rights; and (e) rights to solidarity.

Helping and health professionals, also aware of the importance of human rights principles, have in various ways incorporated these rights into their ethics codes and curricula to assist them in socially just practice. Human rights offers a kind of universal language and set of agreements allowing those involved in helping to engage in dialogue. In Chapter 1, I argue that we must have a culture that supports a "lived awareness" of human rights principles in our minds, bodies, and hearts.

Adhering to such principles will not be easy, for creating and maintaining social justice is a struggle. The prototypical character Sisyphus, condemned by the gods to roll a boulder up a hill, only to watch it roll back down, nevertheless reflects the possibility of joy in the struggle. Working for a socially just world will not be easy, and Chapter 1 concludes with some provisos urging social activists not to demonize the "enemy" or give in to narrow definitions of human rights as a pretext for humanitarian intervention.

Chapter 2 presents the human rights triptych. In the center is the Universal Declaration of Human Rights, with the declarations and conventions that flowed from it on the right panel and implementation measures on the left. Viewing human rights as historical-philosophical compromises among the values of various religions, schools of thoughts, and historical epochs, this chapter outlines the history of the human rights concept, from antiquity through the Middle Ages, Renaissance, Age of Enlightenment, and Age of Industrialization and includes select government input into the drafting of the Universal Declaration.

The chapter then discusses important core principles of major international human rights documents, beginning with the United Nations (UN) Charter and moving to documents ratified by the United States, such as the International Covenant on Civil and Political Rights (ICCPR), the International Convention on the Elimination of All Forms of Racial Discrimination (CERD), and the Convention Against Torture (CAT). It also discusses documents the United States has not ratified, such as the International Covenant on Economic, Social and Cultural Rights (ICESCR); the Convention on the Elimination of Discrimination Against Women (CEDAW); the Rights of the Child (CRC); and the Draft Declaration on the Rights of Indigenous Peoples. It is possible to glean from the core principles of these documents those human rights that have relevance for socially just practice in the helping and health professions.

Finally, after a brief discussion of other human rights regimes, such as the Organization of American States, the African Union, and the European Union, Chapter 2 discusses such international implementation measures as

U.S. reports to human rights monitoring committees, with particular attention to health issues (e.g., disparate infant mortality, longevity, and disease rates among various minority groups). It concludes with a discussion of the viability of various world conferences with attendant platforms of actions to ensure government accountability.

Part I provides the necessary knowledge to understand more fully and implement more effectively the levels of intervention possible in the helping and health professions. Part II focuses on human rights documents as guiding principles for social action and service for helping and health professionals; however, by merely relaying the major principles of and debates over human rights and social justice activism, Part I is in itself a social action. Expanding our consciousness about human rights and social justice can potentially change our symbolic thought processes. Questioning how the present social order adheres to human rights principles could lead to socially just and informed action and service to humanity and the world, of which we are all stewards.

Note

1. *Indigenous Peoples* is capitalized consistent with a burgeoning social movement recognizing those who have had an historical presence on lands prior to colonialism and who wish to transmit to future generations their cultural patterns and identities. Whereas extremely rich and diverse patterns exist among roughly 5,000 such groups known more commonly in the United States as Native American or Alaskan Native, the term Indigenous Peoples is used in such statements by indigenous representatives as the 1996 Report of the Working Group: "We, the *Indigenous Peoples* present at the Indigenous Peoples Preparatory Meeting on Saturday, 27 July 1996, at the World Council of Churches, have reached a consensus on the issue of defining *Indigenous Peoples* [italics added]" (Workshop on Data Collection and Dissagregation for Indigenous Peoples, 2004, p. 4). It must also be emphasized that "naming" something is more specific to Western cultures, such as the naming of "tribes," biological nomenclature, and psychiatric diagnoses. So-called tribes, for example, may have been wanderers (not in a pejorative sense), often as a subsistence lifestyle. Indigenous elders may pass on to youth a dynamic knowledge about trees, birds, animals, and explanations for others' behavior. This knowledge would then need to be unlearned in a Western educational system based on more static nomenclature and terminology. Biological taxonomy, for instance, might break down phenomena into smaller parts, from kingdom, phylum, class, order, family, genus, and species, to variety, an atomistic view of the nature of things as emphasized by the Roman Epicurean philosopher Lucretius. An indigenous understanding might look at the world in a more connected sense, as a tree branch bending, indicative of an eagle's respite for an extended period.

1

Introduction

Ideas move people.

—Eleanor Roosevelt

The purpose of this book is to examine how the powerful idea of human rights can help us create a socially just world. Technically, human rights[1] do not exist. However, human needs do, and human rights provide the legal mandate to fulfill human need. As the preface states, this work is based on the assumption that human rights are the cornerstone—the bedrock, if you will—of social justice. Human rights mirror the social-environmental contexts of the time—values that have more or less crystallized into rights, often embedded in constitutions and/or other ethical codes of conduct, serving as guiding principles for a way of life. In turn, these values mirror a complexity of philosophical, psychological, sociological, anthropological, and other variables. As also discussed, social justice is a struggle to unite friends, allies, and partners in fair and equitable practices, as the term's etymological roots suggest. This book is an effort to grasp some of these underlying complexities, which will provide the framework to implement social action and service initiatives for the helping and health professions.

Rationale for This Work

The rationale for this book is simple: Today, no government would *dare* say it is against human rights. This attitude is quite a switch from the Conference of Evian, called in 1938 by the United States in response to the abuses of the Third Reich. The conclusion of that conference was that no nation had the right to interfere with another's domestic affairs. Was the real issue, however, that many countries did not want to bring attention to the mistreatment of their own citizens—for example, public lynchings in the United States; the Soviet Union's *Gulag,* an area roughly the size of France, in which many political prisoners were kept; and European policies of torture in African colonial countries? After another failed attempt at the Bermuda Conference to deal with wartime refugees, one of the worst pogroms in history—the Holocaust—resulted in the deaths of roughly 10 million innocents, mostly Jews but also Roma, homosexuals, Poles, Jehovah's Witnesses, and others inimical to the Fuhrer's policies. Such conferences were late in coming.

Other atrocities the world failed to reckon with included the transatlantic slave trade, the genocide against Indigenous Peoples, and the massacre of the Armenians, to cite a few. But over the years, human rights issues such as apartheid in South Africa, the killing of civilians in China's Tiananmen Square, female genital mutilation in Somalia, and, in the United States, the death penalty, childhood poverty, and allegations of torture at Guantanamo Bay, have become the concerns of almost the entire world community. For whatever reason—perhaps technological innovations such as the airplane, film, or radio—it has become increasingly easier and quicker to "bear witness" to the abuse of human dignity of other members of the human family. Certainly, such violations "shock the conscience of humanity," as asserted in the Preamble of the Universal Declaration of Human Rights, a document emerging from the ashes of World War II that has become the authoritative definition of human rights standards and is increasingly referred to as customary international law (Buergenthal, Sheldon, & Stewart, 2002; *Filartiga v. Pena-Irala,* 1980; Wronka, 1998a, 1998b). It can also be said that the United States is a rights-based culture (Stone, 2001) in part because of its Bill of Rights, a beautiful but limited document describing rights as they are increasingly understood in the global community.

Whenever gross injustice occurs, something perhaps about the human condition moves us to act on behalf of social justice. The French existentialist Gabriel Marcel (1967) saw this impulse as proof of a Supreme Being, of God; for Paul Tillich (2000), it is our ultimate concern; and Carl Jung wrote about the 2-million-year-old person within each of us who is a seat of wisdom (Hannah, 1981). Whatever one calls it, a spiritual profundity in the

Figure 1.1   A 1934 Photo of Inmates at Dachau Concentration Camp[2]
Listening to a Speech by Hitler. Much of the world looked the
other way during the pogroms of the Third Reich, as it did during
the transatlantic slave trade and genocide against Indigenous
Peoples. It is questionable whether such behavior still exists given
situations in Darfur, the Congo, Kashmir, and Palestine, rampant
discrimination, let alone pockets of extreme poverty worldwide,
and nearly a billion people starving each day. The challenge is to
resolve conflicts in direct, nonviolent, and dignified ways in
accordance with human rights. Out of the carnage of World War II,
the social construct of *human rights* was born, an idea late in
coming.

Source: United States Memorial Holocaust Museum.

human condition calls for action and service to humanity in the face of injustice. This book is an attempt to get in touch with this inner spirit and, paradoxically, to move us outward beyond ourselves.

A major repercussion of World War II, therefore, was the belief that such
outrages should *never again* occur. The United Nations (UN)[3] was founded at
the San Francisco Conference on October 25, 1945. Immediately, the UN
formed a committee to draw up a document to which all member nations
could agree. The word *document* comes from the Latin word *docere*, meaning
"to teach," and human rights documents can be excellent teaching tools to
reinforce the lessons learned from the scars of experience (Rosenstock-Huessy,

1969). An American, Eleanor Roosevelt, chaired the drafting committee, and on December 10, 1948, the General Assembly endorsed the Universal Declaration of Human Rights with no dissenting vote. Since then, other international human rights documents have been developed by not only the UN but also other regional international bodies, such as the African Union and the Organization of American States, as well as nongovernmental organizations[4] (NGOs) such as Amnesty International and the International Fourth World Movement. Examples include the Convention on the Elimination of Discrimination Against Women (CEDAW), the Convention on the Elimination of All Forms of Racial Discrimination (CERD), the Convention on the Rights of the Child (CRC), the African Charter on Human and People's Rights (ACHPR), and the Inter-American Convention on Forced Disappearances (IACFD). An important NGO document is the Declaration on the Rights of Human Rights Defenders and Action Plan, drafted in 1998 by human rights activists at the Human Rights Defenders Summit in Paris, commemorating the 50th anniversary of the General Assembly's endorsement of the Universal Declaration of Human Rights.

It is impossible to discuss all these documents and the mandated government reports on compliance with the declarations and conventions. Instead, I will attempt to identify international human rights law, including major aspects of human rights theory and practice that should have relevance to social justice in general and to the helping and health professions in particular. The International Federation of Social Work, for example, has called social work a "human rights profession, having as its basic tenet the intrinsic value of every human being" (United Nations, 1994, p. 3). The National Association of Social Work has forthrightly stated that it "endorses the fundamental principles set forth in the human rights documents of the United Nations . . . [and that] human rights be adopted as a foundation[al] principle upon which all of social work theory and applied knowledge rests" (Falk, 1999, p. 17).

Other professions have also asserted the importance of human rights in various ways. The American Sociological Association (2005) "urges all governments . . . to uphold the spirit and the substance of the articles of the Universal Declaration of Human Rights and other international agreements that [assert] the importance of full equality of all peoples and cultures" (p. 2). The American Psychological Association (2007) emphasizes in the Preamble to its Ethics Code that "psychologists respect and protect civil and human rights" (p. 2). The first principle of medical ethics for the American Medical Association (2007) states, "A physician shall be dedicated to providing competent medical care, with compassion and respect for human dignity and rights" (p. 1). Provision 1.1 of the American Nurses Association Center for Ethics and Human Rights (2007) asserts: "A fundamental principle that underlies all nursing practice is respect for the inherent worth, dignity, and human rights of every individual" (p. 3). The American Public Health Association (2005) states at length,

> Being cognizant that human rights provide the ethical framework for public health practice . . . and recognizing that human rights refers broadly to those rights . . . articulated in the Universal Declaration of Human Rights, and subsequent international, regional, and national agreements, declarations, charters, and laws, including the right to health . . . acknowledging that human rights conventions have implications for health and health professionals . . . further acknowledging that the right to the highest attainable standard of health is one of the fundamental rights of every human being. . . . [We encourage] schools and educational programs in the health professions to make human rights a fundamental component of their curricula. (p. 2)

Other major organizations, such as the American Anthropological Association, the Association of Human Service Professionals, the American Political Science Association, to mention a few, have also made human rights statements. But one thing is clear: The idea of human rights is slowly seeping into the global consciousness. In these days, when time with our families is at a premium, environmental degradation is ever increasing, the threat of nuclear war constantly looms on the horizon, and roughly 40% of the world lives on less than $2 per day, often making mere survival a challenge, implementing human rights principles has an urgency beyond question.

Toward the Creation of a Human Rights Culture

To deal with and ultimately overcome these pressing issues, it is most important that independent scholar-practitioners be willing to commit themselves to creating what is known as a human rights culture. The challenge is to create a socially just world in which one's lived awareness of human rights principles is known not only cognitively but in one's heart—dragged into one's "vital labors," to coin a term from the French philosopher cum child psychologist, Maurice Merleau-Ponty (1967). It is worth emphasizing that only chosen values endure. Such a culture cannot be forced; it must be chosen. Thus, a just society is possible only if everyone on Mother Earth chooses to implement such principles. We must, then, reflect on some preliminary interrelated, yet distinct, points.

The Importance of Words

First, it is important to understand the etymological roots of the words *culture, instrument,* and *education. Culture* comes from the Latin *cultura,* meaning "tilling, cultivation," or the preparation and cultivation of land for crops. Often, this is an arduous task. Certainly, it requires the right tools. Ultimately, given our connectedness, a good tilling of the soil must be done correctly, with no pesticides or artificial fertilizers, to produce more healthful and nourishing crops. The word *instrument,* from the Latin *instrumenta,* means "tool." Fundamentally, this book is about human rights instruments, which mirror the collective wisdom of the world community as understood by UN membership. Thus, the Universal Declaration and its progeny are our educational tools, through which we positively affect the quality of life for all. Quality of life, however, ought not be improved on the global scale only, but also in our local communities and everyday lives.

Human rights principles, if lived correctly, would definitively affect our educational institutions, places of employment, and practice settings when we engage in social action and service to others. The word *education* has two possible etymological roots: the Latin *educere,* meaning "to lead out," and the Latin *educare,* meaning "to grow, nourish, strengthen." Human rights instruments, then, being primarily educational tools, should help expand our consciousness—that is, lead us from the darkness of the cave, in a Platonic sense, to view the world in a new light and nourish us in the process. For example, as I state in *Human Rights and Social Policy in the 21st Century* (Wronka, 1998b),

> United States constitutions concur fundamentally with the Universal Declaration's first generation or negative rights, which consist of civil and political guarantees. There appear minor correspondences, most notably in states' guarantees for education, with the Universal Declaration's second generation or positive rights, which consist of economic, social, and cultural rights. Apart from some states' concerns for duties to the community, there are no correspondences with the Universal Declaration's third generation or solidarity rights, which consist essentially of the right to a just social and international order in which human rights can be realized. (p. 219)

Many Americans think the United States is the best in regard to implementing human rights. However, a reading of federal and state constitutions demonstrates that numerous constitutional guarantees of many fundamental human rights are lacking. The etymological roots presented here therefore lead us to the basic question of how human rights instruments can serve as educational tools to enlighten us and move us toward social action and service. Such a task might be extremely difficult in that certain actions would need to be groundbreaking.

Information as Power

Second, it is necessary to acknowledge that information is power. To say that homelessness or lack of health care shouldn't exist is one thing. But the Universal Declaration, asserting that adequate shelter and health care are human rights, without a doubt serves as an instrument for social change. And the fact that the U.S. Constitution, the supreme law of the land, does not acknowledge these rights is a compelling argument to move public sentiment toward social justice, at least as defined by international human rights standards.

Though, unfortunately, not many people know what their rights are, the launching of the UN World Program for Human Rights Education (HREA, 2005), emphasizing the right to know one's rights, is auspicious. Ms. Roosevelt, "whose FBI file was thicker than a stack of phone books" and on whose head the "KKK put a price" (Public Broadcasting System, 2000), said it well:

> Where, after all, do universal human rights begin? In small places, close to home—so close and so small that they cannot be seen on any maps of the world. Yet, they are the world of the individual person; the neighborhood he lives in; the school or college he attends; the factory, farm or office where he works. Such are the places where every man, woman and child seeks equal justice, equal opportunity, equal dignity without discrimination. Unless these rights have meaning there, they have little meaning anywhere. Without concerned citizen action to uphold them close to home, we shall look in vain for progress in the larger world. (U.S. Department of State Report on Country's Human Rights Practices, 1993, p. xix)

That woman's courageous understanding that human rights education must go beyond the school setting, to raise awareness of its relevance for the workplace and in everyday life, underscores the need for a radical character transformation, from focusing on the local to the global arena. A major question is whether mere cognitive awareness of human rights can help us create meaningful and long-lasting social change throughout the world.

The Vulnerability of the Human Condition

A third point is the vulnerability of the human condition. Is the study of concepts such as human rights culture, lived awareness, and character transformation merely a privilege of the middle and upper classes? Are these terms, at worst, just elitist, helping-profession babble? Perhaps. In a world where nearly 1 billion people living on the verge of starvation is a daily fact of life, who has the time for what the philosopher Jeremy Bentham called "nonsense on stilts" (cited in Wronka, 1998b, p. 194)? Was our former ambassador to the United Nations, the late Jeanne Kirkpatrick, correct when she referred to the Universal Declaration as a "letter to Santa Claus . . . Neither nature, experience, nor probability informs these lists of 'entitlements,' which are subject to no constraints except those of the mind and appetite of their authors" (Laqueur & Rubin, 1990, p. 364)?

Human rights is a powerful idea, and it is a bizarre stereotype that those living in extreme poverty are too tired to fight and advocate for social justice (Lappe, Collins, & Rosset, 1998). Human rights can assist anyone—the very rich, the very poor—in establishing the framework necessary to create a socially just world. The debate must focus on human rights for all, and we must believe that such a world is possible. It is unfortunate that human rights discourse sometimes "collapses" into elitist language, but perhaps that only mirrors human vulnerability, if not our frailty. Although Eleanor Roosevelt wanted a document, not for the doctors of jurisprudence but rather for the intelligent layperson, the Universal Declaration itself occasionally lapses into elitist and legalistic language. This text, written with the same audience in mind, is not free from similarly unwieldy vocabulary. Ultimately, however, human rights and social justice are simple concepts to grasp; their basic thrust is common human decency. We must constantly ask if we are really speaking *to* or *at* others rather than *with* them as partners in struggle.

Reluctance of Governments and Other Powerful Entities

In moving toward this human rights culture, the foundation of social justice, it is important to keep in mind the general reluctance of governments, which may act collusively with other powerful entities. As a general rule, governments tend to be reluctant to provide for the human rights of their citizens without massive public support of such rights. Former Supreme Court Justice Louis Brandeis (Riak, 2001) may be right in calling government our omnipresent teacher; however, in contemporary times other powerful entities, such as corporations—some with growing concentration of wealth and corresponding power greater than that of governments—the media, and the military, seem to have an even more profound influence on values formation. This new millennium has also witnessed a growth in international agreements, such as the North Atlantic Free Trade Agreement (NAFTA), and the power of international players such as the World Bank (WB), the

International Monetary Fund (IMF), and the World Trade Organization (WTO), who may also collude with governments.

Citing the growing chasm between the richest and poorest people on the planet as today's most serious universal problem, former President Jimmy Carter, in accepting the Nobel Peace Prize, stated that "citizens of the ten wealthiest countries are now seventy-five times richer than those who live in the ten poorest ones, and the separation is increasing every year not only between nations but also within them" (Carter, 2002, p. 18). Indeed, the ratio of wealth between the world's poorest and richest nations is 1 to 103 (UN Development Program, 2005). Furthermore, Lappe and colleagues reported in 1998 that General Motors sales were greater than the gross national product of 169 countries (1998), and by the end of the last millennium, Microsoft market capitalization had even passed that of General Motors (Brown, Flavin, & French, 1999). Such economic disparity also exists within countries like the United States, where chief executive pay is approximately 535 times the average employee's salary and 1% of the population controls 47% of the net financial wealth (Morgenson, 2004). In addition, the United States, with the highest per capita income in the world (Kivel, 2004), dominates the world film industry (UN Development Program, 2005). The media can influence both young and old to uncritically adopt the consumer lifestyle of the rich and famous, especially those of the United States, which has become a primary model for global policy making (Steiner & Alston, 2000). Furthermore, governments spend at least $1 trillion on the military per year, with U.S. spending making up nearly half that amount (*World Almanac,* 2005). The international agreements and players mentioned earlier, who are greatly influenced by governments and corporations, often encourage privatization in exchange for loans given ostensibly to develop infrastructure, such as hospitals and schools.

Numerous questions arise: Where might our social actions be most helpful? How can or should activists work collaboratively, rather than confrontationally, with governments, corporations, the media, the military, and other international players? A most basic question is how to speak "truth," as mirrored in human rights instruments, to the powers that be? Or are those in power already aware of truth, and must our social actions be to unveil truth together?

The Importance of Socialization

Fifth, one must acknowledge the importance of socialization. Only about 10% of Americans have ever heard of the Universal Declaration of Human Rights, putting into serious question the values we transmit to our youth.

Nearly every American child knows the story of Abraham Lincoln's austere beginnings, from birth in a log cabin to later become president. Children also know about George Washington's honesty, telling the truth—that he cut down the cherry tree. The issue is not whether George may have been hungry, put in harm's way by a falling tree, or even why he had access to an axe. Subtly, society teaches that people can rise to the top by telling the truth, but putting children in harm's way is of secondary importance.

Our educational system may also emphasize basic human selfishness, labeling theorists who advocate socially just societies as utopian and unrealistic. But numerous pockets of communities have believed in the value of sharing—kibbutzim, religious communities, and traditional indigenous communities, for instance. In addition, the mirroring of cultural values in schools and the media can teach children to give higher priority to having than to being, which the French existentialist Gabriel Marcel (1965) saw as a growing social problem. Indeed, only a handful of countries allow advertising on children's programming, on grounds that it is unethical to persuade children to consume products of dubious value that fail to fulfill their promises and also lead to obesity and the onset of early diabetes.

The psychiatrist R. D. Laing's (1962) notion of hypnotization to the *lebenswelt* (everyday life) may be relevant here. The helping and health professions come to accept such givens as private or government programs to help the poor, when they should be working to eliminate the poor who need help in the first place. Or they may accept managed care based on corporate models that easily make us dulled, if not blinded, to more amorphous struggles— for example, against an educational system not attuned to building a socially just world on the foundation of human rights. It is only too easy to stay within our comfort zones, making Hannah Arendt's famous phrase "the banality of evil" chillingly true, and bleaker still for those in professions meant to help others.

Moving From the Mind to the Heart to the Body

Finally, to implement human rights principles, we need to make a journey from the mind, to the heart, to the body. Knowing these rights is no guarantee that we learn them, in the true sense of learning, which ought to lead us to reconsider fundamental assumptions of our lives and entail major experiential transformation (Colaizzi, 1978). Acquiring knowledge is infinitely inferior to developing a critical attitude (Freire, 2004); people must come to their own realization of the utility of a particular concept in their lives and the lives of others. It may be possible to teach clients that living well is the best revenge, but unless that concept is lived—dragged into the everyday life—it really has no meaning.

The same can be said for human rights principles. Learning that health care is a human right, then spitting this knowledge out on a multiple-choice exam is a questionable exercise. To create a society that takes such a right seriously and acknowledges its interdependence with other rights, however—that is something! Independent experts have been appointed by government leaders to develop human rights instruments from their collective wisdom, and our struggle is translating this knowledge into lived realities that will enhance the quality of life for everyone. Table 1.1 concisely summarizes these issues, with select corresponding questions they might pose.

Next, we examine some of these human rights in greater depth.

Table 1.1   Preliminary Issues to Consider While Moving Toward the Creation of a Human Rights Culture*

Issue	*Select Question(s) Posed*
The importance of words: etymologies of *culture* as "tilling," *instrument* as "tool," and *education* as "leading out" and "strengthening"	How can human rights instruments effectively serve as groundbreaking tools to lead us out of the darkness of the cave?
Information is power	Does a mere cognitive awareness of human rights lead us to a socially just world? How can such information be powerful, moving people in positive directions?
Vulnerability of the human condition	How can people speak *with* rather than *at* or *to* others as partners in struggle and do so irrespective of class or other differences?
Reluctance of governments and other powerful entities	Should energies be directed at or with governments, corporations, the media, the military, and/or international players such as the IMF and WTO? How can social activists engage collaboratively, rather than confrontationally, with power? Should one speak truth to power, or are the powerful already aware of truth?
Importance of socialization	How can the educational system and other socializing entities be responsive to issues pertaining to social justice? Does the educational system socialize children, adolescents, and adults into accepting selfishness and violence as a given? Is cooperation fundamental to the human condition?

(Continued)

(Continued)

Issue	Select Question(s) Posed
Moving from the mind to the heart to the body	Rather than blindly "banking" knowledge of human rights and social justice, how can we have a critical, yet respectful attitude toward other sets of guiding principles that will positively affect our everyday lives from the local to the global?

*This list is meant to be merely selective. Readers may have their own issues and reflections that they wish to entertain in addition to these.

Five Core Notions of Human Rights

To better appreciate the rest of this work, readers may wish to at least skim the Universal Declaration and select portions of other human rights documents, in particular, CEDAW, CERD, and CRC (see earlier text), which can be found in the appendices. For the time being, please pay particular attention to Articles 22 through 30 of the Universal Declaration, which state, in part:

> Everyone has the right to rest and leisure, including reasonable limitation of working hours. . . . (Article 24)

> Everyone has the right to a standard of living adequate for the health and well-being of himself[5] and his family, including food, clothing, housing, and medical care and necessary social services, and the right to security in the event of unemployment, sickness, disability, widowhood, old age or other lack of livelihood in circumstances beyond his control. . . . Motherhood and childhood are entitled to special care and assistance. All children, whether born in or out of wedlock, shall enjoy the same social protection. (Article 25)

Do these articles sound like the U.S. situation? Roughly 47 million people here lack health insurance, 3 million people are homeless, and 10 million working-age adults are unemployed. Not very socially just, is it? Perhaps the powerful idea of human rights might assist us in dealing with these and other issues.

In brief, then, the Universal Declaration of Human Rights consists of five core notions.[6] I emphasize the word *core*, from the French *le coeur*, meaning "heart." Let us never lose sight that our ultimate quest is a change of heart.

Human Dignity

The first notion is human dignity; Article 1 states in part that "all humans are born free and equal in dignity and rights." This notion appears to emanate from the Judeo-Christian-Islamic tradition, indicative of the preponderance of Western and a few Islamic nations involved in drafting the declaration. Genesis 1:27 states, "God created man in His image," which according to Talmudic scholar Ben Azzai embodies the ultimate and supreme worth of the individual. Christians also accept the sanctity and dignity of the human person proclaimed in Genesis. Similarly, the holy Koran asserts in Sura, "Verily, we have honored every human being." According to Muslim scholar Riffat Hassan (1982), the Koran upholds the sanctity and absolute value of human life.

Nondiscrimination

If all humans are worthy of dignity, we must have nondiscrimination, the second crucial notion. That is, to have rights, the only criterion is that a person is a human being. Consequently, one must act justly toward others "without distinction of any kind, such as race, color, sex, language, religions, political or other opinion, national or social origin, property, birth or other status," as Article 2 asserts, in part. Although a person's humanity is obvious, history is replete with attempts to reject it. The Supreme Court's *Dred Scott* decision ruled that an African American man was "property." The early European settlers in the Americas often debated whether the indigenous people were humans or animals (Zinn, 1990). To this day, the challenge of the helping and health professions is to view humans as human, not as interesting cases, diagnoses, clients, or research subjects, and to create a socially just world where people have rights, irrespective of any peripheral or superficial characteristic that may lead to discrimination.

Discrimination also occurs on the basis of such intangibles as distance and time. For example, the bombers in World War II dropped shells less discriminately when at higher altitudes. Thus, the less visible the results, the more justifiable the horrors of such actions may appear. Similarly, keeping one's distance from others, and spending less time with them, may lead to forgetting their humanity, resulting in their objectification, if not oppression. Although many of us may use diagnostic terms to describe clients, such as having a personality disorder, we resent others referring to our own family members that way because we are physically closer to them and spend more time with them.

Civil and Political Rights

The third core notion is civil and political rights—that is, the liberty to pursue this quest for human dignity free from discrimination and the abuse of political authority. This right is outlined roughly in Articles 3 to 21, which state in part: "Everyone has the right to freedom of thought, conscience and religion" (Article 18), and "Everyone has the right to freedom of opinion and expression" (Article 19). Also called first-generation or negative rights, they essentially stress the need for government *not* to interfere with the basic human need to express oneself verbally or in writing or to practice one's religion. They arose primarily in response to the abuse of tyrannical monarchs in the 17th and 18th centuries and resulted in documents such as the U.S. Declaration of Independence and the U.S. Constitution's Bill of Rights. The major influences behind these documents were the rights expressed by Enlightenment theorists like John Locke to life, liberty, property, and freedom from arbitrary rule and by Thomas Jefferson to the pursuit of happiness.

Economic, Social, and Cultural Rights

The fourth crucial notion is economic, social, and cultural rights, which are second-generation or positive rights. This idea asserts that government provides for basic necessities to ensure an existence worthy of human dignity. Articles 22 through 27 delineate these rights, an example of which was stated earlier in Article 25. Such rights include, but are not limited to, food, health care, education, meaningful and gainful employment, special protections for mothers and children, security in old age, participation in a community's cultural life, and rest and leisure. Economic and social rights arose predominantly in reaction to the abuses of industrialization that became increasingly evident in the 19th century, resulting in massive poverty amid affluence. The Soviet Constitution of 1936 exemplifies these rights. Theorists such as Gracchus Babeuf, Thomas Paine, and Karl Marx were influential in the development of positive rights. For example, in the *Rights of Man,* Thomas Paine advocates rather eloquently for the prevention of poverty so that

> the hearts of the humane will not be shocked by rag[g]ed and hungry children, and persons of seventy or eighty years of age, begging for bread. The dying poor will not be dragged from place to place to breath[e] their last. [And] widows will have maintenance for their children and not be carted away, on the deaths of their husbands, like culprits and criminals. (Fast, 1946, pp. 255–256)

Solidarity Rights

The last crucial notion of the Universal Declaration is solidarity rights in Articles 28 through 30. Although these rights are still in the process of conceptual elaboration, they are the result of the failure of domestic sovereignty, most notably during the final years of the 20th century, to deal with global issues such as pollution, war, development, self-determination, the oppression of indigenous and other peoples, natural and man-made disasters, and the emergence of nationalism in Third World countries that is also concerned with global redistribution of power in international forums, economic prosperity, and other important values (Claude & Weston, 1992). These articles emphasize the fundamental human right to intergovernmental cooperation and the notion that for every right there are corresponding duties and limitations. Thus, international cooperation is necessary for global food distribution, but people also have the duty not to overconsume.

Although these solidarity rights are not explicitly stated in the Universal Declaration, its emphasis, for example, on the right "to a social and international order in which rights and freedoms set forth in the Declaration can be fully realized" (Article 28) sustains them. Some examples are rights to self-determination, cultural diversity, a clean environment, peace, development, international humanitarian disaster relief, international distributive justice and preservation of the common and cultural heritages of humanity, such as the seas, space, cultural and religious monuments, and heritages in general. In *Project for a Perpetual Peace,* the noted philosopher Immanuel Kant recognizes the hypocrisy of nations and asserts that moral actions must come from a profound sense of duty (Curtis, 1981), paving the way for including the idea of solidarity in human rights discussions. Although which human rights are more important is controversial, solidarity rights are generally less well known than the other sets of rights. They are, however, extremely significant; the right to peace, for example, is becoming increasingly abrogated, with expanding wars in the Middle East as of this writing and military spending at the dawn of this millennium reaching record levels (Renner, 2005). Furthermore, the average number of natural disasters in the world in the last 30 years has skyrocketed from approximately 200 in 1975 to 1,700 disasters in 2001 (Montanari, 2005), creating greater urgency not only to provide for victims of hurricanes, earthquakes, and tsunamis but to prevent the escalation of such disasters by reducing greenhouse emissions, educating others about adequate safety procedures, and developing adequate warning systems.

Roughly 20% of the global population controls 86% of the world's gross product (Kivel, 2004), often through entities other than governments. Former President Jimmy Carter, in accepting the Nobel Peace Prize in 2002, articulated well the urgency of this problem:

> The most serious and universal problem [today] is the growing chasm between the richest and poorest people on earth. . . . The results of this disparity are root causes of most of the world's unresolved problems, including starvation, illiteracy, environmental degradation, violent conflict, and unnecessary illnesses that range from Guinea worm to HIV/AIDS. (Carter, 2002, pp. 18–19)

The Interdependence and Indivisibility of Rights

It is important to recognize that human rights are interdependent and indivisible. Hence, freedom of expression, religion, and access to information (civil and political rights) are of questionable value if people lack education, gainful employment, health care, food, and shelter (economic, social, and cultural rights) or live in a polluted environment and a world at war (solidarity rights). The right to food—meaning that it is available at a reasonable cost, nutritious, easily accessible, and culturally appropriate (Eide, 1987)— is also linked to global climate change, which tends to reduce food production by producing more droughts, desertification, and paradoxically excessive rainfall in some areas (Gore, 2006; Montanari, 2005).

Take another right—health care. Good quality health care is possible only if there are educated people to provide it, thus requiring a society committed to the right to education. Also needed is a just social order to pay for it, perhaps through progressive taxation. Simply stated, each person must pay her or his share for the "general welfare," an often neglected phrase in the Preamble to the U.S. Constitution. Meaningful (i.e., socially useful) and gainful (i.e., reasonably paid) employment would also be necessary to help alleviate the social and economic strains of raising a family that could result in domestic violence (Gil, 1992). Children often experience the residual effects of the low wages of their parents, who are under constant pressure to provide for their families and still have security in their old age—another human right. Children might be hard pressed to learn in school or even take part in the business of childhood (i.e., play) because they are worrying about family problems. Such problems could be alleviated by better social protections, many of which are covered in the Universal Declaration.

When we speak of one human right, therefore, we must find ways to integrate others. The United States has argued, however, for the priority of civil and political rights. This attitude is perhaps best exemplified by former U.S. Ambassador to the United Nations Morris B. Abram, who wrote in part that "development is not a right. . . . [and] little more than a dangerous incitement because it implies that fundamental freedoms cannot be fully realized until all people enjoy the right to development" (Abram, 1991, p. 1). Part of our challenge, therefore, is to create an open dialogue on the importance of developing a just social and international order, which would have implications for all human rights.

Before viewing these notions, as summarized in Table 1.2, it may also be necessary to acknowledge that these notions roughly correspond to those expressed in President Franklin Roosevelt's (1941) *Four Freedoms* speech:

In the future days, which we seek to make secure, we look forward to a world founded upon four essential human freedoms. [Human dignity and nondiscrimination are implicit.]

The first is the freedom of speech and expression everywhere in the world [negative freedom].

The second is the freedom of every person to worship God in his own way everywhere in the world [negative freedom].

The third is the freedom from want, which translated into world terms, means economic understandings, which will secure to every nation a healthy peacetime life for its inhabitants everywhere in the world [positive freedom].

The fourth is freedom from fear—which, translated into world terms, means a world-wide reduction of armaments to such a point and in such a thorough fashion that no nation will be in a position to commit an act of physical aggression against any neighbor—anywhere in the world [solidarity right].

Norman Rockwell immortalized these words in his *Four Freedoms* paintings reprinted on page 22 with permission.

The challenge, then, is to provide all human rights for all people—for "every person, everywhere" as proclaimed on a banner over Amherst Common in Massachusetts during Human Rights week, the week of December 10, when the General Assembly signed the Universal Declaration. The banner also urged the public to take part in the annual reading of the Universal Declaration of Human Rights followed by a candlelight vigil, a macro social action strategy to move toward the creation of a human rights culture.

Finally, let it be said that the case of *Filartiga v. Pena-Irala* (1980), which ruled in a U.S. federal court against a torturer for an act committed in Paraguay, was a major breakthrough. Justices Feinberg, Kaufman, and Kearse of the Second Circuit ruled that

official torture is now prohibited by the law of nations. This prohibition is clear and unambiguous and admits no distinction between treatment of aliens and citizens. . . . This prohibition has become part *of customary international law, as evidenced and defined by the Universal Declaration of Human Rights.* [italics added] (630 F.2d 884–885)

In brief, Mr. Pena-Irala, the alleged torturer and police officer, had tried to settle in Brooklyn, New York, as an illegal alien, while Dr. Joel Filartiga was living in Los Angeles. On learning of Pena-Irala's whereabouts, Filartiga

Figure 1.2 Norman Rockwell's *Four Freedoms* Paintings (clockwise from the upper left): "Freedom From Fear," "Freedom From Want," Freedom of Worship," and "Freedom of Speech". These corresponded to Roosevelt's Four Freedoms, which became substantive principles in the Universal Declaration of Human Rights.

Source: Printed by permission of the Norman Rockwell Family Agency. Copyright © 1943 the Norman Rockwell Family Entities.

Table 1.2   Five Core Notions of the Universal Declaration of Human Rights*

Articles of the Universal Declaration	*Crucial Notion*	*Examples*	*Philosophic-Historical Legacy*
Article 1	Human dignity	Equality, freedom, the duty to act in a spirit of brotherhood and sisterhood	Judaic-Christian-Islamic tradition; the U.S. Declaration of Independence
Article 2	Nondiscrimination	Based on race, color, sex, language, religion, political opinion, national or social origin, property, birth, or other status	Judaic-Christian-Islamic tradition; the U.S. Declaration of Independence
Articles 3–21	Civil and political (or first-generation or negative) rights	Freedoms of thought, religion, expression in oral and written form; access to information; rights to privacy and a fair and public hearing	The U.S. Constitution's Bill of Rights; Roosevelt's Four Freedoms speech
Articles 22–27	Economic, social, and cultural (or second-generation or positive) rights	Rights to meaningful and gainful employment, rest and leisure, health care, food, housing, education, participation in the cultural life of the community; special care and assistance for motherhood and childhood	The Soviet Constitution of 1923; Roosevelt's Four Freedoms speech
Articles 28–30	Solidarity** (or third-generation) rights	Rights to a just social and international order, self-determination, peace, preservation of the common and cultural heritages of humanity, development, humanitarian disaster relief, and international distributive justice	The failure of domestic sovereignty, a reawakening of Third World nationalism, and increasing global maldistributions of wealth; Roosevelt's Four Freedoms speech

*The Universal Declaration is increasingly referred to as *customary international law,* by which all countries must abide. All rights are interdependent and indivisible.

**Solidarity rights are still in the process of conceptual elaboration and get their sustenance from Articles 28 to 30, which emphasize the right to a just social and international order and that rights have corresponding duties and limitations.

brought him to a U.S. court for the torture and death of his son, Joelita, then 17 years old and held in prison in Pena-Irala's custody. The federal court ruled against Pena-Irala. Although he left the United States before damages, ranging in the millions, were collected, this case is very symbolic. The Universal Declaration thus, as customary international law, means that all nations must abide by its principles. What has become known as the Filartiga Principle has never been overturned. An impressive body of law has evolved from that decision, with the hope that not only torture but other human rights—such as health care, security in old age, and special protections for motherhood and children—will, with support of a growing public consensus, become legally mandated (Wronka, 1998a, 1998b, 2004).

The conclusion must be "Human rights for every person, everywhere." Socialized to think global social justice is merely a utopian ideal, our initial reaction might be that it is impossible. But who would have thought that with the invention of gunpowder, submarines, jets, and rockets would someday have the firepower they now have—as much as all the munitions released in World War II? Presently, the entire human race can literally be destroyed in a matter of days, if that long. If nightmares can become reality, why not dreams of social justice? There is no reason humanity cannot share visions of peace at the table of brotherhood and sisterhood, becoming a truly Beloved Community, as often proclaimed by the late Rev. Dr. Martin Luther King, Jr.

Social Justice as Struggle

Human rights documents, then, are tools that can help create a human rights culture, which is a lived awareness of human rights principles from the global to local levels. Ultimately, social policies, administrative decision making, and other practice interventions ought to reflect essential human rights principles such as human dignity and nondiscrimination. As stated earlier, however, to correctly till the land to create a socially just world, metaphorically, the soil must be free from insecticides, pollutants, and artificial fertilizers to produce an abundant crop—that is, a socially just world. It is very easy, however, to distort this idea of human rights, to pollute it, without awareness of certain provisos or warnings. To say that rhetoric about human rights, as well as free trade and democracy, has taken over the world is an understatement! One hears, for example, of Saddam Hussein's wanton killing of the Kurds, a worthy concern certainly. But rarely does one hear about domestic human rights violations, such as children living in extreme poverty. Before discussing these provisos more fully, we need to regard social justice as struggle, with a brief consideration of Albert Camus' portrayal of the mythical character Sisyphus.[7]

Sisyphus as the Prototypical Human Rights Defender

Myths, which tell stories and speak of struggles since the beginning of time, can serve as models for social action. Carl Jung uses the Odysseus myth to illustrate the struggles of the consciousness against the powerful and often sinister forces of the animus and anima, represented by the beautiful call of the Sirens and the monsters Scylla and Charybdis (Hannah, 1981). More specifically, Paul Ricoeur (1967) calls those myths "traditional narration[s] . . . which can provide grounds for . . . [a]ll the forms of action and thought by which man understands himself and his world" (p. 5). Sisyphus was condemned by the gods to push a rock up a hill, never quite reaching the top before it rolled back down, whereupon he resumed his endless struggle. Camus (1991) states that because of a "certain levity in regard to the gods," Sisyphus had gone so far as to trick Death by putting "death in chains," causing death to cease on Earth for some time. Pluto had to dispatch the god of war, to liberate Death from the conqueror's hands (p. 119). After being granted permission to leave the underworld to chastise his wife for betrayal, followed by an overly prolonged stay on Earth, the gods later had to issue a decree for his return to the underworld, where his rock was ready for him.

But Homer describes Sisyphus as the "wisest and most prudent of mortals." Indeed, Camus calls Sisyphus

> the absurd hero . . . [a]s much through his passions as through his torture. His scorn of the gods, his hatred of death, and his passion for life won him that unspeakable penalty in which the whole being is exerted toward accomplishing nothing. This is the price that must be paid for the passions of this earth. (p. 120)

Camus reminds us, too, of Oedipus's final cry that "the nobility of my soul, makes me conclude that all is well." He ends by telling us that

> Sisyphus's silent joy is contained therein. . . . [He] teaches the higher fidelity that negates the gods and raises rocks. He too, concludes that all is well. . . . The struggle itself toward the heights is enough to fill a man's [and woman's] heart. One must imagine Sisyphus happy. (p. 123)

Myths exist so the imagination can run with them, giving them continuing significance. Sisyphus, indeed, teaches us that, despite the possibility that the gods or the powers that be will rebuke or punish us for our passions, there is joy in struggle. Or as Norman O. Brown, a countercultural leader of the 1960s, used to say, "*In hilaritas tristia; in trisita hilaritatis*" (Lectures on Giambattista Vico, Duquesne University, 1973). Translated literally, this means, "In happiness, there is sadness; in sadness, there is happiness." This is the paradox of joy in struggle. Ultimately, we may even have to grapple with the possibility that the gods will unleash death on us in our quest for social justice, as happened to Malcolm X, Martin Luther King, Jr., Mahatma Gandhi, Crazy Horse, and the lesser known Olympe de Gouges, whose courage in writing a Declaration on the Rights of Women led to her execution by guillotine on November 6, 1793.

Also, our struggle is ultimately ambiguous. As Sisyphus never quite reached the top with his rock, we may never have complete certitude that the quest is the right and only one. Yet despite the ambiguities, we must be consoled that, like Sisyphus, "the absurd" person must in "silent joy" be "still on the go. The rock is still rolling" (Camus, 1991, p. 123).

Chapter 3 discusses this struggle in more depth. Briefly, if initiatives focus one's energies on engaging in social action and service for whole populations, they will always be problematic. Thus, if a person engages in a macro, or *primary*, intervention—for instance, implementing a right to adequate shelter as an amendment to the U.S. Constitution—many people would still be homeless and in need of adequate shelter. On the other hand, engaging in a *secondary* intervention, such as writing a grant proposal for a homeless shelter, then opening such a shelter or perhaps a soup kitchen, would leave undone development of strategies such as a constitutional amendment that might have longer-lasting effects. In other words, human rights defenders and social justice advocates will never quite reach the pinnacle of success. Their efforts, like the Universal Declaration of Human Rights, will never be perfect and always open to criticism. But the struggle itself should be enough to fill one's heart.

Thus, those wishing to create a socially just world, built on a foundation of human rights, can obviously be described as absurd heroes or heroines—absurd in that their work, often riddled with ambiguity, is neither completely nor precisely done. But Sisyphus is also wise and prudent. He has learned wisdom from his efforts and found joy in them. Maybe more important, however, Sisyphus has a higher sense of fidelity, transcending even the gods. Indeed, the helping and health professions call for the highest fidelity (plausibly from the Latin *fido,* meaning "faith") to the healing powers of clients and patients themselves so that they too might put "death in chains" and find joy in doing so.

Some Initial Provisos for the Human Rights Defender

For a socially just world, local and global, to flower in a soil rich in human rights, our grounding must be free from the rhetoric, if not falsehoods, surrounding human rights discourse. War, for example, is bad . . . very bad.

But isn't invasion often presented as the only way to help another country's people advance their human rights? True, there are evil people in the world who must be stopped. But surely, there are more creative ways to provide for the human rights of others than killing people, a most obvious human rights violation.

These provisos, caveats, and warnings can also emphatically demonstrate that human rights work is not as perfect or cut-and-dried as it might seem. It is easy, for instance, to equate human rights work with concrete actions, such as eliminating the death penalty or the abuse or torture of prisoners. But protecting human rights ultimately means implementing the entirety of the Universal Declaration of Human Rights. This calls for a vision of a socially just world, to wrestle with the numerous uncertainties and intangibles, the structural forces, "an unjust social and international order" (Article 28), that result in violations of human rights. These caveats also show that those in power might abuse this powerful idea of human rights, and it is therefore necessary to demand a reckoning. True, activists, like Sisyphus, may suffer for such insolence toward the powerful. To suffer is a person's individual choice, a decision arrived at in one's meditative life. It is also important to acknowledge the wisdom of Gandhi and Martin Luther King, Jr. that unearned suffering can be redemptive.

The Doctrine of Humanitarian Intervention

The first proviso is that governments have often used human rights as a justification to invade other countries, a doctrine known as *humanitarian intervention,* which has recently been discredited (Boyle, 2004). There may be much truth to the mistreatment of Germans in the Polish Corridor or the genocide against the Kurds by Saddam Hussein, but one can easily argue that the invasions of Poland in World War II or, more recently, of Iraq had hidden agendas. The situations were different, but world domination or control of Iraq's plentiful natural resources (such as oil) may have played more important roles than humanitarian concerns. Indeed, the U.S.[8] policy model, as of this writing, is gradually taking over Iraq, with increasing reports of managed care in the hospitals, high tuition fees in universities, and increasing use of private transportation. Previously, health care and higher education were universal entitlements paid for by taxes rather than privately financed as in the United States. Certainly, the grotesque activities of a dictator need to be dealt with. Yet it's important to keep in mind that the model of health care and education in Iraq before the invasion and in Europe more closely approximates the principles of the Universal Declaration.

Also, why was female genital mutilation so much in the public eye only during the U.S. invasion of Somalia, a strategically located country? Violence is antithetical to human rights principles. Only nonviolent actions can have a lasting effect, as evidenced by King John's signing of the Magna Carta with the Barons of Runnymede. Our model ought to be Gandhi, who said, "Non-violence is the first article of my faith. It is also the last article of my creed" (cited in Partington, 1992, p. 297). One must be cautious. Wholehearted opposition to the abuses of the Kurds is important, but the question is whether violence can effectively remedy such human rights violations, especially in the form of contemporary war, in which roughly 90% of casualties are civilians.

The Hypocrisy of Governments

A second caution emanates from the first. Put bluntly, one must always be alert to the *hypocrisy of governments* (or other powerful entities, as previously discussed) as the major driving force in the human rights arena, rather than true humanitarian concern. As the famed community organizer Saul Alinsky was fond of saying, he wanted the establishment to sit on "their own petard"(Alinsky, 1989, p. 152). The word *petard* in the French means "firecracker." In other words, if policy makers want to make a noise, they must listen to the roar of their own words. If the powerful talk about human rights in foreign countries, as they often do in political discourse, then they must also make a noise about their own country's human rights violations. President Bush has said, for instance, that "human rights are non-negotiable." It is important to remember Eleanor Roosevelt's response to Eric Sevareid's question, "Would you say then that the Universal Declaration of Human Rights is dangerous to governments?" She replied: "Yes . . . oh, yes" (cited in Wronka, 1998b, p. 89).

Profit, narrowly defined as immediate monetary gain rather than the fulfillment of human need vis-à-vis human rights principles, may also underlie human rights arguments. Thus, free speech arguments can be pretexts for violence in the media or advertising on children's television. Freedom of speech, though a human rights value, is questionable if it means continually exposing people to violence in the media. It is only too easy to model behavior on violent heroes, and now heroines, in video games and other media, dulling people's senses to the horrors of war. Pointing out such hypocrisies ought to be part of the work of human rights defenders.

The Sanitization of Oppression

Third, the human condition is such that we constantly seek meaning, trying to make sense of the world, especially in the face of uncertainties, horrors, and a human-initiated hastening of death.[9] Thus, it is important to be on the lookout for the *sanitization of oppression*. In our quest for meaning, it is easy to think we understand something by naming, or categorizing it. Such reasoning, however, may convince one of "knowing" something when the category itself may be merely a euphemism-masking oppression. The helping and health professions are replete with diagnostic categories or other forms of classification, such as intelligence quotients, scores on achievement tests, or axes of understanding. It is easy to engage in what Lifton (2000) calls the human propensity to call a cabbage a rose or a rat a rabbit. Despite the best of intentions, cataloging people based on color, class, culture, or gender may create a self-fulfilling prophecy (Zola, 1983). Labeling someone with a personality disorder (e.g., schizophrenic, paranoid, oppositional-defiant) may actually be a veiled insult.

Human rights is certainly a worthwhile value in helping people. Yet it is important to constantly be on the lookout for use of flowery or technical language that masks oppression. Is the world, despite our increasing discourse about human rights, democracy, and global free trade, a better place now than prior to the Universal Declaration of Human Rights? The gap between the world's richest and poorest is growing each day, yet we often hear of the need to "fight for democracy" to implement human rights for all. Furthermore, roughly 2.5 billion people in the world live on less than $2 per day, constituting 40% of the world population, making each day a struggle merely to survive. In the middle of the 20th century, the ratio of the gross domestic product of the 20 richest countries was roughly 18 times that of the poorer countries. At the turn of the current millennium, this ratio has more than doubled to 37 times, a situation evoking the image of a champagne glass with a large concentration of income at the top and a thin stem at the bottom. In fact, the ratio of income of the poorest to the richest people in the world as a whole is 1 to 103 (UN Development Program, 2005).

Is a world wrought by free trade and human rights a democratic world? Looking at the United States, Supreme Court Justice Louis Brandeis said it well: "We can either have democracy in this country or we can have great wealth concentrated in the hands of the few, but we cannot have both" (cited in Danaher, 1996, p. 36). Yet in the United States, "1% of the population controls 47% of the net financial wealth" (Kivel, 2004, p. 19). Are these instances of class and global apartheid?

The point is that to truly take human rights seriously in the quest for social justice, the gauge must be the fulfillment of human need and human development. The human need to be treated with dignity is always apparent, and treatment modalities of the helping and health professions ought to be consistent with a need so fundamental to the human condition. Yes, knowledge of human needs is imperfect. Yet one can easily argue that people have biological needs for food and clean water; social-psychological needs for affiliation, care, and love; productive-creative needs for meaningful participation in the community; security needs for trust; self-actualization needs to develop to one's potential; and spiritual needs for human dignity and an existence with meaning and coherence (Gil, 1998). If such needs are fulfilled, social justice is achieved. Veiled insults and euphemisms will not fulfill human need. However, used as a guide to fulfill human need, human rights ought to undo the burdens of oppression that surround us, whether in the form of expert-oriented (Katz, 1982; Wronka, 1993), hierarchical helping and health professions or the pretext of human rights to engage in "free" trade that actually masks oppression, as global data indicate.

Narrow Definitions of Human Rights

Fourth, it is very easy to define human rights in *narrow terms*. The human rights movement owes a lot to the painstaking work of groups such as Amnesty International. Its initial case-by-case approach and adoption of political prisoners has led to growing public awareness of the importance of human rights as a force for social change. Such an approach brought to light the human rights abuses in the former Soviet Union, and the eventual destruction of the Gulag. A case-by-case approach has its merits, but some integration of cases is still needed to reveal how they are inextricably linked to other violations of human rights and a socially just domestic and international order. Similarly, in addition to concern for imprisonment for religious practices, allegations of torture, and implementation of the death penalty, these concerns must also be integrated with social order issues such as structural violence and questionable economic and social arrangements.

The point is that some groups and the media often define human rights in rather narrow terms, focusing on the prolonged detainment and allegations of torture of prisoners of war in Guantanamo Bay, for example. Certainly cruel and unusual punishment violates fundamental human rights standards. It is important to treat all humans with justice, tempered with mercy. But if peace were considered a human right and war eliminated, there would be no prisoners in Guantanamo in the first place. Another case in point is apartheid in South Africa; although legally forbidden, de facto (i.e., in fact), the practice continues. The question becomes, why are activists more concerned about South Africa than about high infant mortality rates in Burkina Faso, where one in five children dies before the age of 1? Is this because South Africa has a sizeable white population and human rights work in general has a "Eurocentric bias" (Steiner & Alston, 2000)? These questions are not simple to answer. Perhaps the point to keep in mind is that, like Sisyphus, who found joy in struggle and ambiguity, we may never to reach the heights of perfection. People can, however, share the struggle and the happiness of reflecting together on such issues (Merleau-Ponty, 1964).

Demonization of the Other

Fifth, one must be on guard to *avoid demonizing the Other*.[10] Rights talk can easily become a means of taking cheap shots at one's "enemy." This was perhaps more apparent during the Cold War between the United States and the Soviet Union in the 1980s. Reports of the imprisonment of political prisoners and the misuse of psychiatric medications in Soviet hospitals flooded the American media. Similarly, the communist press was inundated with images of homelessness, unemployment, and Ku Klux Klan gatherings and stories of the long strand of broken promises and treaties with the U.S. government. It is doubtful that Tiananmen Square would have been in the media if China were not a communist country. Today, we often hear about the denial of the women's right to vote in Muslim countries.

The challenge, however, is to find a way to use "humility not arrogance"— the words of former President Bill Clinton, inscribed on the walls of the Holocaust Museum in Washington, DC—to provide human rights for all. The enemy must be demystified, so to speak, and we must engage in constructive dialogue in ways that also acknowledge human rights violations in our own country. So talk of forbidding women the right to vote in a Muslim country ought to be balanced by acknowledgment of a paucity of women legislators in the United States, fewer than in certain Muslim countries. The challenge is to somehow extricate oneself from parochial viewpoints, engage in constructive dialogue with different cultures, and recognize a shared humanity rather than to engage in spurious finger pointing. Jane Addams, sometimes referred to as the mother of social work, a peace and social justice advocate, proponent of an ethic of reciprocity and world citizenship, and first president of the Women's International League for Peace and Freedom (WILPF), is an excellent example of someone who refused to give into evil images and stereotypes of even those government officials and corporate heads in power. She listened unceasingly to the oppressor and the oppressed, confident in the importance of listening to all views, however unfavorable. Ultimately, her efforts were successful, as evidenced by the famed Settlement Houses she established and her excellent work as Sanitation Commissioner for Chicago. She is shown in Figure 1.3 with Eleanor Roosevelt and Elinor Morgenthau, both devotees of Addams's work.

Human Rights Documents as Human Creations

Sixth, let us always be aware that *human rights documents are human creations* themselves. Independent experts appointed by governments to comment on human rights reports (discussed in Chapter 3) may have privileged situations in the system and lead lives divorced from struggle. That is

Figure 1.3   Eleanor Roosevelt (center), Chairperson of the Drafting Committee of the Universal Declaration of Human Rights, With Jane Addams (right), Sometimes Called the Mother of Social Work, and Elinor Morgenthau (left), Teacher and Director of Plays at the Henry Street Settlement House in NYC, at Westport, Connecticut, 1929. They refused to demonize others and recognized the importance of creative dialogue and social action to eradicate social injustice.

Source: The National Archives.

not always the case, and a privileged life certainly does not always translate into lack of concern for the underdog. And many underdogs, after attaining better positions, wave good-bye to their neighborhood cronies. The challenge, therefore, is always to include public participation in the actual formulation and implementation of human rights documents. These documents are by no means perfect, and the voices of the marginalized are needed to construct and implement human rights principles. Eleanor Roosevelt admitted the Universal Declaration was

> not a perfect document . . . Being, as it must be, a composite document to meet the thoughts of so many different peoples, there must be a considerable number of compromises. On the whole, however, it is a good document. We could never hope for perfection no matter how many times we revised the Declaration, for one could always see something a little better that one might do. (UN Department of Public Information, 1950, pp. 15–16)

The Universal Declaration, for example, did not mention the rights of people with disabilities or gays, lesbians, bisexuals, transsexuals, or the intersexed (the 1 in 2,000 infants born with ambiguous genitalia). Interpretations of human rights evolve, as do human rights documents. Human rights is not the silver bullet to slay the werewolf of an ugly social order preying on the human family; it will not wholly transform the world into a society more amicable to human development. Something about the human species continually searches for the silver bullet, the quick fix.

There is no quick fix, but the human rights concept is a powerful tool. But who knows? Maybe in the next century (or even tomorrow, next month, or next year) another idea will come along that is as powerful as, or even more powerful than, human rights or social justice. Maybe visitors from another galaxy, travelling perhaps 1 million light-years, will land on Earth, and the Earth will join forces with these beings to thwart the growth and development of the human species. Perhaps the rallying cry will be "Planetary species rights!" In the latter part of the last century, the movement was from civil to human rights, as Malcolm X eloquently stated, in the context of the African American experience:

> The problem of the Afro-American . . . should be taken out of the national context into the international arena. . . . It is a world problem. . . . *Instead of calling it a civil rights struggle . . . look at it as a struggle for human rights* [italics added] . . . and use the United Nations' avenues, its Human Rights Commission . . . [as] more of a chance of getting meaningful results . . . and the moral support of the world. (Sterling Entertainment Group, 1992)

Martin Luther King, Jr. echoed this sentiment when he said, "I think it is necessary to realize that we have moved from the era of civil rights to the era of human rights" (cited in Cho, Crooms, Dorow, Huff, Scott, & Thomas, 2006, p. 4). For the time being at least, the debate must ultimately be about human rights for all.

Cultural Relativism as Possible Pretext

Humans obviously are embedded in cultures, which at times are themselves inimical to fundamental human rights principles. There should be no discrimination based on culture, ethnicity, or religion. Yet, some cultural practices purposefully inflict pain—foot-binding in traditional China; *sati,* the tradition of a woman throwing herself on her husband's funeral pyre; *devdase,* the tradition of a woman being sacrificed to the gods; or female genital mutilation—failing to meet the "just requirements of morality, public order and the general welfare in a democratic society," as enunciated in Article 29 of the Universal Declaration. But we must question such cultural practices with humility, for a culture condemning female genital mutilation in another culture may promote anorexia nervosa among its young women, not to mention an arms buildup that could result in the massacre of millions of innocents. Only with humility and through open discussion and debate with groups most affected by such practices can we have any meaningful and creative dialogue.

Table 1.3 summarizes the seven provisos discussed in this chapter.

Table 1.3   Seven Provisos for the Human Rights Defender/Social Justice Advocate*

Caveat	Explanation
The doctrine of humanitarian intervention	Preemptive invasion of another country for ostensible human rights abuses
The hypocrisy of governments	The failure of one government to acknowledge human rights abuses in its own country while lambasting another for violations
The sanitization of oppression	The giving of a category or diagnosis based more on class, religion, political opinion, or administrative expediency than on illness
Narrow definitions of human rights	The refusal to view one right within the entire context of other human rights principles
Demonization of the other	The need to extricate oneself from parochial viewpoints and spurious fingerpointing, refusing to give in to stereotypes and evil images, acknowledging a shared humanity of both oppressor and oppressed

Caveat	Explanation
Human rights documents as human creations	The need to see human rights documents as reflecting the context of the time—limited at times but with tremendous potential for personality transformation from the individual to the national to the global community
Cultural relativism as possible pretext	The need to engage with humility and creative dialogue with cultures whose practices appear inimical to human rights standards

*These provisos are testimony to the fact that the work of activists will always be fraught with numerous difficulties and ambiguities. However, realizing that social justice is a struggle, which may cause rebuke from the powers that be, human rights defenders must decide to take them on in a joyful spirit, like the mythical character Sisyphus, as popularized by Albert Camus.

Summary

The purpose of this book is to examine how the social construct *human rights* can serve as a foundation for a socially just world. These rights, legal mandates to fulfill human need, are interdependent and indivisible. The book's rationale is that today, no government would dare say it is against human rights, an almost complete turnaround from the conclusion of the Conference of Evian (1938). Although late in coming, given the experience of Indigenous Peoples and African Americans, to mention just a couple of human rights violations, it was called in response to the atrocities of the Third Reich, but it concluded that no country had a right to interfere with another country's domestic affairs. Out of the ruins of World War II was born the United Nations and the Universal Declaration of Human Rights, the authoritative definition of human rights standards, signed by the General Assembly with no dissent on December 10, 1948. The Universal Declaration contains five crucial notions: (a) the right to human dignity; (b) the right to be free from discrimination; (c) civil and political rights; (d) economic, social, and cultural rights; and (e) solidarity rights.

This idea of human rights has become so powerful that the helping and health professions have acknowledged, in various ways, the importance of incorporating human rights into their curriculum and practice. Ultimately, the aim is to create what is called a "human rights culture," a lived awareness of human rights principles, so that every person, everywhere can have his or her needs met and be treated with dignity, fundamental to social justice. Such a culture can exist, not only globally but also at the local level, even in our communities, schools, places of employment, and everyday interactions. As activists work toward implementing human rights principles, it would help to reflect on certain ideas—for one, that the journey from the mind to the heart is a long one. Human rights instruments can serve as tools to "till the soil" and create a foundation from which human needs can flourish.

Mindful of the joy in struggle, as in the myth of Sisyphus, it is important to understand that, just as the Universal Declaration is not a perfect document, neither are social actions perfect. We need a broad vision, because numerous ambiguities will emerge as we work toward social justice. One needs to work on a case-by-case basis; but also to change unjust social order. Keeping our eyes on the prize—that is, the creation of a human rights culture—will also necessitate keeping our eyes on the lies. We must be constantly vigilant to a number of provisos and caveats—pretexts by the powerful for humanitarian intervention, government hypocrisy, use of violence to advance human rights, the sanitization of oppression, narrowly defined human rights, the demonization of the Other, certain cultural practices—and aware that human rights documents, as creations themselves, are constantly evolving.

Ultimately, the question to ask is not necessarily "Wouldn't the world be a better place if everyone had a good job, health care, and security in old age?" Rather, such questions would be more powerful couched in human rights terms. Employment, medical care, and security in old age are undeniably human rights that would help us create persuasive arguments to fulfill human needs and enhance human development. It is important to never lose sight of the power of this idea of human rights. Recall Malcolm X's statement that the struggle is no longer about civil rights, but human rights (Sterling Entertainment Documentary, 1992).

Because human rights discussions cannot take place in a historical-philosophical vacuum, we now need to present a history of the human rights idea, culminating in the endorsement of the Universal Declaration, a historical-philosophical compromise. Following this discussion, the book elaborates some essential themes from major human rights instruments issued after the Universal Declaration. For the sake of expediency, the appendices summarize in tabular form the themes of the human rights documents discussed in this book. This scaffolding of rights ought to give helping and health professionals a solid sense of human rights principles that can provide a basis for social justice, and corresponding social action and service initiatives.

Questions for Discussion

1. A major theme of this book is the interdependence and indivisibility of human rights. Are time limits or other restrictions for welfare benefits in the government-sponsored welfare program, Temporary Aid to Needy Families

(TANF), and the emphasis of the presidential initiative, the No Child Left Behind Act, on standardized testing consistent with the principles of the Universal Declaration of Human Rights? Why or why not? What other policies are consistent and/or inconsistent with human rights principles as discussed so far? Comment on the following statements: (a) Human rights is fashionable. Wherever one goes one hears about human rights. But nothing gets done. It is time to move on. (b) It would be great if human rights were fashionable. Then we would truly have health care for all, meaningful jobs at living wages, security in old age, and no child living in poverty.

2. Does the doctrine of humanitarian intervention represent noble principles, or is it actually an excuse to invade another country for hidden agenda? In war, does one side "demonize" the other, or does each feel that it is fighting for a just cause, the furthering of human rights principles? If the former, how can relations be improved so that there is openness, dialogue, and resolution of conflict? Can the same principles be used for groups that demonize each other, such as the Left demonizing the Right and vice versa? Do you feel that the helping and health professions to some extent demonize one another or do they act out of true humanitarian concern? In public discourse, for example, one hears of psychiatry, lambasting the American Psychological Association for its endorsement of interrogation techniques at Guantanamo, noting that the U.S. military is the largest employer of psychologists. Psychology also appears to have expressed concern of the overmedicating of our children by psychiatry. Furthermore, one is more prone to hear about the former, as the pharmaceutical industry is the most profitable sector since World War II, arguably having more control over the shaping of public opinion. And where do social work and nursing, more female-dominated professions, fit into this scenario of caricature? What do you see as the greatest obstacles to implementing human rights principles? How would you overcome them?

3. Have you ever received a diagnosis? How was it helpful? Was it unhelpful in any way? Did it contribute to your understanding? Is the story of the fairy tale character Rumplestiltskin relevant in any way? (When named, he tore himself up.)

4. Abraham Lincoln, author of the "Emancipation Proclamation", often emphasized the importance of being a sincere friend in one's writing, speech, and actions. This is not different from the etymological meanings of "social justice" (as described in the Preface) as equitable treatment among friends. Think of those who were sincere friends to you; now think of your words and actions as a sincere friend to others. What are some similar themes?

How can you translate this spirit of friendship so that it has meaning in your everyday life and community?

5. Does your profession adequately integrate human rights standards in its curriculum and in practice situations in the field? Has your profession ever engaged in the "sanitization of oppression"? Give some concrete examples.

6. If only chosen values endure, what nonviolent and noncoercive strategies might be most effective for realizing human rights principles by having a human rights culture, moving from the mind to heart to the body, that is, dragging its principles into one's everyday life and becoming part of the collective consciousness of the community? Or do you feel it is not necessary to strategize anything, that things should just happen? Or do you feel it is necessary to have such a culture in the first place?

7. How should one respond to a dignitary who says that the Universal Declaration of Human Rights is like a "letter to Santa Claus," as did our former ambassador to the United Nations, Jeanne Kirkpatrick? Does it represent nothing but "airy" and "utopian" ideals, hardly realizable in a world so full of war and strife? Or are its principles realizable for every person, everywhere?

8. How would the Universal Declaration look if it were drafted today? Would it include additional categories of discrimination? What other rights might it also assert? Where would the notion of duties and limitations of rights fit in? Comment on the following scenario: Sarah recently read the Universal Declaration and now feels energized to confront discrimination in all its forms as enunciated in Article 2. But not only does she want world peace, she desires, as Gandhi says, to "be change you want to see in the world." She then goes to an Internet dating site and enters various criteria for a partner in regard to age, race, income, health, height, body weight, and so on. She oscillates between feeling guilty for her perceived hypocrisy and thinking that dating is just another thing. After scouring the personals, half jokingly, yet half serious, she asks her friends to help organize a convention of good-looking, financially secure, emotionally stable men. (Of course, Sarah could be Tom, and the convention needn't be the opposite sex.)

9. Describe a situation in which someone helped you—really helped you. What happened exactly? Now describe a situation in which someone thought he or she was helping you, but the intervention actually hurt you in some way. What happened exactly? Did that person act like he or she knew what was best for you? Did you feel demeaned—for instance, like a "poor weak" person in need of "help"? What can be learned from these experiences for the helping and health professions? Now describe a situation in which you felt

someone treated you with dignity. Then describe a situation in which you treated someone with dignity. Now think of a situation in which someone treated you in an undignified way and one in which you treated someone without dignity. Is it easier to think of situations in which you were treated with dignity or no dignity? What does this show about our culture? What can be done about it?

10. This book argues that human rights is the cornerstone—the bedrock, if you will—of social justice and that human rights ought to be discussed in relation to other guiding principles of major spiritual and religious belief systems, humanistic manifestos, and indigenous teachings. What other guiding principles have you found helpful in your everyday life that you feel can help in creating a socially just world? How do you think these principles are similar and/or different from human rights principles you've learned so far? Try to keep those principles in mind while reading the rest of this book and continue to compare human rights with the values you have learned to cherish throughout your life.

Activities/Actions

1. Organize a reading of the Universal Declaration of Human Rights on December 10, Human Rights Day. Try to be where and when many people are around, such as downtowns and parks during lunchtime or soon after work. Afterward, just stand around, have a candlelight vigil, and ask if anyone would like to say something . . . anything. Stand and stand and stand. For many conducting this action, it will be very cold outside. Standing there itself may be a sign of commitment to stand up for human rights. Be ready to speak with the media with a prepared statement or extemporaneously about the Universal Declaration as customary international law, a document drafted under the leadership of an American, or a document that needs to be incorporated into U.S. law.

2. Scour the newspapers looking for articles that deal with a human rights situation in another country. Write a letter to the editor commending her or him for raising public awareness about that particular human rights issue. But integrate the idea that there are also human rights issues in the United States, such as millions lacking access to health care, adequate shelter, and security in old age. If you are brave, bring up peace as a human right, suggesting that the world's largest arms supplier is violating this right.

3. If you are from the Left, believing in government responsibility to provide for human need, go to a meeting of people on the Right, who believe in

privatization of social programs. Show them the Universal Declaration and tell them that an American, Eleanor Roosevelt, was chairperson of the drafting committee of that document. Begin a dialogue about its principles. See if you can agree on ways to achieve those principles.

4. Begin a movement in the helping and health professions to catalogue endorsements of the Universal Declaration and the seven major conventions following it. In the left-hand column, list, for example, the Council on Social Work Education, the National Association of Social Work, the American Psychological Association, the American Nurses Association, the American Public Health Association, and the American Medical Association. Mark with Xs those documents (listed across the page; see Table 1.4) that correspond to the professional organization's respective endorsements.

Table 1.4   A Human Rights Endorsement Grid: Endorsements of Human Rights Documents by Professional Organizations

	Human Rights Document						
Organization	*Universal Declaration*	*ICCPR*	*ICESCR*	*CRC*	*CEDAW*	*CERD*	*CAT*
CSWE							
NASW							
APA							
ANA							
APHA							
AMA							

As you progress in the next chapter, basic principles of documents following the Universal Declaration will become clearer. You may wish, at some later time, to see how your organization feels about specific principles, such as CEDAW, which calls on governments to provide the means for parents to balance family and work life. You may also wish to include other documents more pertinent to a professional organization, like the Protection of Persons with Mental Illness or Principles of Medical Ethics. In addition to professional organizations, what NGOs might be included? If organizations have endorsed documents, how would you, or should you, monitor an organization's compliance with human rights documents?

5. To borrow from Gandhi, imagine the poorest, most helpless person you have ever seen and ask yourself if the next step you take can be of use

to that person. Now try to change your life so that your next step would be of some use to that person. Do this exercise with other classmates. See who can make the first step. If you are able to get up from your seat, discuss how you might plan to change your life. If you have trouble leaving your seat, discuss some of the obstacles that prevent you from doing so.

Notes

1. Although for grammatical reasons the words *human rights* are treated here as plural, the term should be understood as singular in meaning. Rights are interdependent, equal, and indivisible. Ultimately, one right is meaningless without taking into consideration other rights. Freedom of speech, for example, is of questionable value if a person is homeless or lives in a world at war. Adequate shelter and peace are also considered human rights.

2. *Concentration camp* is actually a misnomer. They were really death camps. Questions arise concerning other concentrated areas, such as our inner cities and reservations where African American and Native American men have a longevity rate of roughly 43. Although these are not death camps per se, unjust social and economic arrangements may have taken the place of barbed wire, amorphous brute forces leading to premature deaths. But given widespread and pervasive human rights violations like extreme poverty, including nearly 1 billion who go to bed starving each night, rarely mentioned in public discourse, what may really be closed off is our minds, products of questionable socialization processes emphasizing profit and the inevitability of war rather than human development for all as a viable possibility. From the Latin *campus,* meaning "theater of action," such camps may have also provided a setting for a kind of observation, if not voyeurism, on the part of personnel, including helping and health professionals, to engage in research with a merciless pleasure, purportedly to improve the human condition.

3. It is a great irony that the United Nations, of which the United States was a major architect, does not appear to be as valued here as it is in many parts of the world. One can easily argue that the UN has its share of issues. Restructuring of that global institution is a worthwhile goal, yet it might be wise to heed the age-old injunction to "examine the log in one's eye, before plucking the speck from another." Nearly every community organization has its share of issues. The UN, however, deals in conflict resolution with entire nations, not merely individuals, groups, street gangs, or professional committees. The UN, a voluntary organization, is also only as strong as its member states want it to be. Besides, "If it bleeds, it leads." Violence sells; and prevention, which is much of the work of the UN, does not. Often an unseen actor in world affairs, it is extremely influential in numerous ways, such as the eradication of polio and worldwide efforts to combat the AIDS pandemic and global poverty.

4. It is unfortunate that the negative connotations of the prefix *non* are associated with such important citizens' groups fighting on behalf of human rights and social justice. Similarly, there are *non*profits or groups for *non*violence, which also

has negative connotations. Terms such as NGO and nonviolence, therefore, are used with some hesitation, but they are the terms most commonly recognized.

5. Eleanor Roosevelt wanted nonsexist language in the final version of the Universal Declaration but was unsuccessful in her attempt. Despite this limitation, it is commonly understood that words such as *he, him, himself,* and *brotherhood* also mean *she, her, herself,* and *sisterhood.* The Universal Declaration also asserts the importance of motherhood requiring special protections as it should. It is conceivable that if drafted in this new millennium, fatherhood and/or parenthood would also merit worthy consideration.

6. For an in-depth discussion of these crucial notions, the history of the idea of human rights, and national debates about each specific article prior to the endorsement of the Universal Declaration, see *Human Rights and Social Policy in the 21st century: A history of the idea of human rights and comparison of the United Nations Universal Declaration of Human Rights with United States federal and state constitutions* (Wronka, 1998b). A succinct overview of human rights can be found in my entry in the *Encyclopedia of Social Work* (1995a), an updated version of which is scheduled for the 2008 edition.

7. This book uses *human rights defender* interchangeably with terms such as *social activist* and *social justice advocate* for reasons mentioned in the Preface. Perhaps Jose Marti's words, popularized in the song "Guantanamera," *un hombre sincero,*" loosely translated as a "sincere person," aptly describe someone aspiring to create a world of human dignity, rights, and social justice.

8. Although it is customary to use the adjective *American* as pertaining to the United States, this book will often use the more accurate *United States* or *U.S.* as the correct modifier. A cursory glance at any map would show that numerous countries make up the Americas, both North and South. Also, for an in-depth discussion of this doctrine and issues pertaining to cultural relativism in the context of U.S. foreign policy, see Noam Chomsky's *The Umbrella of U.S. Power* (2002).

9. See particularly Viktor Frankl's *Man's Search for Meaning* (1984) and Robert Lifton's *The Nazi Doctors* (2000) and *Death in Life: Survivors of Hiroshima* (1967).

10. The "Other" in this work refers to Emmanuel Levinas's (1906–1995) notion that another person is inextricably linked to one's self by concerns for social justice. The Other therefore is in no way apart from the experiencing person, but rather inextricably linked. Germanic notions of *dasein, mitsein,* and *mitwelt,* loosely meaning that being in the world is being with others, also echo this notion of human interconnectedness. Ultimately, the presence of the Other is shared, calling for responsibility and challenging the self to question indifference in the face of social injustice. See particularly Levinas's *Totality and Infinity* (2001).

2

Before and Beyond the Universal Declaration of Human Rights

My country is the world and my religion is good deeds.

—Thomas Paine

This chapter provides a bridge between our initial understanding of the power of the idea of human rights, with the Universal Declaration of Human Rights as the centerpiece, and certain major developments after its endorsement with no dissent by the UN General Assembly. It is Janus-faced, looking back and forward, as in the instant when Sisyphus, who is "superior to his fate," nears the top of the mountain and contemplates the stone rolling backward, only to have to push it up again, which "crowns his victory" (Camus, 1991, p. 121). Discussions of human rights cannot take place in a historical-philosophical vacuum; they must be attuned to history as they take up the struggle to engage in action and service in the name of social justice.

Perhaps philosopher George Santayana is right that what we learn from history is that we do not learn from history; that history books mirror only the stories of the victorious. Success has many parents, seeking credit for their roles in successful historical outcomes, but few acknowledge their roles in failures, which are orphans. We also need a dialogue of understanding among various interpretations of the historical record, fully aware that some may have simply jockeyed themselves into the limelight. Truth may remain elusive; searching for truth is always a struggle. Falsehoods can easily become part of a people's collective consciousness—for instance, that the land now known as the Americas, and inhabited by millions of people, was "discovered" by a man with three ships and a map. Does discovery mean ownership? Is it even important? We can never know *the* definitive history of anything, but any event or place can have a number of histories. Given the vicissitudes of the human condition, one hopes that humanity will remain willing to learn from the past; we must confront it, as Santayana reminds us, so that the world is not condemned to repeat it.

Toward a History of the Idea of Human Rights

Humankind has been searching for immutable truths since time immemorial. Even in the beginning, this search for a universal, unchanging reality may have been a Western attempt to understand the world, while Eastern approaches acknowledged that the only certainty is uncertainty. The human species, a "flaw in the diamond of the world" (Merleau-Ponty, 1964), lacks the kind of genetic programming in other life forms (Gil, 1998) that, for example, prompts certain species, such as whales, to migrate long distances, or, like bees, to do a dance directing other members of the colony to a field of flowers containing honey. In *Homo sapiens*, that is, the human species, issues aren't as clear-cut. The human mind seems to differentiate us from other life forms; humans must *choose* ways of life that protect them from extreme vulnerability to the elements and the frailty of the human condition in general. Perhaps that explains why, as the sage Friedrich Nietzsche said, humans had to invent laughter, and Nikos Katzanzakis, through his playful character, Zorba, reminds us that whatever adversity we face, humans always have the power to dance and play.

Cultures as Reflective of Human Choice

History reflects the choices humans have made in this dance of life. The myriad social structures and cultures in the world reflect the multidimensional mosaic of human choices, crystallized into ethical and legislative frameworks embedded in documents such as the Universal Declaration and major international covenants. Not surprisingly, the etymological origins of both *religion* and *constitution* (*religare* and *constitare*), which often provide the guiding principles for our ways of life and reflect the social-environmental contexts of the time, mean "to choose." It's worth noting that the Greek etymological root of the word *heresy* also means "to choose," suggesting that one person's freedom fighter may be another's terrorist; one person's iconoclast, another's religious leader. St. Augustine, in his classic *City of God,* illustrated this paradox with the example that taking over a ship makes you a pirate, but if you take over a fleet, you are an admiral. If groups with massive, well-equipped and well-financed armies kill close to 30 million people, as in World War II, or more recently, roughly 2 million in the war in Vietnam, they are called governments. Groups not as well endowed are called terrorists.

Violence may be understandable, as in the Newark riots in the late 1960s—a kind of counterviolence to racist and classist structures in the United States. Yet a major theme of this work is that violence engaged in by governments, terrorists, or oppressed groups should not be condoned. Stooping to another's level, perhaps the greatest challenge of the 21st century, will only result in more violence. It is a sad statement on the human condition and our culture that people too often begin to listen only when the channels of communication are closed. As Eric Fromm, author of the *Art of Loving* (and former patient, then husband, of the psychoanalyst Freida Fromm-Reichmann), asserts, "unlived life leads to destruction" (Hornstein, 2000). Soon after the Newark riots, the U.S. government formed a commission whose report acknowledged that white institutions have established, condoned, and maintained racist structures in the United States.

Counterviolence needn't be on such a grand scale, however. Another example is the senseless homicide/suicide at Virginia Tech in April 2007, committed by a youth proclaiming his anger toward and hatred of the wealthy, that claimed 33 victims. That individual was ultimately responsible for this uncondonable act. Yet, society may need to come to grips with the possibility that its profit-motivated system, which subordinates human needs, rights, and dignity, creates the frustration and violence, residues of unlived lives, that leads to atrocities.

As the historical record has often shown, humanity's greatest challenge, in groups and as individuals, is to choose nonviolence over violence; the latter, Gandhi reminds us, has not worked for centuries. Surely, a major aim of understanding historical processes is to see the interplay between the environment and human choice in ways that uncover the reasons, however elusive, for violence, and to seek an alternative social justice constructed from precepts of human dignity and rights.

Although the term was officially coined by the United Nations at its founding in 1945, the human rights concept is rooted in the complex struggle between contending choices to ensure survival of the human species, which at times, has been a violent response to oppressive structures. Violence is obvious in massive killings, such as the Massacre of St. Bartholomew's Day, celebrated at a Thanksgiving Mass in which thousands of French protestant Huguenots were killed in Catholic France (Ebenstein, 1960). But violence is also often masked with euphemistic language. Thus, neutral words like *restructuring* and *downsizing* might really mean the firing of persons over 50, whistleblowers, marginalized groups, and the like. Talk of *forgiving* or *canceling* Third World debt easily obscures the historical violence inflicted by the rich on the poor countries of the world: centuries of enslavement in the Americas, broken promises with Indigenous Peoples, and more recently, triumph of the postindustrial First World in the Cold War that has produced a kind of global apartheid. Indeed, the so-called race to the bottom—that is, corporations searching for the lowest wages for every worker in any country, often under the auspices of international trade agreements among elites such as NAFTA and organizations such as the World Trade Organization (WTO)[1]—may actually be an orchestrated global alliance of "haves" to violate the basic human right to socially useful work, at a reasonable wage, that contributes to the development of the human personality.[2] Understanding history, then, may require looking at the struggle of humanity's failures and successes as it attempts to eke out a socially just, nonviolent world.

A History of Human Rights From the Humanistic Tradition

Violence does not have to exist on such a macro scale, however. People also act violently in their everyday and professional lives. For example, it is easy to view stereotypes of people as "actualities" rather than "possibilities": that is, women are not actually good at mathematics; African Americans can actually perform only menial tasks. Such prejudicial attitudes pollute relations with others, whose human dignity and rights, and all the possibilities for human development, are thwarted in such a discriminatory atmosphere. Professionals may see Indigenous Peoples as inferior intellectually because they may have not performed well on intelligence tests, generally culturally biased on white standards such as quick reaction times, planning for the future, or even mathematical acumen—values not traditionally associated with some cultures. If Inuits living in the Arctic tested whites on skill in gauging whether ice is too thin for fishing or knowledge of what to do if a moose's ears move backward,[3] they would find similarly low intelligence scores.

Sartre (1993) lamented that research in the social or human sciences often seeks meaningless facts rather than meaningful essences, and perhaps we ought to acknowledge how numbers and categorizations, though certainly useful in some contexts (e.g., in administrative functions), nevertheless can do a disservice to human dignity. It is all too easy to define a person by a score on an IQ test that measures not necessarily intellectual potential but rather, class. Alfred Binet, whose work led to the development of the Binet Intelligence Test, expressed concern about this issue, fearing that test results could be used to further class interests, if not produce a kind of fascist mentality. It was not long after his test was developed that Hitler began gassing people with disabilities, many having scored low on intelligence tests, and with the collusion of helping and health professionals! Diagnoses, as discussed in Chapter 1, can also sanitize oppression; the poor may be diagnosed as "juvenile delinquent" or as having a "personality disorder," whereas the wealthy are seen as "suffering from a 'situational adjustment of adolescence'" or perhaps as "anxiety neurotic." Health professionals know only too well that knowing people's blood pressure, height, weight, and cholesterol levels doesn't mean you understand them entirely. These numbers serve as markers, but the challenge is to understand an individual's world of experience that may have played a role in producing such measurements.

Thus, we may violate people's human rights by placing them and their multiple ways of experiencing and acting as a being-in-the-world (Heidegger, 1959), devoid of environmental-social context, into a theoretic system's framework, whatever sanction that system might receive from the academic, professional community. People do not engage with each other solely as "schedules of reinforcement," like Pavlov's dogs or Skinnerian rats, shaping one another's behavior through sophisticated processes of rewards and punishments. People can love one another with all the mysteries and intangibles such profound interconnectedness involves. The problem, however, may be that it is easier to discern such concrete entities as easily distinguishable rewards and punishments than to reflect on and try to understand the lived world of the experiencing, loving person.

What we need is a humanistic approach that is phenomenon bound rather than systems bound. This approach is discussed in more depth in Chapter 5, in the context of integrating research methodology into the helping and health professions in a human rights framework. For the time being, it is important to acknowledge that human rights do indeed emerge from this tradition, the human being constantly struggling to be seen as a potentiality with the ability to transcend any straightjacket of categorization or prejudice based, for example, on gender, class, race, national origin, or religion. Is that not what discrimination is: seeing a person as an actuality rather than as a possibility who is more than a score, a diagnosis, or a stereotyped character trait of his or her group. We may sum up the history of the idea of human rights by saying it represents a struggle of the human race to transcend any actuality thrust upon it, to proclaim loudly that people are human beings, *more than just* numbers, diagnoses, subjects of a schedule of reinforcement, wage slaves, second-class citizens, or poor defenseless persons who must be helped by those who have no understanding of the indignity of their favors and handouts. Undeniably, this concept has a lot to do with the human need for self-actualization, which, as Abraham Maslow (1987), a major architect of the humanistic movement, asserts, is intimately intertwined with human dignity.

Human Rights Documents as Historical-Philosophical Compromises

Human rights documents are really historical-philosophical compromises in response to violence, in which human development is thwarted. These documents are indeed teaching tools (recall that *docere* means "to teach"), representing choices, kinds of constitutions, that reflect the wisdom of many members of the global community, most often governments, ideally with input from the "will of the people," a phrase found in every state constitution in the United States (Wronka, 1998b). Indeed, some human rights documents are called conventions or covenants, whose Latin root, *convenire*, means "to meet, to come together." But in some cultures, such documents, which ultimately crystallize values into legally mandated rights, are not written down, for example, indigenous cultures in which sharing was traditionally highly valued, as in the Inupiat Illitqusiat movement in the Arctic region of Alaska. Other handed-down values were knowledge of language, sharing, respect for elders, love for children, hard work, knowledge of one's family tree, avoidance of conflict, respect for nature, spirituality, humor, family roles, successful hunting, domestic skills, humility, and responsibility to the tribe (Wronka, 1993). Ultimately, human rights documents are variations of a theme, representing choices in response to broadly defined violence. The Inupiaq value of sharing reflects the need for communal responsibility in a harsh environment; the U.S. Bill of Rights' emphasis on freedom of religion reflects the colonists' terror from the religious wars in Europe.

It would be a mistake, however, to view the history of human rights as merely a struggle between the forces of good and evil. The world is more complicated. Such a Hobson's choice[4] may be tempting, but it could easily result in a kind of evil imaging of the other, which is hardly a productive way to engage in positive social action and service. Such a dichotomy could also result in a holier-than-thou attitude on the part of the human rights defender or social justice advocate. The helping and health professions may be prone to such self-righteous attitudes. The helper, for example, may feel more self-actualized than thou, better psychoanalyzed than thou, more in touch with feelings than thou, more able to empower than thou, healthier than thou, or more organic than thou.

Indeed, a little humility might help. Historically, human rights defenders have had their share of issues. An obvious case is the beheading of an early feminist activist, Olympe de Gouges (Healy, 2001), by those supposedly concerned about human rights. Concerned that the French Declaration of the Rights of Man and Citizen, drafted soon after the French Revolution, was limited by excluding half of the human race—that is, women—she drew up a document on the Rights of Women. For her heresy, she faced the guillotine. Thus, the history of the idea of human rights involves a struggle, yes, but not necessarily between the forces of good and evil. Rather, to paraphrase Zorba, it is a story of the people's agony in making sense of their lives as they deal with the basic ontological question: What does life mean in the face of death? Shall we, asked Shakespeare, "suffer the slings and arrows of outrageous fortune" or rise against them? The story of human rights is about the struggle of the human race to ascend to the heights rather than cave in to circumstance. Indeed, human rights documents have emerged as guiding lights in a world of darkness.

Figure 2.1   Olympe de Gouges, Author of the French Declaration on the Rights of Women and the Female Citizen, Facing the Guillotine. Fearful that the French Declaration on the Rights of Man and Citizen failed to include half the human race, Olympe de Gouges drafted a Declaration on the Rights of Women, for which she faced the guillotine.

Source: Wikimedia Commons/Mettais/1793.

The Human Rights Triptych

To get a further sense of this journey, it is now necessary to examine what René Cassin sometimes referred to as the "true father of human rights" (Szabo, 1982, p. 23), the *human rights triptych*. This triptych is akin to works of artists like Peter Breughel and Hieronymus Bosch, such as the latter's *Garden of Earthly Delights,* in which the central panel depicts the main theme, the descent of humanity; the right panel depicts the seven deadly sins; and the left, the Garden of Eden. The side panels elaborate on the essence of the main theme. In the human rights triptych (Table 2.1), the central panel, the most important in understanding human rights, is the Universal Declaration of Human Rights, whose five crucial concepts are discussed in Chapter 1. (Included here also is the UN Charter, which preceded the Universal Declaration, but has emerged as an extremely powerful voice in world affairs, especially because of its status as a treaty. It is important for the social activist to have some awareness of the Charter's major principles as well.) On the right side are the declarations and covenants that followed it; on the left are the means of its implementation, which consist largely of filing reports pertaining to human rights committees, and world conferences. Both side panels embellish the essence of the Universal Declaration.

The following are eight major human rights instruments that came after the Universal Declaration, along with their acronyms and the dates they entered into force (that is, became law in the international community): (a) the International Covenant on Civil and Political Rights (ICCPR, 1976); (b) the International Covenant on Economic, Social and Cultural Rights (ICESCR, 1976); (c) the Convention on the Rights of the Child (CRC, 1990); (d) the Convention on the Elimination of Discrimination Against Women (CEDAW, 1981); (e) the Convention Against Torture and Other Cruel, Inhuman, or Degrading Treatment or Punishment (CAT, 1987); (f) the International Convention on the Elimination of All Forms of Racial Discrimination (CERD, 1969); and (g) the Convention on Migrant Workers (CMW, 2003). Recently drafted was the Convention on the Rights of People with Disabilities (CRPD, 2006). These conventions have the status of treaty and, when ratified, according to Article 6 of the U.S. Constitution, the Supremacy Clause, they must be considered "Supreme Law of the Land" and "judges bound thereby" (Weissbrodt, Fitzpatrick, & Newman, 2001). The United States has ratified the ICCPR, CAT, and CERD, but with the caveat that they be "non-self–executing"—that is, nonenforceable in U.S. courts (Buergenthal, Shelton, & Stewart, 2002). Given this notion of "non-self–executing," the argument could easily be made that the United States has ratified none of these conventions. One hopes human rights defenders will one day succeed in removing this shameful caveat. Ratification ultimately should be more than a mere symbolic gesture, even though U.S. ratification at this time may still provide fodder for social action vis-à-vis human rights reports soon to be discussed.[5] Symbols can move people, but legally binding documents buttressed by the will of the people are preferable.

Occasionally, optional protocols are added, generally to address issues that governments felt needed further articulation but were dealt with only briefly, if at all, in the document. Examples are the Optional Protocol to the ICCPR Aiming at Abolition of the Death Penalty (1991), the Optional Protocol to the CRC on the Involvement of Children in Armed Conflict (2000), and the Optional Protocol on the Sale of Children, Child Prostitution, and Child Pornography (2000).[6]

Generally, documents in the right panel of the tryptich elaborate on rights the Universal Declaration only touches on. Thus, whereas the Universal Declaration may say simply, "Motherhood and childhood are entitled to special care and assistance" (Article 25), CEDAW and CRC establish what this special care and assistance means. For example, the CEDAW states that this special care and assistance means governments ought to "encourage the provision of necessary supporting social services to enable parents to combine family obligations with work responsibilities and participation in public life, in particular through promoting the establishment and development of a network of child-care facilities" (Article 11). They should also ensure "to women appropriate services in connection with pregnancy, confinement and the post-natal period, granting free services where necessary, as well as adequate nutrition during pregnancy and lactation" (Article 12). Examples in CRC are the right of the child to "be registered immediately after birth . . . and the right from birth to a name, the right to acquire a nationality and, as far as possible, the right to know and be cared for by his or her parents" (Article 7); to "assure to the child who is capable of forming his or her own views the right to express those views freely in all matters affecting the child, the views of the child being given due weight in accordance with the age and maturity of the child" (Article 12); and "the establishment of social programmes to provide necessary support for the child and for those who have the care of the child" (Article 19).

The left panel, undoubtedly the weakest part of the triptych with its emphasis on implementation, consists primarily of charter- and treaty-based approaches to implementing human rights principles. The former primarily consist of the appointment of special rapporteurs to examine and report on a particular theme and/or country that gained prominence in the global community. Such themes include racism and xenophobia (1993), violence against women (1994), extreme poverty (1998), the right to food (2000),

Table 2.1   The Human Rights Triptych

Implementation	The Authoritative Definition of Human Rights Standards	Documents Following the Universal Declaration
1. Thematic and Country-Based Reports for Charter-Based Concerns 2. Dialogue with the Human Rights Monitoring Committees of Major Human Rights Conventions consisting of: a. the filing of reports; b. the response of the human rights monitoring committee; and c. the informing of the appropriate governmental bodies of the positive aspects and concerns of the committee. 3. World Conferences and Action Plans	1. The United Nations Charter, which has the status of Treaty 2. The Universal Declaration of Human Rights (UDHR)—the Authoritative Definition of Human Rights Standards, increasingly referred to as Customary International Law and consisting of five crucial notions: a. human dignity b. nondiscrimination c. civil and political rights d. economic, social, and cultural rights e. solidarity rights	1. Eight Major Human Rights Conventions having the status of Treaty a. The International Covenant on Civil and Political Rights (ICCPR) b. The International Covenant on Economic, Social and Cultural Rights (ICESCR) c. The Convention on the Rights of the Child (CRC) d. The Convention on the Elimination of Discrimination Against Women (CEDAW) e. The Convention Against Torture (CAT) f. The International Convention on the Elimination of All Forms of Racial Discrimination (CERD) g. The Convention on Migrant Workers and Their Families (CMW) h. International Convention on the Rights of Persons with Disabilities (CRPD) Other human rights protocols and documents, like the Genocide Convention and the Draft Declaration on the Rights of Indigenous Peoples

the situation of Indigenous Peoples (2001), the highest attainable standard of physical and mental health (2004), and torture and other cruel, inhuman, or degrading treatment or punishment (2006). The latter, treaty-based mechanisms involve a human rights monitoring committee that examines, with a spirit of creative dialogue, a country's progress vis-à-vis each article of the eight major conventions. Such implementation mechanisms can be extremely powerful tools for creating awareness of human rights principles and, ideally, a collective change of character for entire nations. One example is the plethora of laws and policies that have arisen in roughly the last decade to combat violence against women, not long after the special rapporteur's report on violence against women.

There are also world conferences, often under the auspices of the United Nations, but in concert with numerous NGOs that have become a powerful force governments must reckon with. Some examples are conferences, with their attendant action plans, on overpopulation in Cairo (1993), women in Beijing (1995), food in Rome (1997), racism in Durban (2001), sustainability in Johannesburg (2002), and the information society in Tunisia (2005). Implementation mechanisms are discussed later in this chapter.

This introduction to the human rights triptych gives you perspective for examining the history of the human rights concept, which has emerged in the public consciousness and remains a powerful force not only in world affairs but also in our professional and everyday lives.

The full history of human rights is beyond the scope of this book. This sketch, however, highlights some of the major developments. Although the term *human rights* was formally legitimated by the United Nations only in 1945, the concept is actually a legacy of centuries of struggle for survival of the human species against its own vulnerabilities in a sometimes inhospitable environment.[7]

Antiquity

Given that human dignity and the fulfillment of human need are at the core of human rights, one could easily say human rights began somewhere along the Tigris and Euphrates rivers, where human civilization purportedly began. The first time one person acted decently toward another human in distress—that is, acted dutifully in ways that fulfilled human need and dignity—human rights began. Many cultures did not codify such obligations in texts, but this section arbitrarily begins with the Code of Hammurabi, which is a representative long-established ethical and legal system.

In this Code, King Hammurabi (1795–1750 BC) proclaimed groups of laws that people could readily understand in relation to their communal obligations. It had a prayerful format, beginning and ending with incantations to the gods. Close to 300 laws or codes of ethical conduct included numerous admonitions against, for example, false witness, failure to pay debt, physical violence toward one's parents and others, and willful poor construction of an abode. Such infractions were to be met with death or a punishment equal to the crime. For example, if a person stole, he would be put to death (Code 22); if a son struck his father, his hands would be cut off (Code 195); and if a man put out the eye of another man, his eye would also be put out (Code 196). The code also had an air of superstition. The accused, for example, were allowed to throw themselves into the Euphrates, and if the current bore them to the shore alive, they were declared innocent (Horne, 2006). Apparently, swimming was unknown at the time.

Certainly, the harshness of the Code of Hammurabi in no way represents the Universal Declaration's call for peace, tolerance, and friendship. Yet its relatively succinct statement of laws that were understandable to the educated layperson as a means of illustrating how people ought to act toward one another may have paved the way toward precursors to the Declaration, which also succinctly stated codes of conduct in educated layperson's language.

One can see the possible influence of that code in Judaism; Exodus 21:23 says, "Life for life, eye for eye, tooth for tooth, hand for hand, foot for foot, burning for burning, wound for wound." Meting out justice in such a retaliatory fashion is now largely discredited. The death penalty, for one, can easily lead to a culture of violence, especially when an innocent person is executed. Legal costs to prosecute someone in capital punishment cases are roughly twice those of life imprisonment. Sanctioning such punishment may even lead some to view the act of murder as an action in the service of a noble cause, and execution a means to their own immortalization.

The Judaic code, however, is most noteworthy for its notion of duties toward one another: "When you come upon your enemy's ox or ass going astray, see to it that it is returned to him. When you notice the ass of one who hates you lying prostrate under its burden, by no means desert him; help him, rather, to raise it up" (Exodus 23:4–5). In fact, this notion of duties is fundamental to human rights discourse. To reemphasize, the right to health care means eating foods that are nutritious, not overconsuming, and exercising. However, given the interdependency of rights, government must provide for the effective "social and international order" for the entitlement of such rights, such as the accessibility of parks for walking, swimming pools, bike paths from Maine to the Aleutians, as well as meaningful and gainful employment (also a predictor of longevity) to be able to afford foods that are nutritious and culturally acceptable (Eide, 1987).

The first crucial notion, then, is that of human dignity, with some of its religious/spiritual historical precedents part of this "Magna Carta for humanity," as Ms. Roosevelt called the Universal Declaration. The preponderance of the Judaic-Christian-Islamic tradition appears to have paved the way for this first crucial notion of human dignity. Judaism proclaims, for example, in Genesis 1:27, that "God created man in His image. In the image of God He created him." Christianity also accepts the dignity of the person, adding in John 1:1–4, "In the beginning was the Word, and the Word was with God; He was in the beginning with God. All things were made through Him, and without Him was made nothing that has been made. In Him was life and the life was the light of men." The Koran also states succinctly in Sura 17:70, "Verily we have honored every human being."

If all humans have dignity, it goes without saying that nondiscrimination is also fundamental to these three major religions. Although it is not within the scope of this section to discuss all further references to human dignity and nondiscrimination in scripture, one can also see these notions perhaps originating in Genesis 5:1–2: "When God created man, He made him in the likeness of God. Male and female He created them, and He blessed them and called them Man when they were created." Proverbs 22:2 states that "rich and poor have a common bond: The Lord is giver of all." Revered in most if not all major religious teachings, these fundamental human rights concepts are essential to the Universal Declaration and all its progeny. And certainly, if all humans are to be honored, human dignity and its corollary nondiscrimination for every person, everywhere ought to be continually invoked.

Continuing with this synopsis of my previous study (Wronka, 1998b), major precursors to notions of civil and political rights in antiquity appear in the works of major Greek writers such as Pericles (490–429 BC) and Sophocles (469–406 BC). In his famous oration on democracy, for example, Pericles spoke of being able to "serve the state . . . not hindered by the obscurity of his condition" (Kagan, 1965, p. 125). The right to expression and civil disobedience was expressed in Sophocles's *Antigone,* whose protagonist, in opposition to official decree, followed her conscience by burying her brother, Polynices (Palumbo, 1982). Also expressed in these ancient sources is the notion of hospitality toward beggars, who are "under Zeus' care" (Lloyd-Jones, 1971, p. 30). To be sure, the Greeks owned slaves, who may have outnumbered freemen (Curtis, 1981), and women had very few rights, illustrating the perennial problem of the gap between words and action that exists to this day.

After conquering Greece, the Romans largely built on the foundations of Greek ethical systems. A major development was the growing popularity of Stoicism, to which the sage Cicero was a convert (Higginbotham, 1967). Regarding its emphasis on the brotherhood of Man (finding its way into Article 1 of the Universal Declaration), Cicero expounded that "nature . . . unites man with man and joins them in bonds of speech and common life" (p. 43) and called for international binding principles that "ordain that no one is justified in harming another for his own advantage" (p. 144). Another influential thinker was Marcus Aurelius, whose *Meditations* paved the way for the notion of duties into human rights discourse: "What need for guesswork when the way of duty lies there before you" (Aurelius, 1984, p. 156). He also said most eloquently, "Put your whole heart into doing what is just . . . know the joy of life by piling good deed on good deed until no rift or cranny appears between them" (p. 186), and, finally, "Neither can I be angry with my brother or fall foul of him; for he and I were born to work together, like a man's two hands, feet, or eyelids . . . to obstruct each other is against nature's law" (p. 35).

In a nutshell, Aurelius's words speak to the essence of what it means to live in a socially just world. It may also be said, finally, that Marcus Aurelius's teachings exemplify a generalist model, or what in social work is more formally called an advanced generalist practice model; he was a social change advocate interested in world citizenship, an administrator as emperor of Rome, and a counselor and sage. The psychologist/ethicist Lawrence Kohlberg praised Aurelius's extremely high, if not impeccable, ethical standards as Roman Emperor—an administrator always aware of the needs of his employees, constituents, and even enemies. He was a precursor to the rational-emotive psychotherapy movement (Moss, 2001), which always acknowledges the importance of a person's reaction to difficult circumstance.

The Middle Ages

The most influential precursors to the Universal Declaration during the Middle Ages were the thinkers St. Augustine (354–430), St. Thomas Aquinas (1225–1274), and John of Salisbury (1120–1180). Augustine's classic work, *City of God*, laid the foundation for the inclusion of solidarity rights into the Universal Declaration. It notes, for instance, that people who take over a ship are called pirates. But should they take over a fleet, they are admirals. A case in point is the slaughter of millions of Indigenous People; presidents and governments do not "occupy," but rather "manage" the lands that were actually stolen. It is no wonder there is an outcry for self-determination today.

Aquinas's *Summa Theologica* reiterated the principle of human dignity. But he also added the "power of man . . . to participate intellectually and actively in the rational order of the universe" (D'Entreves, 1959, p. 21). In fact, through reason, humans can comprehend the "divine" nature of things, an indispensable expression of the dignity of the human person (Ebenstein, 1960). John of Salisbury again emphasized the common good, comparing humankind to the body: "The eyes, ears and tongue . . . claimed by judges . . . soldiers correspond to the hands . . . husbandmen correspond to the feet" (Ebenstein, 1960, p. 200).

Undeniably, the most significant document of this period was the Magna Carta, drawn up by the barons at Runnymede in 1215 in response to the abuses of King John. This document may have also been a legacy of the *Assizes of Jerusalem* (1099), drafted during the Crusades, in which the barons subordinated the power of the king in that holy city to themselves. Many of those surrounding King John at Runnymede had already seen terrible bloodshed during the Crusades and wanted an end to violence. They could have easily killed King John and his small entourage. But instead, they drew up a document that has stood the test of time as a testimonial to the efficacy of the power of nonviolence, which Gandhi and Martin Luther King, Jr. later referred to as "soul force." The document itself is replete with references to the rights incorporated into the Universal Declaration. Clause 30 of the Magna Carta, for example, states, "No person shall take the horses or carts of any free man." There is an obvious correspondence here with Article 12 of the Universal Declaration: "No one shall arbitrarily be deprived of his property" and, for that matter, his "standard of living," as asserted in Article 25. The safety of family life was also important in the Magna Carta, just as it is in the Universal Declaration. Clause 8 states that "no widow shall be disdained to marry herself, while she is living without a husband." And in the Universal Declaration, Article 16 declares the right to enter into marriage "with free and full consent" and "protection" of the family by society and the state.

The Renaissance

Gutenberg's invention of the printing press (1450), and Columbus's landing in what has become known as the Americas (1492), helped spread the notion that some humans were merely property, as was the case with African slaves, as well as provoking debates about whether Indigenous Peoples were themselves animals (Zinn, 1990). The printing press was used largely to spread viewpoints of elites, leading to untold misery in slave ships and the massacre of millions of Indigenous Peoples. But such mistreatment has finally created some backlash, fueling a present-day *Cry of the Oppressed* (Drinan, 1987) that *never again* should such pogroms occur. Much of the art of the Renaissance period also reinforced Eurocentrism. Thus, the beauty of the smile of Da Vinci's "Mona Lisa" or the steadfast grace, sensuality, and poise of Michelangelo's "David" were qualities attributed to one group, an attitude still alive today, as evidenced by the gross global maldistribution of wealth between the North and South, as well as between white and nonwhite cultures.

Four major social theorists of the time addressed major human rights issues: Petrarch (1304–1374), Giovanni Pico (1463–1494), Desiderius Erasmus (1466–1536), and Martin Luther (1483–1546). Petrarch emphasized that education ought to have a "sober use"—to educate the moral and upstanding person rather than serve as merely a "glittering shackle" (Jones, 1952, p. 564). Pico, in his *Discourse on the Dignity of Man,* spoke of humans as "worthy of all admiration" (Jones, p. 565). Erasmus was extremely concerned with the corrupting influence of power, asserting that for the ruler "every effort must be directed toward providing him with a proper education" (Gilmore, 1952, pp. 129–130). His well-known *Praise of Folly* attempted to expose the snobbishness, vanity, and immorality of many of the scholastic works of the time, calling for a nonelitist approach to learning scripture. He believed one needn't have scholastic degrees to practice virtues such as love and humility, major aspects of the Judaic-Christian-Islamic heritage. Folly was at times necessary to nourish the soul. Martin Luther called for freedom of conscience in religious matters. According to him, faith could not be forced on anyone. These notions of human dignity, as the legacies of these thinkers, are obvious in Eleanor Roosevelt's call for a document not for the doctors of jurisprudence but for the educated layperson, educational systems that teach tolerance and appeal to one's conscience in matters of religion.

An extremely influential document of the time was *The Vindiciae Contra Tyrannos (Defense of Liberty Against Tyrants),* written in 1579 under the pseudonym Stephen Junius. The document was actually a mass of precepts published by French Huguenots, many later murdered and others forced into exile. It focused mainly on the problem of obedience to the state, emphasizing the priority of individual conscience. Its precepts included "the whole body of the people is above the king" (Laski, 1925, p. 124); "subjects are the king's brethren and not his slaves" (p. 156); "the aims of justice are first that none be wronged, secondly, that good be done to all" (p. 225); and "justice requires that tyrants and destroyers of the commonwealth be compelled to reason; and that charity challenges the right of relieving and restoring the oppressed" (p. 229).

The *Vindiciae,* widely distributed thanks to the invention of the printing press, became a vehicle of bearing witness to the abuse of authority, urging others to respond to the dictates of their conscience that, among other things, arbitrary executions and exile should not be tolerated. Such principles are fundamental to human rights discourse.

The Age of Enlightenment

This period is perhaps best described by the motto *Sapere aude!*—that is, "Have the courage to use your own understanding" (Goldmann, 1973, p. 3), reflecting a growing disillusion with government and ecclesiastical authorities who engaged in various forms of religion- or class-based oppression. In the United States, it must first be said that the American Founding Fathers were influenced not only by European writers such as Locke, Rousseau, and Montesquieu, as well as ideas expressed in the Magna Carta and Greek and Roman thinkers, but also by the powerful, well-organized Haudenosaunee (Iroquois) [and] Kaianerekowa (Great Law of Peace). The Constitution's framers, therefore, adopted certain aspects of the Iroquois Confederacy, such as equal representation of nations (states), checks and balances, and the concepts of freedom, peace, and democracy (Mihesuah, 1996). Many of those concepts also eventually found their way into the Universal Declaration. Certainly, if the international community paid more attention to indigenous knowledge, they might lessen the global maldistribution of wealth (Wronka, 2007), a violation of solidarity rights. As Sitting Bull (Tatanka Iyotanka, 1831–1890) of the Sioux Nation observed, "The White man knows how to produce goods, but not how to distribute them" (Safransky, 1990, p. 74).

John Locke's (1632–1704) writings were extremely pervasive at that time. He wrote often of the rights to "life, liberty (freedom from arbitrary rule), and property" (Weston, 1989, p. 14) and had a major influence on Thomas Jefferson's *Declaration of Independence,* although the latter dropped the word *property,* substituting "the pursuit of happiness." However, although Locke advocated natural rights to not have to submit oneself to arbitrary rule, his writings lacked any notion of positive rights. In fact, Locke saw poverty as a result of moral failure rather than symptomatic of structural malaise (Cranston, 1961)—that is, social and international disorder.

Thomas Paine (1737–1809) appears to have provided an antidote to Locke's thinking about moral weakness as a reason for poverty. In his *Rights of Man,* he argued that government has a duty to provide for progressive taxation, education for all, and full employment so that "the haunts of the wretched will be known . . . and the number of petty crimes, the offspring of distress and poverty, will be lessened . . . and the cause and apprehension of riots and tumults will cease" (Fast, 1946, pp. 255–256).

Francois Marie Voltaire (1694–1778) was a strong proponent of freedom of the press and religious thought. To him, "Every private individual who persecutes a man, his brother, because he is not of the same opinion, is a monster" (Laquer & Rubin, 1990, pp. 79–81). Jean Jacques Rousseau (1712–1778) and Gracchus Babeuf (1760–1797) differed from their French colleague in adding compassion for the lower classes in Europe. Rousseau, in his *Social Contract,* wrote that no citizen "shall ever be wealthy enough to buy another and none poor enough to be forced to sell himself" (Ebenstein, 1960, p. 440). Babeuf, in his *Manifesto of Equals,* asserted, "We demand the communal enjoyments of the fruits of the earth: the fruits are for all" (Harrington, 1972, p. 24).

Major documents during this time were the Declaration of Independence (1776), the U.S. Constitution (1789), and the Bill of Rights (1791). Whereas the Declaration of Independence speaks of the equality of man, not only did it not recognize women, but it blatantly referred to Indigenous Peoples in the Americas as "Indian savages," revealing once again the hypocrisy of government, if not the frailty of the human condition. Revelatory of the philosophical *zeitgeist* of the time, however, these documents were fundamental to negative freedoms found in the Universal Declaration. The French Declaration of the Rights of Man and Citizen went beyond notions such as freedom of thought and conscience to more definitively assert economic rights, as in Article 6:

> The law should be the same for all, whether it protects or punishes; and all being equal in its sight, are equally eligible to all honors, places and *employments* [italics added] according to their different abilities, without any other distinction than that of their virtues and talents.

In spite of the beheading of Olympe de Gouges (1745–1793), her Declaration of the Rights of Women and the Female Citizen may have had an influence at that time, however slight. Article I of that document states that "woman is born free and lives equal to man in her rights. Social distinctions can be based only on the common utility."

The Age of Industrialization

A major characteristic of this epoch was the growing maldistribution of wealth, due in large measure to the rapid advancement of technology, which created limited ownership of capital and a depersonalized, if not dehumanized, the workforce subject to the whims of their employers, generally the owners of capital. Perhaps the predominant theorist of this time was Karl Marx (1818–1883), who collaborated with Friedrich Engels (1820–1895) in writing the *Communist Manifesto*. Marx was aware that, by themselves, civil rights were merely the rights of "egoistic man" (Tucker, 1978, p. 42), and he viewed them as a façade of capitalism (Kolakowski, 1983). In the *Manifesto,* he advocated for a "heavy progressive or graduated income tax . . . equal obligation of all to work . . . free education for all in public schools . . . [and] abolition of child factory labor in its present form" (Ebenstein, 1960, pp. 702–703). Later, the famed Muslim African American leader Malcolm X referred to civil rights as a watering down of the true notion of human rights.

However, it was not only Marx, Engels, and later, their follower Vladimir Ilyich Ulyanov (Lenin; 1870–1924) who were aware that civil, political, economic, social, cultural, and solidarity rights—that is, human rights—are

Figure 2.2   Malcolm X. Like Martin Luther King, Jr., he felt that it was no longer about a civil rights struggle, but a struggle for human rights. He urged oppressed peoples to use UN human rights bodies as a way of garnering the moral support of the world.

Source: Library of Congress.

interconnected with the need, expressed more recently by Malcolm X, for governments as well as an international authority to guarantee such rights. Papal encyclicals, such as Pope Leo XIII's *Rerum Novarum (On the Condition of Labor)* (1891) and Pope Pius XI's *Quadragesimo Anno (Reconstructing the Social Order)* (1931), have also advocated for such interconnectedness. *Rerum Novarum,* for example, states that

> whenever the general interest of any particular class suffers, or is threatened with harm, which can in no other way be met or prevented, the public authority must step in to deal with it. Now, it is to the interest of the community, as well as of the individual, that peace and good order should be maintained. (Sec. 36)

Indeed, the late Pope John Paul II spoke of the "grain of truth in Marxism" (Kwitny, 1997).

Perhaps the major document of this time was the Soviet Constitution of 1936, a rather liberal document, written perhaps as an alternative to the economic system that led to the Depression in the United States. Its articles assert certain economic and social rights:

> Article 118, the right to guaranteed employment; Article 119, the right to rest and leisure; Article 120, the right to maintenance in old age; and Article 122, that women are accorded equal rights with men. It is also replete with duties, such as those stated in Article 12: From each according to his ability, to each according to his work. (Chafee, 1952, pp. 911–916)

A major institutional development was the League of Nations, established at the Treaty of Versailles in 1919 in response to the horrors of World War I. The League later dissolved, largely over bickering about which country treated its own citizens or foreigners better. Yet, it did set up a Minorities Protection System, create the International Labor Organization (ILO), and endorse the Geneva Declaration of the Rights of the Child (1925), legacies that remain, for example, in the Convention on the Rights of the Child. It is worthwhile to recall once again the hypocrisy of governments, as nation-states attempted to resolve disputes among themselves. Poland, for example, on September 13, 1934, after numerous complaints from minorities, asserted it would no longer comply with the League's minority protection system. Germany withdrew from the League on October 14, 1933, refusing to acknowledge mistreatment of its own citizens while lambasting Poland for its alleged abuse of Germans in the Polish Corridor.

After the collapse of the League and the ensuing devastations of World War II, numerous conferences were held: the London Declaration, 1941; Atlantic Charter, 1941; Moscow Declaration, 1943; Dumbarton Oaks, 1944; and Yalta, 1944. But only with the establishment of the United Nations at the San Francisco Conference in 1945 did nations begin to work formally through this new international institutional structure to acknowledge human rights violations in other countries while beginning to look at violations in their own. Confronting countries' double standards remains a challenge to this day. The phrase *human rights*, in fact, did not appear in the original UN Covenant and was later mentioned only in the UN Charter as "a passing reference" (Farer, 1989, p. 195).

Select Input Prior to the Endorsement of the Universal Declaration

Thanks largely to the 42 private organizations the United States brought in as consultants, a Human Rights Commission was specifically provided for in

Article 68 of the UN Charter: "The Economic and Social Council shall set up commissions in economic and social fields and for the promotion of human rights" (Farer, 1989). The Commission had its first meeting on April 29, 1946, and listened to notables such as the author H. G. Wells. Previously, Wells had drawn up a draft "Declaration of the Rights of Man," which was translated into 10 languages, dropped in microfilm to the Resistance in occupied Europe, and distributed worldwide to 300 editors in 48 countries. It was a definite forerunner to the Universal Declaration, urging, among other things, right to life, protection of minors, duties to the community, freedom of movement, and freedom from violence (Dillow, 1986).

Several articles concerned human dignity and nondiscrimination rights. South Africa felt that notions of human dignity in Article 1 might destroy the whole basis of the multiracial structure of South Africa. Regarding Article 2, Russia wanted a more definitive statement of nondiscrimination by "class" rather than by "property or other status," which appeared in the final document (Department of Public Information, 1950). In regard to civil and political rights, it is noteworthy that the Soviet Union wanted a definitive statement in Article 3 (on the right to life, liberty, and security) on abolishing the death penalty, and called public lynchings in the United States human rights violations. France, a U.S. ally, retorted that sentences in Soviet concentration camps were like slow death penalties, to which Russia responded that properly run camps led not to inmates' death but rather to their reform. Regarding the notion of freedom of religion, thought, and conscience in Article 18, it is worth noting Russia saw many religious practices as leading to religious fanaticism, such as savage mortification and sacrifices of humans. Saudi Arabia was also concerned that missionaries had often abused the right to freedom of religion as a pretext for political intervention. Some Muslim countries also expressed much concern about the "freedom to change one's belief," which is forbidden by the Koran. Greece expressed concern that freedom to manifest religion might lead to unfair practices of proselytizing. In regard to freedom of speech in Article 19, the Soviet Union opposed freedom of speech for the propagation of aggression, accusing the American press of encouraging a war psychosis. In regard to freedom of assembly in Article 20, the Soviet Union wanted all antidemocratic gatherings to be forbidden by law so that the "monster of fascism" would not rise again. Haiti also felt that evildoers could easily justify their activities under this article (Department of Public Information, 1950).

Nations also responded to articles concerning economic and social rights. Commenting on Article 23 regarding the right to work, the Soviet Union described unemployment as one of the great misfortunes of the working class, a misfortune that cannot occur in the USSR's socialist economy. All states agreed that every person had the right to work, but disagreed over the extent of the state's responsibility to make that happen and whether joining a trade union should be obligatory. The right to rest and leisure in Article 24 was largely supported, although some states did not want to make it appear that such a right implied laziness. The United Kingdom wanted a definitive statement on the right to periodic holidays with pay. Concerning Article 25 on rights pertaining to a standard of living adequate for the well-being of the family, Yugoslavia urged inclusion of the equality of legitimate and illegitimate children. The United States also favored a guaranteed minimum standard of living and seemed to support the USSR's notion of social insurance being provided at the expense of the state and/or the employer. In regard to the right to education, Article 26, major issues arose over the right for a parent to choose children's education, to avoid replicating the compulsory indoctrination in Nazi Germany, where children were forced to join the Hitler Youth Movement. The right to participate in the cultural life of the community (Article 27) was added following the lead of Mexico, which asserted that progress is possible through not only intellectual but also cultural life (Department of Public Information, 1950).

Duties and solidarity rights covered in other articles were also debated. The USSR felt that as long as private ownership of the means of production existed, the social order mentioned in Article 28 would never be a good one. Australia believed endorsing the article did not imply an endorsement of capitalism. Cuba and India also urged definitive statements of duties to the community. But Belgium reminded the committee that mankind had yet to improve on the Ten Commandments, the cornerstone of which was "Thou shalt love thy neighbor as thyself" (Department of Public Information, 1950). Of the 56 member states of the UN at that time, on December 10, 1948, the General Assembly endorsed the Universal Declaration of Human Rights with no dissenting vote. There were eight abstentions: Byelorussia, Czechoslovakia, Poland, Ukraine, USSR, Yugoslavia, Saudi Arabia, and South Africa. In brief, members of the Soviet bloc were concerned that there was insufficient stress on economic, social, and cultural rights; Saudi Arabia felt that the freedom to change one's religion was inimical to Islam; and South Africa felt members of the committee were insensitive to the plight of foreigners living in a foreign land. (*Yearbook of the United Nations, 1948–1949*).

With this more in-depth understanding of some of the religious, historical, and philosophical antecedents to the Universal Declaration, it is now possible to move toward an understanding of the fundamental tenets of the major conventions following it (the right panel of the triptych). These conventions, of course, have their own history, beyond the scope of this text. The conventions on civil and political and economic, social, and cultural rights reflected deep divisions at that time (the Cold War) between the United States and its allies and the Soviet Bloc: The former generally preferred civil and political liberties, whereas the latter preferred economic, social, and cultural rights.

But these documents also arose from a general feeling among the global community that the needs of particular groups, manifested in human rights discourse, should be further addressed. The blind spot toward massive global discrimination against women, children, and people of color, for example, led to human rights documents for these respective groups. But here, too, blind spots persisted. For example, in the eight major conventions following the Universal Declaration, *indigenous* is used once, in Article 17 of the (CRC), asserting that states "should encourage the mass media to have particular regard to the linguistic needs of the child . . . who is indigenous" and briefly in the Preamble to the Convention on the Rights of People with Disabilities. No wonder Indigenous Peoples recently presented a Draft Declaration on the Rights of Indigenous People to the General Assembly calling attention to, among other things, the need to strengthen the "distinctive spiritual and material relationship with lands, waters, seas and other resources . . . [which shall include] . . . sea ice, flora, fauna" (Article 25) and the "right to traditional medicines and health practices" (Article 24). A blind spot, indeed! This declaration is discussed in more depth later in this chapter. A major criticism of this emphasis on particular groups is that it sets one group against another, a divide-and-conquer strategy. Yet, acknowledging the interdependence of rights and our global interconnectedness, these progeny of the Universal Declaration taken together have much potential to construct a socially just world.

Select Major International Human Rights Initiatives

The remainder of this chapter discusses and summarizes, in tabular form, the core principles of some the major progeny of the Universal Declaration, chosen somewhat arbitrarily but nevertheless, of paramount importance: the UN Charter, six major relatively long-standing human rights conventions, the Genocide Convention, and the Draft Declaration on Indigenous Peoples. Although the UN Charter came before the Universal Declaration, it is included here because it has the status of treaty, as do the eight major human rights conventions mentioned earlier and the Genocide Convention. It is important to stress that when ratified, these documents, at least in the United States, ought to be considered the "law of the land," according to the Supremacy Clause, Article VI, Sec. 2, of the U.S. Constitution.

The Genocide Convention is not generally considered a "major" human rights convention, primarily because it does not have ongoing monitoring committees, to be discussed later in this chapter. But it is included here because many of the conflicts in the world today are *intranational killings* among different groups, often living in the same nation (the term *genocide* comes from the Latin, *caedere,* "to cut down, to kill" and *genus,* "race, stock, family, kind"). It is an extremely important human rights document, which the United States ratified in 1988 and, therefore, must abide by. We, the people, must know about this document to ensure that our government, or any government for that matter, recognizes genocide when it occurs and implements the means to stop it. Unfortunately, this was not the case in Rwanda, when the governments of the world looked askance during the Rwandan massacres. President Clinton was reluctant to get involved then. Yet, with growing pressure President Bush has referred to the pogroms in Darfur as genocide, entailing governmental obligations and international accountability.

The Declaration on Indigenous Peoples, although presently not a treaty, is also included in this discussion, given its extreme importance to populations traditionally disregarded and a substantive achievement of the newly formed Human Rights Council. These populations often live in environmentally threatened areas and increasingly bear the burdens these threats pose, such as the loss of traditional cultural practices of a subsistence lifestyle of hunting and fishing, the use of traditional medicines in healing, and communal helping practices in general (Katz, 1982).

In creating the tables in this chapter, which assess the core principles and essential themes of the documents under discussion, I have attempted to keep the original wording, including such technical terms as *self-government* and *self-determination* and, at times, legalese like *nonrefoulement*. These nine tables, then, summarize for an educated layperson the documents' major principles that should be readily understandable to the general public. The article numbers in parentheses after the principles indicate where one can find them discussed in the documents. Given that these documents tend to be rather lengthy, at times 10 pages or more, these synopses can make major human rights principles accessible to more people and make them aware of how their government complies with them. I omitted the lengthy organizational procedures in some documents, such as reporting qualifications for membership in monitoring committees and the like.

My essential aim is to relay for the educated layperson principles based on the five core human rights concepts of the Universal Declaration—human dignity, nondiscrimination, and negative, positive, and solidarity rights. It would be worthwhile, as you read them, to think about how to make these principles a reality in the nation and the world (the macro); in local communities and workplaces (the mezzo); and in clinical practices and everyday life (the micro), points elaborated on with select examples in Part II. What are the implications for the helping and health professional, for example, of CEDAW's call for states to engage in the "encouragement of the provision of necessary social services to enable parents to combine family obligations with work responsibilities and participation in public life in particular through the development of child-care facilities"? Should helping professionals, as administrators, help employees juggle family with work life? Or is the UN Charter's call for a "due respect for the culture of peoples" not so much a state obligation as the obligation of helping and health professionals to respect the cultures of workers and clients, as they work collaboratively toward individual transformation and social change to create a socially just world? Also, phrases such as "self-determination," "respect for culture," "the elimination of stereotyped concepts of men's and women's abilities," "the promotion of understanding, tolerance, and friendship," "right to due process," "freedom of conscience and thought," "right to self-help groups," and "the treatment with humanity and respect for the inherent dignity of the human person" are integral to these documents. The challenge for helping and health professionals, or for any educated layperson, is to implement such concepts in the mutual struggle for social justice.

Occasionally, there is also some commentary, usually around issues of ratification of the document. Later chapters examine other documents pertaining to medical ethics and protections of persons with mental illness that have more specific implications for the helping and health professions. Client empowerment and cultural, racial, and gender biases integral to the helping and health professions are just a few topics more specific human rights documents entertain. Yet the documents discussed in this chapter certainly provide a catalog of guiding principles in service of social justice. One may intuitively sense that no person should be homeless, lacking in health care, or insecure in old age, but these documents legitimize, if not enshrine, social justice concerns in the language of human rights, a powerful idea whose time has come.

The principles of the Convention on Immigrants and Persons with Disabilities are of extreme importance, but because of their newness I have chosen not to include them at this time. Nevertheless, it is worth noting that 80 countries signed on immediately when the Convention on Persons with Disabilities opened for state signature on March 30, 2007. This is testimony to the power of human rights and the remarkable progress much of the world has made from the global *zeitgeist* during the 1938 Conference of Evian.

Select Core Principles of Some Major Human Rights Documents

The UN Charter

The United Nations Charter (Table 2.2) entered into force[8] in 1945. This Charter, like the seven major conventions following it, has the status of law, by which the United States is bound, according to the Constitution's Supremacy Clause. The United States has ratified three conventions with monitoring committees that followed the Charter—ICCPR, CERD, and CAT; CEDAW, CESCR, and the CRC were signed by the United States and are being considered for ratification in its legislative framework. Finally, the Genocide Convention and the Draft Declaration on Indigenous Peoples are very important and timely human rights initiatives.

Table 2.2   Select Core Principles of the United Nations Charter

Essential Theme (Article[s])	Elaboration
The maintenance of peace and security (1)	This shall take effective collective measures for the prevention and removal of threats of peace and to bring about by peaceful means, in conformity with principles of justice and international law, the settlement of international disputes.
The development of friendly relations among nations (1)	This shall be based on respect for the principle of equal rights and self-determination of peoples.
International cooperation in solving international problems of an economic, social, cultural, or humanitarian character (1, 55)	This shall be done by promoting respect for human rights and fundamental freedoms for all, without distinction as to race, sex, language, or religion.
The promotion of full employment (55)	This shall include the promotion of higher standards of living and the development of conditions of economic and social progress.
A due respect for the culture of peoples (73)	This shall include their political, economic, social, scientific, and educational advancement; their just treatment; their protection against abuses; and the encouragement of research to enhance development.
The development of self-government (73)	This shall take into account the political aspirations of the peoples and the progressive development of free political institutions.

Questions to ask in relation to the UN Charter are whether the United States[9] promotes the development of friendly relations among nations and full employment, engages in international cooperation, and has due respect for the culture of different peoples. Ultimately, these questions must be translated into social actions, to eradicate gaps between a country's words and actions.

Conventions With Monitoring Committees That the United States Has Ratified

The International Covenant on Civil and Political Rights (ICCPR; see Table 2.3) entered into force in 1976.

Table 2.3   Select Core Principles of the International Covenant on Civil and Political Rights (ICCPR)

Essential Theme (Article[s])	Elaboration
The right to self-determination (1, 27)	The right of people to freely determine their political status, freely pursue their economic, social, and cultural development, and dispose of their natural wealth based on the principle of mutual benefit; persons belonging to ethnic, religious, or linguistic minorities shall not be denied the right to enjoy their own culture or to use their own language.
The obligation of states to take necessary steps to realize civil and political rights through legislative and other means (2–5)	States must provide effective remedies by competent authorities if rights are violated; there shall be nondiscrimination of all people in regard to the law, in particular the equality of men and women.
The right to life (6–7)	No one shall arbitrarily be deprived of the right to life; those sentenced to death shall have the right to seek pardon; no person who committed a crime under 18 or a pregnant woman shall be given the death penalty; no one shall be subjected to torture or cruel and unusual punishment; medical experimentation shall require free consent.
The prohibition of slavery (5)	The slave trade in all its forms and forced or compulsory labor are prohibited.

The ICCPR has two optional protocols. The first, entering into force in 1976, relates to receiving individual complaints concerning human rights violations, and the other, adopted by the General Assembly in 1989, deals with the abolishment of the death penalty. The United States has ratified neither. As with CERD (Table 2.4), the United States has expressed concerns, preferring a broader reading of freedoms of speech than that enunciated in the ICCPR.

The Convention on the Elimination of Racial Discrimination (CERD) entered into force in 1969.

The United States had the following reservation regarding this document:

The laws of the U.S. contain extensive protections of individual freedom of speech, expression, and association. Accordingly, the U.S. does not accept any obligation under this Convention, in particular under Articles 4 and 7, to restrict those rights, through the adoption of legislation or any other measures. [And] the laws of the U.S. establish extensive protections against discrimination, reaching significant areas of non-governmental activity. Individual privacy and

Table 2.4   Select Core Principles of the International Convention on the Elimination of All Forms of Racial Discrimination (CERD)

Essential Theme (Article[s])	Elaboration
Definition of racial discrimination (1, 5)	Exclusion based on race, color, descent, and national or ethnic origin having the effect of nullifying the recognition on equal footing of human rights in the political, economic, social, cultural, or any other field of public life.
Special measures to secure advancement shall not be construed as racial discrimination (1, 2)	When circumstances warrant, states shall take special and concrete measure to ensure the adequate development and protection of certain racial groups; after objectives have been achieved, such measures shall discontinue; measures must not lead to the maintenance of separate rights of different racial groups.
The condemnation of racial discrimination and apartheid and the promotion of understanding among all races (2–3)	States will not sponsor, defend, or support racial discrimination, taking effective measures to nullify any laws that have that effect; states will encourage, where appropriate, means of eliminating barriers among races and discourage anything strengthening racial division.
The condemnation of propaganda and organizations based on ideas or theories of superiority and the adoption of immediate and positive measures to eradicate all incitement to this end (4)	Public authorities shall not permit, promote, or incite racial discrimination; dissemination of ideas based on racial superiority or hatred, incitement to racial discrimination, acts of violence, and provision of assistance, including financing, shall be prohibited by law.
The equal enjoyment of civil and political rights (5)	The right of equal access to participate, vote, and stand for election; equal treatment before tribunals; rights to travel, nationality, marriage and choice of spouse, inheritance, freedom of thought, conscience, and religion, freedom of opinion and expression, peaceful assembly and association, and to own property alone and in association with others.
The equal enjoyment of economic and social rights (5)	Rights to work, just and favorable conditions for work, protection against unemployment, equal pay for equal work, just remuneration, form and join trade unions, housing, public health, medical care, social security, social services, education and training, and equal participation in cultural activities.

Essential Theme (Article[s])	Elaboration
Equal access to any place or service intended for use by the general public (5)	Examples of such places are transport, hotels, restaurants, cafes, theaters, and parks.
Rights to effective remedies, if right is violated (6)	Rights shall include competent national tribunals and other state institutions to assist in remediation of rights.
The undertaking of immediate and effective measures (7)	These measures should be particularly in the fields of teaching, education, culture, and information to promote understanding, tolerance, and friendship among nations and racial or ethnic groups.

freedom from governmental interference in private conduct, however, are also recognized as among the fundamental values which shape our free and democratic society. To the extent that the Convention calls for a broader regulation of private conduct, the U.S. does not accept any obligation under the Convention to enact legislation or take other measure under paragraph (1) of Article 2. . . . The specific consent of the U.S. is required [before] a dispute . . . may be submitted to the jurisdiction of the International Court of Justice. (Weissbrodt, Fitzpatrick, Newman, Hoffman, & Rumsey, 2001, pp. 285–286)

Some of these reservations are legalese, yet a major issue appears to be problems of hate speech that might incite to violence, if not war. The United States has acknowledged that hate speech is the "cancer of the soul" at the ICCPR hearing, which I attended, yet it is well known that, in the United States, Nazis can have rallies. In some countries, like Germany, such rallies are forbidden, as is Holocaust denial. It is obvious how these documents expand the debates. In the United States, for one, it is often argued that an idea, however repugnant, should not be repressed. The challenge is to discuss and debate ideas in such a way that moves toward dignity and tolerance for all. Debate does not need to mean one party wins and the other loses. Rather, frank discussions and open debates are ways that persons can collectively seek truth by eliciting and responding to questions while moving toward a socially just society.

Next in Table 2.5 is the Convention Against Torture (CAT), which entered into force in 1987.

The United States has asserted its understanding that, to constitute torture, an act must be specifically intended to inflict severe physical or mental pain resulting from prolonged mental harm; the intentional infliction or threatened infliction of severe physical pain or suffering; the administration or application or threatened administration or application of mind-altering

Table 2.5   Select Essential Themes of the Convention Against Torture and Other Cruel, Inhuman, or Degrading Treatment or Punishment (CAT)

Essential Theme (Article[s])	*Elaboration*
Definition of torture (1, 4, 16)	Any act by which severe pain or suffering, whether physical or mental, is intentionally inflicted for the purposes of obtaining information, administering punishment for a crime someone or a third person has committed or is suspected of committing, intimidation, or discrimination of any kind. This act is done by the consent, acquiescence, or complicity of an official or other person acting in an official capacity. States shall also undertake to prevent other acts of cruel, inhuman, or degrading treatment or punishment.
The noninvocation of exceptional circumstances (2)	States or threats of war, internal political instability, any other public emergency, and order from a superior officer or public authority cannot justify torture.
The principle of *nonrefoulement* (no return) (3)	No state shall extradite a person if there are substantial grounds for believing there is danger of that person being tortured. Competent authorities will take into account the state's consistent pattern of gross, flagrant, or mass violations of human rights.
Principle of due process for the accused (6–9)	On examination of information, the accused shall be taken into custody and should be assisted in communicating immediately with the nearest appropriate representative of his or her national state. Time in custody shall only be the necessary time to enable criminal prosecution or extradition. If not extradited, the accused shall be guaranteed fair treatment in all proceedings in the state where the offense was committed. States shall engage in the greatest measure of assistance with criminal proceedings.
Education regarding the prohibition against torture in the training of law enforcement, military, medical personnel, and public officials involvedin custody and interrogation (10)	States shall keep systematic review of interrogation rules, methods, and practices used in the arrest, detention, and imprisonment of persons.
The right of due process to a person alleging torture (13–14, 16)	This right shall include the right to complain and to a prompt and impartial hearing. States shall ensure that the complainant and witnesses are protected. The victim shall have a right to fair and adequate compensation, including the means of full rehabilitation. In the event of death, defendants shall be entitled to full compensation. Any statement made under torture shall not be invoked as evidence.

substances or other procedures calculated to profoundly disrupt the senses or the personality; the threat of imminent death; and the threat that another person will imminently be subjected to death, severe physical pain, or suffering. The United States has also asserted that it "does not consider this Convention to restrict or prohibit the U.S. from applying the death penalty consistent with the Fifth, Eighth, and/or Fourteenth Amendments to the Constitution, including any constitutional period of confinement prior to the imposition of the death penalty" (Weissbrodt et al., 2001, pp. 282–283).

The General Assembly adopted an optional protocol to CAT in 2000 that would allow for "a system of regular visits undertaken by independent international and national bodies to places where people are deprived of their liberty, in order to prevent torture and other cruel, inhuman or degrading treatment or punishment." The United States has not ratified it.

Conventions With Monitoring Committees That the United States Has Signed

Signing a document is a major step a country takes to consider ratification in its legislative bodies. Of the human rights conventions with monitoring committees that the United States has signed, the first to be discussed in Table 2.6 is the Covenant on Economic, Social and Cultural Rights (CESCR), which entered into force in 1976. Although the United States has not ratified it, it is an extremely important document, considering the country's widespread poverty, lack of health care, and homelessness, in the midst of plenty—major human rights violations.

Table 2.6   Select Core Principles of the International Covenant on Economic, Social and Cultural Rights (CESCR)

Essential Theme (Article[s])	Elaborations
Right to self-determination (1)	The right of people to freely determine their political status, freely pursue their economic, social, and cultural development, and dispose of their natural wealth based on the principle of mutual benefit.
The progressive realization of human rights principles (2)	Through the undertaking of steps individually and through international cooperation and assistance, a view toward achieving progressively the full realization of rights in this Covenant, particularly through legislative measures. States shall undertake to guarantee nondiscrimination in the enjoyment of economic, social, and cultural rights.

(Continued)

Table 2.6 (Continued)

Essential Theme (Article[s])	Elaborations
The right to work (6–8)	Full and productive employment; fair wages to ensure a decent living for families; just and favorable conditions of work; the opportunity to gain a living by work; safe and healthy working conditions; opportunity for promotion based on seniority and competence; the right to rest and leisure, including reasonable limitation of working hours, such as periodic holidays with pay; the right to protect workers' interests through trade unions; fair wages and equal remuneration for work.
Protections for the family, particularly while responsible for the care and education of dependent children (10)	Paid leave for working mothers before and after childbirth; the prohibition of economic and social exploitation of children harmful to morals or health, likely to hamper normal development.
The right to an adequate standard of living for a person and her or his family (9, 11)	The right to social security, including social insurance; adequate food, clothing, and housing and the continuous improvement of living conditions; the improvement of the methods of production, conservation, and distribution of food and the dissemination of the principles of nutrition.
The right to the highest attainable standard of physical and mental health (12)	The reduction of the infant mortality rate; the improvement of environmental hygiene; the prevention, treatment, and control of epidemic, occupational, and other diseases; the assurance of medical attention in the event of sickness.
The right to education (13)	Education ought to be directed to the full development of the human personality and the sense of its dignity and the respect for human rights; it shall enable all to participate in society and promote tolerance among all nations, racial, ethnic, and religious groups; primary education shall be compulsory; secondary education shall be generally available and accessible to all; higher education shall be made equally accessible on the basis of capacity and in particular by the progressive introduction of free education.
The right to take part in cultural life and benefit in the advancement of science (15)	Steps must be taken to conserve, develop, and diffuse culture consistent with the goals of this Covenant; states must respect the freedom indispensable for scientific research and creative activity and encourage the development of international cooperation in the scientific and cultural fields; everyone has the right to benefit from scientific progress and its applications.

The United States has failed to ratify this convention largely because it does not perceive such economic and social rights as rights, per se, but the responsibility of the individual and the family. In effect, the United States does not acknowledge government financial obligations to take care of such human needs as the right to the highest attainable standard of physical and mental health. Human needs in the current economic system, with its emphasis on privatization, profit, and capital, are commodified—that is, treated like a commodity to be traded in the marketplace. In the most austere sense, good health care would thus go to the highest bidder; those unable to pay would have to go without.

The Convention on the Elimination of Discrimination Against Women (CEDAW) entered into force in 1981 (see Table 2.7).

Table 2.7   Select Core Principles of the Convention on the Elimination of Discrimination Against Women (CEDAW)

Essential Theme (Article[s])	Elaboration
Definition of discrimination against women (1)	Exclusion of women that nullifies their recognition of civil, political, economic, social, and cultural rights.
The equality of men and women (2–3)	States must adopt appropriate legislation, legal protections, and competent tribunals to eliminate discrimination and ensure the full development and advancement of women.
The modification of social and cultural patterns of conduct to eliminate the idea of superiority or inferiority of either sex (5)	The common responsibility of men and women in the raising of children with the interest of the children as the primordial consideration.
Participation of women in policy formulation (7)	The right to vote, right to be eligible for public office, and right to participate in nongovernmental organizations.
Equality of men and women in education (10, 13)	Similar access to same curricula, teaching staff, scholarships, and studies from the preschool to the professional, higher technical levels; the elimination of stereotyped concept of men's and women's abilities; enactment at the earliest possible time of programs to eliminate any gap in functional literacy; same opportunities to participate in sports; information and advice on family planning.
Equality of men and women in employment (11)	Similar access to all benefits and conditions of service, promotion, job security; the right to equal remuneration and the protection of health and safety, including safeguarding the function of reproduction.

(Continued)

Table 2.7 (Continued)

Essential Theme (Article[s])	Elaboration
Nondiscrimination on the grounds of maternity and marital status (11–12)	Introduction of maternity leave with pay without loss of former employment or seniority; prohibition against dismissal on the basis of pregnancy or marital situation; encouragement of the provision of necessary social services to enable parents to combine family obligations with work responsibilities and participation in public life, in particular through the development of child care facilities; appropriate services in connection with pregnancy, confinement, and the postnatal period, granting free services when necessary and adequate nutrition during pregnancy and lactation.
Elimination of discrimination in areas of economic and social life (13)	Rights to family benefits, bank loans, mortgages, other forms of financial credit, and participation in recreational activities and all aspects of cultural life.
Particular attention to the situation of rural women, including their work in nonmonetized sectors of the economy (14)	Right to obtain all types of training and education, formal and nonformal, as pertaining to technical proficiency and functional literacy; right to self-help groups and cooperatives to obtain equal access to economic opportunities through employment or self-employment; access to agricultural credit and loans, marketing facilities, appropriate technology, and equal treatment in land and agrarian reform and land resettlement; right to enjoyment of adequate living conditions, particularly in relation to housing, sanitation, electricity and water supply, transport, and communications.
Equality of men and women before the law (15)	Equal rights to conclude contracts and administer property; equal treatment in all stages of procedure in courts; equal rights in regard to movement of persons and freedom to choose residence; the nullification of all instruments restricting the legal capacity of women.
Equality in marriage and the family (16)	Rights to marry and freely choose a spouse with free and full consent; similar rights, irrespective of marital status in matters relating to their children, with the interests of the child as paramount; right to decide freely and responsibly the number and spacing of children and access to information and the means to secure this right; right to choose a family name, profession, occupation; similar rights in respect to ownership, acquisition, management, administration, enjoyment and disposition of property; compulsory official registration of marriage.

Given the failure to pass the Equal Rights Amendment, and that there are antidiscrimination clauses pertaining to gender in the constitutions of only 11 states (Wronka, 1998b), the United States' failure to ratify CEDAW reflects a culture perhaps inimical to gender issues. Also, the United States expressed some concerns that (a) it "would not be required to provide paid maternity leave or ensure the continuation of other benefits" under the convention, (b) an understanding that the convention did not establish a right to an abortion, and (c) that it "would be able to determine which health care service was appropriate and which services would be free" (Weissbrodt et al., 2001, p. 128). The United States has also not ratified the Optional Protocol to CEDAW, adopted by the General Assembly in 1999 and entered into force in 2000. This protocol would allow for the human rights monitoring committee to hear complaints from individuals and groups who felt they were discriminated against on the basis of gender.

The sixth major human rights convention that has a human rights monitoring committee is the Convention on the Rights of the Child (CRC) in Table 2.8. Only the United States and Somalia have not ratified this document. The latter country, however, does not appear to have the governmental capacity to do so. Although lengthy, this document's lucidity and thoroughness can be particularly helpful as a set of good and solid guiding principles for the helping and health professions and certainly for anyone aspiring to a socially just world for these defenseless ones, who will eventually inherit the earth.

(Text continues on p. 81)

Table 2.8   Select Core Principles of the International Convention on the Rights of the Child (CRC)

Essential Theme (Article[s])	*Elaboration*
Nondiscrimination of the child (1–2)	Generally, every human being under 18 shall be respected irrespective of the child's or the parents', or legal guardian's, race, color, sex, language, religion, political opinion, national, ethnic, or social origin, property, disability, birth, or other status.
Best interests of the child as the primary consideration (3, 5, 9, 18)	Parents, legal guardians, and where applicable, members of the extended family or community as provided by local custom, all public and private social welfare institutions, services, and facilities responsible for the care of children shall conform to standards established by competent authorities, particularly in areas of safety and health; separation shall take place against the child's will only if by competent authorities it is seen as in the child's best interest

(Continued)

Table 2.8 (Continued)

Essential Theme (Article[s])	Elaboration
	and all parties are given due process; the child must also have the right to maintain contact and personal relations with both parents, unless contrary to the child's best interests; in cases of imprisonment or detention, information must be given to the child of the parents' whereabouts unless it is detrimental to the child's well-being.
Economic, social, and cultural rights for all children (4–5, 24, 26–29)	Measures must be undertaken to the maximum extent of available resources and where needed within the framework of international cooperation to ensure the maximum survival and development of the child; this shall include recognition of the right of the child to the enjoyment of the highest attainable standard of health; the state shall ensure provision of necessary medical assistance, with emphasis on the development of primary health care, including attempts to diminish infant and child mortality and to combat disease and malnutrition, applying readily available technology, the provision of adequate nutritious foods and clean drinking water, the provision of appropriate pre- and postnatal health care for mothers, and the provision of appropriate health care information, such as the advantages of breastfeeding, hygiene, environmental sanitation, and the prevention of accidents; traditional practices prejudicial to the health of children must be abolished; every child has the right to social insurance and a standard of living adequate for the child's physical, mental, spiritual, moral, and social development; states shall take appropriate measures to assist parents unable to financially take care of their children, particularly in regard to nutrition, clothing, and housing; the child shall have the right to education, including, among other things, free and compulsory primary education and the availability of secondary education; states shall offer financial assistance if not free education, make higher education accessible to all on the basis of capacity, make educational and vocational information and guidance available, and encourage of regular attendance and the reduction of dropout rates; school discipline must be consistent with the child's dignity; education of the child shall be directed to the respect for the child's parents, his or her cultural identity, language, the country from which he or she may originate, and for civilizations different from his or her own; the preparation of the child for responsible life in a free society with respect for human rights and in the spirit of understanding, peace, tolerance, equality of sexes,

Essential Theme (Article[s])	Elaboration
	and friendship among all people, and development and respect for the national environment.
Right to registration and respect of identity (7, 8, 30)	This shall be carried out immediately after birth, which shall include the right to a name, nationality, and as far as possible, the right to know and be cared for by his or her parents; identity, including nationality, name, and family relations, must be preserved and speedily reestablished if illegally deprived; minorities or Indigenous People shall not be denied the right to enjoy their own culture, to profess and practice their own religion, or to use their own language.
All treatment of the child shall be done in a positive, humane, and expeditious manner (10–11)	This is particularly important in regard to family reunification; there shall be no illicit transfer and nonreturn of children.
Respect for the views of the child (12)	In any issue pertaining to the well-being of the child, his or her views, expressed freely, must be taken into account, giving due weight to the maturity of the child.
Respect for the civil and political rights of children (13–16)	This includes the right to freedom of expression, regardless of frontiers, either orally, in writing, in art, or any other media of the child's choice, restricted in part for the rights or reputations of others and the protection of public health or morals; the child shall have the right to freedom of thought, conscience, and religion; regarding religion, the rights of parents need to be respected; the child also has the right to freedom of association and peaceful assembly; no child shall be subjected to arbitrary interference with his or her privacy, family, home, or correspondence or to unlawful attacks on his or her reputation.
Respect of rights and duties of parents and when applicable, legal guardians (14)	This right particularly concerns the need to provide direction to the child in a manner consistent with the child's evolving capacities.
The importance of the media in the promotion of the child's social, cultural, spiritual, and moral well-being and physical and mental health (17)	Material in the media must be available from a diversity of national and international resources; the media must have particular regard to the linguistic needs of the child who belongs to a minority or is indigenous; the child must be protected from materials injurious to his or her well-being; children's books must be encouraged, produced, and disseminated.

(Continued)

Table 2.8 (Continued)

Essential Theme (Article[s])	Elaboration
States shall render assistance to parents and legal guardians in the performance of child-rearing responsibilities and shall ensure the development of institutions, facilities, and services for the care of children (18)	This right acknowledges that states must recognize that both parents have common and primary responsibilities for the upbringing of children, where the best interest of the child shall be the primary concern; this assistance shall include the right to benefit from child care services for working parents.
The state shall take appropriate measures to protect the child from mental and physical abuse and to provide care for the child in the event of being deprived of his or her family (19, 20, 25, 33, 39)	Abuse shall include any neglect or negligent treatment, maltreatment, exploitation, sexual abuse; protective measures shall include social programs to provide necessary support for the child and for those who have care of the child, as well as other forms of prevention, identification, reporting, referral, investigation, treatment, and follow-up; all children have the right to periodic review of treatment; if the child is temporarily or permanently deprived of his or her family, the state shall ensure alternative care for such a child, which shall include, among other things, foster placement, *kafalah* of Islamic law, adoption or, if necessary, placement in suitable institutions; due regard shall be paid to the desirability of continuity in a child's upbringing and to the child's ethnic, religious, cultural, and linguistic background; states shall protect children from the production, illicit use, and trafficking of narcotics and psychotropic substances; any child abused has the right to recovery and social reintegration in a manner fostering health, self-respect, and dignity.
States shall take appropriate measures to give humanitarian assistance and appropriate protection for refugee children (22)	The child shall be treated with appropriate protections and with humanitarian assistance with the cooperation of the United Nations and other competent inter- and nongovernmental organizations to protect and assist the child and to obtain necessary information with an eye toward reunification; if no family can be found, the child shall be given the same protections as a child deprived of his or her family environment.
A child physically or mentally disabled should enjoy a full and decent life (23)	Such a life would ensure dignity, promote self-reliance, and facilitate the child's active participation in the community; assistance to the child shall be extended to those in care of her or him free of charge whenever possible, taking into account the financial resources of

Essential Theme (Article[s])	Elaboration
	those caring for the child; the child shall receive education, training, health care, rehabilitation, preparation for employment, and recreational opportunities in a manner conducive to the child's fullest possible social integration and human development; states will, in the spirit of international cooperation and taking particular account of developing countries, share information about the preventive health care and rehabilitation in general in this regard.
The right to rest and leisure (31)	This shall include the rights to engage in play and recreational activities appropriate to the age of the child and to participate fully in cultural and artistic life with equal opportunities for cultural, artistic, and recreational and leisure activity.
The right to be protected from exploitation of any kind (32, 34)	This shall include economic exploitation in work that is hazardous or will interfere with a child's education; this will include appropriate regulation, among other things, of hours and conditions of employment; sexual exploitation of children is strictly forbidden, including, but not limited to, prostitution, use of children in pornographic materials or performances, and any unlawful sexual activity.
A child must be treated with dignity if alleged or accused of infringing penal law (37, 40)	No child shall be subjected to torture, degrading punishment, nor life imprisonment without the possibility of parole; he or she shall be given due process, including, but not limited to, presumption of innocence, treatment with worth that reinforces the child's respect for human rights, to have legal and appropriate assistance, free assistance of an interpreter, if necessary, and a speedy trial; a variety of dispositions must be made available, such as counseling, probation, and educational and vocational training programs to ensure children are dealt with in a manner appropriate to their well-being and proportionate to their circumstances, and the offense detention must be a last resort and for the shortest possible period; given the best interests of the child standard, he or she shall be separated from adults and have the right to maintain contact with his or her family.

(Text continued from p. 77)

Some of the major reasons for the U.S. refusal to ratify the CRC are: (a) child labor limitations may be broader than current U.S. standards; (b) an acknowledgment that it is not the state's duty to provide for the "promise of economic/ health/special needs/education support" of children as enunciated throughout the convention; and (c) the subsequent limitations on state control over policy on ratification (Fellmeth, 2002, p. 587). The United States, however, did ratify the two optional protocols to the CRC—one in 2002 on Children in Armed Conflict, prohibiting persons under the age of 18 to participate in hostilities, and the other in 2003 on the Sale of Children, Child Prostitution, and Child Pornography.

Two Select Timely Human Rights Documents

The Convention on the Prevention and Punishment of the Crime of Genocide (CPPG), or the Genocide Convention, in Table 2.9 entered into force in 1948; the United States ratified it in 1988. Although it does not have a human rights monitoring committee, the Convention's importance is obvious considering present-day attempts at ethnic cleansing, such as in Rwanda, Bosnia, Iraq, and now Darfur, not to mention historical precedents such as slavery and the extermination of Indigenous Peoples.

Table 2.9   Select Core Principles From the Convention on the Prevention and Punishment of the Crime of Genocide (CPPG)

Essential Theme (Article[s])	Elaboration
Genocide must be prevented and perpetrators punished (1, 3, 4–6)	Genocide is a crime under international law, whether in time of peace or war. Punishment shall also be for conspiracy to commit genocide, direct and public incitement to commit genocide, attempt to commit genocide, or complicity in genocide; perpetrators shall include constitutionally responsible rulers, public officials, or private individuals and shall be tried by competent tribunals; states will enact necessary legislation to provide effective penalties.
Definition of genocide (2)	Acts with intent to destroy, in whole or in part, a national ethnic, racial, or religious group, such as killing members of the group, causing serious bodily or mental harm, deliberately inflicting conditions of life calculated to bring about the group's physical destruction in whole or in part, imposing measures intended to prevent births within the group, transferring children of the group to another group.

The United States had a reservation about this document, requiring the specific consent of the United States in each case before any dispute is submitted to the International Court of Justice. It had also asserted that the term *mental harm* should be defined as "permanent impairment of mental faculties through drugs, torture or similar techniques" and that acts committed "in the course of armed conflicts committed without the specific intent" are not sufficient to constitute genocide as defined by this Convention (Weissbrodt et al., 2001, p. 181).

Finally, there is the most recent document, pertaining to Indigenous Peoples, the Draft Declaration on the Rights of Indigenous Peoples in Table 2.10 endorsed by the General Assembly in September 2007. This document is a major achievement of the new Human Rights Council, reflecting extensive input from Indigenous Peoples.

Table 2.10   Select Core Principles From the Declaration on the Rights of Indigenous Peoples

Right to self-determination (3–4, 8, 12, 14, 18–19, 21, 31, 32–39)	Free determination of political status and the pursuit of economic and social development; right to strengthen distinct cultural characteristics, yet should they choose, to participate in the political, economic, social, and cultural life of the state; right to be recognized as indigenous; right to develop past, present, and future manifestations of culture, such as archeological sites, artifacts, ceremonies, literature, and visual and performing arts; right to revitalize, develop, and transmit languages, oral traditions, philosophies, literatures and to retain own names for communities, places, and persons; right to participate fully in all levels of decision making affecting their rights, lives, and destinies; right to maintain indigenous decision-making institutions and participate fully at all levels of decision making; right to develop their own political, economic, and social systems; right to autonomy and self-government regarding culture, religion, education, information, media, health, housing, employment, social welfare, economic activities, land and resources, environment, and entry by nonmembers; right to retain own citizenship and citizenship of the state; right to develop institutional structures; right to determine responsibilities; right to develop contacts and cooperation across borders; shall include cooperation by the state to achieve these rights.
Full guarantees against genocide (6–7, 10, 36)	Shall include the removal of indigenous children under pretext; shall include ethnic and cultural genocide; no relocation shall occur without full informed consent, agreement on just compensation, and where possible, the option to return; right to enforcement of treaties.
Redress for deprivations of cultural values and ethnic identities (7, 12–13, 21, 27, 30)	Redress shall be for deprivation of lands, assimilation or integration imposed by the state, propaganda against them; restitution shall include cultural, intellectual, religious, and spiritual property taken without free and informed consent; the right to repatriation of human remains; shall include compensation for deprivation of means of subsistence; restitution shall include lands, territories, and resources traditionally owned but confiscated; shall also be redress for the exploitation of mineral and water resources.
Special protections in periods of armed conflict (11, 28)	No indigenous children shall be recruited into the armed forces; shall be no forcing of Indigenous Peoples to abandon lands for military purposes or serve in the military under discriminatory conditions; shall be no use of indigenous land for military activities or disposal of hazardous materials; shall be no recruitment of indigenous individuals against their will, and in particular, for use against other Indigenous Peoples.

(Continued)

Table 2.10 (Continued)

Right to control the education of indigenous children (15–16)	Shall include the right to be educated in own language in a manner appropriate to cultural methods of teaching and learning; the dignity and diversity of culture, traditions, histories, and aspirations shall be reflected in education and shall promote tolerance and understanding among Indigenous Peoples and all segments of society.
Right to establish own media (17)	Shall be in their own language, but with access to nonindigenous media, which ought to reflect indigenous cultural diversity.
Nondiscrimination in labor (18)	Shall include labor, employment, and salary.
Special measures for immediate, effective, and continuing improvement in economic and social conditions (22–23)	Shall include areas of employment, vocational training and retraining, housing, sanitation, health, social security, and rights of indigenous elders, women, youth, children, and disabled persons; Indigenous Peoples shall determine strategies and priorities for economic and social programs and administer them as far as possible.
Right to traditional medicines and health practices (24)	Shall include protection of vital medicinal plants, animals, and minerals and access to all medical institutions.
Right to maintain and strengthen distinctive spiritual and material relationship with lands, waters, seas, and other resources traditionally owned (25–26)	Shall also include sea ice, flora, fauna; with effective measures to prevent the state from interference, alienation, and encroachment on such rights.
Full recognition of cultural and intellectual property (29)	Special measures are necessary to control, develop, and protect human and other genetic resources, seeds, medicines, and knowledge of cultural traditions.

The United States voted against the document in 2006, largely because it felt the notion of self-determination is too strong, preferring the term *self-management* in regard to particular resources.

The lack of any international human rights document on discrimination based on sexual orientation must be mentioned; this is unfortunate, but it illustrates again that social justice is a struggle. It is worth noting that at the Fourth Session of the Human Rights Council in Geneva, on March 2007, the United Kingdom of Great Britain and Northern Ireland urged the world community to examine persistent discrimination against this group. Citing the 40th anniversary of the Sexual Offenses Act in the UK, they state: "We pause to remember that the majority of gay people around the world still live in countries where simply being themselves is a crime. Human rights belong to everyone" (McCartney, 2007, p. 3).

The brutal killing of a gay teenager, Matthew Shepard, in 1998, is an extreme case of human rights violations, but the refusal of some employers to hire people based on sexual orientation, which has nothing to do with bona fide occupational qualifications, is also an example of discrimination violating the rights to life and work found in almost every human rights instrument. At the December 1998 Human Rights Defenders' Conference, commemorating the 50th anniversary of the General Assembly's endorsement of the Universal Declaration, the general consensus of the NGOs was that such a document, while needed, was still too controversial. Unfortunately, the United States recently voted to deny two gay human rights groups, the Danish National Association for Gays and Lesbians and the International Lesbian and Gay Association based in Belgium, consultative status (presently 3,000 nongovernmental organizations have such status) with the United Nations (Hoge, 2006). Such status could eventually have led to a document that would prevent further bloodshed. No person, no matter what their sexual orientation, should be treated without dignity as occurs in places like Iran, where in 2005 two teenagers were executed simply for engaging in gay sex and where, according to the Persian Gay and Lesbian Organization, 4,000 gays and lesbians have been executed since the 1979 revolution (Iran, the Facts, 2007). Surely, much work remains to be done.

Other Human Rights Regimes

Before addressing the left panel of the human rights triptych within the UN system, a word must be said about some of the so-called human rights regimes mentioned earlier, such as the Organization of American States (OAS), the African Union (AU), and the European Union (EU). These groups also have their triptychs. The OAS, for instance, has the American Convention on Human Rights, with its Additional Protocol on Human Rights in the Area of Economic, Social, and Cultural Rights (Protocol of San Salvador) at the center and a number of other conventions on the right panel, such as the Inter-American Conventions to Prevent and Punish Torture, on the Prevention, Punishment and Eradication of Violence Against Women, and on the Elimination of All Forms of Discrimination Against Persons with Disabilities. Roughly 30 years ago, President Carter signed the American Convention, which his secretary of state, Warren Christopher, called "a significant advance in the development of the international law of human rights" (Weissbrodt et al., 2001, p. 127). To date, the United States has not ratified it or any of the additional protocols and conventions that followed. On the left of this triptych are also reporting mechanisms and reports by special rapporteurs (to be discussed within the UN system) on such themes as migrant workers, freedom of expression, and the rights of women. It is difficult to generalize about the OAS human rights machinery, but, perhaps because of rampant extreme poverty predominantly in southern countries, the emphasis seems to be primarily on economic, social, and cultural rights, such as the right to social security, health care, a healthy environment, food, education, the benefits of culture, the formation and protection of families and children, protection of the elderly, and protection of the handicapped. Speaking of the family (Article 15), for example, the Protocol of San Salvador asserts that states

> hereby undertake to accord adequate protection to the family . . . in particular: to provide special care and assistance to mothers during a reasonable period before and after childbirth; to guarantee adequate nutrition for children at a nursing state and during school attendance years; to adopt special measures for the protection of adolescents in order to ensure the full development of their physical, intellectual and moral capacities; [and] to undertake special programs of family training so as to help create a stable and positive environment in which children will receive and develop the values of understanding, solidarity, respect and responsibility.

The African Union has at its heart (the center of its triptych) the African Charter on Human and Peoples' Rights, with its documents on the Rights of Women in Africa, the Establishment of an African Court on Human and Peoples' Rights, the Convention Establishing the African Economic Community, and the African Charter on the Rights and Welfare of the Child. As expected, given the horrors of the transatlantic slave trade and in relation to major UN documents, the Union appears more concerned with rights to solidarity, noting, for instance, "the unquestionable and inalienable right to self-determination" (Article 20) and asserting that "colonized or oppressed peoples shall have the right to free themselves from the bonds of domination by resorting to any means recognized by the international community" (Article 20). It also calls on states, for example, to "undertake to eliminate all forms of foreign economic exploitation particularly that practiced by international monopolies" (Article 21). Various committees and reporting procedures are also included in the Charter's left panel.

Perhaps because of the centuries of conflict and wars waged on the European landscape, and its collective scars, the European Union, through its Council of Europe, appears to be the most developed of the human rights regimes as a possible preventive strategy. For instance, the European Convention on Human Rights and Fundamental Freedoms has at least 12 protocols dealing with issues such as prohibiting the collective expulsion of aliens and general prohibitions against discrimination. The document most discussed, however, is the European Social Charter of 1999, which very strongly supports second-generation rights, asserting roughly 40 rights in areas such as safe and healthy working conditions, vocational guidance and training, social welfare services, equal opportunities and equal treatment, dignity at work, and the right to protection against poverty and social exclusion. Generally, extreme poverty in Europe is not so much viewed as a product of low wages, although that is important, nor as a sign of failure that is somehow just; rather, it is defined in terms of social exclusion—that is, the barring of individuals and groups from participation in and building of community, an essential aspect of the human condition.

Implementation

For the most part, implementation mechanisms are extremely weak and ultimately must be left to the will of the people. However, paradoxically, there may be strength in weakness. Throughout this book I emphasize that only *chosen* values—in this case, human rights principles—endure. No one can impose a human rights culture on anyone. It must make sense to people. Surely, the collective wisdom of nearly the entire global community is testimony to the importance and efficacy of a society's commitment to human rights. It may take time, however, to implement human rights documents, and forcing them on a people will only make for superficial, if not totally artificial, change. Although theoretically and technically having the force of law, reporting mechanisms, especially conventions regarded as treaties, are often very difficult, though possible, to implement, for example, human rights committee recommendations.

The problem is that people are unaware of these reports. For example, after attending a hearing of the human rights monitoring committee of the ICCPR, Elizabeth Ewatt, an independent expert from Australia, commented that NGOs were having trouble getting the 1994 U.S. report to the committee. The United States said it would make more copies available. However, the Springfield College bookstore manager reported that, despite repeated calls, the U.S. Government Printing Office said it had never heard of the report. With the advent of the Internet, however, these reports have become available.[10]

These periodic reports, to be submitted roughly every 4 to 7 years, are excellent means of monitoring a government's progress toward implementing its treaty obligations. For example, the Periodic Report of the United States to the UN Human Rights Monitoring Committee on the Elimination of Racial Discrimination, submitted in April 2007, had to answer to the committee's concerns in the previous 2001 report about excessive police brutality toward some racial minorities and foreigners. The U.S. responded that, especially in light of 9/11, it has stepped up its training of law enforcement officers with particular attention to combating prejudices against Arab Americans and Muslim Americans. Also of concern in 2001 were major disparities in housing, equal opportunities for education and employment, and health care. The U.S. responded, in 2007, that minority-owned businesses represent the fastest growing segment of the economy, with evidence suggesting that gaps in educational attainment are beginning to close, especially at the elementary and middle school levels. Generally, governments comprising the UN are often reluctant to implement recommendations, unless it appears that the will of the people supports them. Social activists, therefore, have a major role in informing others about these reports and working with governments to ensure the implementation of human rights committee recommendations.

Country and Thematic Reports

These reports are sustained by Articles 55 and 56 of the UN Charter, which state that all governments "pledge themselves to take joint and separate action" to "promote . . . higher standards of living . . . full employment . . . development . . . solutions of international economic . . . and related problems; and . . . universal respect for, and observance of human rights and fundamental freedoms." The UN, essentially through its High Commissioner of Human Rights, an office established in large measure through efforts of the Clinton administration serves as the major overseer and facilitator of human rights initiatives, issues reports on states' progress toward implementation of human rights documents. These reports may be discussed at the annual Human Rights Council meeting. Presently, the Council answers to the General Assembly, where each country gets one vote. The commissioner often requests the drafting of reports on a specific country's compliance with human rights standards and/or various themes, such as violence against women, the situation of extreme poverty, and violations of the rights to food. Such reports are referred to as "charter based."

Although numerous procedures exist to deal with human rights violations, a prominent one is the 1503 Confidential Procedure, based on a country's adherence to internationally accepted human rights norms. What country is considered is obviously political, but this decision is made behind closed doors.

The criteria for a country to be considered are that the violation must be (a) gross and extremely severe in nature, (b) a consistent pattern and widespread, and (c) reliably attested. It must also be apparent that all domestic remedies have been exhausted—that is, every legal avenue has failed to resolve the area of contention (Steiner & Alston, 2000; Weissbrodt et al., 2001). Although deliberations are secretive, working groups generally get the cooperation and information they want from a country. After these deliberations, countries that continue to violate human rights are listed publicly. Since the inception of the 1503 procedure, roughly 80 countries have been considered, involving issues such as torture, political detention, summary or arbitrary killing, and disappearance (Weissbrodt et al., 2001). While this is certainly not a perfect world, the end of *de jure*—that is, legally sanctioned—apartheid in South Africa and the diminution of the "dirty" civil wars in Latin America may be testimony to the efficacy of this method.

Thematic procedures, moreover, can be extremely enlightening, and on occasion, such procedures also include investigation by a special rapporteur concerning the human rights situation in a particular country. If information is power, certainly knowing about disseminating, and using these reports to create open dialogue within a country and among countries is an excellent way to reach proper conclusions about and a general consensus on how to rectify human rights violations. These thematic mechanisms begin a process of scrutinizing countries' practices, which in this case, are in the public forum. In 1985, for example, the thematic procedure concerned itself with torture. The special rapporteur, who consults with NGOs as well as government bodies, uses his or her discretion, as an independent expert,[11] to transmit allegations of torture to governments. Since 1985, for example, these efforts have led to international scrutiny of at least 60 countries, including El Salvador, Haiti, India, Indonesia, Jamaica, and the Philippines. These procedures appear to have led to a growing international consensus on the prohibition against torture in this new millennium; the present international furor over alleged mistreatment of prisoners in Guantanamo is a case in point.

One noteworthy country report concerning U.S. compliance with CERD, ratified in 1994, was from special rapporteur Maurice Glélé-Ahanhanzo, whose 1995 *Report on Contemporary Forms of Racism, Racial Discrimination, Xenophobia, and Related Intolerance in the USA* mentions, for example, that

> in white areas, the houses are in good state of repair, the highways and public infrastructures are well maintained and the household garbage is collected regularly—quite the opposite of what may be seen in those districts where ethnic minorities predominate. (p. 14)

In response, the U.S. Department of State (1995) asserted, "Evident in this observation is Mr. Glélé's perception of apartheid-like 'white areas' in the U.S. There are no such demarcations. . . . The report fails to acknowledge the country's civil rights enforcement efforts in the field of housing" (p. 19). The report also mentions U.S. "harassment" of African Americans, such as Julian Bond, Clarence Mitchell, Ron Dellums, Charles Rangel, Andrew Young, David Dinkins, Maynard Jackson, Marion Barry, and others: "Elected government officials . . . may face various forms of harassment. . . . A number of Black officials were placed under surveillance, their telephones tapped, subjected to investigations, spied on by cameras for corruption or embezzlement" (pp. 16–17). The Department of State responded:

> [This] list of some 17 [allegedly harassed African Americans] is a curious point in light of the fact that in 1993, over 13,000 African Americans and other minorities served in elected governmental positions. This line of argument goes beyond over-simplification by deliberately ignoring the many protective and facilitating steps authorized under U.S. law to deal with obstacles to equal participation in the political life of the nation. (p. 22)

In addition to country reports, theme-oriented procedures by special rapporteurs can provide informative and productive means to investigate and rectify global concerns worldwide. Topics include reports on issues such as the sale of children (1992), internally displaced persons (1993), freedom of opinion and expression (1993), violence against women (1994), extreme poverty (1996), the right to food (2000), the right to adequate housing (2001), and the rights of Indigenous Peoples (2001). Addressing extreme poverty, for example, Leandro Despouy's *The Realization of Economic, Social, and Cultural Rights* (1996) notes poverty as "the world's most efficient and pitiless murderer and executioner" (p. 3). He examines, among other things, "some of the fundamental principles of human rights in the light of the experiences of very poor people" (p. 24). Such principles include, but are not limited to, the equal dignity of all human beings, the principle of equality and nondiscrimination, the "concatenation of misfortunates demonstrate[ing] the indivisibility and interdependence of human rights" (p. 25), the right to a decent standard of living, and the rights to housing, work, and health care, all as asserted in varying capacities in international human rights instruments. Calling poverty "the new face of apartheid" (p. 37), he integrates the voices of those in extreme poverty. For instance,

> I was in a shelter with my children. I was so closely watched by my children that I did not dare do anything. If they heard us shouting, someone from the child welfare office would come to see what was happening. . . . I was so afraid that my children would be taken away from me. (p. 31)

Another woman with a lung problem was afraid to get treatment because she feared her children would be "placed in an institution if she goes to the hospital" (p. 30). Despouy urges UNICEF (United Nations Children's Fund), WHO (World Health Organization), UNCTAD (United Nations Conference on Trade and Development), UNEP (United Nations Environment Programme), ILO (International Labor Organization), and NGOs to coordinate initiative and work cooperatively, which is also a recommendation of the noted economist Jeffrey Sachs (2005). Although it is difficult to state precisely the effectiveness of these country and thematic reports, Clinton's initiative on race in 1997 and the passing of the Violence Against Women Act in 1996 may have been direct consequences of such initiatives.

It is noteworthy, furthermore, that one of the most recent thematic reports by the new Human Rights Council—of which the United States is merely an observer, not even having run for membership, perhaps because of the international outcry over Guantanamo—is on extreme poverty (2006). The special rapporteur, Arjun Sengupta, noted the following:

> Despite the economic wealth of the United States and the efforts of the government, the poverty rate remains high compared to other rich nations and there is no evidence that the incidence of poverty, and especially extreme poverty, is on the decrease. . . . Government programs and policies have not effectively remedied the vulnerable situation of those groups most at risk of extreme poverty, notably African Americans, Hispanics, immigrants and single mothers. (UN Human Rights Expert, 2006)

Reports on Compliance With Human Rights Conventions

As stated, if the United States ratifies a convention, it ought to become law as mandated by the Supremacy Clause, Article VI of the U.S. Constitution. To move toward compliance with an international convention, a country must file periodic reports (which, as a general rule, are always late) noting strengths and weaknesses of their domestic policies with respect to internationally accepted standards. The country appears before the UN human rights monitoring committee, which then offers its final comments. As stated, the United States has ratified ICCPR, CERD, and CAT. These periodic reports are an excellent means for expanding consciousness about internationally accepted definitions of human rights standards so that people can come to their own conclusions. Reports discussed here are "treaty based," as opposed to the Charter-based mechanisms just described.

One might expect countries to present themselves positively, and this certainly happens to some extent; yet it is honorable that countries develop and submit such reports for international scrutiny, with the aim and hope of creating a better world, not only for their own citizens but for the entire global community. Whatever form the new Human Rights Council takes, it is generally acknowledged that such these are often done with good cooperation with governments, which, according to a *New York Times* commentary, ought to be encouraged and continued (Hoge, 2006). Although the United States has not ratified CESCR, it is worth noting that some countries such as Russia have cooperated with the human rights monitoring committees by ratifying CESCR and committing themselves to its principles. The committee welcomed Russia's adoption of laws aimed at enhancing women's participation in political life and abolishing the worst forms of child labor; it was also forthright in stating the subjects of its concern. The committee is, for example, "deeply concerned about the poor living conditions in the Republic of Chechnya and notes with regret that sufficient information was not provided on this problem in the State party's report" and "the precarious situation of indigenous communities in the State party, affecting their right to self-determination under article 1 of the Convention" (Committee on Economic, Social and Cultural Rights, 2003, pp. 1–2).

Having attended the hearing of the United States before the UN human rights committees monitoring for the ICCPR in March 1995, I can speak to good-faith attempts of the United States and the UN to truly engage in a spirit of creative dialogue (Wronka, 1995b) to move toward rectifying domestic problems. Certainly, these reports and hearings are not perfect. However, it was impressive that the UN monitoring committee spoke of the U.S. Bill of Rights as a "beacon of hope for humanity" and acknowledged the broad array of freedoms of speech and expression in the United States; members even personally commented positively on their college experiences in what they called Bean Town (Boston). Yet they also urged that "hate speech be raised to the level of an obscenity." Moreover, they expressed concerns that one out of four children lives in poverty (an observation not substantive to the ICCPR); that no definitive study advocated a general consensus on the death penalty, which they felt could be racially motivated; and that the legacy of McCarthyism still persisted.

More recently, the United States filed a report to the human rights monitoring committee of CERD (2000). After some general comments, it relates how the country is doing in regard to each article. It honestly acknowledges, for instance, that the United States

> engaged in a series of Indian wars in the nineteenth century, which resulted in significant loss of life and lands among Indian tribes. In the 1880's over the protests of Indian leaders, including Sitting Bull and Lone Wolfe, the United States embarked on a policy of distributing tribal community lands to individual

Indians in an attempt to assimilate Indians into the agrarian culture of our nation. This Allotment Policy resulted in a loss of almost 100 million acres of Indian lands. (p. 6)

It then acknowledged "significant disparities with regard to certain health measures." For example,

infant mortality rates are 2.5 times higher for Blacks than for Whites and 1.5 times higher for Native Americans. . . . Black men under age 65 have prostate cancer at nearly twice the rate of White men. . . . The death rate from heart disease for Blacks is 41 percent higher than for Whites. . . . Diabetes is twice as likely to affect Hispanics and Native Americans as the general population. . . . Black children are three times more likely than White children to be hospitalized for asthma. . . . the maternal mortality rate for Hispanic women is 23 percent higher than the rate for non-Hispanic women. . . . Blacks experience disproportionately high mortality rates from certain causes, including heart disease and stroke, homicide, and accidents, cancer, infant mortality, cirrhosis and diabetes. . . . Native Americans are 579 percent more likely to die from alcoholism, 475 percent more likely to die from tuberculosis and 231 percent more likely to die from diabetes than Americans as a whole. (pp. 85–86)

The human rights committee's Concluding Observations (CERD, 2001) expresses positive aspects and concerns and recommendations. On the positive side, it notes the "extensive constitutional and legislative framework for the effective protection of civil rights in general provided by the Bill of Rights and federal laws, the "1997 Initiative on Race," the "establishment of the Minority Business Development Agency," and the "continuous increase in the number of persons belonging to, in particular, the African American and Hispanic communities in fields of employment" (p. 2).

Some of its concerns are "that the majority of federal, state and local prison and jail inmates . . . are members of ethnic or national minorities, and that the incarceration rate is particularly high with regard to African Americans and Hispanics." The committee recommended that the United States "take firm action to guarantee the right of everyone, without distinction as to race, color or national or ethnic origin, to equal treatment before the courts and all other organs administering justice." It also noted, with concern, the "disturbing correlation between race, both of the victim and the defendant and the imposition of the death penalty"; "persistent disparities in the enjoyment of, in particular, the right to adequate housing, equal opportunities for education and employment, and access to public and private health care"; "incidents of police violence and brutality, including cases of deaths as a result of excessive use of force by law enforcement officials, which particularly affect minority groups and foreigners" (pp. 2–5).

Where these reports go from here is anybody's guess, although they are supposed to be taken up by the appropriate legislative bodies. There is definitely a need for a coordinating body between these international initiatives and domestic policies, which is why some have advocated for a Human Rights Cabinet to define human rights with the vision implicit in human rights principles rather than the narrow definitions, often riddled with hidden agenda, discussed earlier. Furthermore, the United States must respond to concerns of the committee, which now, on behalf of the United States, are available for the entire world to see on the Internet. Some countries do not have their reports so readily available, and the United States ought to be commended for being willing to air its dirty laundry, so to speak.

It is also extremely important that NGOs provide input into those reports, because official records sometimes tell only part of the story. For example, the "real number of hate crimes in the United States is more than 15 times higher than FBI statistics reflect," according to a study by the Bureau of Justice Statistics (Southern Poverty Law Center, 2005, p. 4). A thorough accounting of data is paramount, as this knowledge winds its way to international forums. Often, NGOs write what are called shadow reports, to fill in gaps left by official reports. One such report on forced drugging, use of electroshock, and overmedication of children can be found in Chapter 4. Although official human rights reports are not perfect, what is? These reports, however, can serve as a guide for social justice activists to show a country how it is doing in regard to human rights standards and to work collaboratively for adequate solutions. Certainly, activists can use them as guides for direct nonviolent actions for government implementation.

World Conferences

Since the Rio Conference on the Environment and Development (the Earth Summit) in 1992, these world conferences with action plans have become a high water mark of participation, continually opening up possibilities for fuller and deeper integration of governments with ever-growing civil society (Cooper, 2004). With the proliferation of international civil society—that is, the growth of numerous groups dedicated to social justice issues—has come a chipping away at traditional notions of state sovereignty (Steiner & Alston, 2001). In large measure, the development of technology—the Internet, video-conferencing, and the like—has strengthened the viability of global conferences as a force that the powerful need to reckon with. As the UN comments:

To some, the series of large-scale United Nations conferences held in the 1990s seemed like an extravagant talk-fest. But most of the world's leaders and policymakers have viewed these events as a worthwhile investment—and even a watershed—in shaping our global future. (United Nations, 2006, p. 4)

In addition to Rio, there were the World Conference on Human Rights (1993, Vienna); the International Conference on Population and Development (1994, Cairo); the World Summit for Social Development (1995, Copenhagen); the Fourth World Conference on Women (1995, Beijing); the Second UN Conference on Human Settlements (1996, Istanbul); the World Conference Against Racism, Racial Discrimination, Xenophobia, and Related Intolerance (2001, Durban); the World Conference on Sustainability (2002, Johannesburg); the World Conference on the Information Society (2003, Geneva); and the World Conference on Disaster Reduction (2005, Kobe, Hyogo, Japan). Often they have follow-up conferences, usually 5 or 10 years later, such as the 2002 World Food + 5 Summit in Rome and the 2002 Rio +10 World Conference in Johannesburg.

A word must be said about the 1998 World Conference for Peace, which met at The Hague, Holland. It was *not* under UN auspices, perhaps because the United Nations consists of governments, separated almost entirely through lines, that is, state boundaries, most often symbolic of force and violence. NGOs, however, worldwide, decided to gather for a conference that drew Nobel Prize winners and a plethora of members of international civil society.

World conferences make their own declarations, such as the Beijing Platform of Action for the Women's Convention. The United States, in that instance, committed itself to a platform of action that would

> establish a White House Council on Women to plan for the effective implementation within the U.S. of the Platform for Action, with full participation of NGO's; Launch a six year $1.6 billion initiative to fight domestic violence and other crimes against women; lead a comprehensive assault, through the Department of Health and Human Services, on threats to women's health and security, AIDS, smoking, and breast cancer; conduct a grass-roots campaign through the Department of Labor to improve conditions for women in the workplace, including working with employers to develop more equitable pay and promotion policies and helping employees balance the twin responsibilities of family and work; have the Treasury Department take steps to promote access to financial credit for women. (Beijing Women's Conference, 1997, p. 3)

Of course, substantive principles and actions can emanate from human rights documents, such as the necessity of government to provide for the balancing of family life and work, as asserted in CEDAW, just one of many documents. Given the historical reluctance of governments to provide for human rights, it is now up to us to work toward social justice in positive, nonviolent ways, yet with direct actions to ensure that human rights are realized for every person, everywhere.

Summary

With the Universal Declaration of Human Rights as the centerpiece, this chapter provided a Janus-faced look back at the history of the idea of human rights and some consequent major developments. Viewing history itself as struggle that reflects human choice and is not free from a myth of total objectivity, the chapter began by examining some major religious teachings. An arbitrary selection of such major documents as the Code of Hammurabi, the Magna Carta, the French Declaration of the Rights of Man and Citizen, and the U.S. and Soviet constitutions were reviewed as precursors to the Universal Declaration, mirroring the zeitgeist, or spirit, of their times, as voiced by philosophers and political theorists. Then it examined the core principles of the progeny of the Universal Declaration (the right panel of the human rights triptych), including the Convention on the Elimination of Discrimination Against Women (CEDAW); the Covenant on Economic, Social and Cultural Rights (CESCR); and the Convention on the Rights of the Child (CRC). Following this review, the chapter looked at the left panel of the triptych and weakest part of the human rights framework, the means of implementation. These instruments consist of reports by special rapporteurs on themes such as Indigenous Peoples, racism, and the environment; country reports to human rights monitoring committees of major conventions; and world conferences, such as the World Conference on Women in Beijing (1995) and the World Conference on Sustainability in Durban (2003). Action plans of these conferences can provide succinct strategies for the social activist.

Building on this preliminary knowledge, the following chapters examine how this powerful idea relates to major foci of the helping and health professions: whole population, at-risk, clinical, and research dimensions.

Questions for Discussion

1. Look at all UN human rights documents, navigating from the UN Web site (www.un.org) or more directly from my home page (www.humanrightsculture .org), clicking on the Human Rights Links and then Link to All UN Human Rights Instruments. What human rights instruments are missing from the list

of documents? Is there a document, for example, on the rights of gays, lesbians, transsexuals, intersexed, or even asexual? Is there one on security in old age, the rights of men, the eradication of extreme poverty, international distributive justice, peace, or humanitarian disaster relief? What could such documents be called to form easily recognizable acronyms, like CEDAW or CERD, or CESCR, that could assist in creating international social movements? How about calling it the Convention to Abolish Extreme Poverty (CAEP), a title considered at the Human Rights Council meetings in September 2007? Begin discussing what some of these documents might look like. What would be their core principles? Begin writing the documents, and go to the U.S. human rights network (www.ushrnetwork.org) to engage in coalition building.

2. Presently, a priority of the Department of State—the federal agency charged with the promotion, ratification, and implementation of human rights instruments—is the ratification of CEDAW. Why? Should the Department of State have the CRC as a priority, given that the United States is one of two nations in the world that have not ratified that document? Also, given the high incidences of violence against children and their extreme vulnerability, would the "mobilization of shame," a common action strategy among human rights defenders, be an effective strategy to ensure its ratification? How should one determine which human rights document takes precedence in domestic forums? In 2006, the newly formed Human Rights Council drafted a document on Guiding Principles for the Eradication of Extreme Poverty with an eye toward an international binding convention. Comment on the following statements: (a) Oh no, not another human rights document! Nothing but words, words, words. What we need to do is implement the documents we already have. (b) Public discourse rarely mentions extreme poverty that exists nationally and globally. Given its devastating effects, which can easily lead to violence and war, it is necessary to expand people's consciousness about this issue by moving toward an internationally binding convention, which in turn would assist in its implementation. (c) If we learned how to love one another and lived together in peace, human rights documents would not be necessary. (d) Human rights documents can assist in teaching us how to love one another and live together in peace.

3. One of the most controversial aspects of CERD, at least in the United States, is what amounts to a prohibition against hate speech that can incite violence. Even in regard to the ICCPR, the human rights monitoring committee has, in the spirit of creative dialogue, urged the United States to raise hate speech to the level of an obscenity. Do neo-Nazis or the Ku Klux Klan have a right to assemble in the town common, or should a Holocaust denier

be granted a forum at a university? Should they be arrested, as the law requires in some European countries? Are such arrests at best merely token, small efforts to compensate for a hideous past? What limitations, if any, should there be on freedom of expression?

4. How do the history books and the media deal with the historical treatment of Indigenous Peoples in the United States? Is genocide ever mentioned? Were the Indians the "bad guys"? Do the history books emphasize "Indian attacks" or "white attacks"? Have you heard of the Trail of Tears, a forced march by the U.S. government, resulting in the displacement and deaths of thousands of Indigenous Peoples? Do you feel that the treatment of Indigenous Peoples in history books is a sin of omission, not dissimilar to denying the Holocaust? Or is it an honest mistake made by hundreds, if not thousands, of historians? Does the current situation of Indigenous Peoples meet some, if not all, of the criteria of the Genocide Convention and the Draft Declaration on the Rights of Indigenous Peoples? Are there any other similar "oversights," such as the treatment of African Americans, women, gays, and lesbians in this country? Is it OK to forgive historians as being, for example, products of their times? Or is society slowly beginning to grapple with this issue by finally acknowledging the dignity of groups previously oppressed and now slowly moving toward a socially just community? Are museums, for example, now depicting the situation of Indigenous Peoples and other groups in a more truthful light?

5. Given that history always has a subjective element, what does this synopsis of the history of the human rights concept leave out? Given the growing popularity of this idea of human rights, does the adage "success has many parents, but failure is an orphan" account for a preponderance of European thinkers seen here as contributing to its history? Can one argue that many entities, including the United States in its depiction of Eleanor Roosevelt's role, are scurrying to take credit? Are there any unsung heroes or heroines in the history of human rights?

6. Although capitalist countries generally favored passage of the ICCPR, and socialist countries were generally more favorable toward CESCR, the history of the Cold War is replete with instances of both sides taking cheap shots at one another. In the 1980s the United States would lambast the Soviet Union for the misuse of psychiatry to oppress political prisoners; the Soviet Union would condemn the United States for breaking treaties with its Indigenous Peoples. Do some historical research on this issue, using, for example, a content analysis of historical materials from the *New York Times*, available on the Internet at www.nytimes.com. How can that information be

constructively used? Today, does a similar kind of "cold war" exist, divided not along political but religious lines—a kind of standoff between fundamentalist Christian and Islamic religious forces—perhaps making the stakes even more powerful? Comment on the following statements: (a) Capitalism, which transfers wealth through speculation, is an example of the promotion of human dignity in action. (b) State-sponsored socialism, such as in the former Soviet Union, even with its gulag and imprisonment of political dissidents, was necessary to promote human dignity. (c) The historical record is replete with instances of people living collectively, sharing the results of their labor in decent and meaningful ways.

7. CEDAW speaks of self-help groups as a human right. Does calling self-help groups a human right move you to (a) petition professional organizations to formally endorse their efficacy, if they haven't done so already; (b) form such groups in your communities; and/or (c) lobby your governmental agencies to form them? Do the helping and health professions tend to downplay the effectiveness of support groups because that would perhaps interfere with their practices, which are often market driven? Or do these professions support such groups because professionals are basically committed to their clients' growth, irrespective of financial threat to their practices? One would be hard-pressed, for example, to find a professional who would not recommend the many "anonymouses" out there for alcoholic, overweight, depressed, and sex- and love-addicted persons. Or do professionals committed to such groups face an ethical dilemma because they must support themselves and their families with dignity? If the latter is correct, what societal or other changes might be necessary?

8. Why might the U.S. government refuse to take up the social and economic obligations for health care, education, and paid maternity leave enunciated in some major international human rights documents? By and large, the U.S. government sees these obligations as family obligations. Yet isn't it the domain of government to provide a social order that ensures families of the opportunities for such fundamental rights? Or is this not the domain of government? Or does the U.S. government, in fact, take up this challenge through a vast array of social welfare programs and services? Comment critically on the following statements: (a) The U.S. Bill of Rights is an exemplary document serving as a beacon of hope for humanity. (b) The United States, given its leadership in the drafting and ongoing implementation of the Universal Declaration, is a major leader in providing human rights around the world. (c) If peace is a human right, then the United States, which spends nearly half of the entire world's spending on armaments, violates this right indiscriminately and may be the worst offender of human rights.

9. Go over all of the elaborations of essential themes of all the human rights documents listed with a "fine-tooth comb." Highlight themes and portions of the elaborations regarding which you feel your country is most negligent. Discuss your findings with classmates, noting how you disagree or agree and what can be done to rectify what appear to be major human rights violations as defined by those documents. Now go to the Internet[12] and read the U.S. reports to the human rights monitoring committees. After reading a report, contact the Department of State and ask to provide input. What do they say? Do they even respond to your phone call and/or e-mail? If they do not respond, how could one make them listen? Now read, in its entirety, one of the shadow reports found on the U.S. Human Rights Network Web site (www.ushrnetwork.org). Does the shadow report adequately address issues not dealt with in the official human rights reports?

10. Do the major human rights documents emphasizing race, gender, or age set one group against the others, a skillful machination of government? Or have they indeed been helpful in advancing the rights of people of color, children, and women, for example? Does advancing the rights of one group, in fact, advance the rights of another? Or does it take away from the rights of other groups? Simply put, when advancing human rights, does one easily end up robbing Peter to pay Paul? How can this dilemma be resolved so that, when we engage in a social action for children, for example, we are also mindful of those discriminated against on the basis of race or gender? And how about those in multiple jeopardies, simultaneously discriminated against on the basis of race, gender, age, class, national origin, political opinion, and the like?

Activities/Actions

1. Think of a group you are prejudiced against. Now find and stare at a picture or pictures of people from that group. If no pictures are available, meditate on an image of someone from that group, and let the prejudices rise within you, using a kind of active imagination developed by Carl Jung. Then try to have it out with them, not to let such demons control you. If, for some reason, you wish to hold on to these prejudices or just cannot let them go, ask where this gets you. Is dealing with such demons a lifelong process, or can individuals be rid of them overnight if they really put their minds to it? Discuss your experiences, but please be careful to share only what you deem necessary and not to be offensive in your comments. Begin doing something to combat these prejudices in your everyday life and to implement social actions to eradicate them.

2. Begin a social movement to set up a Human Rights Cabinet, similar to the cabinet agencies that answer to the president, such as the Department of Homeland Security. Would such a cabinet be a bottomless pit, in which everything might be considered a human rights violation, dulling sensitivity to the very idea of human rights as a helpful tool in the struggle for social justice? Or could such a cabinet become easily co-opted by groups interested in only some rights, particularly those that affect only elites? Can one argue, for example, that concern for a right to a clean environment, which dominates public discourse, is in line with the interests of the wealthy seeking pristine vacation spots? Should one pay more attention to the plight of those in extreme poverty?

3. Place a referendum on your state's ballot pertaining to the Universal Declaration of Human Rights or to other human rights documents important to you. Have it read something simple like, "Do you urge your representatives to endorse and support the principles of the Universal Declaration of Human Rights (or one of the documents following it)?" or "The people of the state of . . . urge its legislators to monitor progress toward complying with the principles of the Universal Declaration of Human Rights." It can be legally binding or nonbinding. A lot of human rights work is education, so make sure to include a paragraph or two explaining in layperson's terms that the Universal Declaration endorses rights such as medical care, security in old age, availability of college education at reasonable tuitions, and meaningful and gainful employment at a reasonable wage, which Americans are largely unaware of as rights per se. You may wish to also throw in freedoms of speech and the press, which most Americans equate with human rights.

4. Do you see a human rights violation in the United States that is gross, widespread, and reliably attested to for which domestic remedies have been exhausted—primary criteria of a human rights violation as commonly understood in international law? Write a "communication" (the preferred word in the UN system rather than "complaint") to the United Nations. Send it to the Human Rights Commission and put on the envelope, perhaps, "Attention: 1503 Procedure." Send it via registered mail and see what happens. Be sure to send a copy to the State Department and the president. Do you have any trepidation in doing the latter activity? Share your experience with the class. You can certainly send the communication via e-mail, but generally, written communications receive more notice.

5. Occasionally, it is possible to provide input into implementation of human rights conventions through general discussions. You can join these discussions by clicking on the appropriate convention from the Human Rights Links on my home page (www.humanrightsculture.org). You will find, for

example, an e-mail address, such as CRCgeneraldiscussion@ohchr.org, or the human rights blog at www.ushrnetwork.org. See what general discussions are currently under way and provide input. Is this an effective way to participate in community building or just a façade, giving the impression of public participation? What would be the most effective method to ensure such discussions positively affect the human rights situation in a particular country, as defined by human rights documents?

Notes

1. See particularly Danaher (1996) for further analysis of this issue.

2. This definition of employment is borrowed from the U.S. delegation's definition of the right to work during the debates that led to the UN's endorsement of the Universal Declaration (Wronka, 1998b).

3. The answer here is to be very careful, run, and seek cover if possible. I found this out when I chanced on a moose with her calf while hiking in Denali National Park. I thank my Inuit students for instructing me about the need to take such actions.

4. Hobson sold horses. He would offer customers the choice between two horses he had in the front of the store. However, savvy customers would look around and notice in the back there were others available. The choices thrust on them, therefore, did not entirely encompass the myriad choices possible.

5. Examples of guiding principles, declarations, and covenants following these major instruments are the (a) Principles for the Protection of Persons With Mental Illness and the Improvement of Mental Health Care; (b) Declaration on the Rights of Mentally Retarded Persons; (c) Principles of Medical Ethics Relevant to the Role of Health Personnel, Particularly Physicians, in the Protection of Prisoners and Detainees Against Torture and Other Cruel, Inhuman, and Degrading Treatment or Punishment; (d) Geneva Convention for the Amelioration of the Condition of Wounded, Sick, and Shipwrecked Members of Armed Forces at Sea; (e) Convention Against Discrimination in Education; (f) Declaration on the Elimination of All Forms of Intolerance and of Discrimination Based on Religion or Belief; (g) Declaration on the Elimination of Violence Against Women; (h) Standard Minimum Rules for the Treatment of Prisoners; (i) Rule for the Protection of Juveniles Deprived of Their Liberty; (j) Declaration of Fundamental Principles Concerning the Contribution to the Mass Media to Strengthening Peace and International Understanding; (k) Declaration on the Right to Development; (l) Code of Conduct for Law Enforcement Officials; (m) Convention on the Reduction of Statelessness; and (n) the Genocide Convention. Obviously, this long list underscores the need for interdisciplinary understanding and collaboration while attempting to implement human rights for all.

6. A list of all these documents can be found by clicking on Human Rights Links at my home page: www.humanrightsculture.org. Then, click on List of All U.N. Human Rights Instruments. Unless otherwise specified, other information pertaining

to human rights, such as country reports to human rights monitoring committees, can be found by navigating from that Web site.

7. A more in-depth analysis of this history, including input from countries prior to the endorsement of the Universal Declaration, appears in my previous work, *Human Rights and Social Policy in the 21st Century* (1998b).

8. "Entered into force" simply means that members of the UN must abide by its principles.

9. As stated in the Preface, readers may wish to insert any country of interest; the United States is mentioned here and throughout the text merely as an example.

10. They can be accessed from my Web site, by clicking on Human Rights Links, then Reports to the UN Human Rights Monitoring Committees.

11. The aim is to be independent. Although this is often the case, disappearances of persons directly confronting their own governments have been documented. Thus, some may act independently but with trepidation for obvious reasons.

12. As in Question 1, unless otherwise specified, it is possible to access documents through the UN portal or my Web site.

PART II

Building From the Foundation

A rmed with knowledge of the need for the creation of a human rights culture, some struggles involved in this quest for social justice, the historical-philosophical legacies of human rights documents, crucial notions of the Universal Declaration of Human Rights, essential themes of select major conventions and declarations, and implementation procedures, Part II builds upon this basic foundation.

Chapter 3 poses a model for helping and health professionals, albeit an advanced generalist social work and public health model of intervention to social and individual malaise. From the Latin *intervenire,* meaning "to come between, to interrupt," human rights principles can serve as guides for socially just interventions to change an unjust social order, but also, if necessary to provide a framework for dealing with its symptoms. The helping and health professions ought to then tackle issues such as alcoholism, mental illness, AIDS, or obesity by a five-pronged, often overlapping approach. In brief, the meta-macro level speaks of global interventions, the macro level addresses whole populations at the national level, the mezzo level addresses at-risk populations, the micro level deals with people requiring clinical and direct practice interventions, and the meta-micro level addresses the healing power of everyday life. Taking its cue from human rights documents, for instance, many social problems could be ameliorated by a national consensus about the right to meaningful and gainful employment in the federal constitution. Emphasizing the macro, whole population approach, it gives examples of other social actions, such as the drafting of declarations and resolutions and the introduction of human rights bills in legislatures that might serve to educate others about this powerful idea. It concludes by paying particular attention to the use of the arts, broadly defined, for social justice and mentioning other select nonviolent strategies. For one, it depicts as a viable social change strategy, the holding of a truth commission by the Poor People's Economic Human Rights Campaign.

Chapter 4 examines at-risk and clinical interventions. It makes particular mention of select principles, like parental leave with pay and the integration of the abused child into the community, as worthwhile venues for the helping and health professions to achieve the highest attainable standard of health. It also includes business and human rights, humanistic administration, social entrepreneurship, and grant writing within the context of human rights and social justice. The San Francisco CEDAW gender analysis serves as an illustration of a social action strategy that assisted in moving toward gender equality in the workplace. The clinical section first examines two major human rights documents, Principles of Medical Ethics relevant to the role of Health Personnel, particularly Physicians in the Protection of Prisoners and Detainees Against Torture, and Other Cruel, Inhuman, or Degrading Treatment or Punishment and the Protection of Persons with Mental Illness with primary attention to psychotherapy; it then offers human rights principles that have particular implications to this mode of intervention including, but not limited to, human dignity, nondiscrimination, a nonhierarchical approach to helping, cultural sensitivity, use of support groups, and the need for a systems oriented approach.

Chapter 5 discusses a human rights and social justice approach to research-action projects with attention to quantitative and qualitative approaches. Making note of the Universal Declaration of Human Rights Project, this chapter discusses a content analysis of the Universal Declaration in comparison with U.S. federal and state constitutions. One could easily see in graphic terms the lack of human rights principles in U.S. constitutions. Much attention is also paid to ethics, the need to develop a culture of informed consent, and the legacy of the atrocities mentioned at the Nuremburg trials after World War II, in part carried out by helping and health personnel. It also discusses a qualitative study pertaining to Native American children and examples of student projects that integrated human rights. Because research without action is vacuous, it concludes with information on effective speaking and writing skills, always mindful that evil triumphs because the good say and write nothing.

Chapter 6 concludes by offering some ground rules for social action borrowed from a number of sources, like Marcus Aurelius, Martin Luther King, Jr., Mother Teresa, Mahatma Gandhi, and Crazy Horse, ever mindful of the latter's indigenous wisdom to have the vision, hope, and courage of the eagle.

3

An Advanced Generalist/Public Health Model and Whole Population Approaches to Human Rights and Social Justice

Good words do not last long unless they amount to something.

—Chief Joseph

A Helping and Health Profession Model of Intervention

St. Augustine wrote *Ama et fac quod vis,* or "Love and do what you will" (cited in Partington, 1992, p. 37). Joseph Wresinski, founder of the International Fourth World Movement, an organization dedicated to eradicating extreme poverty and responsible for the UN declaration of 1996 as the International Year for the Eradication of Extreme Poverty (Vos van Steenwijk, 1996), himself had grown up in dire circumstance and experienced firsthand the indignity of taking handouts, standing in line as a child waiting for free Suchard chocolates. Yet he emerged from these circumstances with the madness of love. In 1987 he placed a stone in front of the Palais de Chaillot, where the General

Assembly had endorsed the Universal Declaration of Human Rights in 1948, which read: "Wherever men and women are condemned to live in extreme poverty, human rights are violated. To come together to ensure that these rights be respected is our solemn duty" (International Fourth World, 2007). This commemoration further solidified a burgeoning global understanding of poverty as a violation of human rights. If everyone loved and behaved decently toward one another, simply followed the Golden Rule to "do unto others," books such as this and a sizeable portion of the helping and health professions would probably be unnecessary. And certainly, this love must, as Martin Luther King, Jr. stated, not be "sentimental and anemic" (Washington, 1986, p. 247). Love, said Dr. King, must have "Power [which] at its best is love implementing the demands of justice and justice at its best is power correcting everything that stands against love" (p. 247). Such notions may not be much different from Pope Benedict XVI's most recent Encyclical *Deus Caritas Est,* which asserted the inseparability of love and truth and urged believers and nonbelievers to come together to fight poverty and injustice (Albacete, 2006). All professions, religions, concerned citizens—every person, everywhere—can fight against injustice for every person, everywhere.

However, as psychiatrist and concentration camp survivor Bruno Bettleheim asserts in the title of his well-known book on childhood schizophrenia, *Love Is Not Enough.* To love, sometimes madly, to be decent, and to treat others as we would like to be treated are necessary, but listening to the collective wisdom of those who have learned from the scars of experience may also be required (Rosenstock-Huessy, 1969). King, who saw love as the "supreme unifying principle of life" (Washington, 1986, p. 334), was also aware of what he called the "human rights revolution" (p. 280). This book argues that collective wisdom is found in human rights instruments that followed the carnage of World War II and continue to be developed today in response to ongoing injustices like the ever-widening gap between the rich and poor countries. An intuitive understanding of social justice could be further solidified by human rights principles that provide adequate definitions and goals to act as frameworks or guiding principles to develop effective strategies in action and service to others.

Broadly defined to include being an example for others, by words and actions, as parents, family members, and professionals; what the media teaches; and learning in schools, colleges, and universities, education plays an important role in this struggle for human dignity and social justice. But education fails, on many occasions, "to lead" and "to nourish," as its etymological origins dictate. Before discussing educational and other related strategies in creating a socially just world, it is important to discuss various levels of intervention, consistent with the notion of a systems-oriented approach, a substantive concept in the helping and health professions, particularly advanced generalist social work and public health.

Levels of Intervention

Before discussing the meaning of a whole-population approach to intervening in a social problem, it is necessary to describe three levels of intervention that are generally accepted in the helping and health professions: the macro, mezzo, and micro. "Levels" may be a misnomer, as distinctions among them are often blurred. Furthermore, the concept of levels is hierarchical, largely a Western, if not masculine, way of dividing the world into neat categories, much like floors and cubicles in an office building. Other indigenous or Eastern ways of knowing may be less hierarchical, more concentric, free-flowing, horizontal, and expansive. Language is always limited, constantly evolving. For the time being, the world may be stuck with concepts like levels that obscure the interrelatedness of things. But acknowledgment of this conceptual bias may invite exploration of other venues to tackling such complex issues.

Macro Level

Briefly, the *macro* level, sometimes called a *primary intervention strategy*, may be referred to as a whole-population approach. It is a strategy of helping that aims to impact the quality of life of groups as largely as possible. These groups do not have to be pathological or near the pathology that would label them physically or mentally ill, or prone to illness, as in mezzo- or micro-level interventions. Rather, a macro social action strategy aims to prevent people from falling through the cracks and to improve everyone's quality of life and standard of living, not just monetarily, which would entail economic justice, but also in ways that promote social justice quite literally as friends united, respectful of each other's developmental capacities and right to participate equitably in community building. Universal implementation of a national graduated taxation policy that taxed the rich proportionately more than the poor and/or fines levied based on ability to pay (for example, speeding tickets issued in parts of Scandinavia) would lessen the gaps between the haves and have-nots. Another example is instituting a national school curriculum that would teach responsible choice regarding the use of alcohol and drugs, to prevent substance abuse or reduce the harm caused if substances are used. In the first scenario, graduated taxation should help eliminate violence, as tensions between haves and have-nots are reduced; the second might lessen substance abuse, with its attendant complications like an underground culture of unemployment, theft, and trafficking, which are inimical to a young person's growth and development. The Universal Declaration, with its concern for the right to work at a reasonable wage (Article 23) and a just social order (Article 28), and the Convention on the Rights of the Child (CRC), with its concern for the protection of children "from illicit use of narcotic drugs and psychotropic substances" (Article 33), can provide human rights guidance with these interventions.

Mezzo Level

The *mezzo* level, or secondary intervention, deals primarily with interventions in groups at risk. Given the relationship between domestic violence and lack of collective bargaining in the workplace (Gil, 1992), a stratagem might be to set up an ombudsperson's office or form a bargaining unit, in which workplace issues could be aired confidentially and possibly resolved before tension in the employment setting gets out of hand and perhaps displaced onto a spouse or child. More selective than the previous approach, it might also target children growing up in abusive households who might be at risk for depression, substance abuse, or juvenile delinquency. The helping and health professional could develop support groups in the school and/or have children learn ways to cope with an alcoholic parent or dysfunctional living situation. The children could learn to prioritize safety; speak with someone they can trust like a godmother or grandfather; and seek peer or professional help. Interventions allowing children to talk about their issues ought to prevent acting out. Article 23 of the Universal Declaration—"Everyone has the right to form and to join trade unions for the protection of his interests"—provides fodder for the first intervention; for the second, Article 39 of the CRC speaks of the obligations of governments "to promote physical and psychological recovery and social reintegration of a child victim of any form of neglect, exploitation or abuse."

Micro Level

The *micro* level would basically entail a more or less clinical intervention, generally on an individual, or possibly even group, level. This intervention might entail direct counseling with a substance abuser, depressed child, juvenile delinquent, or domestic violence perpetrator. If working with people addicted to alcohol, a group might provide support and feedback from other members about possible pretexts for drinking and point out the infamous pity pot. It can be quite revelatory to hear group members say, "I drink because I'm happy; I drink because I'm sad." Others might focus on such excuses for an obviously maladaptive lifestyle by responding, "So are you saying, poor me, poor me, pour me another one."

As yet there are no major human rights documents on substance abuse. However, in working with a depressed or acting-out child, a guiding principle for intervention might be Principle 10 of the Principles for the Protection of Persons With Mental Illness and the Improvement of Mental Health Care, that "medication . . . shall never be administered as a punishment or for the convenience of others." This would ensure the child's best interests are central to any intervention, a substantive principle of the CRC. Overmedicating for the convenience of staff would be strictly verboten. Other principles relevant to interventions for juveniles are Articles 31 and 35 of the Rules for the Protection of Juveniles Deprived of Their Liberty, one of a series of documents on Human Rights in the Administration of Justice: "Juveniles deprived of their liberty have the right to facilities and services that meet all the requirements of health and human dignity" (Article 31), and "The possession of personal effects is a basic element of the right to privacy and essential to the psychological well-being of the juveniles" (Article 35).

Micro interventions do not have to be clinical in a pure sense. Generally, this level deals with symptoms after all else fails, often referred to as direct practice. Opening up a homeless shelter, and setting up a job referral and counseling service or peer support groups for men and women would be a micro intervention. Forming a trade union to aid workers at risk of losing their jobs would be a mezzo strategy. Lobbying for a right to adequate shelter and meaningful and gainful employment in the federal constitution would be a macro social action.

These levels can be illustrated with the story of rescuers working to save people on the verge of death as they float downriver, perhaps from a burning or sinking ship at the river's mouth. After numerous attempts to save the survivors (the micro), someone gets the idea to go upstream to find the source of the problem—a strong current or, further upstream, that wrecked ship. They could put out the fire or teach the people to swim in the strong currents (the mezzo and macro).

Meta-Macro Level

Beyond these three commonly understood levels, there are other "meta" levels that this book will refer to and are still in the process of conceptual elaboration. First is the *meta-macro*. Here interventions go beyond the nation-state, sometimes *really* beyond it. Again using the sinking ship and rescuers example, we look beyond the stream itself to its origin. Imagine that much of its water had evaporated as a result of the greenhouse effect. Sandbars would be a much greater hazard to vessels in its shallow waters. An effective intervention would necessitate going beyond the ordinary confines of the ship or stream in the first place, or, metaphorically, beyond the nation-state.

For the most part, macro interventions take place on the national level. But considering our growing global interdependence, some have argued the nation-state is a fiction (Davis, 1984), and global interventions may be more fitting. It costs roughly $1.3 trillion in military armaments annually to keep national borders intact. Interventions that aim to dissolve lines between countries might be necessary to move us toward a general consensus of world citizenship, or as Nobel Prize winner Joseph Rotblatt (1997) put it: "Allegiance to Humanity." Loyalty to Mother Earth, broadly defined, should result in spending money on bread, not arms; as former President Dwight Eisenhower eloquently expressed it, "Every gun that is made, every warship launched, every rocket fired, signifies in the final sense a theft from those who are hungry and not fed, those who are cold and not clothed" (cited in Peace Pilgrim, 1991, p. 114).

One could say that state boundaries have already dissolved, as the International Monetary Fund (IMF), World Bank (WB), and World Trade Organization (WTO) have largely taken over as prime movers in global policy making (Danaher, 2004), forcing poor states to adopt structural adjustment policies, like the privatization of health care and education, in exchange for projects such as roads or ports of questionable utility masquerading as aid. Such projects may indeed serve the interests of rich countries quickly moving oil and cheap products through cheap labor. A global culture based on allegiance to humanity and world citizenship should, on the other hand, legally mandate the fulfillment of human need vis-à-vis internationally accepted human rights norms, which are antithetical to treating human need as a commodity traded in the marketplace. As numerous protests at the meetings of these powerful groups—in Seattle (1999) and Cancun (2005), for example—evidence, the vast array of groups that have arisen in the twilight of the last millennium and dawn of the new one, such as the IMF, WB, and WTO, are not likely to be sensitive to civil society. In Davos, Switzerland, a relatively isolated canton in the Alps where government leaders and heads of corporations like Coca-Cola and Forbes met in 2007 for the World Economic Forum, protest is forbidden and security is high.

Going beyond the nation-state may also require use of a world currency. While regional currencies in the African Union and the Caribbean, modeled on the Euro, are being discussed, an obvious meta-macro intervention, it may also be worthwhile to consider a basic unit of currency for the entire world, perhaps called the Mondo. Ever stand on a long line waiting to exchange a dollar for Swiss or French francs, or a Euro? Not a very good use of time, is it? Some credit card companies are now adding a fee for any purchases made with foreign currency. Couldn't time and money be better used doing a good deed, perhaps? One might say that the U.S. dollar is already a universal currency, but it is questionable whether this currency reflects social justice concerns rather than consumerism, nearly half the entire world's military budget, as well as a long legacy of colonialism and imperialism evidenced by slavery and genocide against Indigenous Peoples. The challenge is to develop a currency backed by human rights, dignity, and social justice while keeping in mind a previous caveat about viewing human rights initiatives in overly narrow terms. A world currency will work only if there are mechanisms for equitable global distribution of economic and social wealth within the human family.

Should social activists wish to engage in such a global meta-macro intervention, anticipating a nonviolent yet slow disbanding of the nation-state, it is important to keep in mind that economics alone and a higher standard of living will not entirely solve global malaise due to international distributive injustice. Millennia of wisdom tell us that a person does not live by bread alone. It is an understatement that many children in the industrialized world live in loveless affluence. Yet world citizenship might also create a sense of the importance of sharing cultures, learning from each other's ways of life, best practices models aimed at enhancing family well-being and unity. Individual well-being and family cohesion are not entirely dependent on economic stability. Strong evidence suggests that the history of ethnic interchange is not one of conflict, but rather cooperation (Boulding, 2000). This idea of world citizenship promoted by thinkers from Marcus Aurelius, to Cicero, St. Augustine, Dante, Erasmus, Thomas Paine, Jane Addams, H.G. Wells, and Ralph Waldo Emerson, as well as many of the Papal Encyclicals, has stood the test of time. It will not go away (Heater, 1996).

To summarize, the meta-macro level acknowledges the global interconnectedness of things: The local is connected to the state; the state is connected to the country; the country is connected to the continent; the continent is connected to the world; and the world is connected to the universe. Recall that solidarity rights regard the oceans, mountains, space, and the heavens as the common heritage of humanity, to be used for peaceful purposes. The world, not one country, must be a master of the universe.

Meta-Micro Level

The *meta-micro* level speaks to the realm of the everyday life. Although it's true problems can get out of hand, requiring clinical interventions with persons diagnosed with a physical or mental illness, everyday life itself may provide tremendous healing power. Still in the process of conceptual elaboration, this level acknowledges that not all problems require clinical professional interventions. This level, pertaining to what existential phenomenologists call the *lebenswelt*, poses an important challenge to enhance our everyday interactions with family, friends, and even strangers, those thousands of miles away living in dire poverty who are also part of the human family. Conversations with one's grandmother on the porch on a hot summer day, slowly rocking back and forth while listening to the faint creaking of the chairs, just watching the world go by, may have more therapeutic benefit than an entire army of social workers, psychologists, psychiatrists, psychiatric nurses, and doctors combined. So, too, can a smile to a homeless soul—a complete stranger seeking a human connection, however slight—have a tremendous impact. Helping and health professionals have a duty to transcend the professional to relate as humans to other humans.

When doing intakes, triage, or utilization review, it is important to ask for strengths in a person's environment, which obviously touches on this level. There is an evident acknowledgment that family, friends, peer interventions, and even perhaps kind comments by strangers (especially to some children who may have never heard a kind word in their life) are themselves healing. This level is not that distant from Eleanor Roosevelt's notion of human rights as beginning "In small places, close to home . . . the neighborhood he lives in" (U.S. Department of State Report on Country's Human Rights Practices, 1993, p. xix). Yet the helping professions are replete with studies on the efficacy of clinical interventions rather than the healing properties of everyday encounters. Undeniably, this metalevel has relevance for each of us. A smile, a concerned glance, a "good morning" can have immeasurable curative impact on abused children. How people discriminate in their everyday lives, failing to afford others the human dignity every human deserves, might be one of the most pernicious forms of human rights violations. Are some people kind only to good children? Do people hold doors open for African American women as much as for white women? Or should women hold doors open for men?

Helping and health professionals, although obviously supportive of this idea of nondiscrimination, ought not be blind to the curative impact of the everyday life even though it cannot easily be operationalized or measured. Professionals do not have a monopoly on helping and healing. Being able to measure something does not mean one has found truth. Truth may be elusive, but the journey is more fruitful with genuine questioning together, an actual sharing of each other's perspectives in the world community. The challenge is to have a forum where such an exchange is possible. The paradox is that the answer is in the questioning together; as the cliched, yet profound expression says, we *are* all in this together.

The Struggle to Implement Levels of Intervention

The demarcation among levels is not entirely distinct. Research, sometimes referred to as a *quaternary intervention*, is necessary to provide informed knowledge for interventions at each of these levels, however blurred the boundary between them. In turn, these levels impact research questions and methodology. Each level also has its own difficulties, revealing once again that struggle is always involved in working for social justice. None of these levels of intervention offers a perfect solution, and there is no easy answer regarding which to choose. Everyone must meditate on and choose which level or levels to expend his or her energies on to work for social action and service to others.

To illustrate some implementations, on the micro level, activists might set up homeless shelters and soup kitchens to help the chronically homeless, or counsel depressed children unable to concentrate in the school setting because of constant daydreaming about troubles in the home situation. On the mezzo level, one could identify persons at risk for homelessness or children for depression, an often neglected group, especially if their anger is turned inward. Yet one must also work on the macro level to change the national and global economic and social structures that result in exorbitant rents, unemployment, and parents needing to work at three jobs just to make ends meet, with the unintentional neglect of their children. Yes, some homeless persons will die in the streets while activists lobby for a right to adequate shelter in the federal or state constitution (the macro). But success in making these rights constitutional would inevitably help many others on the verge of homelessness. Consequently, attending to the needs of the homeless, by setting up soup kitchens, homeless shelters, and employment referral services (the mezzo and micro) is important; however, as long as the global cultural and economic structures are still in place, the homeless will keep coming. Concerning depressed children, activists could find effective ways to counsel them and elicit peer assistance. In an appropriate forum, other children could share their stories of how they got over their depression (the micro). Yet, introducing an amendment to the federal or a state constitution, calling for special protections for children (the macro), as asserted in the Universal Declaration, is also important.

Levels are also fraught with their own difficulties. Macro interventions may take too long. How many centuries did it take Europe to realize that a single currency might help alleviate the conflicts that have scarred its history? At the mezzo level, professionals attempting willy-nilly to diagnose all children who may be suffering from depression might produce a self-fulfilling prophecy. The clinical face-to-face encounter may be an inefficient use of time and resources.

A basic point is that no matter what helping and health professionals do or at which level they choose to intervene, their actions can always be open to criticism. It may help here to remember Mother Teresa's wisdom (more on this in Chapter 6), that when you do good, you may "get kicked in the teeth." Ultimately, each step can be fraught with difficulty, and it's always a tough call where to spend one's time working for social justice. Perhaps the only choice is to listen to one's conscience, or as Joseph Campbell, renowned authority on myth and legend, puts it, "Follow one's bliss."

In folk singer Peter Seeger's well-known song, the refrain "To everything there is a season" popularizes the wisdom of the ancient adage. At various times in our lives, we experience a range of draws in different directions; human rights defenders, using human rights documents as guiding principles, must be fully aware of these conflicting pulls and tugs to make an informed decision about where they want to direct their time and energies. The answer to how to make the best contributions comes by getting in touch with one's inner soul. Like the mythological character, Sisyphus, human rights defenders must be willing to take up this struggle. In his essay, Camus concludes that "Sisyphus was happy" in this endless struggle. If activists acknowledge that social justice is a struggle, they too can be happy in the broadest sense, experiencing the timeless joy of a good deed that nothing can take away. The Stoic philosopher, Marcus Aurelius (1984), wrote beautifully about this joy in his *Meditations:*

> Let every action aim solely at the common good. . . . For a life that is sound and secure . . . put your whole heart into doing what is just, and speaking what is true; and for the rest, know the joy of life by piling good deed on good deed until no rift or cranny appears between them. (pp. 183, 186)

Table 3.1 summarizes the levels of intervention, with examples and select concerns for each.

Based on the definitions, examples, and concerns listed in the preceding table, Table 3.2 presents some select interventions for specific issues in the helping and health professions: alcoholism, mental illness, AIDS, and obesity. But note the table moves from the meta-macro to the meta-micro, then to the research level, for each particular issue. The interventions are not exclusive, but merely illustrative of the multiple ways of dealing with individual and social malaises that are interrelated. Without specific mention of human rights principles, one can easily see how interventions, such as creating an open forum to question an economic order that puts profit above human need; destigmatizing the mentally ill; creating awareness of and sharing scientific advancement; and ensuring global access to nutritious foods, are consistent with human rights documents.

Figure 3.1 is a diagrammatic representation illustrating how human rights principles ought to serve as the bedrock of social justice, with implications for intervention levels from the meta-macro to the meta-micro. Research, both quantitative and qualitative, would also provide and receive input from social action and service initiatives.

With these preliminary remarks on the relevance of human rights for social justice from the meta-macro to the meta-micro levels, it is now possible to

Table 3.1 Levels of Intervention for the Helping and Health Professions*

Level	Definition	Example(s)	Select Concerns
Macro or primary intervention	An approach primarily dealing with whole populations to alleviate an individual and/or social problem	Working for rights to adequate shelter, education, and/or meaningful and gainful employment as amendments to state or federal constitution	Strategy may necessitate massive human rights education, coalition building, and tremendous amounts of time and money; people may be reluctant to deal with ambiguities and lack of immediate results
Mezzo or secondary intervention	An approach primarily dealing with at-risk populations to alleviate an individual and/or social problem	Employee protections and/or assessment of people at risk for depression, substance abuse, or HIV	Possible creation of a self-fulfilling prophecy; intervention may mask hidden agenda
Micro or tertiary intervention	An approach primarily dealing with populations whose symptomology is full blown	Counseling the depressed person, substance abuser, or person with AIDS; setting up a homeless shelter	Servicing generally a small number of people; homeless, for one, will continue to appear due to structural violence
Research or quaternary intervention	Qualitative and/or quantitative approaches providing input into effective strategies for other dimensions	Understanding teen pregnancy from the perspective of mothers and/or administering self-image measurements	Questions of size and kind of sample with numerous issues pertaining to a culture of informed consent
Meta-Macro	An approach truly global, perhaps transcending taken-for-granted assumptions about entities like the nation-state and a national currency	Nonviolently attempting to create an allegiance to humanity; working toward a world currency constructed from pillars of social justice; attempting to work with supranational organizations like the IMF and World Bank in accordance with human rights principles	Years of socialization viewing war, rather than world peace, as inevitable; human needs for affiliation based on language, culture
Meta-Micro	An approach that transcends professionalism, acknowledging the healing power of family, friends, and everyday life in general	Therapeutic impact of conversations, long walks with significant others; saying hello and smiling to a homeless person or someone in distress	Therapeutic impact is not entirely amenable to professional intervention as commonly understood; may be perceived as negating professionalism

*Levels of intervention are often blurred, interacting not necessarily in linear, but rather concentric ways. Each level, a viable strategy, can easily elicit its own set of expectations and criticisms, once again fortifying the notion that social justice is a struggle.

Table 3.2 Select Interventions for Some Individual and Social Issues From the Meta-Macro to the Meta-Micro and Research Levels*

Level	Alcoholism	Mental Illness	AIDS	Obesity
Meta-Macro	Providing a global open forum on the viability of profitability in alcohol sales	Global movements to destigmatize those considered mentally ill who, as humans, also have a right to human dignity	Creating global awareness to share in scientific advancement by sharing medication regimens with poor countries	Ensuring easy access globally to foods that are nutritious, culturally appropriate, and reasonably priced
Macro	Teaching responsible choice curriculum to all students at the high school level	Teaching children to find viable ways to change moods	Lobbying for a right to nondiscrimination based on medical condition in a national constitution	Lobbying against advertising on children's television urging the consumption of fatty foods
Mezzo	Providing support groups for children experiencing neglect in dysfunctional families	Creating awareness in schools that nondisruptive children may also need help	Providing education to high school girls, which could lead to adequate employment	Incentives for overweight children to exercise
Micro	Working through rationalizations for drinking in individual or group therapy	Dealing with adequate coping strategies in group and/or individual settings	Incorporating the patient in treatment planning to ensure better compliance with medication	Monitoring diets, finding alternative ways to deal with stress
Meta-Micro	Helping an alcoholic found sleeping on the streets in an extremely cold climate	Supporting siblings and having an understanding attitude to persons emotionally challenged	Letting a person with AIDS know someone is there to help in case of emergency	Compassion and kindness to an obese person
Research	Determining effective outcomes of above interventions	Determining effective outcomes of above interventions	Determining effective outcomes of above interventions	Determining effective outcomes of above interventions

*Levels and interventions are not precise and intersect in multifaceted ways.

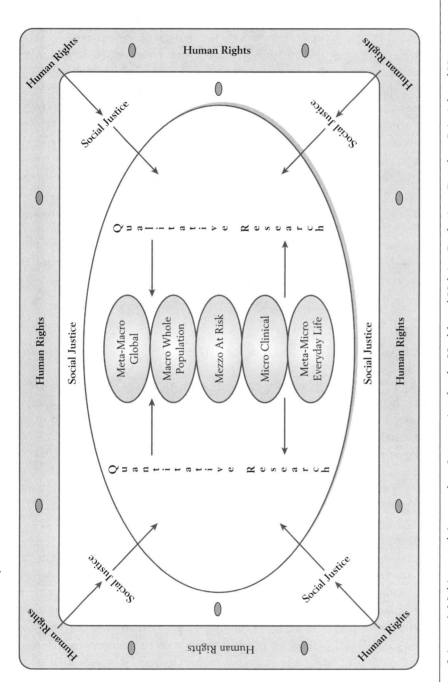

Figure 3.1   A Multipronged Approach to Intervention for the Health and Helping Professions Based on Principles of Human Rights and Social Justice. This diagram depicts the multifaceted interplay among human rights, social justice, and the five levels of intervention for the helping and health professions.

propose interventions more specifically—a kind of human rights scaffolding to enhance helping strategies. Just talking about such a framework with friends and colleagues can also serve as a teaching tool for human rights instruments, as the helping and health professions have slowly begun to include human rights, and commitments to social justice, in their curricula. Historically this culture has evoked few international human rights principles in the helping and health professions, but these professions in contemporary times have demonstrated an interest in integrating such principles in their interventions. The helping and health professions may also influence the culture in multiple ways. Such offenses as slavery, genocide against Indigenous Peoples, and the Holocaust, for example, may have been committed with the collusion of those in an alleged helping capacity. But now, with an almost global consensus that human rights concern the world community, these professions have a duty, amply expressed in ethical and other professional codes of conduct, not to collude with policy makers and others deaf to the cries of the oppressed (Drinan, 1987) and to take constructive social action as responsible members of the human community.

Education Toward the Creation of a Human Rights Culture

Apart from the everyday education people share with their children, family, and others through their words, actions, and examples, formal schooling can play a major role in creating a human rights culture, socializing children to work for social justice. Once values are instilled at an early age, it is very difficult to change them. Various curricula slowly evolving since 1948 consist of exercises, role-plays, dissemination of information, and the like, intended to expand consciousness at all ages about ways to enhance human rights and dignity. The UN declared 1995–2005 the Decade for Human Rights Education, but found such education so worthwhile it launched the World Program for Human Rights Education in 2006.

Human rights curricula and its cousins, violence prevention and diversity training, are *not* silver bullets, especially if a culture accepts social injustice as a given (Gil, 1995, 1998). A social order which condones vast transfers of wealth through capital speculation (gambling perhaps?) could easily provoke resentment among those not fortunate enough to reap monetary gain in that way. One aim of human rights education is to be open to other venues that will move toward a societal acknowledgment of work—a good day's work for a good day's pay that will enhance human dignity—as opposed to wealth from capital accumulation alone. The former kind of society would offer reasonable wages, adequate benefits, and retirement packages for security in old age to ultimately cement a collective commitment to social justice, as defined by human rights criteria. One thing human rights education can teach is that human dignity from work is a communal obligation that is antithetical to an "I've got mine" mentality.

Select Examples and Resources

Following are some examples from an emergent human rights literature. There should be more. First, if we take world citizenship seriously, it would be necessary to translate the Universal Declaration of Human Rights and other documents in as many languages as possible. Figure 3.2 shows Eleanor Roosevelt with a Spanish version.

Figure 3.2   Eleanor Roosevelt With a Copy of a Spanish Version of the Universal Declaration of Human Rights. It is important to translate that and other human rights documents into as many languages as possible to educate others about the true meaning of human rights, their interdependence, and their indivisibility.

Source: The National Archives.

For educating others about human rights principles, one helpful book is *ABC, Teaching Human Rights* (United Nations, 1986). One exercise called "Wishing Well" is appropriate for preschoolers: Arrange students in a circle. Suggest that it is the edge of a wishing well. Propose that each child in turn makes the following wishes (this can also be done in small groups or in pairs):

If I could be an animal, I'd be _____ because . . .

If I could be a bird, I'd be _____ because . . .

If I could be an insect, I'd be _____ because

If I could be a flower, I'd be _____ because

If I could be a tree, I'd be _____ because

If I could be a musical instrument, I'd be _____ because

If I could be a car, I'd be _____ because

If I could be a movie, I'd be _____ because

If I could be a food, I'd be _____ because

If I could be a TV show, I'd be _____ because

If I could be a foreign country, I'd be _____ because

If I could be a cartoon character, I'd be _____ because

Afterward, it is very easy to start a discussion about how everyone is different; yet, despite their differences, people all have the same desires, likes/dislikes, and so on. Obviously, this exercise is about unity in diversity, which is fundamental to any discussion of social justice.

This book published by UNESCO, long an advocate for human rights education, includes numerous other activities like (a) washing machine (children pass through a line of other children, who just say good things about them), (b) planning the world community (children speak about how they would plan the world, not knowing whether they would be born male, female, rich, poor, or a member of a particular race, ethnicity, culture, or religion), (c) the Universal Declaration of Human Rights in plain English (with examples, teachers read the Universal Declaration in ways that children can understand and ask children what they think), and (d) imaginary friend (with eyes closed, children imagine going to a special place, anywhere in the world, opening the door, and seeing a special friend who is always there to talk to). Such exercises and the viewpoints they elicit are excellent teaching tools.

Another resource with examples of educational approaches is Reardon's *Educating for Human Dignity: Learning about Rights and Responsibilities, a K–12 Teaching Resource* (1995). In the first grade children learn the importance of a social contract, in which limits are set for the common good. After the teacher reads certain class rules, children decide which rules they feel are most important. In the second grade, students reflect through visual imagery what needs children have when born. Both of these exercises can prepare children to understand the importance of human rights instruments as social compacts, historical-philosophical compromises,[1] and legal mandates (what must be done) to fulfill human needs. Examples of exercises for grades 3 to 6 are drawing a tree of life describing the roots as children's human needs and the branches as principles of the Convention on the Rights of the Child, and discussing the relationship between the Universal Declaration and the Declaration of Independence and the Bill of Rights. At the junior high level, emphasis is on the relationship between rights and duties. Students read the Universal Declaration and discuss duties necessary to implement each article. At the senior level, students learn in depth about other human rights instruments, like the Genocide Convention and the African Charter on Human and People's Rights, reflecting on such issues as apartheid in South Africa, the Holocaust, and how the domestic situation compares with rights enunciated in human rights instruments.

Amnesty International, a major human rights organization, also has excellent materials, including visual aids, which are also listed in the Annotated Media Resources. Worth noting is their quarterly periodical *Fourth R*. It is complete with ready-to-use lesson plans, a plethora of articles on innovative ways to teach human rights through film, poetry, and mathematics, and numerous other resources. One issue, for instance, had an "Ideas to Steal!" (Amnesty International, 2004, p. 11) section consisting of excellent Internet sites for lesson plans and manuals, including www.hrea.org/erc/Library/visualaids.htm (for Web-based visual aids for human rights learning); www.facinghistory.org/Campus/ (examining the role of radio as a means to promulgate hate as in Rwanda); www.pbs.org/wnet/wideangle/classroom/lp5.html (on resolving religious conflict); www.michigan.gov (examining how literature and art can enhance human rights); and www.arrc-hre.com/mydrawing_frameset.html (a portal for the Asian Regional Resource Center). The Web site www.amnestyusa .org/education is an excellent portal for further information about Amnesty's outstanding materials. The International Labor Organization (ILO) also can serve as an excellent resource. They have, for example, an excellent resource on supporting children's rights through education and arts. The full text can be accessed from ILO's Web site at http://www.ilo.org/global/lang—en/index.htm and entering the word "scream" in the search box.

On the postsecondary level, resources that incorporate human rights into various disciplines have also slowly evolved. Of note are Link and Healy's *Teaching International Content: Curriculum Resources for Social Work Education* (2005) and Aspel's *Teaching About Human Rights* (2005), which also have numerous resources for the creative human rights educator. Another good resource is Fisher and MacKay's *Gender Justice: Women's Rights are Human Rights* (1996), published by the Unitarian Universalist Service Committee. This book examines, among other things, the Beijing Platform of Action drafted after the World Conference on Women, and summarizes eight major U.S. commitments to its implementation: (a) establishing a White House Council on Women; (b) the Department of Justice launching a 6-year initiative to fight domestic violence; (c) the Department of Health and Human Services launching a comprehensive battle against threats to women's health; (d) the Department of Labor launching a grassroots campaign to improve working conditions for women; (e) the Treasury Department promoting better access to credit for women; (f) the Agency for International Development increasing women's political participation; (g) the Department of Education removing barriers to quality education for girls and women with low incomes; and (h) continuing to speak out without hesitation on behalf of human rights of all people. Reichert's exercise book on understanding human rights (2006) compares social work ethics codes with human rights principles. A good training resource specifically for economic, social, and cultural rights is *The Circle of Rights* (2000) by the International Human Rights Internship Program. For those interested in implementing human rights locally, an excellent training manual is *Human Rights for All* (Northeastern University, Program on Human Rights and the Global Economy, 2007). Hopefully, *this* book will also serve as a practical means to advance human rights and social justice.

On the occasion of the 50th anniversary of the General Assembly's endorsement of the Universal Declaration, the Jacob Blaustein Institute (1998) came out with an excellent action kit with such ideas as national letter-writing campaigns and community organizing to form local human rights groups. Amnesty International is also launching a Global Campaign for Human Dignity in 2008, which would deal substantively with economic, social, and cultural rights, a more recent concern of this excellent human rights organization. An activist's toolkit can be found at http://www.amnestyusa.org/Activist_Toolkit/page.do?id=1031046&n1=4&n2=63.

Human rights reports discussed earlier, and the Concluding Observations of the Human Rights Committee, are also excellent educational tools on both secondary and postsecondary levels. These reports were written primarily with the cooperation of governments, NGOs, academics, and researchers. Whereas no report is perfect, the United States ought to be commended for its open acknowledgment of the "legacies of racism, ethnic intolerance and destructive policies relating to Native Americans" and that "issues relating to race, ethnicity, and national origin continue to play a negative role in American society" (United Nations, 2000, p. 4). In response, the Human Rights Committee noted "the persistence of the discriminatory effects of the legacy of slavery, segregation, and destruction policies with regard to Native Americans" (United Nations, 2001, p. 1). Such documents containing the humble admissions by a powerful country to a small committee of independent experts can be extremely powerful teaching tools. This kind of interchange between a government and independent committee offers an excellent springboard from which to launch open and frank discussions about directions to pursue together toward social justice.

Commemorating Major International Days

One way to move toward a lived awareness of human rights principles that eventually may influence cultural values and crystallize into legally mandated rights is to commemorate major international days. Following is a select list, with commentary (Human Rights Education Associates, 2007, p. 1). Social justice advocates may wish to have community events in their schools, town commons, places of employment, or any public place. Often there is not much to celebrate, which is why commemorating (literally, a "remembering together") may be preferable.

1. **Good Morning and Mean It Day**[2] **(January 2)**—Although this should be an everyday greeting, this commemorative day, approximating the beginning of the new year, symbolically illustrates the profound impact of simple words in everyday transactions.

2. **Martin Luther King, Jr. Day (January 15)**—In the United States, this is celebrated on the Monday after the birthday (January 15, 1929) of the civil rights leader, who challenged racial discrimination through boycotts, marches, and a commitment to nonviolence.

3. **International Holocaust Remembrance Day (January 27)**—To commemorate all the victims of the Nazi genocide.

4. **International Women's Day (March 8)**—Celebrated for the first time in Europe in 1911; in December 1977, the General Assembly adopted a resolution proclaiming this day in recognition that peace and social progress require the active participation and equality of women.

5. **International Day for the Elimination of Racial Discrimination (March 21)**—Commemorating the killing by police of 69 people who were peacefully demonstrating against apartheid, on March 21, 1960, in Sharpeville, South Africa.

6. **World Day Against Child Labor (June 12)**—Result of a global movement creating awareness of the forced induction of millions of children to work under some of the worst conditions imaginable as scavengers in small-scale mining and quarrying, and in grand-scale textile and agribusinesses around the world.

7. **World Refugee Day (June 20)**—A global movement drawing attention to the plight of refugees, and their enduring courage and contributions to host societies despite continuing dangers.

8. **International Day of the World's Indigenous Peoples (August 9)**—Officially commemorated annually in recognition of the first meeting of the United Nations Working Group on Indigenous Populations in Geneva in 1982.

9. **International Day for Remembrance of the Slave Trade (August 23)**—A global movement remembering that day in 1781 in Santo Domingo, which saw the beginning of the uprising that would play a crucial role in the abolition of the transatlantic slave trade.

10. **International Day of Peace (September 21)**—Declared by the UN General Assembly in 2001, this is a call for all nations and peoples to observe a day of global ceasefire and nonviolence.

11. **International Day of Older Persons (October 1)**—In this fast-aging world, in which one third of the population is expected to be over 60 in this millennium, this day commemorates the contributions of the elderly in caring for sick persons, transmitting their knowledge and experience, and participating in the workforce, and also urges a society incorporating people of all ages.

12. **World Day Against the Death Penalty** and **World Mental Health Day (October 10)**—Initiated by the World Coalition Against the Death Penalty, the World Day Against the Death Penalty brings attention to, among other things, the capriciousness of the death penalty along regional and racial lines, legal costs above and beyond life imprisonment, the culture of violence it produced, and its intractability, as well as the possibility it will provide a perverse incentive to those seeking to be immortalized for a cause. It may not be coincidental that this day also commemorates the struggles of those considered mentally ill, who continue to be disproportionately represented in prison populations.

13. **World Food Day (October 16)**—Bringing attention to the day-in-day-out hunger that nearly 1 billion people suffer every day and its related preventable diseases, this day also urges policies consistent with sustainable development and a just global distribution of food.

14. **International Day for the Eradication of Extreme Poverty (October 17)**—Initiated when International Fourth World Movement founder Joseph Wresinski placed a stone in front of the Palais de Chaillot, asserting that where men and women "are condemned to live in poverty," their "human rights are violated," this day calls for a just social order in which everyone lives with human rights and dignity.

15. **International Day of Tolerance (November 16)**—Initiated by UNESCO, this day emphasizes the role that education, including modeling of adults, plays in teaching children tolerance toward others, rooted in genuine friendship,

a commitment to learning about other groups, demystifying of stereotypes, and examination of exaggerated self-importance and group pride.

16. **Universal Children's Day (November 20)**—Commemorating the day that the General Assembly adopted the Convention on the Rights of the Child in 1989, this day brings attention to the need for global fraternity and sorority among the world's children, urging the world to promote the welfare of all its children.

17. **Mondo or World Currency Day[3] (November 23)**—In anticipation of major holiday spending in many parts of the world, this day is intended to create awareness of not only the ease of monetary transactions with one world currency, but the savings in time and wealth, which should and could be transferred to those less fortunate.

18. **International Day for the Elimination of Violence Against Women (November 25)**—Commemorating a General Assembly resolution on this day in 1999, this day promotes global recognition of gender violence, recalling the assassination of the Mirabel sisters, political activists in the Dominican Republic.

19. **National Day of Mourning (On Thanksgiving in the United States)**—Observed generally on the third or fourth Thursday in November, this day commemorates the legacy of genocide that took place after the landing of Columbus in what today is almost universally referred to as the Americas.

20. **International Day of Disabled Persons (December 3)**—Estimating 600 million people with disabilities, or alternative ways of being, the General Assembly proclaimed this day to increase awareness and mobilize support for practical action to allow persons with disabilities to live with fundamental freedoms and human dignity.

21. **Right to Development Day[4] (December 4)**—Alternatively called **Open Forum Day,** this day commemorates the endorsement of the Right to Development on December 4, 1986. It calls on all the people of the world to engage in open and creative dialogue on structural changes and economic and social reforms needed to ensure equality of opportunity and the eradication of all social injustices. It is an excellent lead-in to International Human Rights Day.

22. **International Human Rights Day (December 10)**—Commemorates the endorsement of the Universal Declaration of Human Rights by the UN General Assembly with no dissent in 1948.

23. **International Migrant's Day (December 18)**—Originated by Filipino and Asian migrant organizations on December 18, 1990, the International Convention on the Protection of the Rights of All Migrant Workers and Members of Their Families was adopted by the United Nations.

Human rights issues are also commemorated with various internationally recognized years and decades: 2005 was the International Year of Microcredit, extolling low-interest loaning to the poor; 2006 was named the International Year of Deserts and Desertification to bring attention to burgeoning arid lands throughout the world; 2008 is the International Year of Languages to call attention to the importance of learning languages and to the extinction of many of the world's languages, and the International Year of Sanitation, a growing public health concern given increased pollution and global warming; 2001–2010 is the International Decade for a Culture of Peace and Non-Violence for the Children of the World; 2003–2012 is the International Decade for World Literacy; 2005–2014 is the Second International Decade of the World's Indigenous People and the Decade of Education for Sustainable Development; and 2005–2015 is the International Decade for Water for Life as well as the World Decade for Human Rights Education. These commemorative days, years, and decades provide excellent opportunities for the human rights defender/social justice advocate to create awareness of major issues facing the world today, debate them, and arrive at collective decisions to implement social actions and service that promote a socially just world.

Proclamations, Resolutions, Declarations, and Bills[5]

One social action strategy to commemorate these days is simply to issue proclamations and resolutions, as depicted in Practice Illustration 3.1.

Practice Illustration 3.1
The Issuance of Proclamations and/or Resolutions

The Amherst Human Rights Commission, in order to create awareness of December 10 as Human Rights Day and March 21 as the International Day to Eradicate Racism, held a reading of the Universal Declaration in its Town Commons on December 10 and of select portions of the Convention on the Elimination of Racial Discrimination on March 21. They also issued official proclamations. Following are these two proclamations that may serve as an example to create awareness of internationally recognized values.

Proclamation of Human Rights Day

Whereas, the General Assembly of the United Nations endorsed the Universal Declaration of Human Rights, with no dissenting vote, on December 10th, 1948, under the able leadership of an American, Ms. Eleanor Roosevelt; and

Whereas, the Universal Declaration asserts the dignity of the human person; nondiscrimination based on race, color, sex, age, language, religion, political opinion, nationality, social origin, birth, or other status [medical condition, sexual orientation, disability]; civil and political rights, such as freedoms of thought, speech, belief, and the press; economic, social, and cultural rights, such as rights to employment, food, shelter, and health care; the solidarity of the human race; the notion that every right has a corresponding duty; and the interdependence and indivisibility of all human rights; and

Whereas, the Universal Declaration is referred to as the authoritative definition of human rights standards and increasingly referred to as customary international law, which all countries must abide; and

Whereas, the Universal Declaration gave birth to a long train of other declarations and covenants further defining human rights standards, such as the Rights of the Child, the Convention on the Elimination of All Forms of Racial Discrimination, and the Convention on the Elimination of Discrimination Against Women, which have the status of treaty and are to be considered "Law of the Land" in accordance with the Supremacy Clause of the U.S. Constitution, Article VI(2); and

Whereas, the Universal Declaration avows legal mandates to fulfill human need, NOW, THEREFORE, BE IT RESOLVED, that the Select Board of the Town of Amherst does hereby proclaim

December 10, 2002, and every December 10th hereafter as Human Rights Day in Amherst and the Select Board encourages all Amherst citizens to be mindful of human rights principles and urges all municipal, state, federal, and international bodies to incorporate said principles into their laws and policies as a means to move toward the creation of a human rights culture, which is a "lived awareness" of human rights principles.

Voted and signed this 2nd day of December 2002.

Proclamation of March 21st as the International Day for the Elimination of Racial Discrimination in the Town of Amherst

Given that the Secretary General Kofi Annan and the General Assembly of the United Nations recently declared March 21st as the International Day for the Elimination of Racial Discrimination;

Whereas on that day on March 21st, 1960, police opened fire and killed 69 people in the township of Sharpeville, South Africa, who were peacefully demonstrating against apartheid;

Whereas the United Nations has called upon the international community not only to commemorate that tragedy, but also to work together to combat racism and discrimination wherever they exist;

Whereas the United States signed the Universal Declaration of Human Rights, the authoritative definition of human rights standards, increasingly referred to as customary international law;

Whereas the Universal Declaration of Human Rights asserts the interdependence and indivisibility of human rights and prohibits all forms of discrimination, including race;

Given that the United States has ratified the International Covenant on the Elimination of All Forms of Racial Discrimination in 1994, a progeny of the Universal Declaration of Human Rights, and submitted its report on racial discrimination to the United States in 1999, and according to Article VI of the U.S. Constitution that Covenant is considered a Treaty thereby being Law for the United States and the "judges bound thereby";

The Town of Amherst, thereby, recognizes the importance of an international day to eliminate all forms of racial discrimination and recognizes the efforts of the United States for attempting to eliminate racial discrimination and urges the United States to continue with these efforts,

Hereby declares March 21st, 2003, as the International Day for the Elimination of Racial Discrimination and urges the community to commemorate this day to take constructive steps to advance human dignity for all, the essential thrusts of human rights instruments, and, if possible to attend a reading of select portions of the International Convention on the Elimination of Discrimination to be read in the Town Common on 7 PM on March 21.

Following is a Warrant Article, which is still in discussion.

Town Human Rights Warrant Article 25
as Amended for Town Meeting on June 1, 2005

Whereas human rights principles represent the highest aspirations of the human race and their violation has resulted in acts that have outraged the conscience of humanity;

Whereas such principles can be found in the Universal Declaration of Human Rights, the ultimate standard of human rights and a document increasingly referred to as customary international law;

Whereas such principles are further elaborated in its progeny, such as the Convention on the Elimination of Discrimination Against Women; Convention on the Elimination of All Forms of Racial Discrimination, Convention on the Rights of the Child, Declaration on the Rights of Disabled Persons; and Convention on the Prevention and Punishment of the Crime of Genocide;

Whereas everyone is entitled to the rights found in these documents, including, but not limited to health care, security in old age, meaningful and gainful employment, rest and leisure, adequate shelter, education, participation in the cultural life of the community, and peace;

Whereas being human is the only criterion for such rights, which have corresponding duties, no distinction shall be made on the basis of race, ethnicity, color, gender, language, religion, sexual orientation, political or other opinion, culture, social origin, property, birth, military or any other status,

Town Meeting in Concert with the Select Board and the Human Rights Commission for the Town of Amherst resolve that it will commit itself to the progressive realization of human rights principles within the resources of the town, state, nation, and world community and urges all municipalities, states, nations, the international community, that is, every person, everywhere to work together in a spirit of cooperation and harmony to realize human rights for all.

It is noteworthy that in the town of Amherst, run by a select board and town meeting, the general consensus was that everyone's human rights should be guaranteed. The problem in guaranteeing all those rights, including health care, is it could easily bankrupt the town. It was having enough difficulties financing school programs. The sentiment for universal human rights obviously existed, but concerted national and international efforts are necessary to guarantee them.

Declarations and Bills

More forceful are other social action strategies that declare human rights documents law for a city, state, or nation. Passing bills is also a way to assert the viability of human rights principles. Practice Illustration 3.2 depicts two such action strategies.

Figure 3.3   A Banner Reading "Human Rights for Every Person, Everywhere" Hanging Over the Amherst Town Commons, Human Rights Day, December 10th.

Practice Illustration 3.2
Asserting Human Rights Principles as Laws Through Declarations

The Coalition for a Strong United Nations (CSUN) in concert with the mayor and city council of the City of Cambridge, Massachusetts, issued the Cambridge Declaration of Human Rights, initiated by Jock Forbes and written by this author with Prof. Winston Langley of the University of Massachusetts. The document declared the Universal Declaration of Human Rights law in that city:

The Cambridge Declaration of Human Rights

In City Council
September 28, 1998
Mayor Duekay
Councillor Born
Councillor Davis
Vice Mayor Galluccio
Councillor Reeves
Councillor Russell
Councillor Sullivan
Councillor Toomey
Councillor Triantafillou

WHEREAS continuing disregard and contempt for human rights have resulted in barbarous acts which have outraged the conscience of humanity; and

WHEREAS the advent of a world, where humans can live with dignity and enjoy their civil and political rights, such as freedom of thought, speech, belief, and the press; economic, social and cultural rights, such as rights to employment, food, shelter, and health care; and solidarity rights, such as rights to peace, self-determination, development, and clean environment, is the highest aspiration of humanity; and

ACKNOWLEDGING the interdependence and indivisibility of human rights as enshrined in the United Nations Universal Declaration of Human Rights, approved in 1948 without dissent by the UN General Assembly, including the United States, and today increasingly referred to as *customary international law,*

RECOGNIZING the necessity to mandate legally the protection and enforcement of these rights in the promotion of human development, without discrimination of any kind such as race, color, sex, language, religion, political or other opinion, nationality, social origin, birth or other status,

INVOKING the spirit of our time which calls upon the peoples of the world to rededicate themselves to the global task of promoting and protecting human rights,

DETERMINED to take new steps in a recommitment to sustained efforts to ensure co-operation and solidarity in the promotion of human rights,

The Cambridge City Council, hereby

DECLARES the Universal Declaration of Human Rights the Law of the Land, urging its implementation in accordance with the Will of the People and by all executive, legislative, judicial and other public bodies;

ENDORSES the development of a human rights culture, which is a lived awareness of these rights and principles, entailing corresponding duties;

COMMENDS all previous and future efforts that are in compliance with the Declaration;

URGES other municipal, state, national and international bodies to move toward implementation of the Declaration; and

REACHES out to the people of the world in a spirit of co-operation, certain that together we can create a just social and international order in the effective realization of human rights for all.

In City Council September 28, 1998.
Adopted by the affirmative vote of nine members.
Attest: D. Margaret Drury, City Clerk.

Bills, which often have more force than declarations, are also a good way to initiate discussion is to develop talking points. Practice Illustration 3.3 has some talking points that I had written prior to the development of House Bill 706.

Practice Illustration 3.3
Asserting Human Rights Principles Through Bills

Soon thereafter CSUN, the U.S. chapter of the International Fourth World Movement (IFWM), and the Massachusetts chapter of the Women's International League for Peace and Freedom (WILP) initiated a Human Rights Bill, now known as Human Rights Bill 706. It was constructed in part from the following talking points, which, more or less, are brainstormed ideas that might be included in more formal statements. It is often a good strategy to have group members individually and collectively think about what points they wish to include in more formal official documents. Following are some talking points that emerged prior to the development of House Bill 706:

1. The United Nations drafted the Universal Declaration of Human Rights, the authoritative definition of human rights standards and a document increasingly referred to as customary international law, under the able leadership of the Chairperson of the Drafting Committee, an American, Eleanor Roosevelt.

2. Given the early leadership in the field of human rights, the United States ought to continue as a leader and be on the cutting edge of providing for human rights for all people.

3. The Universal Declaration, while endorsed with no dissent by the General Assembly in 1948, was first declared *customary international law* in a federal court in *Filartiga v. Pena* (1980) 630 F.2d 884–885, which ruled against a torturer, living in the United States, for an act committed in Paraguay.

4. The *Filartiga* decision appears to have spearheaded a global movement resulting in other cases worldwide, such as *Pinochet v. Spain*, based on which it can be said that in the future torturers may have no safe haven, a major goal of the noted human rights group Amnesty International.

5. In addition to the right not to be tortured (Article 5), however, the Universal Declaration declared other rights that should be guaranteed, such as rights to employment at a reasonable wage and under favorable working conditions (Article 23); rights to health care, shelter, security in old age, and special protections for children and motherhood (Article 25); and the right to education (Article 26).

6. The Universal Declaration asserts that every right has a corresponding duty, for example, the right to health care also requires the duty to eat healthfully, exercise appropriately, not overconsume, and produce food sustainably—lifestyles to which we all generally aspire. Government must also assist in providing the necessary opportunities for this to happen (Article 28).

7. In addition to the Universal Declaration, the United States has also ratified other major human rights treaties, including the Convention Against Torture, the International Covenant on Civil and Political Rights, and the International Convention on the Elimination of All Forms of Racial Discrimination. According to Article VI of the U.S. Constitution, these documents, which have the status of treaties, ought to become "law of the land and the judges bound thereby." In brief, these documents describe the Universal Declaration articles in more depth.

8. The United States has not ratified three other major human rights treaties: the Convention on the Rights of the Child, the Convention on the Elimination of All Forms of Racial Discrimination, and the International Covenant on Economic, Social, and Cultural Rights. Failure to ratify these conventions, especially the Convention on the Rights of the Child, appears to have played a major role in the ousting in 2001 of the United States from the UN Human Rights Commission, and the current ousting of the United States from the Human Rights Commission of the Organization of American States.

9. The United States has a rights-based culture, as evidenced by its Bill of Rights, which the UN monitoring committee of the International Covenant on Civil and Political Rights referred to as a "beacon of hope for humanity," and the state of Massachusetts' Patients' Bill of Rights, drafted by the late Senator Jack Backman.

10. The state of Massachusetts also has a traditional commitment to international human rights initiatives, as evidenced by its official declaration of October 24 as United Nations Day (when the United Nations was founded) and December 10

as Human Rights Day (when the UN endorsed the Universal Declaration). Enacting House Bill 2840 into law would continue that tradition.

11. It was Eleanor Roosevelt's dream that "One day school children would know the Universal Declaration of Human Rights, as much as the Bill of Rights." Sadly, her dream does not yet appear to have become a reality, and this bill would help assist educating others about what human rights actually are.

12. Enacting Human Rights House Bill 2840 into law would be one step toward what has been called the Creation of a Human Rights Culture, which is a "lived awareness" of human rights principles, where every person, everywhere can live with human dignity, as asserted in Article 1 of the Universal Declaration.

Following is the bill that emerged, initially written in concert with Massachusetts State Representative Ellen Story.

The Commonwealth of Massachusetts in the Year Two Thousand Five Human Rights Bill 706

RESOLVE to establish a special commission to investigate the integration of international human rights standards into Massachusetts state law and policies.

Be it enacted by the Senate and House of Representatives in General Court assembled, and by the authority of the same, as follows:

WHEREAS, the Commonwealth of Massachusetts has an interest in ensuring the protection, safety, prosperity and happiness of all its residents; and

RECOGNIZING that respect for the inherent dignity of all people is the foundation of freedom, justice and peace in the world; and

ACKNOWLEDGING that the United Nations Universal Declaration of Human Rights, approved in 1948 without dissent by the UN General Assembly, including the United States, establishes a baseline standard for human rights both domestically and internationally; and

REMEMBERING the leadership role that Eleanor Roosevelt and other prominent Americans have played in articulating global human rights standards and in establishing United States' commitment to honor and protect human rights in this country; and

RECOGNIZING the progeny of the Universal Declaration of Human Rights, including, but not limited to: the Convention on the Elimination of All Forms of Racial Discrimination; the Convention on the Elimination of All Forms of Discrimination Against Women; the Convention on the Rights of the Child; the Convention on Economic, Social, and Cultural Rights; the Convention on Civil and Political Rights; and the Convention Against Torture; and

INVOKING the spirit of our times which recognizes the increasingly global nature of our society and calls upon the peoples of the world to rededicate themselves to the task of promoting and protecting human rights and providing opportunities for freedom, liberty and opportunity in all corners of the world,

BE IT RESOLVED by the Senate and the House of Representatives in General Court assembled, and by the authority of the same, to take steps to review international human rights standards and evaluate integration of such standards into the policies and laws of the Commonwealth of Massachusetts by establishing a special commission for the purpose of making an investigation and study relative to the integration of international human rights standards in the commonwealth's laws and policies. This commission shall be composed of nine members, two of whom shall be appointed by the Speaker of the Senate, one of whom shall be appointed by the Minority Leader of the Senate; two of whom shall be appointed by the Speaker of the House, one of whom shall be the chairperson, and one of whom shall be appointed by the Minority Leader of the House. In addition, the chairperson of the Massachusetts Commission Against Discrimination, the head of the Civil Rights Division of the Attorney General's office and the executive director of the Massachusetts Commission on the Status of Women shall serve on this commission; and be it further

RESOLVED, that the special commission shall hold hearings and take testimony at such places as it deems necessary in this Commonwealth; and be it further

RESOLVED, that said commission shall report to the general court the results of its investigation and study and its recommendations, if any, together with drafts of legislation necessary to carry its recommendations into effect by filing the same with the clerk of the House of Representatives on or before the 30th of September, 2006.

Providing NGO Input

Recently, the International Federation of Social Work (IFSW) provided input (Practice Illustration 3.4) into the Expert Seminar on Human Rights and Extreme Poverty, March 22–23, 2007, sponsored by the Special Rapporteur on Extreme Poverty, Dr. Arjun Sengupta. NGO input is very important in developing and implementing socially just policies:

Practice Illustration 3.4
International Federation of Social Workers
Statement on Human Rights and Extreme Poverty

Contribution of the International Federation of Social Workers to the Expert Seminar on Human Rights and Extreme Poverty, 22–23 March 2007

The International Federation of Social Workers (IFSW) wishes to thank the Special Rapporteur on Extreme Poverty, Dr. Arun Sengupta, for convening this Expert Seminar on Extreme Poverty and asking for input from select academics, NGOs, and policy advocates. We also wish to thank Mr. Xavier Verzat, Special Representative of the International Fourth World, for eliciting input to be submitted to the Expert Seminar for creative dialogue with other members and organizations. IFSW feels that social work from its inception was a human rights profession, and looks forward to providing input into this extremely important meeting.

In response to Dr. Sengupta's emphasis on experiences and programmes that "could contribute to eradicating extreme poverty as a human rights entitlement," IFSW wishes to make some preliminary comments, followed by specific examples which it views as ways to eradicate extreme poverty. Unfortunately, such poverty still persists after the General Assembly's unanimous endorsement in 1948 of the Universal Declaration of Human Rights, and this despite the considerable economic and social progress witnessed during the past decades. Indeed, as the Human Development Report (2005) asserts, at present roughly 40% of the world lives on less than two dollars per day, and the ratio between the wealth of the world's richest and poorest country is roughly 1 to 103! Such realities are unacceptable and, once again, we welcome any attempts to change such a distressing scenario.

The Importance of Choosing a Human Rights Culture

In brief, despite the world's continuing inability to provide for the poorest of the poor, we feel that given the means, both financial and technical, that are at the disposal of governments, and despite the setbacks caused by diseases and armed conflicts in some regions, we can and must choose a world where human needs can be met satisfactorily. Human rights constitute the legal mandate to fulfill human needs. Whereas knowledge of human needs is imperfect, it can be said perhaps that the human condition is such that humans have *spiritual needs* to be treated with human dignity and respect as they live their lives according to meanings they have derived from fundamental religious, spiritual, and/or philosophical beliefs and systems. Humans also have *cognitive needs,* to have access to knowledge and information and to engage freely without fear of retaliation in dialogue with others about ways to create a socially just world. They also have *physical needs* for adequate food, water, and shelter, as well as *social needs* for affiliation with others in cultural and ethnic groups as well as the family, and ultimately, *self-actualization needs* to live up to one's potential. Such needs, like human rights, are interdependent.

IFSW feels, therefore, that the aims of all poverty reduction programmes ought to be the creation of a human rights culture, which we see as a "lived awareness" of human rights principles that ultimately mirror human needs. Such awareness ought to exist not only in a cognitive sense, that is, one's mind, but in literally a "heartfelt" sense where such principles are lived and dragged into one's everyday life. Research repeatedly asserts that only chosen values endure. One cannot force such a culture on anyone. It must make sense to the entire global community and be chosen on its own merits.

Thus, using the Universal Declaration as the authoritative definition of human rights standards, a document fortunately and increasingly referred to as *customary international law,* such a culture would acknowledge the interdependence, indivisibility, and equality of all human rights. Roughly, the Universal Declaration stresses five crucial notions: (1) human dignity (Art. 1); (2) non-discrimination, based on race, property, religion or other status (Art. 2.); (3) civil and political rights like freedoms of speech, the press, and peaceful assembly (Art. 2–21); (4) economic, social, and cultural rights, like food, medical care, adequate shelter, meaningful or acceptable work, and security in old age (Art. 22–27); and (5) solidarity rights, such as the right to a just social and international order, which scholars have argued to include, for example, rights to peace, development, and humanitarian disaster relief, and international distributive justice, that is, the right of the poorest of the poor to the wealthiest of the richest nations (Art. 28–30). Freedom of speech, for instance, is meaningless and hardly dignified if a person lacks adequate shelter, is hungry, and lives in a world at war.

IFSW views the primary challenge in the eradication of extreme poverty, therefore, as moving the global community toward an acceptance of values and interrelationships among rights, that reflect human needs, found in the Universal Declaration, as well as its "long train of declarations and covenants," as stated by the late Pope John Paul II. The Chairperson of the drafting committee of the Universal Declaration, moreover, Eleanor Roosevelt, had a dream that every school child would know about the Universal Declaration of Human Rights, much as students learn about their own country constitutions. In order for such values to endure, learning must begin at an early age. Furthermore, after the laying of such a foundation, human rights ought to continue to serve as "guiding principles" for socially just policies.

The Need for a Multi-Pronged Approach

With these comments in mind, IFSW would like to offer the following comments in a spirit of creative dialogue with other members of this group with the aim to free humanity from the scourge of extreme poverty. We have chosen to adopt a public health medical and advanced generalist social work model, calling for multi-pronged interventions, with human rights serving as guiding principles. Thus, we need strategies that may be effective with "whole populations" (also referred to as "macro" approaches); "at risk populations" ("mezzo" approaches) and "direct practice" ("micro") levels of intervention. To be sure, distinctions among levels are blurred, yet, they may provide the necessary contours to assess, and then act upon strategies to eliminate extreme poverty. Briefly, then, homelessness, could be dealt with by perhaps adding a "Right to adequate shelter" in a state constitution (a macro approach, getting its sustenance primarily from Article 25 of the Universal Declaration); organizing workers to engage in collective bargaining to assist in the prevention of job loss or, if that is not feasible, to be assisted to acquire further skills for other jobs (a mezzo approach, with sustenance from Article 23); and setting up a homeless shelter and soup kitchen, if previous measures had failed (a micro approach directly dealing with symptoms when other measures have failed). As the above example demonstrates, programmes such as the setting up of homeless shelters are certainly necessary, but are only one aspect of a need for a multi-pronged approach to dealing with extreme poverty that also takes into account the interdependency of rights. Thus, while obviously it is important to help the poor through programmes, the poor must also "stop coming" so to speak. Ultimately, there should be no poor to help. The homeless, moreover, need to have equal access to education, medical care, and meaningful work at reasonable wages so they can live becomingly and with human dignity. With these levels in mind, additional suggestions to deal with extreme poverty are offered below.

Additional Strategies With Commentary

Interventions ought to impact not only everyone in a particular country, but throughout the world. What is needed is a major spiritual transformation, broadly defined, that will place human need before profit with human dignity at its core.

A major macro strategy thus is to add rights found in human rights documents to national constitutions worldwide. The word "constitution" is from the Latin *constitare,* meaning "to choose." As such, they represent societal choices, and the values they represent, in regard to enhancing the quality of life. In the U.S.A., for example, with estimates of three million homeless, there is no right to adequate shelter in its federal or any of its state constitutions. In fact, the only economic, and social, right asserted in the majority of state constitutions is the right to education.

But, in order to have these rights in the constitutions, which must be chosen, it is necessary to acknowledge that socialization processes play a major role. Thus, IFSW concurs with the World Decade for Human Rights Education (2005–2015) and encourages education about human rights documents not only in the post secondary levels, but the primary and secondary as well. (See particularly UNESCO, 2006 for additional teaching materials.) Furthermore, recognizing that education must go beyond formalized institutions, IFSW encourages the media to inform others about human rights documents. In that regard, we recall an "MTV like" skit where in France actors and actresses would dance to music as they recited Article 1 of the Universal Declaration of Human Rights calling, among other things, for human dignity and a spirit of brotherhood among all the peoples of the world. We also note that in select Scandinavian countries at times a right from a human rights document like the Rights of the Child, asserting for example that no child shall be physically or emotionally abused, is flashed on a children's show followed by discussion. Such practices are necessary in order for values ultimately to be chosen, then later reflected in constitutions, and therefore implemented. Ultimately, if children learn about doing duties to others, anywhere where they live in the world, they may at a later point come to a realization that the richer countries of the world have abnegated their responsibilities to those in extreme poverty, but who may also live in their same countries.

Such practices in Europe appear totally different than in the U.S.A. where advertising on children's television encourages children into consumerism, rather than a spirit of fraternity and sorority, paving the way for a society to value profit instead of human need, thereby leading ultimately to extremes in wealth. Fortunately, movements have evolved that commemorate international days, such as October 17, the International Day to Eradicate Extreme Poverty, and the International Day to Eradicate Racism.

In the U.S.A. chief executive pay is roughly five hundred times higher than the average worker's pay. Yet, in the U.S.A. there are burgeoning movements to add human rights in state constitutions, such as the Massachusetts House Bill 708, an Act Relative to Incorporating Human Rights Standards in Massachusetts Laws and Policies. Presently, 60 NGOs in the state support that bill and a similar bill was passed unanimously in the Pennsylvania Legislature. IFSW encourages bills in legislative bodies and declarations as means to educate others about human rights, which ultimately ought to move people to action.

When engaging in such macro strategies, it must be kept in mind, furthermore, that such strategies must transcend domestic sovereignty. IFSW recognizes, therefore, that the one and one half trillion dollars spent on defense to keep lines on the map intact is a questionable enterprise, as such monies could be spent on alleviating the plight of the poor, and the poorest of the poor. Consequently, we urge broad based social movements emphasizing world citizenship and allegiance to humanity, in the words of the late Joseph Rotblatt, a former Nobel Prize Winner.

Finally, considering the acceptance of Guiding Principles for the Eradication of Extreme Poverty, IFSW encourages the development of an International Convention on the Eradication of Extreme Poverty, legally binding upon all Member States, taking into consideration the need for a global redistribution of the earth's wealth and resources.

For populations at risk, we also offer human rights as guiding principles to prevent job loss, and symptoms of job insecurity. Thus, IFSW urges that States encourage workers to engage in collective bargaining and the formation of trade unions to protect their interests as enunciated in such documents as the Universal Declaration and the Convention on Economic, Social and Cultural Rights. Mothers and children are particularly vulnerable to poverty and IFSW encourages States to provide for paid maternity leave before and after childbirth with government sponsored day care as enunciated in the Convention on the Elimination of Discrimination Against Women.

Should all of the above attempts fail to halt extreme poverty, we would need to have recourse to programmes such as shelters for the homeless; distribution of food that is nutritious, easily accessible, culturally appropriate, and at a reasonable cost; provision of loans at reasonable rates; and even the handing out of at least minimal amounts of money to those in dire straits. We should also never forget that education is one of the major means to overcome poverty and extreme poverty.

Certainly, all levels of intervention have different issues and approaches. They often require vast amounts of time with scarce immediate results forthcoming. Furthermore, we need to remind ourselves that extreme poverty, at least poverty in spirit, may also exist among the affluent, as according to a recent *State of the World*, instances of alienation are highest in some of the world's richest countries.

Thank you for your consideration of our viewpoints. We look forward to listening to other approaches in the hope that together we can advance on the road toward the elimination of extreme poverty.

This paper was drafted by Joseph Wronka, PhD, Professor of Social Work, Springfield College; Researcher, Brandeis University, Heller School for Social Policy, in collaboration with Ellen Mouravieff-Apostol, the main IFSW Representative at the United Nations Office at Geneva.

Such proclamations, resolutions, declarations, talking points, bills, and NGO input are excellent means of engaging in creative dialogue, which human rights monitoring committees urge. It is important to stress, no government today would dare say it is against human rights. Government officials often issue proclamations during human rights week, usually the days preceding and following December 10. A proclamation by President George W. Bush in 2002 asserted: "We cherish the values of free speech, equal justice, and religious tolerance. . . . The United States is a country where all citizens have the opportunity to voice their opinions, practice their faith, and enjoy the blessings of freedom" (U.S. Department of State, 2003, p. 1). Such statements are commendable, but they overlook other rights like health care, shelter, security in old age, special protections for motherhood and children, and peace, not to mention a social and international order in which those rights can be realized. Rights are interdependent. The challenge is to work with governments to expand on their knowledge of rights, as commonly understood, to include economic, social, cultural, and solidarity rights in their discourse.

The Arts, Human Rights, and Social Justice

Undeniably, the arts can be a powerful force as a macro intervention for social justice. This section considers the arts broadly defined to include not only art, per se, but also music, literature, poetry, storytelling, sculpture, dance, theater, film—that is, any creative means of expression, an activity apparently unique to the human species. The term *art* comes from the Latin *ars*, meaning, in part, "skill, way, and method." A lesser-known meaning, in a bad sense, is "cunning." Taking this etymology to heart, then, art can be used both positively and negatively. The challenge is to choose the former.

On the negative side is the whole notion of art as cultural facade. That is, by praising the art of an oppressed group, an entire culture is able to hide behind beautiful pieces of art while continuing its exclusionary practices.

Airports worldwide often rather ostentatiously display indigenous art, like majestic totem poles or carved tusks. Yet, not far away, extremely high unemployment and poverty rates among the Indigenous Peoples may exist. Praising the artistic work of a culture might subtly obscure more substantive issues. Oppressors are not deliberately trying to con the public into thinking everything is fine among an oppressed group. Quite the contrary, the general consensus may very well be that it is important to display and extol cultural art in the spirit of dialogue and mutual admiration. The point, however, is that people ought not blind themselves to the complexity of issues involved in producing and displaying art. These issues are anything but transparent.

The lack of prominent displays of Judaic art during the Renaissance and the newly industrialized Europe may have played a major role in the Holocaust. Did Europeans display African art before and during the transatlantic slave trade or indigenous art while colonizing the Americas? Excluding the art of groups from the mainstream is a sin of omission, subtly teaching that one culture is better than another, creating an out-group ripe for scapegoating. On the other hand, Leni Riefenstahl's pro-Hitler film, *Triumph of the Will*, deliberately attempted to stir up hate, while presenting efficiency arguments that following the Fuehrer would make Germany great. Acknowledging that social justice means struggle, when it comes to art, one must move with caution. It may be a "way, skill, and method" to promote social justice. But artists and displayers of art are not immune to the human condition, and their creative attempts do not necessarily guarantee social justice.

Revisiting this powerful idea of human rights, it is one thing to say the arts are important for human development and it is therefore foolish to abandon art programs in the educational system, increasingly a reality in the struggle for funds among forces for war, peace, and social justice. More powerful, however, is asserting that participation in the arts is a human right as guaranteed in Article 27 of the Universal Declaration: "Everyone has the right freely to participate in the cultural life of the community, to enjoy the arts and to share in scientific advancement and its benefits." Acknowledging the interdependence of rights, with economic and social rights equal to cultural rights, it is necessary to make the arts available for all—not only the art of the powerful, but the art of the powerless, too. Has humanity progressed in complying with Article 27 of the Universal Declaration? Seats for Broadway plays and movie tickets appear to have outpaced inflation, such that only the well-to-do may have the opportunity for such luxuries. Complying with Article 27 would mean having museums, films, concerts and the like culturally appropriate and readily accessible, if not free on some days, possibly subsidized by graduated taxes. Subsidies requiring people to pay their share is directly consistent with the clause to "promote the general welfare" in the Preamble of the U.S. Constitution. Unfortunately, the Supreme Court had ruled that that clause cannot be invoked to justify a right (Wronka, 1998b).

The Role of the Media

The media could also play a major role in making the arts more readily available. MTV skits can alert viewers to human rights and their violations. In France, for example, one relatively short skit has actors and actresses dancing to music as they speak the words of Article 1 of the Universal Declaration: "All [dancing continues after each word] . . . human . . . beings . . . are . . . born . . . free . . . and . . . equal . . . in . . . dignity . . . and . . . in . . . rights. . . . They . . . are . . . endowed . . . with . . . reason . . . and . . . conscience . . . and . . . should . . . act . . . toward . . . one . . . another . . . in . . . a . . . spirit . . . of . . . brotherhood." Then, dancing a bit more, they join hands and say, *"Réfléchissez-Vous!"* ("Think about it!"). On Norwegian TV, between cartoons, a right specified in articles of the CRC is flashed on screen, followed by a brief discussion in language a child understands, for example: "Every child has the right to read books which will benefit the child" (Article 17) and "Every child has the right to a decent life with dignity and to take part in decision making" (Article 23). This is quite a difference from the United States, where the media bombards children with the importance of possessions and encourages eating foods of dubious nutritional value! This does not mean that France or Norway can sit back and relax, having created a human rights culture. It only illustrates that some countries, whose quality of life appears more consistent with the Universal Declaration, have engaged in teaching and learning about human rights principles at an early age. When attending the Human Rights Defenders Conference in 1998, I saw the entire copy of the Universal Declaration of Human Rights on the front page of Air France's magazine. Given the role of the media in values formation, the social activist should learn how to use the media to promote responsible citizenship and common human decency as mirrored in human rights principles, the essential thrusts of social justice.

Other Artistic Venues

Paintings, films, plays, dramas, comedy, street theater, and documentaries are all excellent tools for responding to the clarion call of social justice, to move toward public sentiment in accord with the timeless values that human rights documents often assert. Norman Rockwell's *Four Freedoms* paintings— "Freedom From Want," "Freedom of Worship," "Freedom of Speech," and "Freedom From Fear"—reflect President Franklin Roosevelt's vision, discussed earlier, and Rockwell's *Golden Rule*—given to the United Nations as a gift from Nancy Reagan, wife of the late president—bring awareness of human rights principles. *Lysistrata,* the hilarious play by that dramatist/jokester Aristophanes, which opened the 2004 Olympics in Greece, is another example. Lysistrata, a committed and savvy community organizer, organized women in Greece to go on a sex strike until the men agreed to stop fighting in wars. Absolutely hilarious! As a social action strategy, prior to the U.S. invasion of Iraq in 2003, the Women's International League for Peace and Freedom (WILPF) organized a global reading of that play in cities and campuses around the world. Not very effective, perhaps, but better than doing nothing. Leaving one's comfort zone to take risks for social justice is perhaps the greatest challenge facing any social activist.

Music can also be a potent tool for social action. Songs like "We Shall Overcome," "Imagine," "From a Distance," and "He Ain't Heavy . . . He's My Brother [or Sister]" "hath charms to soothe a savage breast," to tame forces that encourage what Nietzsche called a herd mentality, which tramples the world in near-wanton abandon. Singing and dancing to other people's ethnic tunes, dancing the Macarena, a polka, a tarantella, or tango can teach appreciation of different cultures, while acknowledging our common humanity expressed in the universal language of music. Beethoven's classic, "Ode to Joy," can serve as a siren call of hope. The heaviness of the lyrics from "Ole Man River"—"Body all achin' and racked with pain"—create quite a powerful image! And the eerie theme from the movie *Schindler's List* can imprint the stamp of "Never Again" on man's inhumanity to man. And the song "Strange Fruit," a haunting evocation of public lynchings in the South, sung by such luminaries as Billie Holiday, Diana Ross, Pete Seeger, and Sting, was a powerful clarion call to end such atrocities committed in full view of the public, who often perceived them as entertainment! The Third Reich may have wanted to hide its atrocities behind walls, but public lynchings were carried on openly and unashamedly. Jumping to the meta-micro level, everyone can attest to the power of the arts and music as an outlet, an alternative mood enhancer to psychotropic medication. "Smile tho' your heart is aching, smile even though it's breaking, when there are clouds in the sky, you'll get by," go the lyrics to the theme song from Charlie Chaplin's *Modern Times,* a classic commentary on workers' stresses in these days of automation; the comedian and filmmaker dared, while Hollywood looked the other way and making the most of his strengths, to take on Hitler in his farcical *The Great Dictator,* and in part for his courageous mockery of the McCarthy era in *King in New York,* he was not allowed back into the United States until 1972.

On the other hand, music can cause harm even at an early age. There is the line in that children's song, "Three Blind Mice": "She cut off their tails with a carving knife" . . . Really! Isn't it so easy to socialize children into accepting the banalities of evil at a very early age? Should visually challenged people be so dispensable? Did Mendelssohn's powerful "War March of the Priests" play a role, however minor, in the Holocaust? Does the theme to *Star Wars* encourage youth to resolve conflict only through violence, totally inimical to the thrust of the Universal Declaration? Shakespeare was right: "Music oft hath such a charm to make bad good, and good provoke to harm" (*Measure for Measure,* 1604, act 4, scene 1).

The power of sculpture, particularly in memorials, should not be dismissed lightly. War memorials dotting the landscape dull our sensibilities. It is not uncommon to pass at least one war memorial while commuting to and from work. Honoring veterans is important, but civilians killed in war should also be honored; both groups have been caught up and victimized in a vortex of classism, racism, ethnic, and religious strife. But where are the peace memorials? There is at least one of a vulnerable-looking Gandhi, at the Peace Abbey in Sherbourne, Massachusetts. Another is the Boston Irish Famine Memorial. Sculptures are one way to symbolically admit a culture's failures, a form of reparations, however minimal. The sculpture of Crazy Horse in the beautiful black hills of South Dakota is another example. We need others.

Museums can help us remember the horrors of the past so that they are not repeated. In Greek mythology, the Muses were the daughters of Mnemosyne, whose name means "memory." They were the inspiration of poetry, music, dance, and other intellectual activities (Cotterell & Storm, 2003). Elie Wiesel, survivor of Auschwitz, has it right when he states in his poignant *Night:* "In the end, it is all about memory, its sources and its magnitude, and, of course, its consequences" (2006, p. xv). In Austria, there is Terezin, a holding tank where people waited to be transported to larger camps of extermination. There is also The Holocaust Memorial Museum in Washington, DC, where visitors can view actual apparel of concentration camp inmates and read stories of immeasurable horror. In Massachusetts, the Deerfield Museum and the Plymouth Plantation, not far from the actual Plymouth Rock, both openly testify to the genocide of Indigenous Peoples, recounting kidnappings and massacres as they were often caught in the middle of religious wars between the English and French, who viewed them as expendable pawns.

Art should lead to action. The philosopher and concentration camp survivor Emmanuel Levinas writes that, if the artistic experience says,

> Do not speak, do not reflect, admire in silence and in peace, [as] such are the counsels of wisdom satisfied before the beautiful. There is something wicked and egoist and cowardly in artistic enjoyment. There are times when one can be ashamed of it, as of feasting during a plague. (Ayer & O'Grady, 1992, p. 254)

Other Select Direct Nonviolent Strategies

Nonviolent strategies for social change do not always need to mention human rights. But integrating this powerful idea can enhance them. A human rights culture calls for vision, an idea directly consistent with what has been called the spirit of Crazy Horse. Tashunkewitko (his Native American name), an "uncommonly handsome man . . . a gentle warrior, a true brave who stood for the highest ideals of the Sioux . . . [such as] big-heartedness, generosity, courage, and self-denial" (Indigenous Peoples' Literature, 2006, p. 2), said: "A very great vision is needed and the man who has it must follow it as the eagle seeks the deepest blue of the sky" (p. 1). Limited definitions of human rights in opposition to such violations as torture in Guantanamo Bay, the death penalty, and the imprisonment of people of conscience are extremely important, but keeping the vision, what may be called a vision of hope as enunciated in the Universal Declaration, is still vital. If all people had jobs with reasonable wages allowing them to support their families with dignity, a fundamental concept in human rights documents, surely there would be more hope for a brighter future. We hear much talk of terrorism and suicide bombers today, but the world population is currently experiencing a youth bulge, and a burgeoning global economic system that places profit before need. Given that hopelessness is a major predictor of suicide, one aim of social justice is to create structures where people can engage in peaceful rather than warlike activities, to give them a sense of affiliation and ultimately human dignity, which is fundamental to human rights. Hope is a spiritual-philosophical concept, often camouflaged perhaps within medical rubric. Yet the creation of hope is also fundamental to engagement in therapeutic relationships with clients and patients. Creating a human rights culture entails vision and should provide hope by converting socially unjust structures to structures more amenable to the fulfillment of human need.

The noted peace activist Gene Sharp (2005) discusses a number of social actions to enhance strategies in the service of social justice. This book is not meant to be a primer on all social action strategies. Nevertheless, mention of some, in addition to those focused primarily on human rights, ought to provide a sense of the importance of any direct nonviolent strategies. Such strategies, however, require tremendous courage, the courage of the eagle Crazy Horse talks about. The eagle is notorious for flying straight into the storm and may well serve as a model.

Sharp covers the following strategies: (a) actions to send messages; (b) actions to suspend cooperation and assistance; (c) actions to suspend economic relations; (d) actions to suspend political submission; and (e) methods of nonviolent disruption. Formal statements include declarations by organizations and institutions and group petitions. Truth commissions bring public attention to social injustice. Communications with a wider audience include banners, sky-writing, earthwriting, slogans, and symbols (written, painted, drawn, printed, in gestures, spoken, or mimicked). There are also group presentations such as mock awards, picketing, and mock elections; symbolic public acts such as the wearing of symbols, signs, and names, symbolic reclamations, reminding officials of an unjust policy; drama and music through the performance of plays, music, and humorous skits; processions such as marches and parades; honoring the dead, as in paying homage at burial places; and public assemblies like teach-ins with several informed speakers. Finally, there is withdrawal and renunciation, like renunciation of honors, walkouts, and turning one's back. Sharp's discussion of methods makes a good read, which can be enhanced by integrating human rights principles.

Some students in the social action class here held the first Hispanic Human Rights Conference in Hartford, Connecticut. They had music and guest speakers, and came up with various human rights declarations on health care, security in old age, and the like for every person, everywhere. In fact, they were so successful that officials came to them! That is quite different from going to the politicians to convince them of an idea, as is often taught in policy classes. But the idea of human rights is already convincing. Practice Illustration 3.5 depicts a National Truth Commission, part of the excellent work of the Poor People's Economic Human Rights Campaign, a loose affiliation of human rights and social justice groups such as Arise for Social Justice (Springfield, Massachusetts), Center for Economic and Social Rights (New York), Kensington Welfare Rights Union (Philadelphia, Pennsylvania), Social Welfare Action Alliance (national), Southerners for Economic Justice (Durham, North Carolina), People Organized to Win Employment Rights (San Francisco, California), and Youth Action Research Group (Washington, DC). This vast array of organizations, as well as those mentioned supporting the Massachusetts Human Rights Bill, are a few examples of how human rights can easily assist in coalition building.

Practice Illustration 3.5
Holding a National Truth Commission as a
Social Action Strategy: An Example From the Poor People's
Economic Human Rights Campaign (PPEHRC; Poor People's, 2006)

In July 2006, PPEHRC held the first national Truth Commission in Cleveland, Ohio. Modeled after similar commissions in Africa and Latin America, it brought people together from across the United States and the world to bring to light the actual suffering of people living in extreme poverty, a human rights violation. Many social leaders throughout the world were there, including the UN Independent Expert on Extreme Poverty for the Office of the High Commissioner of Human Rights, people from the Center for Constitutional Rights in New York, a member of the Indian Parliament, and one of the Mothers of the Plaza de Mayo from Argentina.

People presented testimonies detailing economic human rights violations on various panels: (1) right to health care panel, (2) living wage struggles panel, (3) right to housing panel, (4) right to water and basic utilities panel, (5) right to education panel; and (6) unjust child removal panel. Lori Smith, from Tennessee, spoke of being dropped from her health insurer after she was diagnosed with lupus; Donn Teske, from Kansas, talked about the experiences of small farming families struggling against corporate agriculture; Mailon Ellison, from Pennsylvania, spoke of struggling to make a home for himself and his family; Dawn Fucile, from Ohio, spoke of her child being removed from her home simply because she is deaf and poor. This commission was also unique in that it provided an important venue for artists, musicians, dancers, and poets to discuss and display their work, trying to shine a light on economic human rights violations in the United States. Survivors of Hurricane Katrina, artists from Rock-a-Mole, and soulful songs in general reminded the roughly 500 who attended the event of the importance and power of the arts.

In brief, PPEHRD urged other communities to hold truth commissions. Following are some of their suggestions. First is gathering information, that is, collecting stories from people who have been downsized, outsourced, cut off welfare rolls, evicted, or denied health care. Then, it is important to organize, build membership, and develop leaders. Such processes must be widespread, including a press strategy, because it is important to break isolation and gain wide acceptance. Central to setting up a truth commission is educating communities, raising their political consciousness about human rights. Another issue is logistics— setting the time and date for the hearing and making sure you have recording devices, both audio and visual if necessary, that work. Human rights monitors must engage in outreach, knocking on doors in the neighborhood, visiting health centers, welfare offices, schools, labor pools, hospital waiting rooms, immigrant organizations, labor unions, emergency shelters, and the like. Then, persuasive testimonies must be chosen. It is also important to have high-profile people at the hearing, like clergy, city councilmen, professors, labor leaders, and entertainers, who might influence policy makers. Obviously, a translator/interpreter may be necessary, and it is important to incorporate the arts into the event. A follow-up report should be submitted to the press summarizing the event for publicity. This report may also serve to attract possible future funding, enhance credibility for the organization, and educate others about the conditions in the community.

It might be interesting to find entities accountable for economic violations, as was done in South Africa's commissions. Torturers in apartheid South Africa were easily recognizable and confessed to their atrocities. But responsibility for a person dying from lack of health care insurance or shelter is more amorphous. Are insurance companies, governments, or corporations to blame? The appearance at hearings of those possibly responsible for violations could be an extension of such commissions. Most would probably deny any accountability, a point that perhaps would need publicity in the press. Has the world progressed any from the government officials at Nuremberg, who, after viewing pictures of atrocities in concentration camps said, one after the other: "I am not responsible... I am not responsible... I am not responsible" (Resnais, 1955). Who, then, is responsible?

When people speak of human rights, the world listens. The struggle for human rights is a people's movement, to which the helping and health professions must pay attention to make "the will of the people"—a phrase found in all 50 U.S. state constitutions—the basis of government policy making (Wronka, 1998b). A true human rights culture will not be duped by the powers that be, if Herman Goering's words at the Nuremberg trials are correct:

> After all, it is the leaders of a country who determine the policy, and it is always a simple matter to drag the people along, whether it is a democracy, or a fascist dictatorship, or a parliament, or a communist dictatorship. Voice or no voice, the people can always be brought to the bidding of the leaders. That is easy. All you have to do is to tell them they are being attacked, and denounce the pacifists for lack of patriotism and exposing the country to danger. It works the same in any country. (cited in Peace Pilgrim, 1991, pp. 114–115)

If done correctly, nonviolent direct action strategies like truth commissions may be a tool for getting governments to follow the people, rather than vice-versa. The challenge is huge, but it is worthwhile to keep in mind Gandhi's famous words: "First they ignore you, then they laugh at you, then they fight you, and then you win." Martin Luther King, Jr., a devotee of Gandhi's nonviolence, was successful in eventually making government listen to the voices of the disenfranchised. In Figure 3.4, he stands not far from President Kennedy, who felt society lavished too much praise on the warrior rather than the peacemaker.

Summary

This chapter defined macro, mezzo, micro, and quaternary levels of intervention as whole-population (macro or primary), at-risk (mezzo or secondary), clinical (micro or tertiary), and research (quaternary), which, although somewhat distinct, are interrelated. It also introduced meta-macro or global interventions and meta-micro interventions that use the healing power of

Figure 3.4   Martin Luther King, Jr. (third from left) With President Kennedy (fifth from right) and Others During the 1965 March for Jobs and Freedom, More Commonly Known as the Civil Rights March. Governments are often reluctant to implement human rights principles, unless vast social movements demand it.

Source: The National Archives.

helpers in everyday life. It described whole-population approaches in which actions based on human rights principles can benefit nations, such as educating people about human rights from the preschool to the graduate level with exercises from major human rights resources like UNESCO and Amnesty International. Other actions are the drafting of local proclamations and declarations about days meant to commemorate human rights, such as December 10, Human Rights Day. Also mentioned were World Currency

Day and Good Morning and Mean It Day, in addition to more generally acknowledged international days like International Women's Day (March 8) and Day for the Elimination of Racial Discrimination (March 21). Defenders may also wish to draft actual human rights bills, which they can craft from talking points, such as Massachusetts Bill 706, which would set up a committee to monitor in a positive, yet direct way how a state is doing in meeting its obligations as defined by international human rights criteria. The arts are another means of bringing attention to human rights documents and violations. The song "Strange Fruit" helped end public hangings in the United States. Focusing particularly on truth commissions, this chapter concluded with a discussion of other select nonviolent strategies such as symbolic public acts, processions, withdrawal, and renunciation.

Questions for Discussion

1. What other international days should we have? Why are there no days acknowledging rights to self-determination, humanitarian disaster relief, international distributive justice, respect for common heritages of humanity (space, the oceans, etc.)? Are such days too scary for governments, perhaps creating a consensus of the feasibility of debt relief for poorer countries, if not peace and international cooperation in space rather than mastery? Should we have days for health care, education, meaningful and gainful employment, rest and leisure, and freedoms of speech and the press? Or do such days exist already? If they do exist, have they somehow lost their meaning? What was the original meaning of Labor Day, for instance? Should there also be a multiple jeopardy day commemorating those discriminated against on the basis of any combinations of characteristics, such as age, race, gender, class, national or social origin, and sexual orientation?

2. Recently, McDonald's had a spurt of advertising acknowledging the importance of Universal Children's Day, November 22. In the 1990s the *New York Times* ran a series of articles concluding that fast-food hamburgers were not only bad for the environment, but led to obesity among children. McDonald's threatened to withdraw advertising dollars should the articles continue, a threat the *New York Times* publicly acknowledged. Do you see a contradiction between McDonald's touting of Children's Day and its use of intimidation? What does that say about the viability of human rights documents and the media in general? Can human rights documents be used as mere facades, behind which the powerful can hide? Or do they speak truth to power, urging the powerful to the bargaining table, if not bringing them down?

3. Whereas it is commendable for a community to make international human rights law legally binding, can this be said to be impractical? The Universal Declaration, for example, asserts medical care is a human right. Given the lack of a one-payer system in the United States, couldn't one person's illness bankrupt a town? If legally binding international human rights are impractical, what can be done to guarantee human rights for every person, everywhere? Should we have a graduated tax system, for example? Should less money be expended on the *military-industrial complex,* a term popularized by former President Eisenhower, a Republican?[6] Does our educational system really graduate peacemakers? Or does it educate the populace, subtly or not so subtly, to see violence as the major strategy for conflict resolution?

4. Comment critically on the following statements:

(a) Establishing a commission to examine how a state's laws and policies compare with international human rights standards is nothing but fluff, hot air, soft, nonsense on stilts, an initiative with no teeth, something academics, or people lucky enough to have the opportunity to work on such proposals, do to keep themselves employed, wasting a lot of time and energy.

(b) Establishing a commission to examine how a state's laws and policies compare with international human rights standards will create a meaningful nonviolent forum, calling for community participation in the policy debates, which will help expand people's awareness of what their human rights are and possibly the hypocrisy of their governments. Such an expanded consciousness ought to result in socially just policies in accord with the Universal Declaration of Human Rights and other human rights instruments.

5. Given the blocking in 1992 of a UN resolution, largely by the African countries, to commemorate the 500th anniversary of Columbus Day and the more recent observation by Indigenous Peoples of a National Day of Mourning in lieu of the traditional U.S. Thanksgiving, is it practical to do away with those traditional holidays? Should any other holidays take their place? If so, what should they be?

6. Think of historical and contemporary music and songs that bring us together and those that tear us apart. Now think of children's songs that may have influenced a desire to work for social justice and human rights. Why do you think Picasso's "Guernica", a painting depicting the horrors of war, was shrouded during the February 2003 UN hearings called by the United States before the war in Iraq? What does that say about the power of art to influence policy? Do you feel that the media encourage a culture of social justice? What type of culture do they encourage? What can you do to change it?

7. Comment critically on the following statements:

(a) The greatest issue facing humanity today is finding alternatives to structural violence. However, our educational system teaches nothing about peaceful conflict resolution, and thereby puts humanity on the verge of global catastrophe. Nowhere does it emphasize tolerance, respect, and friendship among nations as stressed by the Universal Declaration of Human Rights.

(b) Major transfer of wealth through capital speculation in the stock market, the primary socioeconomic system in the United States and much of the world, is a good way to enhance human dignity and provide human rights for all.

What would a socially just economic system based on fundamental human rights principles look like? How could it be constructed and maintained?

8. React to the following: The minimum age for voting in six countries is 16; in Japan CEOs are disgraced if they downsize; in Europe, by and large, health care and education, from preschool to the doctorate level, are provided at minimal cost, paid for by taxes, and paid maternity leave is a customary practice. If you have never heard of such things, what does that tell you about the education system and the media in the United States? Does general reference to the 1965 March in Washington as a march for civil rights, rather than for jobs and freedom, mirror a culture that rather narrowly defines human rights standards? In a classic work on anti-Semitism, Jean-Paul Sartre (1995) asks why the concentration camps were not in the news during World War II. Do you feel that oppressive practices, if not pogroms, that one never hears about still exist in contemporary times? Why do you think that is so? How could human rights education and the media effectively teach policies that appear more consistent with human rights principles, particularly their interdependence and indivisibility?

9. A major theme of this book is that attaining social justice is struggle that helping and health professionals must undertake. One must learn to live with ambiguity while working at various levels of intervention at different times, depending on circumstances and individual and group proclivity. But are things really that complicated? Shouldn't one just counsel an AIDS patient, open up a soup kitchen, administer to a sick child, or release a political prisoner? Why all this talk about macro, mezzo, micro, and the other metalevels? Comment on the following: Any comparison, even by innuendo, of the helping and health professions today to those in Nazi Germany is absurd. Present-day professionals are dedicated and caring people, whose education and training have prepared them to intervene responsibly with those in need.

10. What would a document look like that portrays the Universal Declaration and the documents following it (CEDAW, the CRC, CERD) in ways and words that children can understand? How could the arts enhance this exercise? Would painting, music, and poetry help? How could children's input be enlisted?

Activities/Actions

1. Commemorate one, two, three, or more of the international days discussed in this chapter. Draw up a proclamation that your town or state might endorse and/or have a public reading of portions of a relevant human rights document. Get support from sympathetic community groups and have the appropriate bodies endorse your proclamation. After the readings, have fun, if you are not having fun already.

2. Write a resolution declaring that the Universal Declaration of Human Rights and any of the covenants ratified by the United States should become law for your municipality or state. Bring it to your appropriate legislative body for official endorsement. Have your municipality or state draft a non-binding resolution submitted to the president that urges the ratification of all human rights documents with an eye toward their ready implementation.

3. Write a law similar to MA 706 that will set up a commission to examine how your municipal, state, or federal body's laws and policies compare with international human rights law. Present it at the appropriate legislative hearing and begin developing a broad community base to support it. Persist, if you can, until the law is passed. Then write a grant (see Chapter 5) and publish newsletters and a daily column in the newspaper monitoring in a positive way any developments being made toward compliance with international human rights instruments. Also form a monitoring committee to assess progress toward compliance with the bill. Should one be positive or confrontative as the state moves toward compliance with human rights principles?

4. Begin to incorporate human rights instruments into educational curricula and your profession. Go to various Web sites and readings referred to in this book and present a proposal to the dean, local school administrator, school board, and/or head of your professional organization. What are their reactions? How can you engage in creative dialogue with them?

5. Make up human rights skits similar to the one described in this chapter. Create, for example, a "mini-MTV" parody emphasizing some articles from a human rights document. Go to a radio and/or television station.

Ask to perform the skit or read an article or two from a human rights document. Push the envelope a little. Ask if it's okay to show the skit (or another, perhaps with the station's input) as an alternative to advertising junk food or toys of questionable value on children's television. If the answer is no, perhaps the skit can be performed in class.

Notes

1. One shouldn't underestimate children! Sometimes they enjoy pronouncing big words like that. The terms can easily be explained as, in this case, "Historical-philosophical compromises are simply agreements among a lot of people who dress differently, eat different foods, listen to different music and the like, but who all want peace and social justice in the world."

2. Although this day, Mondo Day (#17), and Right to Development Day (#21) are not on official lists, they may be worthy of consideration. Good Morning and Mean It Day is a meta-micro level intervention highlighting the importance of decency in the everyday life, which transcends professionalism, by every person, everywhere toward every person, everywhere. Why not? Imagine Jew, Christian, Muslim, Hindu, Buddhist, believer and nonbeliever, rich and poor, humanist and nonhumanist, friend and foe alike wishing each other a good morning and really meaning it! Indicative of the meta-macro level, Mondo or World Currency Day and Right to Development Day might be steps toward a world in which allegiance to humanity and globally agreed-upon economic and social arrangements among rich, poor, young, old, black, white, and other groups become reality in a society of all ages and colors. "Dream dreams and say why not?" said Senator Robert Kennedy. That is the recipe.

3. See Note 2.

4. See Note 2.

5. Except as noted, the following proclamations, resolutions, declarations, bills, and talking points were initially drafted by this author.

6. Actually, the former president wanted to use the term Military-Congressional-Industrial Complex, given that appropriations for arms must come from Congress. Famed expert on communicating with children, Haim Ginott (2005), observed that, in concentration camps, learned engineers built gas chambers, educated physicians poisoned children, trained nurses killed infants, and high school and college graduates shot and killed women and children. Lifton (2000) even comments on gassing of innocents in medical school curricula during Nazi Germany. The question becomes whether one could not add "educational" as well to the term. That is, some of the best schools in the nation have educated our political representatives, yet they continually give priority to military rather than social expenditures. This makes the efficacy of our educational system to graduate human rights and social justice advocates questionable.

4

At-Risk and Clinical Social Action and Service Strategies Toward the Creation of a Human Rights Culture

Whoever fights monsters should see to it that in the process he [or she] does not become a monster.

—Friedrich Nietzsche

After looking at whole-population approaches, this chapter examines at-risk and clinical interventions to improve the quality of life within this context of human rights and social justice. It is often difficult to determine precisely who are at risk and who need clinical or direct practice intervention. Ultimately, these would be any person or group whose quality of life is imminently threatened by denial of human rights. These people could easily become marginalized and objectified in ways that make it increasingly difficult to act with autonomy, good judgment, and self-respect in the pursuit of happiness, to use Thomas Jefferson's pithy phrase. Such groups can be so marginalized that the powerful totally disregard their voices, as if they were not even worthy of the effort to marginalize them! As a case in point, does anyone hear the viewpoints of the roughly one fifth of humanity who live on less than a dollar a day regarding global defense spending policies? Those living in extreme poverty may as well be nonexistent!

It has already been established that meaningful and gainful employment that contributes to the development of the human personality and is socially useful work is a human right, as emphasized by the U.S. delegation to the drafting committee of the Universal Declaration (Wronka, 1998b). The UN Charter, which commits itself to the promotion of "higher standards of living, full employment, and conditions of economic and social progress and development" (Article 55), and the Universal Declaration, which asserts "just and favorable remuneration ensuring for himself and his family an existence worthy of human dignity" (Article 23), further exemplify this right. Creating a social movement to place this right in the federal and state constitutions might be a way to educate people about its importance and promote a society committed to this fundamental social justice principle by ensuring reasonable wages and restructuring work to enhance human development and society. Acknowledging the interdependence of rights would also necessitate provisions for health care, security in old age through guaranteed pensions, and unemployment protection, all rights found in the Universal Declaration.

One preventive strategy against at-risk groups falling through the cracks and eventually becoming homeless is to implement the right that "everyone has . . . to form and to join trade unions for the protection of his interests" (Article 23), asserted in the Universal Declaration. An employee couldn't get fired easily without due process. Research has also demonstrated that failure to provide for protections in the workplace may lead to frustration and domestic violence against children (Gil, 1973). Similarly, Article 11 of CEDAW imposes obligations on government to

> introduce maternity leave with pay or with comparable social benefits without loss of former employment, seniority or social allowances; [and] (c) To encourage the provision of the necessary supporting social services to enable parents to combine family obligations with work responsibilities and participation in public life, in particular through promoting the establishment and development of a network of child-care facilities.

Providing for maternity leave with pay would undoubtedly help alleviate emotional strains for mothers-to-be, which may affect not only fetal development, but also relations with spouses and other children. Furthermore, if states met their obligations "to organize self-help groups and co-operatives in order to obtain equal access to economic opportunities through employment or self employment [for women]" (Article 14), it would eliminate many stressors for women who want formal meaningful work in addition to the most important job in the world, that of raising children.

Other human rights documents cover rights that deal specifically with at-risk situations. If parents separate, Article 9 of the CRC asserts, "States Parties shall respect the right of the child who is separated from one or both parents to maintain personal relations and direct contact with both parents on a regular basis, except if it is contrary to the child's best interests." Article 18 asserts that "states shall take all appropriate measures to ensure that children of working parents have the right to benefit from child-care services and facilities for which they are eligible." Having contact with both parents (unless against the child's best interests) and good quality child care can produce excellent returns for the well-being of the child. Table 4.1 lists some human rights principles, relative to at-risk populations, and outcomes anticipated if the principle is adequately implemented.

As argued, distinctions among levels are imprecise. Despite this limitation, it is still possible to choose from a plethora of human rights instruments principles that serve as guides to preventing certain populations from plummeting further into despondency. But these documents are not only guides; in this millennium, the popular consensus is that such documents are no longer merely

Table 4.1   Select Human Rights Principles Relevant to At-Risk Populations

Principle (Document)	Population At Risk	Anticipated Outcome(s)
Right to form and join trade unions for the protection of workers' interests (ICESCR)	Employed worker	Job security; fairness in hiring and firing; reasonable wages to raise a family with dignity; less domestic violence
Maternity leave with pay (CEDAW)	Mother and child	Less stress for pregnant mother and family; possibly positive effects on fetal development
Services to assist families to balance work and family life and to participate in public life (CEDAW)	Parents and children	Formal work productivity, which would enhance community development and family bonding with children
Maintenance of contact with both parents on a periodic basis in cases of separation (CRC)	Parents and children	Bonding with parent and child; healthy child development
Integration of abused child into the community (CRC)	Abused child	Increased self-esteem and ability of child to cope
Prohibition against torture by person in official capacity (CAT)	Incarcerated person	Adherence to the dignity of the human person

lofty aspirations, despite socialization to the contrary, but rather documents worthy of implementation.

Mindful that such documents should be lawful mandates to prevent at-risk groups from developing further pathology, the rest of this chapter examines the helping and health professions as a possible at-risk group, the integration of business and human rights principles, humanistic administration, social entrepreneurship, and grant writing. To some extent, these topics are arbitrary, yet they ought to provide enough information for the developing, if not seasoned, scholar-practitioner/social activist/human rights defender/social justice advocate to understand and appreciate the importance of developing a myriad of social action and service skills in the at-risk dimension. Examining the human rights document Principles for the Protection of Persons With Mental Illness, and Principles of Medical Ethics, the chapter pays particular attention to select clinical interventions and looks further at implications of human rights principles to this tertiary level of intervention. Though the topics covered are arbitrary, these choices reveal again the human dimension to any endeavor combining scholarship with action and service in the name of human rights and social justice. Paradoxically, acknowledging such a shortcoming may actually further open dialogue among other perspectives on how to collectively create a socially just world.

The Helping and Health Professions as an At-Risk Group

Much of the literature on working with at-risk populations deals with vulnerable groups such as adolescents who may be at risk for pregnancy, violence, alcoholism, and sexually transmitted diseases. Not much, if any, of the literature studies the studiers, that is, those in the helping and health professions who arrived at the conclusions of the studies. As Plato asked, "Who guards the guardians?"

Preventing an Abuse of Power

There is much truth in the assertion that power corrupts. Well-educated Nazi doctors in collusion with well-educated nurses, social workers, and psychologists, caught up in the injustices of the time, abused the rights and privileges of their occupation by taking part in evaluations that led to mass executions. To take human rights and social justice seriously, one must also heed Nietzsche's lament that we are all masters of self-deception. We need to take on the mantle of humility, which represents the spirit of Crazy Horse, that of "peace, understanding, and everlasting love"[1] (In the Spirit of Crazy Horse, nd) in the realization that the helping and health professionals are not immune to the human condition.

It is important, then, to find strategies that prevent abuse of power so that the helping and health professions can truly heal, instead of hurt. Milgram's infamous study resulting in what became known as the Eichmann Effect[2] (2004), where subjects were prone to obey experimenters in prestigious settings, dressed in scientific attire, administering electric shocks to supposedly unwitting subjects, is a stark reminder of the power the helping and health professions can have over individuals. The psychiatrist Viktor Frankl (1984) and the educator Elie Wiesel have recounted their experiences in the concentration camps. Wiesel writes, "Was there a way to describe . . . the discovery of a demented and glacial universe where to be inhuman was human, where *disciplined, educated* [italics added] men in uniform came to kill, and innocent children and weary old men came to die"? (Wiesel, 2006, p. ix).

This discussion in no way discounts the social conscience, commitment, fairness, and generosity of many in the helping and health professions. One only has to look at such groups as *Médecins Sans Frontières* (Doctors Without Borders), Physicians for Human Rights, the Social Welfare Action Alliance of the National Association of Social Work, Psychologists for Social Responsibility, Educators for Social Responsibility, and the numerous professional organizations with divisions on peace, social justice, and human rights. Being in such a group neither guarantees a social conscience, nor elevates members of such groups to a loftier status. Many in the helping and health professions are aware of the human tendency to abuse power and try to rectify injustice whenever possible. Our tendency to abuse power is accompanied by a tendency to treat others with common decency. But one should not be blind to the possibilities that even well-educated people, in the name of helping others, may perpetrate abuses on those in powerless positions.

Frankl (1984) and Wiesel (2006), therefore, recount the kindness of so many in the camps who did not give in to the pressure of a situation that could easily produce human atrocities. Such kindness is often overwhelmingly apparent among helping and health professionals. Yet it must be said that the "technicizing" of everything (Lifton, 2000), which played a big role in socializing people to killing in the camps, exerts a powerful pull on the helping professional away from the dignity of the human spirit. Although this pull is not as strong in contemporary society as in the camps, the distancing effects of tests, diagnostic procedures, and the healing technologies (Katz, 1982) on helping and health professionals still may have the power to corrupt. Technology can become an idol that divorces helpers from their helping function (Merleau-Ponty, 1964), making it easier to give in to the banality of evil.

Having Ethics Codes
Consistent With Human Rights Principles

One social action strategy to prevent abuse of power is to have professional ethics codes that are reasonably consistent with human rights principles. This is not a panacea for potential exploitation, but such principles could educate people about the collective wisdom of the international community expressed in human rights documents, which reflect a poignant historically based conviction that the kind of violence experienced in the camps, genocidal pogroms in Rwanda, and gassing of the Kurds en masse in Iraq must never happen again. Reichert (2006) relates many of the principles of the National Association of Social Work's *Code of Ethics* to the Universal Declaration, including the ethical responsibilities of social workers to understand a person's culture; demonstrate competency in providing services sensitive to individual and cultural differences; eradicate discrimination based on race, ethnicity, color, sex, sexual orientation, age, marital status, political belief, religion, and mental or physical disability; advocate for living conditions based on the fulfillment of basic human needs; facilitate informed public participation in shaping social policy; engage in social and political action that seeks to ensure all people have access to employment and resources; provide appropriate services in public emergencies; enhance self-determination; and promote conditions that encourage respect for cultural and social diversity within the United States *and globally* are just some principles. Reichert goes so far as to say: "This wide-ranging category of ethical responsibilities contains within itself a mini-Universal Declaration. The language is uncanny in its resemblance to the spirit of the declaration" (p. 238). Professionals must abide by such principles in their practice, but knowing that their ethics codes are consistent with internationally recognized human rights may make them more powerful and convincing.

Other ethics codes of the helping and health professions have a strong resemblance to human rights principles. The Public Health Code of Ethics speaks of developing processes for policies that ensure opportunity for input from community members; incorporating a variety of approaches that anticipate and respect diverse values, beliefs, and cultures; collaborating with a wide variety of agencies and professional disciplines; and implementing policies that enhance the physical and social environment. It also asserts the interdependence among people and between people and their physical environment and calls for the "full range of scientific tools, including both quantitative and qualitative methods [Principle 9; more on that in the next chapter], which should translate into timely action" (Principle 10). This code goes so far as to say, in its comment on values and beliefs underlying the code, that "humans have a right to the resources necessary for health. The public health code of ethics affirms Article 25 of the Universal Declaration of Human Rights, which states in part 'Everyone has the right to a standard of living adequate for the health and well-being of himself and his family.' . . ."

It is easy to see that many of the human rights documents discussed here relate to most ethics codes in the helping and health professions. Nondiscrimination on the basis of race, color, sex, and so on in Article 2 and the right to work in Article 23 of the Universal Declaration are two examples. There are also the right to self-determination in Article 1 of the two covenants on civil and political and on economic, social, and cultural rights and the call for "international cooperation" in Article 23 and the diminishing of "infant and child mortality . . . taking into consideration the dangers and risks of environmental pollution. . . . and access to hygiene and environmental sanitation" in Article 24 of the CRC.

Incorporating Client Voices in Policy and Treatment

The challenge may be to teach ethics codes in conjunction with principles of basic human rights documents so that students who become practitioners can understand that such codes reflect wise and ancient social teachings that are their duty to translate into action. The need to incorporate the voices of the oppressed in the policy debates, as well as treatment plans, such as assessing patients' perspectives on mandatory testing for the AIDS virus during pregnancy and in newborns (Mawn, 1998), is an ethical *and* human rights issue that might prevent health personnel from taking on the mantle of the expert (Katz, 1982; Wronka, 1993) giving orders to patients. It is important to engage in collaborative processes, so that policy makers and clients do not blindly follow the lead of professionals, disempowering instead of empowering them to take the initiatives in promoting their own health and policy development.

Such potential feelings of power, to which professionals are not immune, could easily translate into policies on a global scale, illustrating the long reach of this mantle of professionalism, sometimes in concert with policies by the World Bank or IMF. There is a trend in the developing countries to use pharmaceuticals, the most profitable industry since World War II, as panaceas for mental health issues. The efficacy of such interventions can easily be documented; nevertheless, this trend appears to be growing in countries that have accepted the World Bank's structural adjustment policies, in the form of privatization, if not corporatization, in exchange for aid. But do the people want privatization or corporate control of resources? More ominously, the helping and health professions may be playing a similarly collusive role of indifference by not adequately engaging in social action strategies to stop such shameful initiatives as the globally inequitable distribution of drugs to combat the spread of the AIDS pandemic, especially in the world's poorest countries. Professional schools must teach, at minimum, Article 27 of the Universal Declaration, which emphasizes "the right . . . to share in scientific advancement and its benefits."

Defining ethical principles as human rights mandates can enable people to choose rather than have these principles forced on them, the *sine qua non* for a true human rights culture. This culture, fundamental to social justice, ought to exist not only globally, but also within the helping and health professions. But ultimately, it is important to remember that life itself is the profession for helping professionals. Cultivating a human rights culture in everyday life that would inevitably spill over into formal professional work is perhaps the greatest challenge facing these professionals who take this idea seriously. Treating clients and patients with kindness and human dignity is as important as kindness to coworkers, friends, and strangers.

Business and Human Rights

Business needn't be antithetical to human rights principles. The fair trade movement, which promotes paying workers reasonable wages for products made from essentially recyclable materials in sustainable ways, is one example of incorporating human rights into business. There is nothing wrong with the free market principle of selling a quality product at a reasonable price. Using the example of building a better mouse trap, a free market should compensate the trap's inventor at a higher price for the better product. But germs do not care about free markets. If the mouse were diseased, a poor family unable to pay for the improved snare might get infected and spread the infection to others. Surely, society must revise such a narrow vision of profit.

The helping and health professions, by their very nature, attempt to place need before profit. But, as discussed, the vulnerability of the human condition is such that no one is immune to the exigencies of a social order, which is often inimical to fulfillment of human potential. In other words, while keeping to professional mandates, helpers must also be attuned to the demands of everyday life. Working within this limitation, that is, they can still question the social order and discuss such alternatives as human rights instruments provide to move toward social justice.

Many helping professionals would like a single-payer health care system, in which mental and physical health have parity, and much of the questionable paperwork, marketing, and accountability of the current system would be eliminated. But the fact is, they often need to work within the context of market forces. Merleau-Ponty referred to this as dragging one's contradictions into his or her daily labors (1964). Whereas the aim of human rights and social justice is the fulfillment of human need, it is nevertheless necessary to work within the context of a culture often inimical to these aims. This may mean, paradoxically, not to adopt what Jeffrey Sachs (2005) called an "anticorporate animus," but to work as well as possible within structures that make the rules, however objectionable they may be. While feeding one's family and living becomingly, it is important not to lose the hope of creating a human rights culture and to continue to engage in practical actions to make such a culture a reality.

This millennium, therefore, increasingly requires some knowledge of business skills. This might range from mere bookkeeping of appointments and accounts payable skills to more complicated procedures like expanding and administering an entire helping enterprise, such as developing a cluster of methadone maintenance clinics or substance abuse/mental health treatment, public health, and teen resource centers. Gimmicks abound, like installing lovebirds in a family therapist's office. Those two cute feathery animals huddled together in the waiting room are a perfect marketing tool for one's services. Ultimately, the aim is not to create enterprises in which, for example, chief executive pay is roughly 500 times higher than the average worker's, as in major U.S. businesses today (Morgenson, 2004). Rather, it is to create enterprises sensitive to workers' and communal needs, entirely consistent with human rights and social justice principles.

It is worth noting that businesses are increasingly recognizing the significant role human rights can play in the workplace. In 2004, for example, the UN Human Rights Commission requested the Secretary General to appoint a Special Rapporteur for Human Rights, Transnational Corporations, and Other Business Practices. Sadly, the United States, along with Australia and South Africa, voted against the resolution. Such a person would "develop materials and methodologies for undertaking human rights impact assessments of business activities; and compile a compendium of best practices of states and businesses" (Amnesty International, 2005, p. 1).

An excellent resource is the Business and Human Rights Resource Center (2005), in partnership with Amnesty International and leading academic institutions, which involves at least 92 companies committed to adherence to human rights principles. The famed Cisco Systems, for example, states on its corporate Web site that

> Cisco strives to treat employees and the communities in which we serve with respect and dignity. A supporter of the United Nations Universal Declaration of Human Rights and the Global Compact, Cisco's codes of conduct, employee

policies and guidelines substantially incorporate laws and ethical principles including those pertaining to freedom of association, non-discrimination, privacy, collective bargaining, compulsory and child labor, immigration and wages and hours. . . . Employees are encouraged to promote a safe, healthy and supportive work environment where employees can contribute their skills and participate with local stakeholders in addressing community well-being, social and economic development and environmental preservation. (Cisco Systems, nd)

The Center also lists, among other things, the top 21 human rights reports by such companies as GAP, Adidas, Chiquita, Ford, Nike, Novartis, and Shell. These reports are at times quite forthright. Paul Pressler, CEO for Gap, for example, openly stated in its Social Responsibility Report (2005) how difficult it was to see headlines that Gap admitted to factory abuses. That report then cited progress and challenges, referring to the launching of

Figure 4.1   Prisoners Doing Forced Labor in the Siemens Factory at Bobrek, a Subcamp of Auschwitz. Bearing a bleak resemblance to many sweatshops and other work sites which dot the globe today, it is questionable whether we have really overcome Hitler's atrocities. Human rights may serve as guiding principles out of this cauldron, in this instance the rights of workers to organize for their interests.

Source: United States Holocaust Memorial Museum. Courtesy of Henry Schwarzbaum.

mandatory ethics courses; seeking to enhance diversity programs; lessening employee injury rates; and the need to continue focusing on "packaging, energy consumption, waste and recycling, and water quality" (p. 5) in its environmental impact studies.

It might be easy to dismiss such reports, like countries' human rights reports, as fluff, whitewash,[3] or a kind of façade to make the companies look good. Is the real issue that "human dignity is not inscribed on the walls of the New York Stock Exchange," as Pierre Sané, then Secretary General of Amnesty International, eloquently stated at the 1998 Human Rights Defender's Conference? Both assertions may have some element of truth, but social justice is a bit more complicated. Whatever people do to meet human rights standards ought to be commended. It is important to be positive and applaud their efforts as they move forward and to work with them if they slide backward. It is something like being in a weight loss support group. Members must applaud each other's progress, yet offer support and help for backsliders. Besides, it is only too easy to ignore the ancient injunction to "examine the log in one's own eye, before plucking the speck from another's." While professionals might monitor a company or country's progress, the efforts of their enterprises to meet human rights principles also need scrutiny.

Perhaps the best approach toward living up to human rights principles, in running or monitoring a business, is to keep a positive attitude, of working with rather than against others. Seeking input, especially if this input demonstrates an organization's commitment to human rights—an idea that will not go away— not only makes sense, but a lot of "cents." Nothing beats doing well by doing good!

Humanistic Administration

Administrators interested in using human rights as a guiding framework for their organization, for the purposes of this discussion, can be said to engage in humanistic administration. Training programs such as Advanced Generalist Social Work and Public Health Administration stress the importance of administrative skills, especially as the helping and health professions are often steeped in a managerial (from *manus* meaning "hand"; i.e., the managers must have their "hands" on things) quagmire. All the wetlands are interrelated with streams, lakes, oceans, even the stratosphere, demonstrating once again the world's interconnectedness. The question becomes, metaphorically, how to navigate the managerial wetlands without destroying their beauty, allowing organizational life to thrive in its natural splendor. Many in the helping and health professions work in a clinical capacity but also become administrators

Figure 4.2   The Transport of Jews to Auschwitz-Birkenau Concentration
Camp. Some helping and health professionals colluded with
government in the transportation and extermination of innocents.
It is a continuing challenge to keep to human rights principles as
enunciated in ethics codes of these professions.

Source: United States Holocaust Memorial Museum. Courtesy of Yad Vashem. Photographer:
Bernhardt Walter/Ernst Hofmann.

(from the Latin *administrare,* "to help, assist, manage, direct"). This section
uses that term rather broadly, to mean anyone, including supervisors and
teachers, functioning in a helping capacity to assist, manage, or direct others.

Toward an Alternative to a Major Managerial Style

There must be alternatives to the "leave them alone, zap (or 'gotcha')," perhaps the major managerial style in the United States. Workers are literally left
alone to do their thing until someone complains. Such complaints may be justified. Employees may be just trying to do the best they know how but pushing their
supervisees too hard, urging or demanding case notes in impeccable grammar,
and assiduously questioning interventions documented in process recordings.
Humanistic administration requires alternatives to this all-too- common scenario.

Humanistic administrators with human rights documents in mind commit themselves to core principles, such as the human dignity of each person on staff, nondiscrimination, just and reasonable workplace conditions, development of the human personality, and the rights of workers to organize, have socially useful work, participate in policy making, and have time for rest and leisure. The problem is that a prerequisite for realizing such principles is a just social and international order, which is now often nonexistent. The notion of workers as wage slaves sometimes correctly characterizes the workplace. Obviously, the morale of workers could be improved if administrators were sympathetic to their right to organize. Whereas there are no easy answers to this dilemma of being a humanist in an unhumanistic world, it is beneficial for employees to first acknowledge that administrators also have administrators managing them, who in turn have administrators. As the saying goes, everyone is in this together, and to truly be sensitive to workers' concerns, it is important to develop what Michael Lerner (1991) called "communities of compassion" in the workplace. Community (from the Latin *munire*, "to fortify, to strengthen") and compassion (from *patior*, "to try, attempt, to undergo" and *co*, meaning "together") aptly describe what the humanistic administrator needs: to develop an awareness among employees that everyone must work together in ways that strengthen a sense of community so much needed in the workplace and community today. That is no small order. The Universal Declaration urges "tolerance, peace, and friendship" among nations. It is not difficult to see the importance of similar attitudes in the workplace.

A basic criticism of the need to develop a human rights culture in the workplace is that it is idealistic "nonsense on stilts," as Bentham (cited in Wronka, 1998b) stated. Such values are impossible in the job setting, with its many demands for quotas, billings, and the like. Yet, experience teaches us about, and history recounts, numerous administrators, teachers, and supervisors attuned to the human dignity of employees, students, and supervisees and committed to their growth. High school dropouts revealed a stark lack of teachers who had taken an interest in them. It is easy to blame teachers. But acknowledging again the need for a just social order, it is difficult for teachers with relentless commitments to spend the necessary time with each student, given oversized classes and heavy teaching schedules, not to mention a feeling of student malaise about furthering one's education, given the spiraling costs of college and questionable employment prospects afterward.

Certainly many exemplary supervisors have never heard of human rights. They know one must simply treat others decently. Human rights principles, however, can provide necessary guidance for what is more or less intuitive. Such principles also reflect major spiritual belief systems. The challenge is not only to model exemplary practices of administrators and treat others with decency, but also to live human rights principles in letter and in spirit.

The Need for Nondiscrimination in the Workplace

A word must be said about nondiscrimination in the workplace. Expanded inclusion of women, people of color, and, to a lesser extent, people with disabilities is evidence the world has advanced, but discrimination exists in various other guises; how people present themselves, a disheveled appearance perhaps, can be mistaken for lack of ability—what could be called the "Colombo Effect."[4] But discrimination is not just about appearance. It is just as easy to categorize (i.e., discriminate against) someone based on their willingness to take a risk or acknowledge their ignorance on an issue. Some students, for example, may be seen unjustly as naïve simply for admitting what others were fearful to acknowledge publicly, their ignorance about a specific population, though they want to learn more. Humanistic administrators must be constantly aware of the need to "slay the beast of discrimination" and be willing to advocate for the human rights of their employees.

Unfortunately, the preceding comments may sound like a cookbook approach to humanistic administration: a little bit of human dignity, add some reasonable wages, a community of compassion, nondiscrimination, and . . . voilà, an effective administrator! It should be that easy! Creating a human rights culture and social justice in the workplace is a lifelong struggle, whose path is strewn with risk yet, hopefully, tempered with humility and a constant willingness to learn. But it is one that can be filled with hope not only for a better world, but for a place of employment that has human rights and dignity at its core.

Practice Illustration 4.1 demonstrates how a human rights framework might serve as a means for administrators and employees, in both private and public organizations, to work together to implement socially just principles of human rights documents. In this instance, the primary document is CEDAW, women being the major at-risk group.

Practice Illustration 4.1
A CEDAW Gender Analysis in
San Francisco as a Social Action Strategy

In 1998, San Francisco was the first county to enact a local ordinance reflecting the principles of the UN Convention to Eliminate All Forms of Discrimination

Against Women (CEDAW). This enactment was due to a unique public/private coalition among the Commission on the Status of Women (COSW), the County, and community organizations spearheaded by the Women's Institute for Leadership Development for Human Rights and Amnesty International. The thrust of this ordinance was on three primary areas: (1) economic development and employment; (2) violence against women and girls; and (3) health care, all essential principles of CEDAW.

Five years later, the city faced a budget shortfall of $300 million necessitating major reductions in workforce and services. Recognizing possible discriminatory practices against women in possible layoffs, COSW approached the city to sponsor a resolution urging departments to conduct a gender analysis of proposed budget reductions. As this was the first attempt to integrate CEDAW into the budget process, the resolution itself educated departments about the human rights framework, which aimed to promote the dignity of all people and ensure that both women and men have equitable access to services and employment, especially given that women compose 50% of the county's population.

The resolution explained a five step process. First was the gathering of quantifiable data, like statistics on employment and public services disaggregated by gender, race, ethnicity, sexual orientation and other status and qualitative data, like descriptive information gathered from focus groups and interviews with employees and department staff. Second was to analyze the data collected with the intent of understanding how everyday operations disparately impacted possibly discriminated groups. The third step was to make recommendations. The fourth was to implement them through an action plan. The fifth was to monitor the action plan.

Because this study was hortatory, not mandatory, of 50 departments only 16 responded. Of those, two reported that women employees, especially women of color, would be severely affected by proposed budget cuts. Others stated that possible layoffs were equitably distributed among gender, race, and other status. Contrary to COSW's concerns, the city police department staff reductions through attrition and retirement might actually increase the ratio of women and minorities within its ranks. In terms of services, women, who compose roughly 85% as recipients of services, would be significantly impacted by budget reductions.

Although the response was less than one-third, this voluntary gender analysis was a novel human rights approach and provided valuable information. Departments were able to anticipate possible disparate and discriminatory impacts of budget cuts. Public and private administrators and officials also gained knowledge of core principles of human rights documents and CEDAW in particular and learned to use a gender analysis tool proactively to fight discrimination and create policies based on critical data. Although an international treaty, the CEDAW ordinance enhanced local government accountability.

Source: Burtman and Williams (2006).

In a social order that places profits over people, jobs as administrators may be hard to obtain. Perhaps the ideal is doing well (a reasonable wage with benefits) by doing good (playing a role, however minimal, in advancing social justice). But the primary predictor of finding a job is not competence, but attitude. That means a willingness to be of service to others, but even more important, to cooperate with others. The etymology of the word *cooperation* is the Latin word *opera*, which etymologically speaking is a *completed* work, whereas an *opus* is an unfinished work. Thus, the correct attitude in job searching is a willingness to work with others, to go the extra mile, until a project's completion. Nowhere is going the extra mile more important than in social entrepreneurship.

Social Entrepreneurship

This idea of human rights is strong enough to encourage risk taking and social action that literally goes to the ends of the earth. Social entrepreneurs are "creative, tenacious individuals with unshakable motivation" to propel the innovation needed to tackle some of society's most serious ills (Bornstein, 2004, p. 64). Throughout history such individuals have been driven by love, global visions of a just world, religious and spiritual commitments, or just plain restlessness with the human condition to make positive contributions to the world. St. Francis of Assisi, just one example discussed by Bornstein, built numerous global organizations to advance changing patterns in the field. A social entrepreneur has vision and an obsessive belief in the impossible, and will do everything in his or her power to create a socially just world.

The problems with encouraging social entrepreneurship (as well as grant writing, in the following section) are obvious. If people don't have health care for their families, for example, it is almost impossible to get them to expend energies on social justice for all. The social entrepreneur must also be concerned about security in old age, as pensions for such tenacious individuals are generally not forthcoming (though social entrepreneurs who live in countries where health care and pensions are paid for by taxes, unlike the United States, don't face these obstacles). Another problem for social entrepreneurs is being co-opted (or more colloquially, hoodwinked) by the social order to engage in developing private sector social solutions for issues that should be the domain of governments.

What's more, their actions do not really change the social order. If successful, their activities put a stamp of approval on the efficacy of a social order that places profit above human need. Going to the ends of the earth, for example, to provide sex education and condoms for adolescents to prevent the spread of AIDS is a worthy social entrepreneurial activity. Yet one could also argue that fighting AIDS requires a country to enforce the basic human right to education for the girl child advocated by the CRC. Education would lead to a job with a reasonable salary with which a woman could support herself and consequently, be in a better position to refuse unwanted sexual advances. But to emphasize social justice ad nauseum is a struggle. A social entrepreneur, like Sisyphus, will never reach the summits of perfection in this quest for social justice; it is an eternal struggle for human rights and dignity. Recognizing these ambiguities, the world must have social entrepreneurs only because, historically, governments are reluctant to provide for human need unless they are pushed. The challenge, as always, is to integrate into our work the vision of a socially just world, mirrored in human rights principles.

An example of a prominent social entrepreneur is Jane Addams, who founded Hull House in 1889, a settlement house that was "an attempt to express the meaning of life in terms of life itself, in forms of activity . . . Application as opposed to research; emotion as opposed to abstraction . . . universal interest as opposed to specialization" (Addams, 1994, p. 78). Sometimes called the Mother of Social Work, she was able to expand these houses nationally. She was also founding president of the Women's International League for Peace and Freedom (WILPF), now a very potent and active group with consultative status at the UN and pivotal in garnering support for Human Rights Bill 706 in Massachusetts. An internationalist and pacifist, who saw the relationships among war, the nation-state, discrimination, and global poverty, she received the Nobel Peace Prize in 1931.

Another example is Maria Montessori. The first female physician in Italy, she had a commitment to internationalism and recognized the importance of social, emotional, perceptual, and physical development in addition to cognitive development. Florence Nightingale, whose actions broke many of the stereotypes of female roles of the time, totally reorganized military hospitals with a combination of tact, diplomacy, good sense, political influence, and calmness. She published an 800-page book, at her own expense, that presented an extensive statistical analysis of the causes of sickness and death in the army (Bornstein, 2004). Muhammad Yunus, 2006 Nobel Peace Prize recipient, founded the Grameen Bank, which gives microloans to help those in poverty become self-sufficient. James Grant, former director of UNICEF, is a tireless leader for children's vaccinations worldwide, who, on his deathbed in January 1995, urged Hillary Clinton to get the president to sign the CRC, which the United States did on February 17, 1995. Henry Dunant, founder of the International Red Cross, against impossible odds, got enemies talking and garnered international support for medical personnel on the battlefield to assist the wounded from both sides. Eleanor Roosevelt was also a social entrepreneur, often discouraged that she failed to get member states at the UN to agree on a universal document, but charged on anyway. "Oh, please make Eleanor tired," the members of the Universal Declaration drafting committee would plead (Tomasevski, 1993).

As these examples show, social entrepreneurs are, according to Bornstein (2004, pp. vii–viii), restless people, *really* possessed by an idea, constantly in search of social excellence and new opportunities and challenges. Bill Drayton, CEO and founder of Ashoka, a global nonprofit organization devoted to developing the profession of social entrepreneurship, says that "social entrepreneurs are not content just to give a fish or teach how to fish. They will not rest until they have revolutionized the fishing industry" (Skoll Foundation, 2005, p. 1). Contrary to what one might think, they weren't necessarily overly self-confident or knowledgeable. They believed in something that was deeply meaningful, valuing the long- over short-term gain. Such motivation is at the bottom of all of the characteristics of social entrepreneurs discussed in the following section.

Social entrepreneurship is the motivation to do something, not to be someone. It is here that the vision and power of human rights can help move someone to become a successful social entrepreneur. The desire to create a human rights culture may be the catalyst that pushes social activists beyond themselves, paradoxically finding themselves by losing themselves in a worthwhile enterprise; as Gandhi said, they become the change they want to see in the world.

Characteristics of Social Entrepreneurs

First, social entrepreneurs have a **willingness to self-correct**, that is, acknowledge when they were on the wrong track. The Grameen Bank, for example, which gives low-interest loans to those in extreme poverty, has recently overhauled its program to a more flexible banking system, rather than a one-size-fits-all approach. Second, they have a **willingness to share credit**. Doing so, of course, makes others more willing to help. Another trait is a **willingness to break free of established structures**, such as a university professor who might, with considerable risk, work on social action initiatives rather than become bogged down in the prevailing "publish or perish" mentality. Social entrepreneurs have a **willingness to cross disciplinary boundaries**. This book urges such collaboration, not only among the helping and health professions, but also among various groups like businesses, government agencies, citizens groups, and those in extreme poverty themselves. A case in point is the International Fourth World Movement's conference at the Sorbonne in Paris (1999), Integrating the Voices of Those in Extreme Poverty, which gathered together academics, professionals, and the homeless to garnish ideas on collaboration. Another trait is a **willingness to work quietly**, that is, making a slow and steady effort to produce a cumulative force. James Grant, former director of UNICEF, did just this when he urged all sides in South America to stop fighting so that they could vaccinate thousands of children during wartime. Finally, and summing up all the preceding characteristics, a **strong ethical impetus** is the "bedrock of social entrepreneurship," according to Bornstein (2004, p. 239). Bornstein continues: "Does the entrepreneur dream of building the world's greatest running shoe company or vaccinating all the world's children?" (p. 239). They are driven by the nature of their vision, and the question is: Can human rights be an undergirding matrix that moves others to implement this vision?

Perhaps one could see how integrating the right to peace as a solidarity right for Addams; the right to education directed to the full development of the human personality to promote understanding, tolerance, and friendship; the right to a just social and international order for Yunus; and health care as a human right for Nightingale and Grant could help move and organize people for social justice. There are also times when human rights themselves are the central focus for entrepreneurial activity. For example, entrepreneurs can work toward a human rights cabinet, which might serve as a connection between international initiatives and domestic implementation. Such a cabinet might have the responsibility for writing human rights reports on compliance with international conventions, rather than taking the current higgledy-piggledy approach of putting reports together piecemeal. Such a cabinet could also encourage other departments like Education, Health and Human Services, and even Homeland Security to integrate human rights documents into their curricula, policies, and protocols in general. Then social entrepreneurs can try to create similar cabinets in other countries. Or they can try to have banners in every corner of the world reading: Human Rights for Every Person, Everywhere: Toward the Creation of a Human Rights Culture. With increasing global interconnectedness, there is every reason to go beyond borders to work for social justice. There is already *Médecins Sans Frontières* (Doctors Without Borders). *Travailleurs Sociaux* (Social Workers), *Infirmières* (Nurses), *Psychologues* (Psychologists), and *Psychiatres* (Psychiatrists) *Sans Frontières* are some viable possibilities.

Grant Writing

Grant writing poses another problem for the social activist/human rights defender. On the one hand, it is important to change the social order to realize human rights: to develop a graduated taxation system; to form social movements to add rights to employment, health care, and security in old age to the U.S. Constitution; or to engage in social action strategies to nonviolently dissolve state boundaries and create allegiance to humanity. On the other hand, it is rather difficult to see the results of such efforts within the time frames often required by funding agencies. Some have even argued that human rights may exist only insofar as a funding agency acknowledges their existence (Steiner & Alston, 2000). People have to eat, and there are many grains of truth to that assertion.

Dealing With a Limited Definition of the Problem

It is difficult to imagine federal or state agencies funding a project that calls for allegiance to humanity. However, in this culture committed to freedom of speech and right to peaceful assembly, agencies have granted 501(c)(3), that is, nonprofit status to organizations committed to nonviolent action. But it would be easier to fund a project to teach children good nutrition than to launch a campaign to do away with advertising on children's television to tackle the pandemic of obesity. This kind of marketing, forbidden in much of the world on ethical grounds, tends to socialize children into eating junk and other foods of dubious nutritional value. But would the Kellogg or Hershey foundations ever fund such a project? Who would fund a project to provide an open and public forum to discuss alternatives to capitalism or to examine stock portfolios of executives in the Food and Drug Administration? It would appear reasonable to suggest that policy makers, as heads of corporations or government agencies, would not promote policies inimical to profits in their stock portfolio. Hitler knew very well the importance of providing grants of questionable utility to academics to keep them occupied, as he and his coterie took over an entire country, repressing its citizens.

It is easy to criticize. Even if such projects are funded, is it little more than a public façade to look good by throwing a bone to the dogs (the grant writers), who salivate (to use a Pavlovian metaphor) for the funder's generosity. On the other hand, such malevolent caricatures of funders do a disservice to those who sit on those foundation boards to make a real difference. The challenge is to find such people and establish a spiritual connection based on shared interest that elicits the necessary funding to create social change. The great majority of funding, close to 90%, comes from individuals who often give to organizations with religious and spiritual values similar to those of the funders. Grant writing is about developing shared partnerships, that is, friends united in fair and equitable ways.

Soon after the Columbine school shootings in the 1990s, a lot of money was allotted by the federal government to develop violence-prevention curricula, including strategies for anger control, changing moods, and reflecting on the problem of violent responses to frustrating situations. Keeping in mind Eric Fromm's insight that unlived life leads to destruction and that the United States, mirroring values that place capital gain before need, has more malls than high schools and that a profit-oriented system creates hopeless-ness among youth, who face generally stagnant wages and jobs with fewer benefits, it is unlikely that one would get funding to create an egalitarian social order, the purpose of a proposed grant, although this notion is embed-ded in the Declaration of Independence, and the Universal Declaration, of which the United States was a major architect.

Despite the difficulty in obtaining funding to change the social order, it is important to acknowledge that anger-control groups and violence-prevention curricula can be helpful. They are good and solid mezzo interventions. One can keep to the vision but still develop strategies to effectively deal with at-risk groups. Writing for grants is an extremely time-consuming process, at least one week of full-time work for a federally funded grant. If a person wants to expend such effort, emphasizing the mezzo, but being cognizant of the macro, it may very well pay off. Once funded, if an agency does a good job, it might be funded again. The point is that even if funders will not finance your visions, you should not be discouraged, because steps toward that vision are also worthwhile tasks. A limited definition of the problem, lengthy application forms, and a laborious bureaucratic process should not discourage the social change agent.

The Importance of Sincerity

Sincerity might well be the key in grant writing. It is important to acknowl-edge one's progress, mentioning honest mistakes and possible retreats from goals, but evaluating and moving on. One must also be on guard to not even *give the appearance of insincerity,* despite one's best intentions. This point cannot be overemphasized. However sincere you are in writing for a grant to attend a social justice conference in Hawaii in the middle of January, funders might be suspicious. Only after you have developed some credibility with the funding source can you write such a proposal without raising eyebrows. As the savvy political theorist Machiavelli said: "Everyone sees what you appear to be, few experience what you really are" (1975, p. 101).

To improve possibilities of receiving money for a grant, really a statement about a shared partnership between funder and fundee, it may be important to acknowledge the importance of family. Yes, family! This idea is somewhat akin to the notion of brotherhood in the Universal Declaration. If there are strong feelings of family, a sense of mutual support and caring, partnership, and a general feeling of being together in the fray, funding may be more forthcoming. Family also means inviting the funders to any functions the agency might have and keeping them informed of progress toward fulfilling the goals of the grant.

People generally say that "schmoozing" is important to get a grant. The original meaning of that word is a "friendly, gossipy, prolonged heart-to-heart talk" (Robinson, 2001, p. 355). Unfortunately, that word has taken on a pejorative connotation as manipulation to "suck up" to someone who has the power. But schmoozing in its original meaning can be okay. To get a grant, one definitely needs a heart-to-heart, something like that spiritual connection mentioned earlier.

Article 1 of the Universal Declaration, with its core notion of human dignity, also mirrors the teachings of some of the world's greatest religions. Given the interdependency of rights, one can easily see how notions of human rights can be integrated into almost any grant application. This could be a way to make such a connection, not to get the money and run, but to enhance the spiritual connection among people. If someone wants money for a soup kitchen, one can easily add that such a kitchen could be a step toward achieving the basic human right, asserted in Article 25 of the Universal Declaration, to "food, clothing, housing and medical care and necessary social services."

Nothing infuriates a funder more than applicants selling themselves for funding, not because they believe in the program, but because money is available for it. Grants certainly need to be well written, organized, and targeted to the funder's interests, but the sense of family, shared partnership, sincerity, and schmoozing in its original sense are all important factors in getting the funding. Grant writers need to emanate a kind of "soul force," the meeting of injustice with justice that King and Gandhi speak about, which might even trump a poorly written grant. Mirroring this soul force can reflect one's hunger and thirst for justice, a prerequisite for making a profound spiritual connection with the funder, and perhaps the major predictor of securing a grant.

A Basic Format for Grant Writing

One mustn't underestimate the need for a well-written and organized grant, though. It needs to hang together well, each section directly leading into the next. It is of utmost importance that the potential funder needn't go fishing for information. Everything should be there in plain, simple English. Grants need to be targeted, but the format described here is basic. First is the **Face Sheet,** which ought to provide *all* contact information, time frame, and the exact amount of money requested. Next, the **Cover Page** contains an abstract of no more than 200 words, including the problem addressed, goals, intervention, means of evaluation, agency capability, and the significance of the project. If the grant is relatively long (over 15 pages), a table of contents should be included. Following that is an **Agency Capability Statement,** which summarizes the organization's history, qualifications to carry out the proposed project, populations served, and accomplishments. Next is the **Problem Statement,** preferably well-documented both quantitatively and qualitatively (see Chapter 5); the former includes statistics, and the latter gives voice to those most affected by the problem, speaking to the conscience and heart of anyone reading the document. This statement should also include a theory— why the problem existed in the first place. High infant mortality rates (the problem), for example, might be due to poor nutrition (the theory). Then come **Goals and Objectives** that can be completed within the time frame; these may be (a) immediate, such as teaching expectant mothers about nutrition and/or activities like swimming; (b) intermediate, such as procuring funding for nutritious foods and admittance to the local Y, based on need; and ultimately, (c) long term, such as lowering infant mortality rates to at least approximate those in other areas of the country.

To implement these goals, one needs an **Intervention,** which consists primarily of programs and activities. This section is extremely important, because one needs to demonstrate the feasibility of the project, that the intervention is proportionate to the agency's abilities and theoretic understanding of the problem. Next is **Administration and Staffing**—where the project is located, organizational structure, and job descriptions of major staff, that is, who does what to whom, under whose supervision, and for what purpose. When in doubt about job descriptions, the Dictionary of Occupational Titles, published by the U.S. government, might be helpful. Then, the **Evaluation** must be clear and preferably include quantifiable and qualitative terms with pre- and postassessments and feedback from people served. It is best to establish an evaluation that is formative (that is, to be done at various stages of the program implementation) as well as summative (done at the completion of the project). It would be a good idea to have the evaluator involved at every level of planning. A **Time Frame** may also be helpful and ought to demonstrate when the activities will be carried out, such as every month or every quarter (Lauffer, 1997).

The next extremely important section is the **Budget.** It must be entirely consistent with the previous descriptions and be divided into personnel and nonpersonnel items. If some workers are not full time, discuss their equivalents. Wages also ought to be reasonable. The Web site www.salary.com is a good starting point. Fringe benefits, such as health care, pensions, and sick leave are also appropriate. Nonpersonnel items will include such things as computers, faxes, postage, and travel. Be sure to justify extremely large items. It would be reasonable to add 4% for salaries and items to account for inflation until the grant is funded. In addition, include any in-kind, that is, voluntarily given goods and services, as well as future plans to fund the project. A **Dissemination of Information** section might be helpful as funders generally like to see project replication. Publications, Internet home pages, conferences, and/or listservs where your program might be seen as a best practices model would be appropriate. Technology can be a bane, but also a blessing, especially when access to useful information about good programs to deal effectively with social ills is crucial. An **Appendix** can include letters of support from community leaders and groups; your organization's mission statement, and perhaps news clips (Lauffer, 1997). The general trend in funding in this millennium is toward group cooperation, making such letters extremely important. It may also be important to have pictures that illustrate the "heart" of your organization's purpose. And if you work with children who have difficulties, there is nothing more moving than a piece of art created by a child who many perceived couldn't draw to save his or her life! And sincerity, touching the funder's heart, is what it is about.

Whatever writing-related stress disorder one might have—a lack of self-confidence that one can get grants for hundreds of thousands, or even millions of dollars—now is the time to get over it! Funding is not about you anyway; it is about others, whose presence calls us toward responsibility (Levinas, 2001). In human rights and social justice work, one is not marketing pesticides, toys, or products that will break in an instant. The marketing is about life. Grant writers must push themselves, get out of their comfort zones, to do a good deed. Even if the grant is not funded, the joy one takes away from the attempt is priceless.

Principles for the Protection of Persons With Mental Illness

The next level of intervention is the tertiary level, in which symptoms are readily apparent and require clinical intervention. Such interventions, with human rights and social justice as theoretic foundations, at this micro level deal with persons who have fallen through the cracks, rather than being on the verge of falling through (mezzo level). These persons are struggling to survive. One must be careful here not to blame the victims for forces beyond their control. The social order and its manifestations play a substantive role in propelling them downstream. The influence of an unjust social order is always open to discussion, because some people are born with biological predispositions that may have also led to such illnesses. The increase in teratogens in sperm and toxins in breast milk in the last few decades are just two examples of a social order run amok, and such externalities[5] are entirely within the purview of the helping and health professions.

Before discussing human rights principles relevant to clinical practice for the helping and health professions, it may be worthwhile to acquaint ourselves with some themes from an important document on mental illness, the Principles for the Protection of Persons With Mental Illness and the Improvement of Mental Health Care, proclaimed by the General Assembly on December 17, 1991 (Table 4.2).

Table 4.2   Select Core Themes From the Principles for the Protection of Persons With Mental Illness and the Improvement of Mental Health Care

Core Theme (Principle[s])	Elaboration
Determination of mental illness ought to be based on internationally accepted medical standards (4)	This determination shall never be made on the basis of economic status or membership of a cultural, racial, or religious group, family or professional conflict, or nonconformity with moral, social, cultural, political, or religious beliefs prevailing in the person's community.
Right to life, work, and treatment in the least restricted environment (3, 7, 9)	The patient shall be cared for as far as possible in the community in which he or she lives; treatment can also take place at the patient's home or the home of relatives or friends.
Standards of care ought to be in accordance with the same treatment as other ill persons and internationally accepted standards such as the Principles of Medical Ethics (6–9, 14)	This shall include the right to confidentiality, right to treatment suited to the patient's cultural background; the person must have protection from harm, including unjust medication, abuse by other patients, staff, or others; treatment shall also be adequate, regular, and comprehensive and administered by qualified professional staff.
Treatment shall be based on an individually prescribed plan directed toward preserving and enhancing personal autonomy (9)	This plan shall be discussed with the patient, reviewed regularly, revised as necessary, and provided by qualified professional staff.
Medication shall meet the best health needs of the patient, given only for therapeutic or diagnostic purposes (10)	Medication shall never be administered as a punishment or for the convenience of others; practitioners shall administer only medication of known or demonstrated efficacy.
Informed consent to treatment, including experimental treatment and clinical trials, must be obtained freely without threats or improper inducements (11)	A patient shall never be invited or induced to waive the right to informed consent. However, if the patient is involuntary, and an independent competent authority, having in possession all relevant information, is satisfied that the person lacks capacity, or if domestic legislation provides and is in danger to the patient's own safety or the safety of others and the treatment plan is in the best interest of the patient's health needs, informed consent may be waived. If treatment is authorized without informed consent, still every effort shall be made to inform the patient about the nature of treatment and involve the patient as far as practicable in the development of a treatment plan.

(Continued)

Table 4.2 (Continued)

Core Theme (Principle[s])	Elaboration
There must be appropriate disclosure of treatment in form and language understood by the patient (11–12)	This disclosure shall include diagnostic assessment, the purpose, method, likely duration, and expected benefit of proposed treatment, alternative modes of treatment, including those less intrusive, and possible pain or discomfort, risks, and side effects of the proposed treatment, and the information of the patient's rights as pertaining to these principles as soon as possible after admission.
The patient shall have the right to full respect in a mental health facility (13)	This shall include the right to privacy, freedom of communication, visits from counsel and visitors at reasonable times, access to information from the media, and freedom of religion. The environment shall also be as close as possible to the normal life of persons of similar age, including facilities for recreation, education, engagement in active occupations suited to the patient's social and cultural background, and, as appropriate, rehabilitation measures and placement services to promote reintegration into the community.
Certain practices are prohibited (11, 13)	Sterilization shall never be carried out as a treatment. In no circumstances shall a patient be subject to forced labor. The labor of a patient shall not be exploited and she/he has the right to fair remuneration of his or her work.
The patient shall have the right to procedural safeguards (17–18, 21)	This shall include the right of the patient to choose representation in any complaint procedure, which shall be heard by a competent review panel; the right to an interpreter if necessary; the right of the patient to his or her records and documents except where it is determined that specific disclosure would cause serious harm to the patient's health or safety or that of others. The decision not to disclose information shall be subjected to judicial review if necessary.
Criminal offenders shall also receive the best available mental health care (20)	This shall also include persons otherwise detained in the course of criminal proceedings or investigations against them, who have a mental illness or are believed to have a mental illness.

It is important to keep this document in mind when reading the next section discussing implications of human rights for clinical work. Apart from adhering to basic principles of human dignity, the helping and health professional must be culturally sensitive, describe treatment in layperson's terms, incorporate the client's input in treatment modalities, describe alternative methods of treatment, and not administer medication for the convenience of others; these are all core themes of the Principles for the Protection of Persons With Mental Illness. It is beyond the scope of this book to examine principles for other illnesses, but one can easily see how such principles can be incorporated into many clinical interventions. Criminal offenders as well as victims of AIDS or other illnesses should receive not only the best available mental health care, but also the best physical health care. Personnel must also discuss alternatives to treatment in nonelitist and understandable language.

Principles of Medical Ethics

Significantly, the document in Table 4.2 mentions Principles of Medical Ethics. Table 4.3 shows another important medical ethics document pertaining to the role of helping and health professions in protecting prisoners and detainees against torture and other cruel and degrading forms of punishment. Those imprisoned often mirror a failed system. A major predictor of imprisonment is lack of meaningful and gainful employment, a human rights violation. Inadequate or lack of education, often a predictor of unemployment, is also a human rights violation interrelated with imprisonment.

Without discounting the complex interplay between human choice and circumstance, prisoners often represent a larger population symptomatic of failures of a structurally violent system that require tertiary interventions in accordance with socially just principles based in human rights. People *can* rise above dire circumstances, and professional intervention could assist that possibility. For example, the CRC requires state parties to integrate into society abused children at risk for depression and acting out, not to mention unhappiness. Without such integration, the responsibility of state parties, these children may turn their violence inward, becoming extremely shy, introverted, and lonely—a marginalized group often neglected by the health and helping professions. Or the violence can be turned outward, resulting in more violent behavior that brings them to the attention of law enforcement and the helping and health professions, unfortunately, often in that order. Certainly, some resilient children have dealt satisfactorily with dire circumstance without state and professional intervention. Yet it is reasonable to think overcoming difficult circumstance would be easier if structures were in place to provide adequate opportunity for this to happen. Those who experience the effects of difficult life circumstance, whether abused children, newly divorced spouses with no formal employment skills, or victims of an environmental catastrophe, have a right to be reintegrated into society. People can overcome emotional or physical trauma, but one mustn't overlook the healing powers of the human community in the form of helping and health professionals, family, friends, support groups, or significant others (more the domain of the meta-micro level, to be discussed shortly).

If a person is incarcerated, therefore, the helping and health professionals need to adhere to socially just principles like human dignity, nondiscrimination, and medical ethics principles such as those presented in Table 4.3, which assert that prisoners and detainees deserve the same rights as the non-incarcerated to mental and physical health.

Practice Illustration 4.2 is an example of a shadow report, that is, an alternate government report to a human rights monitoring committee. It asserts that the helping and health professions may not be in compliance with internationally accepted human rights standards, and suggests violations of some of the principles for the Protection of Persons with Mental Illness and of Medical Ethics.

Table 4.3   Select Core Principles of Medical Ethics Relevant to the Role of Health Personnel, Particularly Physicians, in the Protection of Prisoners and Detainees Against Torture, and Other Cruel, Inhuman, or Degrading Treatment or Punishment

Core Principle (Article)	Elaboration
Protection of same mental and physical health standards (1)	Protection shall be given to those imprisoned or detained or those not detained or imprisoned.
No complicity in, incitement to, or attempts to commit torture or other forms of cruel or degrading punishment (2)	Complicity must not be active or passive.
No professional relationship with prisoners or detainees (3)	Purpose of relations must be solely to evaluate, protect, or improve mental or physical health.
Interrogation, participation of certification, and certification of prisoners or detainees must not adversely affect their mental or physical health (4)	Such actions must also not lead to any form of treatment or punishment that may adversely affect their mental and physical health.
Retraining of prisoners or detainees must be in accordance with purely medical criteria (5)	Such detainment must present no hazard to the mental and physical health of the prisoner and may also be for the protection of fellow prisoners, detainees, and guardians.
Nonderogation of these principles (6)	Public emergency or any ground whatsoever shall not justify violation of these principles.

Practice Illustration 4.2
A Shadow Report on Forced Drugging, Electroshock (ECT), and Mental Health Screening of Children by a Disability Working Group to the Monitoring Committee of the ICCPR on Behalf of the New York Organization for Human Rights and Against Psychiatric Assault, Mind Freedom International, and Law Project International

Often NGOs draw up alternative reports, which they submit to the appropriate human rights committee. At present there is no monitoring committee for the Guidelines for the Protection of Persons With Mental Illness. Other human rights conventions, nevertheless, may present opportunities for alternate voices to be heard, as opposed to official government reports. This Disability Working Group viewed a number of practices in violation of articles of the ICCPR: Articles 2 (on nondiscrimination), 7 (guarantee against torture or cruel, inhuman, or degrading punishment, 8 (freedom of thought and from coercion), and 26 (equal protection of the law).

The report cited among other things that the United States continues to practice forced drugging among prisoners at Guantanamo and people with psychosocial disabilities. One prisoner, Shah Mohammed, for instance, who had attempted suicide, was forcibly injected with an unknown drug that left him feeling paralyzed for one month. In psychiatric institutions neuroleptics, although promoted in the media as curing illness, can in reality cause illness, brain damage, and early death. In a coercive atmosphere, patients agree to take drugs by mouth in order to avoid injection. If they contest their label "mental illness," they are further labeled as "paranoid," "lacking insight," thereby justifying forced drugging.

Electroshock, the report continues, is administered twice as often to women as men. The former report passivity after electroshock, being easily led and unable to resist rape. A 2001 survey revealed that nearly 40% of electroshock is administered through court order primarily because of severe adverse reaction to drugs or inefficacy of drugs. Although a single course of electroshock is roughly 6–10 treatments, some are prescribed "maintenance electroshock," with no foreseeable conclusion. One man received electroshock 56 times before health personnel determined the treatment had no effect. In terms of informed consent, only two states, Texas and California, require disclosure of the probability of irrevocable memory loss. The American Psychiatric Association's model form states: "Most patients actually report that their memory improved with ECT."

In regard to a widespread use of mental health screening and drugging of children in schools, the report cites a growing movement by groups like MindFreedom USA. They oppose such screenings, based on unreliable assessment instruments that do not require adequate informed consent, and coerce young people into treatment using psychotropics as a primary modality. The great majority of screening is by Teen Screen, developed at Columbia University. Used in 460 communities in 42 states, it results in an unacceptable number of false positives, more than 70% falsely identified as at risk for depression and suicide. Given that a

2002 article in the *Journal of the American Academy of Child and Adolescent Psychiatry* (Stubbe & Thomas, 2002) found that recently trained child psychiatrists will prescribe a psychotropic drug to 9 out of 10 children they see; the Food and Drug Administration's (FDA) requirement to include a "black box warning" that antidepressants increase risk of suicidal ideation and behavior, hallucinations, diabetes, psychosis, and heart failure; and that drugs used to treat ADHD cause increased risk of addiction to amphetamines, the report states forthrightly that any prescription of psychotropic drugs to a child is a violation of human rights. In terms of informed consent, the Substance Abuse and Mental Health Services Administration of the U.S. Department of Health and Human Services (SAMHSA) does not require grantees to provide active informed consent of parents and requires no provision for informed consent of children. Generally, schools use passive consent, where a child can be screened if a parent doesn't object. Sometimes screening is part of the curriculum so that informed consent can be bypassed.

MindFreedom USA is not opposed, however, to identification of children having difficulty managing emotions and behavior, thereby failing school. Obviously, children suffer from developmental trauma, but mass screening with questionable instruments and referral to mainstream mental health practitioners is not the way to deal with it. Rather, it is important, among other things, to sit down with the child and find out what is going on at home, asking what the child is afraid of or troubled about. She or he needs provision of alternative environments to feel more safe and affirmed, knowing that help is available to address such issues as getting along with one's peers and managing strong emotions like anger, hatred, and jealousy. Environments conducive to the child's development of unique talents, abilities, and passions, in addition to learning to read, write, and do arithmetic are also important, rather than taking a one-size-fits-all approach.

Source: From Minkowitz, T., Galves, A., Brown, C., Kovary, M., & Remba, E. (2006). Alternative Report on Forced Drugging, Forced Electroshock, and Mental Health Screen of Children in Violation of Article 7. Retrieved September 21, 2006, from www.ushrnetwork.org/pubs/

Wrapping up this section, it may also be worthwhile to recall Dr. King's belief that the world's salvation is not necessarily in the hands of the well adjusted:

> Psychologists have a word which is probably used more frequently than any other word in modern psychology. It is the world "maladjusted." . . . But, there are some things in our social system to which all of us ought to be maladjusted. I never intend to adjust myself to the viciousness of mob rule. . . . To the evils of segregation . . . The crippling effects of discrimination . . . The madness of militarism . . . And the self-defeating method of physical violence. It may be that the salvation of the world lies in the hands of the maladjusted. (cited in Washington, 1986, p. 89)

The question becomes whether some treatments, such as medication to help patients with mental illnesses like schizophrenia in coping with the world, are socially just. They undoubtedly can be helpful. Undoubted also is the compassion and commitment of so many overworked helping and health professionals, including the prescribers of medication. Yet a study of Minnesota psychiatrists receiving payments of $5,000 or more from drugmakers showed that, from 2000 to 2005, they prescribed these drugmakers' antipsychotics more than 300% more than those of drugmakers whose payments were less than $5,000 (Harris, Carey, & Roberts, 2007). Surely, we need alternatives to a market-driven system based on human rights and dignity, to ensure the fulfillment of human need.

Toward a Socially Just Human Rights–Based Approach to Clinical Practice

Presently, there appears to be no explicit human rights–based approach to clinical intervention to deal with such manifestations of an unjust social order as mental illness or substance abuse. These manifestations can encompass a variety of symptoms including depression, violence, homicide, suicide, or the total blocking out of reality as occurs in the most severe and chronic conditions like schizophrenia. Schizophrenia comes from *schizos* and *phrenia,* meaning literally "broken heart," a poignant term for the chronically mentally ill. The failure of the victim of mental illness to make sense of his or her world or to be able to take appropriate and constructive practical action can be a frustrating if not frightening experience. (The challenge for the "victim," from the Latin *victum,* meaning "conquered, overcome, defeated, subdued, vanquished," is to overcome defeat.)

Working toward a human rights–based clinical approach attempts to integrate such principles in ways that enhance human dignity. It is difficult, certainly, to find clinicians not concerned with the dignity of their clients. Some are talented; others are not. Some are good listeners; others are not. Some have a way of getting to the roots of a person's difficulty; others skirt them. Yet people can get better without professional help, through the support of friends, family, even strangers in support groups. The challenge is to ascertain successful interchanges between caretakers and clients/patients. Such interchanges are not easily measurable, nor should they be. But they may be all one needs to have successful outcomes with patient care that helps the natural healing process in mysterious ways. Perhaps the knowledge we get from these interchanges is what a socially just human rights–based intervention is all about.

Ways of Helping That Can Obfuscate Healing

To understand and appreciate successful interchanges between health and helping professionals and their patients, some comments are in order about possible limitations of helping methods that may obfuscate the healing process. It's worth noting that the term *patient* is from the Latin, *patior,* meaning "to suffer, undergo, to try, to attempt"—not surprisingly, a rare Latin verb that is passive in form, yet active in meaning. Though seemingly passive, patients struggle actively in their minds, hearts, and bodies to resolve conflicts manifested in the physical and/or mental arena.

Regarding limitations in clinical mental health practice, it is easy to get lost within a system divorced from social context. Professional criteria, such as the *Diagnostic and Statistical Manual of Mental Disorders* (DSM-IV), have tremendous administrative and clinical utility in diagnosing clients. Diagnoses provide a basis for reimbursement and a relatively efficient tool for assigning clients to therapy groups or matching them with appropriate professionals. Rational-emotive therapy, for example, may be effective with a depressed client, while working through denial and rationalization may be more effective for a substance abuser. Obviously, diagnoses are useful; however, they may also have the iatrogenic effect of creating a self-fulfilling prophecy that exacerbates the illness rather than curing it. In the mental health field, a label of personality disorder can be perceived as a veiled insult. Professionals may diagnosis patients rather easily, but tend to resent it when others diagnose themselves or their family members. The challenge is to not lose sight of others' dignity and human rights, as codified in professional ethical codes and human rights documents.

The Priority of Human Experience

But prioritizing a system, rather than the experiencing person—as far divorced as possible from theoretic suppositions—poses difficulties in addition to the thorny problem of diagnosis. To extend the thorn metaphor, the flowering of the human personality is the rose lying deep within. Helping and health professionals, like gardeners cultivating growth and human development (what this work has referred to as a socially just human rights culture), must be aware of the thorns as they help others in the healing process. Professionals trained in a particular school may easily come to view all problems from a singular perspective. Freudians, for example, may view a person's troubles as due to "transference," an idea endemic to Freudian consciousness (Keen, 1972). Thus, the helper might consider the loss of the client's job to be a result of the legacy of unresolved anger toward the client's parents transferred to the boss. The actuality, however, may be that the boss downsized, and hired relatives or friends. Given that protection of workers' interests is fundamental to social justice, a concerted effort to organize workers may ultimately have been more therapeutic. Developing a community of compassion is fundamental to an administrator sympathetic to human rights principles (Lerner, 1991) However, astute and skilled helping professionals need to identify when transference is undeniably at work, hindering the person in functioning adequately. This dynamic may be the reality, and the entire school of thought can't be dismissed. Yet it is also important to recognize structural issues that threaten the flowering of tolerance, friendship, and understanding, as asserted in the Universal Declaration, in a community.

Implications of the Etymology of Therapy

It is helpful to examine plausible etymological roots of the word *therapy*, that tertiary intervention central to the helping professions. The beautiful enchantress, Helen—the "fairest woman in the world" (Hamilton, 1942, p. 179), "the most desirable bride in Greece" (Cotterell & Storm, 2005, p. 48), and the half-divine and half-human daughter of Zeus and Lena, whose face launched a thousand ships—was born on the Greek Island of *Therapne*. During those times, the Greeks prized beauty highly. Enduring an extremely difficult life, a near-death experience at birth, and rape on this idyllic Greek island, Helen was able not only to persevere, but to thrive. The word *therapy*, which in Greek also means "service" (a basic theme of this work), may be thought of as a kind of island refuge from the storm, where one can escape the past controlling one's destiny. The struggle, therefore, is to make the therapy session a source of refreshment in taking on the challenges of everyday life.

In the psychotherapeutic clinical arena, notions of relationship therapy (Moustakas, 1997), unconditional positive regard (Rogers, 1995), working through (Bruch, 1976; Fromm-Reichmann, 1950; Hornstein, 2000), the communicative relationship (Kaiser, as cited in Fierman, 1965), the playroom as space for exploration and regression within set limits (Axline, 1989), and active imagination (Jung, as cited in Hannah, 1981) ensure the therapeutic situation is one where a person can emerge gracefully, yet with wisdom, liberated from the chains of the past. The helping professions refer to such emergence as self-actualization (Maslow, 1987) or, in the substance abuse field, a quality sobriety. These are not ends in themselves, but reflect the person's continual commitment to individual transformation. The therapeutic notion of free spaces where groups can openly discuss issues of concern, leading to practical action, is similar to that of an island in a storm.

The social justice approach advocated here is also timely, as many leaders in the field of psychotherapy have come of age and are in search of new directions. That was the general consensus at a recent conference attended by many luminaries, such as Albert Ellis, Thomas Szasz, Albert Bandura, Martin Seligman, and even the infamous Dr. Hunter "Patch" Adams, the charismatic doctor played by Robin Williams. Dr. Adams even fell to the floor, calling for "a last stand of loving care" to prevail over the misery of the world (Carey, 2005).

The collective wisdom of the global community, mirrored in human rights documents such as guiding principles, declarations, and conventions, may provide the direction needed by the broadly defined psychotherapeutic helping professions. This is not to say that incorporating human rights into the therapist-client interaction, alone, will slay the damaging vestiges of one's past. It is not the sole panacea. Yet, by at least being cognizant of human rights principles, psychotherapists might see these documents as a stamp of approval for many things they already do. For example, fundamental to social justice is the guarantee of human dignity, as defined in Article 1 of the Universal Declaration. Certainly successful therapists treat their clients with dignity. Certainly human dignity is fundamental to any kind of well-being, the essential aim of therapeutic intervention. Successful helping and health professionals ought to also respect patients, irrespective of their race, class, gender, sexual orientation, or medical condition—the essence of the nondiscrimination principle fundamental to social justice and asserted in Article 2 of the Universal Declaration. They should also treat patients in the context of their environments, taking a holistic approach to helping that is entirely consistent with the notion of the interdependency of rights, an essential tenet of human rights and social justice principles.

Human Rights Principles That Have Implications for the Therapeutic Relationship

This section discusses some human rights principles that are especially pertinent to the art and science of therapeutic help. The helper is like an artist who also is a subtle scientist. The painter applies the brush to canvas with a mixture of spontaneity, indicative of artistic temperament, and reflection, indicative of scientific inquiry. Likewise, a helper, using the insights of human rights, needs a healthy combination of spontaneity and reflection to treat someone. Sincerity or a concerned smile cannot be rehearsed. They must emerge from an unprompted true desire to be of service. But the professional also needs honed knowledge of fair and just practice to have a therapeutic effect.

The principles discussed here, in the best of all worlds, are necessary for a just social order and the realization of human rights. In a managed care system (from the Latin, *manus,* meaning "hand," that is, someone else has a "handle" on what helping professionals are doing), often involving layer upon layer of quantifiable bureaucratic accountability (e.g., numbers of people seen and billed), it is an understatement that such an order does not exist. Some strategies already discussed to change the social order are developing laws for parity of mental and physical health coverage; forming vast social movements to make health care a constitutionally guaranteed human right; incorporating human rights principles into educational and professional curricula; and tirelessly advocating for clients and staff. But what many consider lofty ideals in the macro arena must now be considered legally mandated rights. In the therapeutic setting, too, principles protecting the mentally ill and medical ethics must not be considered mere ideals, but rather guiding principles that need to be legally mandated.

The following principles represent a composite of basic human rights principles, based on documents discussed earlier, that are especially pertinent in the therapeutic process.

The first principle is that **creating a human rights culture is therapeutic in itself**. This confirms Aristotle's ancient wisdom that "we become just by the practice of just actions, self-controlled by exercising self-control, and courageous by performing acts of courage" (cited in Wilson, 2005, p. A27). One *must* go beyond oneself to put the common welfare over individual preoccupations. Perhaps the best way to deal with one's perceived imperfection is to act more like the person one desires to be rather than be preoccupied with self-analysis. Authors such as Real (1997) write that finding something beyond themselves is therapeutic in itself. This echoes millennia of wisdom that we find ourselves by losing ourselves (Matthew 10:39). The notion of therapeutic community bespeaks such age-old knowledge, which advocates participation by clients in activities that lose themselves in others. This approach may not be that different from Frankl's (1984) notion of paradoxical intention to do, with the help of the therapist, the very activity a person fears.

Second, **human dignity is fundamental to the therapeutic process**, not unlike Martin Buber's concept of I-Thou wherein humans can form deeply felt relationships based on a shared spirituality, rather than the I-It relation increasingly common since the Industrial Revolution (Buber, 1958; Gil, 2004). In the dialogues between Martin Buber and Carl Rogers, the founder of client-centered therapy steeped in the tradition of

Soren Kierkegaard, Buber responded in the affirmative to Rogers's question, "[Is] what you have termed the I-Thou relationship . . . similar to what I see as the effective moment in a therapeutic relationship?" (Anderson & Cissna, 1997. p. 29). Although it may be difficult to define dignity, certainly the therapist's own experience as well as the golden rule can serve as guideposts. Health and helping professionals might benefit from reflecting on their own experiences when they were treated with dignity or treated others with dignity. Knowledge thus gained from an inner dialogue is an experiential foundation for understanding patients' longing for the dignity they are entitled to.

Martin Luther King, Jr.'s reflections on human dignity in relation to the courage of Ms. Rosa Parks are also worth considering. Her sitting at the front of the bus, he wrote, was "an individual expression of a timeless longing for human dignity and freedom . . . planted there by her personal sense of dignity and self-respect" (Washington, 1986, p. 424). As Ms. Parks was the victim of "accumulated indignities" (p. 424), so, too, are many patients whose choices of healthier lifestyle in the face of such indignities are reminiscent of her courage.

Third is the **principle of nondiscrimination**. Despite numerous attempts to implement this principle, discrimination frequently rears its ugly head. The diagnosis of certain types of disorders can itself, if not viewed within context, become a self-fulfilling prophecy. The psychiatrist R. D. Laing had admonished in his *Politics of Experience* (1983) that the very behavior the professional is trying to change is reinforced by the labels assigned to that person. Diagnoses certainly provide useful information about a cluster of qualities that could assist in determining appropriate therapy. Yet the challenge is always to see, understand, and appreciate the uniqueness of each individual transcending any cluster of traits. Again, we need to perceive people as possibilities rather than actualities (Keen, 1972), and be attuned to their multiplicities of experiences, perspectives, and potentials. This may be why many accrediting bodies of helping and health professions, such as social work, require liberal arts integrated into their curricula. *Liberal* is from the Latin *liber,* meaning "free," and the root reflects perhaps the helping professional's aim to free others from the shackles of their past and poor lifestyle choices, but also the straitjackets of elitist terminology that can hurt, rather than heal, if not attuned to the person's unique personal history, present situation, and future possibilities.

Furthermore, diagnoses should never be made on the basis of one's membership in a racial, cultural, religious, and class group or nonconformity with various moral or social beliefs in the community. Unwittingly, because of cultural biases, the helper may view a person living in extreme poverty who comes for help as a failure; this is known as the just-world phenomenon—that one gets what they deserve in life. The helper might think automatically that the client needs to learn how to be empowered, when the client has had to take care of a dying relative. The person may be a victim of an unjust social order, fired by a struggling, unsympathetic employer. Put bluntly, is an African American or Latino, mesomorphic, male teen in T-shirt and sneakers more likely to be diagnosed as a juvenile delinquent than an ecto-morphic, svelte, white female teen dressed in expensive clothing? The perva-siveness of stereotypes is a constant challenge.

In addition to possible discrimination in diagnoses, a similar dynamic may come into play during treatment. Professional credentials are no guar-antee of being able to deal with the exigencies of daily existence. Professionals need to be continually attentive to the wisdom their clients may have gained from their own accumulative indignities. The input of those seeking help is important, whether on the micro (clinical) level or the macro (policy) level. Fortunately, it is increasingly common for professionals to elicit patient input when designing treatment plans. Yet it is important to remember the Milgram studies on prejudice, which he called the Cyrano Effect. In brief, the researcher told teachers to plumb the depths of a child's knowledge on subjects like mathematics, literature, and history. But the teachers didn't know that the children were responding to authorities in their fields via electrodes placed in their ears. Teachers, however, only asked ques-tions pertaining to simple things like fractions, decimals, and multiplication problems when the children could easily have answered questions on physics, calculus, and advanced statistical analysis (Milgram, Sabini, & Silver, 1992). Do helping and health professionals do the same with their clients when they fail to acknowledge clients' infinite capacities to change, remaining comfortable in the clinical setting and complacent in their status as a helping and health professional?

Another basic principle is a **nonhierarchical approach** to helping. As stated, every human rights instrument speaks in no uncertain terms of the need for participation, not only by the public in the policy debates, but also by the client in the treatment process itself. It is important to go beyond a blanket perception of the client as helpless, but it is also impor-tant to discuss the treatment plan with the client, review it regularly, and revise it as necessary. This must be done in ways that the client can under-stand. Therapy is not something one does to another person; rather, it takes place in an interpersonal context.

A nonhierarchical approach is also arguably more feminist than tradition-ally masculine top-down hierarchical structure. In the best of all possible worlds, the client would be informed initially of the various treatment modes and alternatives to treatment available and their length, cost, and possible intrusiveness. This information must be provided in an atmosphere of confidentiality and fully informed consent. Informing the client of alternatives to treatment requires broadly based knowledge among qualified and competent staff, necessitating interdisciplinary collaboration. Such an approach would also give clients access to their records, unless competent authorities have deemed such access would be harmful. Nevertheless, the client has the right to appeal, due process, and an effective remedy and restitution, should his or her human rights be violated.

Cultural sensitivity, a fifth principle, is extremely important. It is fortuitous that accrediting agencies are paying more attention to cultural approaches to helping. Intuitively, most professionals sense the importance of a client's cultural background. But knowing that cultural sensitivity is a human right, mirroring the collective wisdom of many of the world's helping and health practitioners and reflected in human rights instruments, makes this vital notion more profoundly significant. Treatment must never be based on the client's nonconformity with communal cultural values but must be suited to his or her cultural background. Cultural sensitivity should also be understood in a broad sense and cultural factors must be considered in integrating the client into the community. An interpreter must be provided if necessary.

Support groups should be seen as effective adjuncts to treatment, a sixth principle. Groups such as Alcoholics Anonymous, Overeaters Anonymous, Emotions Anonymous, Gamblers Anonymous, Narcotics Anonymous, Love and Sex Addicts Anonymous, or any others as well as the various support groups that have arisen for incest survivors, trauma survivors, the sexually questioning, divorced, and bereaved parents, as well as men's and women's support groups offer opportunities for healing. Unfortunately, such groups may be neglected because the social order today does not reimburse for such groups, making it impossible for their facilitators to earn an adequate living. Fortunately, helping and health professionals have formed, facilitated, and maintained such groups, at considerable personal time and expense, a testimony to their dedication.

A seventh principle is that helping and health professionals ought to acknowledge the importance of a **systems-oriented** approach. This approach has been discussed, in various guises, as a strengths perspective, holistic approach, or humanistic approach to helping. But all these variations, true to the basic thrust of human rights principles, focus on the fulfillment of human need and human development as the keys to understanding. People are not pathologies. They are humans with needs and rights. Professionals have a duty to treat them with dignity, respect, tolerance. This approach, however, asserts that people have strengths not only in themselves, but in their environments. The aim of healing, as stated in the Introduction, ought to be to assist in releasing the wisdom of the million-year-old person at the client's core. The helper should also be sympathetic to exigencies of this millennium, such as the client's need to juggle employment with family life, and the necessity of keeping to a job that fails to develop the client's potential. A systems-oriented approach calls for compassion for the person whose world is limited. Human development can be thwarted by the inability to access one's inner knowledge. But a systems approach acknowledges that the exigencies of everyday life that inhibit human growth also need to be changed.

Eighth is the principle of **self-determination**. Whereas this principle has largely been used in the international arena, such as the right of the Kashmiri, the Roma, and Indigenous Peoples to carve their own destiny, it is also appropriate within the helping and health professions. Certain groups need the opportunity to develop traditional and culturally appropriate ways of meting out justice for crimes committed. Tribal courts, banishment to an island, and shame totem poles are some examples as presented at the First International Conference on Self-Determination in Geneva, in 2000. But clients also have the right to self-determination, to develop and harness enough of their inner resources to carve their own destinies, which the art and science of the helping and health professions can provide. What self-determination actually means may be controversial, with some building upon indigenous wisdom suggesting it is merely being able to live together nicely (Daes, 2001), the argument that cultural groups and clients themselves ought to be able to carve their own destinies and deal with their own personal jihads, that is, inner struggles.

Finally, treatment must also be provided by **qualified, competent personnel**. It is important here to practice within one's area of competency. Paradoxically, people also need to be competent about their incompetency. In other words, they must know what they do not know. Ultimately, professionals do not know how a person heals; only the person being helped can ultimately answer that question. However, helpers must be versed in their profession, aware of its possibilities and limitations. Thus, they can facilitate the growth process as a scientist, using the insights of science and professional knowledge, but also an artist, applying skill and spontaneity in painting a portrait of the human personality.

This is not to say that professionals are competent only when they understand human rights principles. These principles alone will not solve such issues as anorexia nervosa and bulimia; alcohol, drug, and other addictions; juvenile delinquency; depression; schizophrenia; and the like. Professionals ultimately must only treat another fairly, equitably, and with dignity in their practices. Intake workers must be competent to do a good psychosocial assessment and be able to understand strengths and weaknesses in a person's environment. Helpers must also know what approaches work best with what clients and have the skills necessary to assist them in alleviating symptoms. A Rogerian approach, unconditional positive regard, might be most effective with a person suffering from low self-esteem. An Ellisian approach, rational-emotive therapy, might work best with a person suffering from depression, helping him or her learn to examine and then change reactions to difficult life circumstance. It's worth noting that this therapy has been said to to be rooted in Stoicism, particularly the writings of Marcus Aurelius, which was influential in the development of human rights principles. The Stoics, who understood the importance of personal disclosure in self-knowledge and development of self-sufficiency through reason and wisdom regardless of the external tragedies in one's life, anticipated rational-emotive therapy and the present philosophical psychotherapy movement (Moss, 2001). Also, a skilled therapist can assist someone diagnosed with schizophrenia, for example, to engage in active imagination to "have it out with the unconscious" (Hannah, 1981, p. 22).

A group might be an effective means of working with addicts (from the Latin *addicere,* meaning "to give up or over; to doom, dedicate or surrender"). It could not only be a support, but also serve as a sounding board to constructively uncover possible reasons for giving power over to alcohol, drugs, another person, or food and take practical action to relinquish that power and move toward a more fulfilling life. Such human rights notions as human dignity, nondiscrimination, and self-determination merely serve as a framework for what helpers already may intuitively use to assess their practice in light of the collective wisdom of the global community.

Some Words on the Meta-Micro Level

The meta-micro level of intervention is the arena of the everyday life, where random acts of kindness, a honed spirituality within, and good deeds performed by persons who are not regarded as helping professionals or by professionals relinquishing the mantle of the expert (Katz, 1982; Wronka, 1993) have a therapeutic effect. With a mere smile, a solid "hello" in the morning, or a small unsolicited gift, an elevator operator, an orderly, a cook, or a housekeeper, although not professionally trained in the formal art and science of helping, can have a phenomenal effect on the well-being of an abused child. This level also includes the realm of family members—grandparents, great-grandparents, stepparents, stepsiblings, para-moms and para-dads (unrelated people who have taken on parenting roles), and distant relatives whose support and wisdom provides a respite from the stresses of the world. Such respite can come even from strangers and peers, through mutually fulfilling and beneficial, rather than seductive and competitive, encounters (see Fellman, 1998). Finally, meta-micro interventions include self-help peer groups, as well as many interactions among people in community that provide support and celebrate life through dance, song, music, food, and camaraderie. Whatever happened to welcoming committees in condo or apartment complexes?

Finally, let us not forget therapeutic possibilities that animals may provide. To abused children, there is nothing like the horse who neighs and shakes his head and mane upon seeing them. We all know the sense of acceptance that pets can give, which ought not be dismissed lightly.

Unfortunately, the therapeutic benefits of nonprofessional everyday encounters, self-help groups, community interventions, even animals are often neglected simply because they are difficult to measure. But the ability to take numerical measures is no guarantee of understanding something. Often, what people search for in their everyday lives that are indispensable to the human condition, like friendship, love, understanding, and companionship, can only be deeply felt. Also, the effectiveness of "unskilled" helpers may quite possibly undermine the authority of those more commonly understood to be versed in helping. The challenge is to be fully aware of the possibilities that everyday encounters can provide outside the realm of professionalism.

Summary

This chapter first discussed principles from human rights documents that might assist the helping and health professions in developing interventions. At the mezzo level of intervention, human rights documents might provide guiding principles for working with at-risk groups, for example, in fulfilling state obligations to provide for paid maternity leave, good quality day care, and reintegration of abused children into the community.

It discussed the helping and health professions as an at-risk group, susceptible to the corrupting influence of power suggested by the Eichmann Effect. It also examined how domains such as business, humanistic administration, grant writing, and social entrepreneurship could be enhanced by consistent adherence to human rights principles. In the clinical arena, focusing on the Principles for the Protection of Persons With Mental Illness and Principles of Medical Ethics, the chapter explored the implications of such basic human rights principles as human dignity, nondiscrimination, cultural sensitivity, self-determination, and a systems-oriented framework, which are substantive to human rights documents, for the therapeutic relationship and how they could assist clinicians in helping clients overcome trauma and addictions. It ended with a brief discussion of the meta-micro intervention level, that is, the healing powers of everyday life and encounters, an arena of helping largely downplayed that needs further scrutiny.

Before concluding, it is necessary to examine the fourth level of intervention, that of research (quantitative and qualitative), paying particular attention to ethical principles that arose directly in response to atrocities. Research without action is useless, but information is power. The next chapter, therefore, also discusses the notion that evil triumphs because the good do nothing, and suggests positive ways to engage with others to inform them about human rights, dignity, and social justice. Social justice work is not complete without sharing; we need to tell the world and bear witness to the violations of human dignity wherever they may occur.

Questions for Discussion

1. Imagine you are an administrator of a helping or health institution, such as a mental health/substance abuse clinic, juvenile treatment center, adult correctional facility, medical facility, or public health center. You are aware of Hannah Arendt's notion of the banality of evil; essentially she portrayed Adolf Eichmann, a high-ranking Nazi officer who facilitated the herding into concentration camps and mass killings of innocents, as a dull, boring bureaucrat, who became desensitized to the violence in which he played a major role. You get a call from CO (Central Office) stating that productivity has vastly increased as evidenced by a marked improvement in the institution's statistics showing more intakes completed, more clients/patients seen, more billing, and ultimately more proceeds generated for the organization. You notice, however, that case notes have become sparser; more clients than ever are on medication; most therapists run groups, spending less time with individual clients who need special attention; and staff morale is down. A humanistic person, you find yourself losing sleep at night, wondering if you yourself have somehow herded clients through the facility and become dulled to its reduced quality of care. How could you fight these demons that keep you up at night? Are you, too,

engaging in the banality of evil, although certainly not on the scale Arendt describes? To what extent are you, a genuinely hardworking, caring, and ethical person, also a victim of an unjust social order? What, if anything, can be done about it?

2. You are feeling depressed. You go to a therapist who tells you that the only way to get better is to be psychoanalyzed, having sessions three times a week for 3 years. You respond that you do not have the time or the money for such prolonged treatment. The therapist calls you resistant to treatment and questions your sincerity in wanting to get better. Do you feel that the therapist violated the alternative methods of treatment principle in the human rights document on the Principles for the Protection of Persons With Mental Illness by insisting there is only one way to get better? Now imagine that you see a therapist who prescribes only medication and asserts you can deal with your issues through short-term treatment and medication. You state that you feel you have major work to do, have the time and money, and want in-depth character transformation, requiring prolonged treatment, such as psychoanalysis. The therapist reasserts that this is not necessary. Were that therapist's assertions also a violation of the alternative methods of treatment principle? The same document also asserts that medication should be given for the benefit and well-being of the patient, rather than the convenience of the caretaker or facility. Do you think this is the practice in school or other settings? Do children who are depressed and withdrawn, do not act out, and rarely cause a ruckus receive the necessary attention or medication from professionals? What can we do to improve the situation?

3. Think of good and bad bosses you may have had. What made them good or bad? What human rights principles do you feel they were unknowingly either implementing or violating? What can you learn from your reflections on your experiences?

4. Think about people to whom you have given money and who have given money to you. Now think of times you have given voluntarily to others and times that others have voluntarily given to you. What can you learn from these experiences? If someone gave you a million dollars to change the social order, what would you do? If someone gave you billions, what would you do? How can you or should you integrate human rights into a grant proposal? Now imagine the following exaggerated but poignant scenario: After traveling to an extremely poor Third World country, Shennika noticed the devastating effects of guinea worm disease, up to 2-foot-long worms that live inside the bodies of children, causing

excruciating pain as they exit through the skin. For reasons unknown to her, the only organization that funds projects to eradicate this malady is the Ku Klux Klan (this is exaggerated for purposes of discussion). Although Shennika detests the racism, hate, and religious intolerance of this group, she asks them for money and receives it. She even went so far as to don a hood and attend a KKK rally for the sole purpose of getting money for her cause. Word gets out of her actions and her friends ostracize her. She is fully aware of the difficulties involved in her decision; she experiences the joy of doing a good deed, alleviating the suffering of so many, and wonders if a social order must always be just. Unable to get a job in her field because of a questionable reputation, she dies at an early age, the only person present at her funeral is the single father who raised her, his love unconditional and everlasting.

5. If you became a social entrepreneur, what would you like to do to change the world? How would you go about it? Do you think the idea of human rights would be helpful? If so, in what ways? If not, why not and what, then, would be helpful? Why do you think social entrepreneurship has become so popular recently? Didn't such entrepreneurship already exist in the voluntary sector, as evidenced by such groups as the Children's Defense Fund and the Salvation Army?

6. Should there be a document for the protection of substance abusers or persons dually diagnosed? How would issues be similar and/or different from those for persons with mental illness? What would such a document look like? How should it be drafted? How could one get international recognition for it?

7. Imagine that you have just read inspiring texts by survivors of concentration camps, such as Viktor Frankl's *Man's Search for Meaning* or Elie Wiesel's *Night*. You find that their hope, courage, and persistence in the midst of ugliness, hate, and indifference is not that different from some of your clients' experiences. Do you think you can use any of the wisdom of these and similar texts in therapeutic ways in your practice? If so, how?

8. How do the ethics code and practice of your profession compare with human rights documents? Start with the Universal Declaration, then look at other documents. Do you feel your profession lives up to human rights principles, or do they go beyond them? Does, for example, the American Psychiatric Association's periodically updated *Diagnostic and Statistical Manual of Mental Disorders* (DSM) further enhance the human dignity of clients or reduce their experience to categories and numbers, a technological society run amok (Ellul, 1967)? If you are critical, what

alternatives do you suggest? Begin working on those alternatives. Generally, what do you feel you could do to improve the ethics and practice of your profession, and do you think human rights documents could be of assistance in creating a socially just practice?

9. Do you and your colleagues adhere to human rights principles in the work and professional setting? If not, how can the setting be improved? It has been argued that human rights defenders/social justice advocates can have a self-righteous, holier-than-thou attitude when it comes to implementing human rights standards. Is that true? How can you humanize the workplace to make a true community of compassion using human rights as a guide in a spirit of humility and creative dialogue?

10. In general, how can human rights principles help you, as a helping or health professional, develop your skills as an administrator, supervisor, or clinician? How do you envision a human rights–based approach directing practice and/or clinical intervention?

Activities/Actions

1. Go to the Web site for the Business and Human Rights Resource Center (2005). Read any of the human rights reports available. Then write letters to the CEOs commending them on the positive aspects of the report with suggestions on ways to improve areas of weakness. Follow through by monitoring how they may have implemented their reports and your suggestions. Try to creatively engage in a positive dialogue with them, especially if they have not further implemented human rights principles. Reflect on whether your style in interacting with them might be more positive if you were more confrontational. In your communications, you may also consider offering to volunteer or work as human rights/social justice intern to achieve certain human rights goals to which the organization has committed itself.

2. Take out a business license and set up a Web site. Give your organization a catchy name with a good acronym; for example, I have used Human Rights Action International (HRAI), as in "It's time to say HRAI" (Hurray!) for human rights! It may sound corny, but such phrases are memorable. Then begin constructing a home page. In addition to readings mentioned, the following books, listed in the reference section, may be of assistance: Larson (2002), Warwick, Hart, and Allen (2002), Robinson (2001), Burnett (2002), and Prokosch and Raymond (2002).

3. Write a grant to open up an office that will serve as a nucleus for coordinating international human rights initiatives with domestic policies. In other words, it might inform federal, state, and perhaps even private agencies of human rights documents, like the Convention on the Rights of People with Disabilities, adopted by the General Assembly in 2007. Collaboratively work with them to monitor progress toward compliance with that document or any document of your choosing. Or, depending on your time and personal and other commitments, set up an organization that is more in line with your interests and style. It may serve seasonally, for example, providing consulting to schools, institutions, and the like during Human Rights week. Or it could be a think tank creating annual or biannual reports, using the Universal Declaration as the yardstick to assess progress toward that document's goals. Or you may wish to develop a mock grant, a fictional wish list that can serve as a boilerplate, but can be tweaked or substantively modified and targeted to a specific funder. Such a boilerplate might include a mission statement, agency capability statement, goals and objectives, methods to achieve these goals, budget to pay for salaries and benefits of workers, and other nonpersonnel materials such as photocopying, stationery, computers, transportation costs, time frames, means of evaluation, and dissemination of information.

4. Sit back, relax, and dream awhile. If it helps, close your eyes. Research consistently demonstrates that a little daydreaming, taking time off from the hustle and bustle of everyday life, much like yoga and meditation, can enhance health and well-being. If you were a social entrepreneur, what type of activity would you most likely want to engage in? Imagine that you had enough resources at your disposal. What would you do and how would you do it? Would you be able to integrate meta-macro, macro, mezzo, micro, and meta-micro interventions into your activities? Imagine that you are carrying HIV medication to villages in the far reaches of an extremely impoverished country. Would you and could you also try to establish the right to education in that country's constitution and set up a bureau to ensure its implementation, your rationale being that educated women are more able to reject sexual advances, thereby decreasing the spread of AIDS? Stay with these images for awhile. Then slowly come back to the present moment. How do you feel? How does your mind, your body, your "soul" feel? Do you think you can realize your dreams? Why or why not? Share your experience.

5. Go the Internet and read thoroughly the entire documents on the Protection of Persons With Mental Illness, the Rights of the Mentally

Retarded, the International Convention on the Rights of People With Disabilities, and/or any other documents relevant to your profession. What principles might be directly relevant to your practice as a clinician? Is there any appreciable difference between your clinical approaches before and after you became aware of those documents? Should there be any difference? Now do a process recording of a clinical session. Then reflect on whether you have met human rights criteria, such as human dignity and cultural sensitivity, during the therapeutic session. How could clinical sessions be strengthened to adhere to human rights principles? Or should they? What other principles in addition to the ones discussed in this chapter might enhance clinical sessions?

Notes

1. "Crazy" might at first seem a pejorative term, as in "this guy's crazy," or a mocking of an emotionally challenged person. Indigenous culture appears to have an extremely high tolerance for alternative ways of being, entirely different from white culture. If Crazy Horse is "crazy," however, it is in the sense that Joseph Wresinski, founder of the International Fourth World Movement, emerged from his difficult life of extreme poverty with "the madness of love" or that every child needs someone who is "crazy" about him or her.

2. Adolf Eichmann was responsible for the deaths of roughly 1 million innocents in concentration camps. When later tried for these war crimes, his defense was, "I only followed orders." This defense led some, like Arendt (1994) and Lifton (2000), to hypothesize about the dulling effects of bureaucratization on people's senses in response to the violence they perpetrate.

3. Interestingly, "white" in this context is pejorative. Usually, the pejorative term is "black": blacklisted, blackballed, blackout, and so on.

4. Columbo was a savvy detective played by Peter Falk, hair always in disarray and wearing an obviously rarely washed raincoat, often searching feverishly for his pen, only to drop it on finding it. However, he astounded onlookers with his brilliance, at least those who were willing to see beyond appearances, that is, not discriminate.

5. Externalities, in brief, are costs of production that the taxpayer is generally responsible for. For example, mothers who unknowingly drink contaminated water may find toxins in their breast milk. That water may be the direct result of waste discharged into streams by manufacturing companies. Violence, broadly defined, is also an externality, manifested by a social order emphasizing profit at the expense of human need. Ultimately, society must pay a price.

5

A Human Rights/Social Justice Approach to Research-Action Projects for the Helping and Health Professions

There is no worse lie than a truth misunderstood by those who hear it.

—William James

Research is doing what one already does, only more rigorously. When beginning a college or graduate program, some might informally look for the easy graders, because they have always felt that good grades are a ticket to a good job. Taking a more rigorous, structured approach, they could find the easy markers by making an educated guess, or, in scientific parlance, a hypothesis, about what might provide the most information. They could choose a sample, like alumni(ae), develop questionnaires, and hand out surveys asking them to rate their instructors' grading behaviors from a score of 1, being easy, to 5, being hard. They could also do a correlation analysis between professors' grading before and after tenure or between a professor's family size and grading style. They might randomly or selectively choose a few persons, perhaps their peers, if alumni(ae) were too difficult to obtain, to interview in depth about professors' teaching and grading styles; for example, are they more likely to give good grades to students' whose names they know or is class participation high on the list of professors' grading criteria?

In general, numerical methods of finding data, primarily through measurement and operationalizing of variables, is often referred to as quantitative research; eliciting findings through meaningful dialogue and rigorous conversation is often called qualitative research. It is not the purpose of this work to elucidate the differences and similarities of these two approaches. Nevertheless, in general, quantitative research is often concerned with method, manipulation, and control of variables, works with individual subjects, and generalizes data to the broader population; qualitative research is phenomenon bound rather than methodologically centered, seeks understanding and meaning rather than loyalty to a system, works with coresearchers (Moustakas, 1990), and views findings as suggestive, based on the situation studied.

The debate over the superiority of quantitative versus qualitative research, dating back to the Platonic tradition that mathematics is music of the gods versus the Aristotelian tradition of catharsis, has set up an unfortunate division between these two camps of thought on ways of knowing. Each has its own merits, and the best alternative may be a yin/yang approach viewing the former as masculine and the latter as feminine (Reinharz, 1993), and acknowledging the strengths and weaknesses of both.

Human Rights Documents
as a Means of Defining the Problem

A human rights/social justice approach to research is largely the same as the preceding hypothetical example of the easy-grade-seeking student. Robert Lifton (1967), in his classic work *Death in Life: Survivors of Hiroshima*, more eloquently described, research as a kind of recreation, urging researchers to take professional risks to confront great historical and other events that do not lend themselves to established approaches or categories of thought. Acknowledging his "delicate-Kafkaesque" (p. 8) position, as an American psychiatrist talking with Japanese survivors about their feelings toward the atomic blast, he nevertheless, after extensive introductions and exhausting hours walking on the hot Hiroshima streets, interviewed the *Hibakusha*, which means literally, "explosion-affected person," victims of the atomic blast. His extensive interviews revealed the *Hibakusha*'s tremendous sense of guilt, having survived when their families and friends had died needlessly.

Lifton's work is striking in his willingness to tackle difficult questions and risk professional confrontation. He does not mention human rights documents in *Death in Life*. That needn't be a weakness, yet incorporating human rights would have highlighted the urgency of the problem. The concept of nondiscrimination based on national or social origin in Article 2 of the Universal Declaration and right to life in Article 3 are fundamental human rights precepts, both violated by the bombing of Hiroshima. Defining the research problem is one of the most difficult tasks for a research project. Human rights principles could provide tools for defining the problem and researching it with qualitative and/or quantitative approaches.

Closer to home, Americans seem to now be working longer hours than their parents, with barely enough time for family or the pursuit of leisure activities necessary for the development of the human personality and the enhancement of human dignity. We have an intuitive sense that this is a problem, but human rights documents can legitimize this feeling that humans need social interaction with their families and friends and time to rest from work and time for renewal by concretely defining the problem. A researcher could refer to Article 24 of the Universal Declaration: "Everyone has the right to rest and leisure, including reasonable limitation of working hours and periodic holidays with pay." Or one could refer to one or a few of the human rights conventions that followed the Universal Declaration, like CESCR's Article 7, which speaks of "remuneration which provides all workers with . . . a decent living for themselves and their families . . . safe and healthy working conditions . . . [and] rest, leisure and reasonable limitation of working hours and periodic holiday with pay." Researchers could engage in vast epidemiological studies, select people randomly and survey them to determine the number of hours worked, comparing this with data of an earlier generation. That would be a longitudinal survey. In the qualitative approach, they can also ask people if and how they spend time with their families. They could also ascertain if quality time with one's family had increased, although the quantity of time spent had decreased.

The only difference between the first example of the student and the second on right to rest and leisure is that human rights documents in the latter served as a way to define our problem. What we research is as important as how. We may have an intuitive sense of what must be done to get good grades, but human rights research, with human rights documents as guides, can be ways to easily, clearly, and most important, *persuasively* define the problem. Recall that no government wants their citizens to believe they have abrogated human rights! Article 24 of the Universal Declaration and Article 7 of CESCR are clear about the human right to rest and leisure and periodic holidays with pay.

Researchers could show governments how they are doing in regard to this basic human right, share their knowledge with the intellectual community, and develop social action strategies to realize that fundamental freedom.

The Challenge of the Interdependency of Rights

As human rights are interdependent and indivisible, a major challenge in researching a right is acknowledging its interdependence and integrating it with other rights. Social research has found, for instance, that lack of stress can be stressful (Selye, 1978). Watching TV for hours, strolling the malls for hours, or hanging out at a street corner or bar till the early morning hours may be enjoyable for awhile, but forever? Essential to the human condition are human needs to produce, participate in community building, and be part of a team, which can be done in a work setting.[1] Then, of course, as workers we need time to rest, and voilà . . . "the right to periodic holidays with pay."

One may have sympathy with students entering a university program, but the energies spent on finding ways to outsmart what is perceived as a political game may be futile. Why care only about grades in the first place? Are easy graders the same as good teachers? Teachers prone to anger students by opposing killing strangers in faraway lands in wars they consider unjust or by quoting thinkers like Karl Marx, often vilified in academia and the media, might be good teachers but have mediocre student evaluations. Getting back to those hypothetical students, they might have found their college experience was rather superficial. Other students may have followed their bliss, studying with whomever they pleased, without a concern for grades. Those who followed their bliss may have received mediocre grades. But they knew that attitude, when the time came, was the prime predictor of landing a job and were more successful anyway. Some who had to work at two jobs, raise a child alone, or care for an ailing relative during college may have become streetwise later in life, making up for nonstellar academic performances by publishing in mainstream journals and engaging in good and solid networking.

Acknowledging the interdependency of rights in this hypothetical situation, one might use the Universal Declaration as a guide, to explore a possible relation between pressure for good grades and a "social and international order . . . in which rights can be realized" (Article 28). The pressures on students to perform exceptionally well may force them to put their family life on the back burner and give up a part-time job; and professors, especially adjuncts, may have limited protections in their jobs to protect them against subtle pressures to be easy graders. Student debt may follow students throughout their lives, and the jobs they get may leave them barely able to find the time and social supports to engage in social action. The social order is neither easily recognizable nor easily measurable.

The Human Dimension Behind Knowledge

What, then, is a researcher concerned about human rights and social justice, who wishes to integrate notions of the interdependency of rights, supposed to do? A first suggestion is to acknowledge that behind any statistical analysis is always a qualitative world of meaning, the instruments themselves often interfering with the very phenomenon they are used to investigate. This is known as the Heisenberg Uncertainty Principle. Heisenberg wanted to measure the speed of electron in its natural state. But the only way to observe an electron was through a light source, which immediately affected the electron's speed. Electrons can't speak, but humans can. That is why researchers must always be open to the voices of those whose reality they think they are defining in a statistical matrix. Even as researchers talk with people, however, their presence will affect their findings in some way. Practice Illustration 5.1 addresses this issue with my reflections on doing research in Cuba.

Practice Illustration 5.1
Reflections on Research in Cuba

When researching social policy in nonmarket countries, and more particularly the mental health/substance abuse system in Cuba in the late 1980s, I was allowed to walk anywhere I wanted and speak with whomever I pleased. I went there as part of a field trip sponsored by the School of Social Work at Boston College. I was very impressed to see pictures of the Havana Mental Hospital before the revolution of 1959 when Fidel Castro came to power, which showed many patients clothed in rags sleeping in tight quarters, on tattered mattresses with visible springs. After the revolution, the mental hospitals were set in clean landscaped lawns, with patients in well-lit, well-ventilated quarters with soft beds. Psychoanalysis— seen as an elitist treatment modality—was not practiced there, I was told; rather, work therapy was the primary treatment.

At that time, numerous articles were being published in the *New York Times* about the abuse of psychiatry in Soviet hospitals, where dissidents were often diagnosed as mentally ill and sometimes shuttled off to the Gulag, an area nearly the size of France to which rapists, murderers, and the like were exiled. On sharing this information with health personnel in Cuba, I was told that this alleged abuse of psychiatry in the Soviet Union was all lies. At that time Cuba and the Soviet Union were strong allies and reacted strongly to negative criticism of each other. Mental health personnel told me that substance abuse was not a major problem in Cuba, certainly not like in Puerto Rico, a U.S. colony where alcoholism and heroin addiction were major concerns. "Alcohol is just not a profitable industry here. . . . Therefore, we have no alcoholism."

People did tell me that excessive criticism of Castro was not allowed, but in the same breath, they said: "But he gave us everything. Things were so bad before the revolution. Today, we have health care, no homelessness, and security in old age. You think that because of your constitution, you have human rights, because you have a right to criticize government officials. But we have no reason to criticize him. What did your government give you?" I thought of the estimated 3 million homeless in the United States; our elderly having to choose between medication and food; and the roughly 47 million who had no health insurance.

To this day, I am not sure if the information given would have been different if persons interviewed didn't know I was an American. Cuban people were exceptionally *simpatico* (somehow the English "nice" doesn't quite express their wonderful hospitality) to all of us Americans, perhaps indicative of the Cuban commitment to *internationalism,* that is, a concern for all humanity whatever the person's national origin. During my 2 weeks there, I observed (and observation is a form of research) *not one* shopping mall, but only *one* homeless person. "He has a civil right to be homeless," said a professor teaching French to Cuban doctors going to Angola. I also saw *hospital, after hospital, after hospital,* dotting the landscape much as malls do in the United States. Health personnel commented proudly that health care was free, actually paid for by taxes, and motivated by a concern for the common good. Every hotel even had its own doctor.

If one considers that the right to life is a fundamental human right (Article 3 of the Universal Declaration), and that to realize this right, we mustn't discriminate on the basis of "political opinion" (Article 2 of the Universal Declaration), can the U.S. decision to turn down Cuba's offer of approximately 600 doctors to help the victims of Katrina be justified? Despite political differences, human lives must never be used as pawns, and Cuban medical personnel are exceptionally well trained in hurricane humanitarian disaster relief. How many lives could they have saved? Is not the right to life fundamental to all major religious teachings, ethical codes, and basic precepts of social justice?

Nearly 20 years later, having attended the first 2 days of the Human Rights Council meeting in Geneva in March 2007 as an official observer for the International Federation of Social Work, I found it noteworthy that the speech by Cuba's Minister of Foreign Affairs, Mr. Felipe Perez Roque, lambasted the United States for its unwillingness to provide continuing support for its Special Rapporteur on the Right to Food, in a world, he said, "where 852 million people are starving" (p. 3). He continued:

Faced with the reality of international torture centers as the one established in the U.S. Naval Base of Guantanamo and the operation of secret flights for the kidnapping and movement of people through Europe in order to be tortured in underground jails, how could we allow the mandate of the Rapporteur on Torture to be discontinued. . . . How could we turn our backs on the tens of thousands of families that are still demanding justice and the right to the truth on their missing or executed relatives during the military dictatorships imposed and supported by Washington in Latin America. . . . As long as the Palestinian people is prevented from its right to establish its own State and the

Israeli occupiers continue to engage in the serious harassment of the civilian population in the occupied territories, this Council will not be able to do without this relevant issue. . . . We will know how to represent a people that has been able to endure and overcome the aggression of the Empire for nearly five decades, which has resisted with dignity and steadfastness the tightening of the genocidal blockade. (Roque, 2007, pp. 4–5)

I noticed that he received a long and loud applause, totally different from reactions to other government speeches. While I continue to be critical of Castro's endorsement of the death penalty and skeptical of the state of freedom of expression in Cuba, my experiences there and later the positive response at the UN, only reinforced by Michael Moore's observations in his film *Sicko* (2007), strongly suggest that this small island overall has positively taken up the struggle for social justice, especially in regard to economic, social, cultural, and solidarity rights. The challenge is to humanize those we consider the "enemy" and humbly engage in a respectful, creative dialogue to learn from each other how to fulfill human rights for all, ultimately leading us back to the Golden Rule, "to do unto others."

I also recall my then 9-year-old son, Chris, struggling feverishly to get his woolen ski hat off on returning from school on a cold New England day, looking up at me and saying: "Whew! It's over. I feel great!" "What's over?" I asked, looking down at this 40-pound, 4-foot some-odd-inches boy, cheeks chafed red from his woolen hat and still catching his breath from running in from the cold. With apparent utter exasperation, he said, "The MCAS.[2] We had tests all week!" Two years later, my daughter Carolyn, assigned to make a card with reasons for liking her parents, listed one reason that "my dad said 'don't worry,' you'll do OK on the MCAS." Both incidents illustrate a tremendous preoccupation with that exam.

The MCAS, like other standardized tests, is based on research and designed to determine each child's standing in comparison with other children of the same age. Yet the question remains if such tests measure achievement, or merely a person's class and level of opportunity. Furthermore, if a child is watching the snow fall, as many children do when the tests are administered, wouldn't that affect the results? The point is that everything we do has a social and environmental context, which research ought to at least acknowledge. We also need to question whether the way that knowledge is taught and assessed encourages the right to education, which would include "the full development of the human personality and . . . the strengthening of respect for human rights . . . [and does it] promote understanding, tolerance and friendship among all nations, racial or religious groups" (Article 26 of the Universal Declaration). Does education also encourage the "right to know one's rights," a fundamental tenet of the new Declaration on the Right to Education?

The Researcher as Searcher of Truth

It is a truism that a researcher must be a person in search of truth. Ultimately, research must go back to square one, struggling with the most fundamental issue of life: What is Truth? It must bring to light fundamental questions of existence posed by the Oracles at Delphi: Who am I? Why am I here? Where am I going? And how am I going to get there? Those are the essential questions, but researchers too easily resort to elitist language—f-tests, t-tests, laws of probability, log of the odds, chi-square, Spearman's rho in quantitative methodology; heuristic methodology, grounded theory, meaning constituents, and dynamicities in qualitative approaches. Such technical terms infiltrate the research landscape like an ominous cloud of locusts swarming over people who simply want to understand the enigma of human existence, to live the best way possible, cultivating their garden to the best of their ability.

Research can be a terminological quagmire of misunderstanding that prevents our free movement to explore the world unfettered with conceptual baggage. But locusts, f-tests, and dynamicities can serve a purpose in helping us understand the world, as long as we know the danger that always lurks in any crisis, if one acknowledges an ongoing tension between sometimes lofty conceptual tools of a discipline and their ostensible goals to improve the quality of life. There is also unlimited opportunity if one uses research tools wisely. The Sanskrit term for crisis means both danger and opportunity. It may come as no surprise, for instance, that in matching up statistics of infant mortality with incidences of violence, one finds that high infant mortality rates, a proxy for lack of female and child participation in policy making, are correlated with racism, unemployment, poor environment, lack of access to health care—that is, human rights violations in general are prime predictors of violence in a community. Using quantitative and qualitative means, avoiding the dangers of easy retreat to elitist language and an expert-oriented mentality, researchers can obtain information to use wisely in working to undo sexism, ageism, racism, and an unjust social and international order inimical to the fulfillment of human need.

The Universal Declaration of Human Rights Project

These introductory comments stress that research is merely a more rigorous way of understanding the world through quantitative and qualitative approaches that need to take into account social-environmental contexts and use human rights documents as a frame of reference. This section presents the Statement of Purpose of The Universal Declaration of Human Rights Project, which originated in the Center for Social Change at Brandeis University's Heller School. Here it is (Practice Illustration 5.2) with slight modifications, but written initially with Dr. David Gil, who serves as primary consultant to the project. Although this project considers other human rights documents, the Universal Declaration is the authoritative definition of human rights standards, from which all other human rights documents flow. A major aim of human rights work is to expand awareness of at least the Universal Declaration to inspire informed debates on ways to fulfill human need.

Practice Illustration 5.2
The Universal Declaration of Human Rights Project

The Universal Declaration of Human Rights Project

Statement of Purpose

The purpose of this action-research project is to assess progress toward compliance with human rights standards as defined by the Universal Declaration of Human Rights and its progeny, the human rights declarations and conventions which follow it. The Universal Declaration, adopted without dissent by the United Nations General Assembly on December 10, 1948, is gradually being perceived as *customary international law,* which all peoples of the world must abide. International conventions which have the status of treaty must also be considered "law of the land . . . and the judges bound thereby," as asserted in the Supremacy Clause, Article VI of the U.S. Constitution.

Project Aims:

A. Expanding awareness of the Universal Declaration and human rights documents which followed it, as a frame of reference for assessing progress toward the realization of internationally acknowledged human rights;

B. Studying public discourse and actions of legislative, judicial, and executive branches of governments, concerning compliance with standards set by the Universal Declaration and its progeny, in order to trace transformations of human needs into legally acknowledged and enforceable rights;

C. Expanding peoples' awareness of, and concern with, apparent significant violations of human rights standards as defined by the Universal Declaration and its progeny and suggesting potential avenues to overcome them.

While supporting the goals of all human rights organizations, this project, acknowledging the interdependency and indivisibility of rights and that rights entail corresponding duties, concerns itself with the vision as enunciated in the Universal Declaration and subsequent human rights documents. It will concentrate especially on economic, social, and solidarity rights contained in the Universal Declaration, because those rights are often neglected, even when civil and political rights are assured.

This project recognizes the global scope of the issues it addresses, but will focus initially upon advances toward the realization of human rights in the United States. Attempts will be made to stimulate similar projects in other countries, and to cooperate with such projects as they evolve.

Human rights/social justice research and social action and service initiatives emanating from it are inseparable and should inform the other levels of intervention. Research might examine the extent to which educational curricula, federal and state constitutions, administrative fiat, and clinical practice integrate human rights principles, and suggest ways to incorporate them in a lived way. It is important to alert the world in oral, written, or other creative format to these findings. Before giving specific examples of quantitative and qualitative approaches, we need to examine the importance of informed consent in doing research.

Toward a Culture of Informed Consent

The use of informed consent in contemporary research protocols emanated from atrocities committed by Nazi medical personnel, who were prosecuted at the Nuremberg Trials and sentenced on August 20, 1947. The court considered experiments that included, but were not limited to, freezing, infection with malaria, exposure to mustard gas and sea water, sterilization, and poisoning. Health personnel would, for example, force subjects to remain in a tank of ice water for periods up to 3 hours; inject malaria into healthy concentration camp inmates to test various drugs' efficacy; deprive subjects of food, then give them only chemically processed sea water; experiment on inmates with x-rays, surgery, and various drugs to develop a suitable method for mass sterilizations with a minimum of time and effort; and secretly administer poison to experimental subjects in their food (Sebring, Beals, & Crawford, 1999) Social workers also complied with such fascist exclusionary policies of that period, the "profession's unwitting service as pawns of the Nazi state" (Lorenz, 1994, as cited in Van Wormer, 1997, p. 176). Such studies resulted in unspeakable physical and mental anguish and pain. Fifteen of the 23 defendants were found guilty; 7 sentenced to death by hanging, and the rest to serve varying times in prison up to life imprisonment. The only female defendant, Herta Oberheuser, was given 20 years (Sebring et al., 1999).

Most astonishing was that such experiments were not isolated, casual acts of health personnel working solely on their own responsibility. They were the products of coordinated governmental policy making! The trial resulted in basic principles that satisfied the highest standards of public morality, ethics, and legal codes. Principle I of the Nuremberg Judgment is quoted fully here, because its legacy is perhaps the most readily apparent in ethical codes on the research of human subjects. The notion of "subject" may also pose some difficulty as it implies being subjected to the researcher's manipulation and control. The very act of getting information from someone may itself be inimical to human dignity. Certainly it may be seen as robbing if it is done without the person's or coresearcher's informed consent. Principle I states:

> The voluntary consent of the human subject is absolutely essential. This means that the person involved should have legal capacity to give consent; should be so situated as to be able to exercise free power of choice, without the intervention of any element of force, fraud, deceit, duress, overreaching, or other ulterior form of constraint or coercion; and should have sufficient knowledge and comprehension of the elements of the subject matter involved as to enable him to make an understanding and enlightened decision. This latter element requires that before the acceptance of an affirmative decision by the experimental subject there should be made known to him the nature, duration, and purpose of the experiment; the method and means by which it is to be conducted; all inconveniences and hazards reasonably to be expected; and the effect upon his health or person which may possibly come from his participation in the experiment. The duty and responsibility for ascertaining the quality of the consent rests upon each individual who initiates, directs, or engages in the experiment. It is a personal duty and responsibility which may not be delegated to another with impunity. (Sebring et al.,1999, p. 298)

Other Nuremberg principles state that a study should yield fruitful results, unprocurable by any other methods; it should be designed to avoid all unnecessary physical and mental suffering; the degree of risk should never exceed that determined by the humanitarian importance of the problem; the highest degree of skill by qualified personnel should be required through all stages of the experiment; the human subject should be at liberty to bring the study to an end; and the person in charge must be prepared to terminate the study if there is positive cause to believe that continuation will likely result in injury, disability, or death (Sebring et al., 1999).

Fast-forward to the Tuskegee studies in which 400 African American men infected with syphilis were monitored for 40 years (1932–1972) despite availability of a proven cure by the 1950s. Helping and health professionals may be aghast at this blatant violation of the right to life, believing we have moved beyond such experimentation, but medication studies continue to be practiced on subjects in Third World countries. For example, Johns Hopkins (1999) conducted studies in Africa in which pregnant women with HIV were randomly assigned to groups, one of which was given a placebo. The women assigned to this group had double the rate of transmission of the virus from mother to child! Cornell (1999) also conducted a study in Haiti that offered HIV tests and treatment to subjects, but denied the best treatment to study the progression of the disease (Wronka, 2001b). With continued debates over whether widely used antidepressants cause suicide, the inclusion of Pfizer in the Dow Jones Industrial Average, and recent lowering of the informed consent standard for prison inmates, it is questionable whether a culture that often places profit above human need, rights, and dignity has truly moved beyond Tuskegee.

Generic Points in the Construction of an Ethics Consent Form

In spite of the legacy of Nuremberg and revolt over Tuskegee, continued questionable ethical practices among the helping and health professions and a profit-oriented society may necessitate emphasis on informed consent and adherence to the humanistic thrust of human rights documents. The following generic points should be considered in constructing an Ethics Consent Form.

First, it might be more appropriate to refer to **coresearchers** rather than human subjects (subjected perhaps?). The concept of coresearcher is more amenable to the notion of human interconnectedness. Or, if the term "human subjects" is used, it should be with a sense of the need to arrive at mutual understandings with the person studied in ways consistent with human dignity and rights. Second, the purpose of the research protocol should be fully explained in **words that coresearchers can understand**. Third, they must also know the **length, time, and duration** of the project, or perhaps more accurately stated, coproject. Fourth, there must be **full information of possible risks, as well as benefits**. Certainly researchers must be attentive to these risks throughout the project, terminating it if coresearchers appear to be experiencing excessive emotional strain. Coresearchers must know, therefore, that there are safeguards, such as counseling, if they need it. Every effort must be made to minimize risks. Fifth, coresearchers must be aware of possible **remuneration for their time,** at minimum, a token compensation illustrative of the value of their time and viewpoints. Sixth, given that all research has hidden agendas, whether for the researcher to obtain a master's, PhD, promotion, or tenure or to fulfill requirements for a grant, **coresearchers must be aware of these possible hidden agendas,** including an understanding of the researcher's credentials.[3] Seventh, coresearchers need to know who will have **access to the data** and how these data will be used. Finally, they need to have relevant **contact information** for the researcher and an institutional review board (IRB) that might oversee the project. It goes without saying that researchers should be truly concerned about the human dignity of coresearchers; that the research be conducted in safe and secure premises; and that coresearchers have the option to stop the project at any time, no questions asked.

An IRB must also be competent to monitor the study. Members must not have conflicts of interest. Testing the effectiveness of a medication is verboten if the IRB has ties to pharmaceutical companies who market the drug. Researchers also must not go IRB shopping and have the responsibility to ask if the board members have any conflicts of interests. In cases of perceived possible conflict, they have a duty to rectify the situation in the spirit of understanding, tolerance, and friendship as asserted in Article 26 of the Universal Declaration. As helping and health professionals, researchers must always be on guard not to get lost in the banality of evil, a dulling of the mind and senses to the violence inflicted on the human person in the name of the search for knowledge and truth.

Quantitative Research

The etymology of the word *quantitative* is from *quantus*, meaning "of what size, how great." Quantitative research primarily deals with measurement, concepts of what and how to measure constantly haunting the *polis*, community members struggling to create a better life (Stone, 2001). But finding a number, like the score on an achievement or IQ test, a personality profile, or a person's temperature or blood pressure, does not necessarily constitute understanding the person. On the macro scale, knowing a country's per capita income and Gross National Product may be one way to measure its wealth, but this information will not necessarily help in assessing human happiness there. Similarly, knowing the number of state constitutions that incorporate particular rights like health care or security in old age may be of severely limited value if these rights are not implemented. Qualitative data that help us understand people, assess human happiness, and evaluate the implementation of rights in the community are important. Yet quantitative indices, though limited, can also give much-needed information. Numerical indices, statistics, can provide easily measurable and recognizable standards (the word *statistics* is from the Latin *stare*, meaning "to stand") with which one can assess progress in mathematical terms.

The objectives of the American Association for the Advancement of Science (AAAS) are to further scientific understanding, facilitate cooperation among scientists, foster scientific and academic freedom and responsibility, improve the effectiveness of science in promoting the general welfare, advance education in science, and "increase public understanding and appreciation of the importance and promise of the methods of science in human progress" (Spirer & Spirer, 1993, p. xiv). In its publication *Data Analysis for Monitoring Human Rights* (Spirer & Spirer), AAAS expresses the importance of mathematics and statistics for the social activist. Statistics is needed in human rights work to "get the message across to the public, governments, world bodies, non-governmental organizations and the media; make successful presentations in legal cases; assess the magnitude and scope of human rights violations; find patterns of human rights violations that can target perpetrators, regions, victim groups etc., give a basis for decisions and recommendations" (p. 1). Statistics create good visibility, helping others to see the situation as a human rights defender does; provide good credibility, if they are accurate; and lead to understanding, which is largely the capacity to develop general statements from the data.

One often hears that statistics lie. True, total objectivity is a myth. Numbers can easily be manipulated and the human rights defender/social activist must be willing to be a scholar, going beyond mere numbers. Examining government statistics on unemployment, as a case in point, a person is counted as employed if he or she works 1 hour per week in a formalized work setting (Wronka, 1998a). One can easily see that such a method of counting could inflate the actual employment numbers, making an incumbent politician look good. However, using human rights principles as a guide, and taking into consideration the interdependency of rights, a person is actually employed if the work situation has favorable conditions; fair remuneration; the right to join trade unions; adequate time off; benefits, such as medical care and protection in the event of unemployment; and pensions to guarantee security in old age. The challenge is to create ways of including such human rights variables in research that would truly inform the policy debates in ways that enhance human dignity and social justice.

Numbers can give a dimension of reasonableness that ought not be dismissed lightly. But the figures should be based on fundamental freedoms and human rights. For example, I did a content analysis of the U.S. Constitution, as a study of a legislative movement, as stated in the preceding Statement of Purpose, toward compliance with the document increasingly considered customary international law, the Universal Declaration. Comparing the federal Constitution with the Universal Declaration, though not corresponding precisely, various phrases nevertheless agreed in substance and sense; however, this textual comparison found the following phrases and substantive portions of crucial notions in the Universal Declaration *absent* in the U.S. Constitution: human dignity, rights to an effective remedy, the importance of the family as the fundamental unit of society, special protections for motherhood and children, and almost every economic, social, and cultural right, such as rights to work, favorable conditions of work, and favorable remuneration for work, right to join trade unions, rights to rest and leisure, and rights to food, clothing, housing, medical care, security in old age, education, and participation in the cultural life of the community. The only positive freedom in the Constitution was protection of an author's interests. There was also no mention of solidarity rights. The "equal protection clause," furthermore (Amendment XIV of the U.S. Constitution), is really a rather "weak" way of asserting the need for nondiscrimination related to gender, race, class, and national origin as enunciated in the Universal Declaration. The Constitution, however, was exceptionally strong in the areas of civil and political rights and freedoms of speech, the press, religion, and peaceful assembly (see Wronka, 1998b).

Heeding former Supreme Court Justice Louis Brandeis's assertion that states should act as "laboratories of democracy" to extend rights not found in the U.S. Constitution, I continued the comparison with all 50 state constitutions.

Though the federal Constitution contained no explicit statements concerning nondiscrimination based on such characteristics as race or gender, states were more definitive about such categories. The grid in Table 5.1 depicts those states that incorporate categories of discrimination consistent with the spirit of the Universal Declaration. It is important to recall that the Universal Declaration asserts an important, but only select group of characteristics. More work is necessary to cover other areas of discrimination, such as sexual orientation, medical condition, family makeup, or marital status. The table displays phrases in state constitutions that correspond with rights in the Universal Declaration.

Table 5.2 shows which states are in compliance with select economic, social, and cultural rights of the Universal Declaration.

Figure 5.1   Supreme Court Justice Louis Brandeis. Brandeis felt that
               government was our omnipresent teacher and wanted states to act
               as laboratories for democracy to extend rights not found in the
               U.S. Constitution.

Table 5.1 A Human Rights Grid Depicting States' Compliance With Nondiscrimination as Defined by the Universal Declaration of Human Rights

State	Race	Color	Sex	Religion	Political Opinion	National Origin	Property	Birth	Physical Handicap	Aliens	Disability	Social Origin
AL												
AK	X	X	X	X		X						
AZ				X								
AR												
CA												
CO												
CT	X	X	X	X		X			X			
DE												
FL	X			X					X			
GA												
HI	X		X	X		X						
ID												
IL			X									
IN												
IA												
KS												
KY												
LA	X		X	X	X	X		X	X			
ME												
MD												
MA	X	X	X	X		X					X	
MI	X	X		X		X				X		
MN												
MS												

(Continued)

Table 5.1 (Continued)

State	Race	Color	Sex	Religion	Political Opinion	National Origin	Property	Birth	Physical Handicap	Aliens	Disability	Social Origin
MO												
MT	X	X	X	X	X							X
NE												
NV												
NH												
NJ												
NM												
NY	X	X		X								
NC	X	X		X		X						
ND												
OH												
OK												
OR												
PA												
RI	X		X						X			
SC												
SD												
TN												
TX	X	X	X	X		X						
UT												
VT												
VA	X	X	X	X		X						
WA												
WV												
WI												
WY	X	X	X									

Table 5.2   A Human Rights Grid of States' Compliance With Select Economic, Social, and Cultural Rights of the Universal Declaration of Human Rights

State	Right to Work	Favorable Conditions of Work	Favorable Remuneration for Work	Right to Join Unions	Rest	Limitation of Working Hours	Importance of the Family	Food	Clothing	Housing
AL										
AK			X							
AZ						X				
AR										
CA										
CO						X				
CT										
DE										
FL			X	X						
GA							X			
HI				X						
ID							X			
IL										
IN										
IA										
KS										
KY										
LA										
ME										
MD										
MA										
MI										
MN										
MS										
MO			X	X						
MT						X				
NE										
NV										
NH										
NJ				X						
NM										
NY				X		X				
NC			X							
ND										
OH										
OK			X							
OR			X							
PA										
RI										
SC										
SD										
TN										
TX										
UT		X								
VT										
VA										
WA										
WV										
WI										
WY		X								

Medical Care	Security in Old Age	Special Care for Motherhood	Special Care for Children	Education	Respect for Human Rights in Education	Right to Cultural Participation	Right to Share in Scientific Advancement	Right to a Just Social and Int'l Order	Need for Duties
				X					X
				X					
				X					
				X					
				X					
				X					
				X					
				X					
				X		X			X
				X					
X				X					X
				X					
				X					
				X					
X				X		X			
				X					
				X					X
									X
				X					
				X					
				X					
				X					
				X		X			X
				X					
				X					
									X
				X					
				X					
				X					
				X					
				X					
				X					
				X					
				X					
				X					
				X					X
				X					
				X					
				X					
				X					
				X					X
				X		X			X
				X					
				X					
				X					
				X					

Researchers can also review the constitution of one state, as I've done with my present home state of Massachusetts (Table 5.3), and show in tabular format how it is doing in regard to the rights defined by the Universal Declaration.

Pictorial images can also be powerful tools to get one's point across and move others to social action. During the 1980s, at the height of the

Table 5.3   Correspondence of the Massachusetts Constitution With Select Human Rights Principles of the Universal Declaration of Human Rights

Human Right	Massachusetts
Race	X
Color	X
Sex	X
Religion	X
Political opinion	
Disability	X
Physical handicap	X
Right to work	
Favorable conditions of work	
Favorable remuneration for work	
Right to join unions	
Rest	
Limitation of working hours	
Importance of the family	
Food	
Clothing	
Housing	
Medical care	
Security in old age	
Special care for motherhood	
Special care for children	
Education	
Respect for human rights in education	
Right to cultural participation	
Right to share in scientific advancement	
Right to a just social and international order	
Need for duties	X

Cold War between the Soviet Union and the United States, an Atomic Clock was displayed with a minute hand that would move either closer or farther away from midnight, the initiation of nuclear war, depending on the mood of the time, that is, the tensions between the two superpowers. Whether it was successful in halting a hot war is questionable, but the image was compelling. A Human Rights/Social Justice Scale depicting the imbalances between rights in the Universal Declaration and those in the U.S. Constitution, such as that in Figure 5.2, could also be a powerful image.

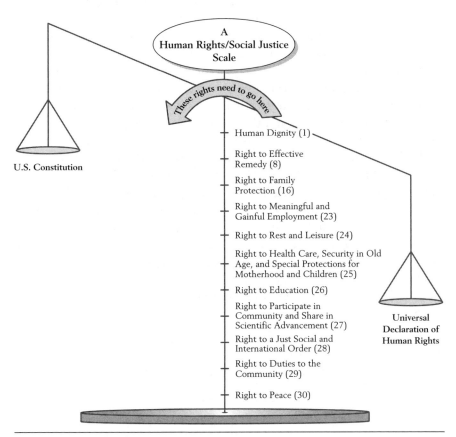

Figure 5.2   The Scales of Justice Depicting a Relationship Between the Universal Declaration and the U.S. Constitution. The challenge is to create a human rights culture that would inevitably result in the incorporation of human rights principles into the federal Constitution.

Those tables and the figure are merely textual comparisons. They are important, certainly, a means of providing valuable information people need to decide for themselves whether their country and state are really committed to human rights. People coming to their own conclusions are perhaps the quintessential policy instrument (Stone, 2001). The possibilities for grids is almost endless. One could, for instance, depict similar comparisons with other international documents, such as the Protection of Persons With Mental Illness and Principles of Medical Ethics with governmental and domestic policy statements and documents. One might also compare ethical and other codes of the helping and health professions, defined as public discourse in the Statement of Purpose of the Universal Declaration of Human Rights Project. Public discourse is often a precursor to changes in government policy. Some documents may even go beyond human rights documents, which can stimulate open dialogue, expanding on definitions of social justice.

What is put on paper is not always implemented; on the other hand, one can behave decently toward others without written statements. Thus, another approach might be to merely list rights, such as health care, employment, and human dignity, and then show how the population is faring in that regard. For example, 46,577,000, or 15.9% of the U.S. population had no health insurance in 2005; 7,591,000 people in the United States were unemployed in 2005, equaling 5.1% of the population; 36,997,000 people in the United States, meaning 12.7% of our population, were living below the poverty level in 2005; 12,896,000 children lived in poverty, that is, 17.6%; and 13,494,000 people, 11.9%, experienced food insecurity[4] (U.S. Census Bureau, 2007). Table 5.4 depicts one way of relating this information, with the proviso of the interdependency of rights.

Hopefully, such tables can be used to expand the debate and assist in community organizing. Questions posed might be: Why doesn't the Universal

Table 5.4   U.S. Implementation of Select Human Rights Principles as Substantive to the Universal Declaration of Human Rights*

Human Right	Percentage Whose Right Is Violated	In U.S. Constitution?
Health care	15.9	No
Employment	5.1	No
Living wage	12.7	No
Well-being of children	17.6	No
Food	11.9	No

*Rights are interdependent, requiring governmental obligations to fulfill them.

Declaration mention discrimination based on sexual orientation and/or medical condition? What does it mean that the United States was a leader in its drafting, but is so negligent in providing some rights to its own citizens? How does the U.S. government count someone as employed? Given the interdependency of rights, is such a counting method consistent with human rights principles of just and favorable remuneration for work? How would one also depict other social malaises in the United States such as an additional 1% of unemployment translating into 3,300 commitments to state prisons and 37,000 early deaths (20,000 of those from heart attacks); one in three children having never seen a dentist; a ranking of 70th worldwide in preschool immunization rates (Anelauskas, 1999); or that one in four Americans has no paid vacation leave? ("Numbers," 2007). It is also useful to compare governmental with nongovernmental data. The Children's Defense Fund (2007), for example, reports that 18.1% of children experience food insecurity. Nothing substitutes for an open, respectful, honed discussion of the issues in a spirit of creative dialogue, and with the intent to guarantee human rights for all.

The preceding information only recounts federal and state constitutional legislation moving toward compliance with human rights standards. Federal and state judicial pronouncements are also concerned with such rights as health care, education, and security in old age. What did presidents, governors, mayors, federal and state judges, and legal cases say regarding human rights that might move us a little closer to a human rights culture? One example is President Clinton's Executive Order 13107 of December 10, 1998, which declared as law "all treaties ratified by the United States," which at that time included ICCPR, CERD, and CAT, further buttressing Article VI, the Supremacy Clause of the U.S. Constitution.

Referring to the Human Rights grids, a major challenge is to fill in the blanks, that is, to have the rights in human rights instruments taken seriously and implemented. It is always amazing that governments based on the will of the people are so often reluctant to provide for such rights. One would be hard pressed to find anyone—radical, liberal, or conservative—who is not in agreement with the principles of the Universal Declaration. Certainly people can have the right to health care, security in old age, special protections for motherhood and children, and the like without going through the rigmarole of human rights. If social justice can occur without human rights, so be it. Such a strategy ought to be encouraged. But, as I've argued throughout, the idea of human rights can move people. The next section looks at how we can use qualitative research to elicit the meaning of human experience to create social justice.

Qualitative Research

The etymological root of *qualitative* is *qualis,* meaning "of what sort, what kind of." It is one thing to know "the size" or "how great" something is, another to know "what kind" it is. For instance, the United States has the greatest Gross National Product in the world. But we need to know "what sort" of meaning this money has. Qualitative information is the meaning that one attaches to things, whether money, events, or situations. Phenomenologically speaking, humans are intentionalities, that is, they are always conscious *of* something (Moustakas, 1994; Sartre, 1957).

Things like money, or any object or situation, cannot be divorced from the meaning we attach to them. Without such meaning, a "thing" is like a tree falling with no one to hear it. In that sense, a tree does not make a sound, unless there is someone to hear it fall. Similarly, money may be meaningless to an Inuit, who lives a subsistence lifestyle; a subsistence lifestyle may be meaningless to a person of European ancestry who values money. Whereas money is generally viewed as a guarantee of happiness, *State of the World* reports that despite its riches, the United States has a general lack of connectedness among its people, showing less and less engagement in civic affairs and trust in government, declining membership in formal organizations, and even fewer informal interactions among friends and relatives such as playing cards, going on picnics, hanging out on stoops in urban areas on summer evenings, and the like. In the industrialized world, the United States has the highest levels of alienation (Gardner, Assadourian, & Sarin, 2004). Quantitatively, one therefore can assess income, but such an assessment is a mere statement of fact, if it is not viewed in a meaningful context.

The ultimate purpose of qualitative research is to elicit meaning, hence attunement to the voices of coresearchers within a culture of informed consent; any form of recreation that takes other viewpoints seriously could enhance human rights principles. Eliciting different voices is important, but any research that does not explicitly deal with numerical analysis can be called qualitative, though there is also some blurring. Results of questionnaires, for example, which are records of people's viewpoints, can easily be quantified. The more in-depth discussion of the issues in qualitative research, however, might ascertain meanings that instruments such as questionnaires alone cannot capture. Wisdom cannot be quantified, but it may be understood to some extent through questionnaires.

Qualitative research can take many forms, each with its own strengths and weaknesses, including: observation, participant observation, individual interviewing, focused group interviewing, document review, narrative, life and oral histories, historical analysis, film, questionnaires, psychological assessment, and unobtrusive measures. Observation has the strength of capturing the subject in a natural setting, and can be useful in obtaining data on non-verbal behavior and communication, providing contextual information, and facilitating nuances of meaning in culture; weaknesses might be that it is fraught with ethical dilemmas such as privacy, subject to the presence of the observer, and highly dependent on the researcher's resourcefulness, systematic approach, and honesty (Marshall & Rossman, 1999)

Whatever the specific strengths and weaknesses of the method used, data from qualitative research is suggestive, rather than definitive as the data from quantitative research, which can be generalized from a small random sample. Some argue that qualitative research has a more feminine orientation (Rheinharz, 1992), emphasizing cooperation over the more macho approach of quantitative methodology (e.g., rejecting the null hypothesis, manipulating and controlling variables, and generalizing to the entire human race from a small sample).

In essence, any eliciting of voices—bearing witness, in human rights/social justice circles—can be seen as qualitative. The rest of this section presents a few examples of the numerous ways of doing this. In the previous illustration of my research experience in Cuba, after 2 weeks' immersion in the country with freedom to speak with anyone and travel anywhere, I found that health care was readily available to everyone and homelessness was nearly nonexistent. It is difficult to imagine that by taking the same approach in the United States, with a per capita income more than five times that of Cuba, one would find adequate shelter and health care were available to all, principles of the Universal Declaration.

Toward Implementing Rights of Indigenous Peoples

Qualitative studies can be more formal. One example is a Michigan study on American Indian grandparents who are parenting their grandchildren (Gross, 2005). The study consisted of 31 individual interviews and 27 focus groups (an average of 9 per group). Although grandparents raising children is part of a growing phenomenon in the United States, as Gross points out, in Native American culture grandparents raising grandchildren is a long-held tradition. Elders are highly respected in the culture, and often viewed as historians, transmitters of culture and language. There is also a strong legacy of fear from centuries of Indian children being removed without informed consent to foster placements, often in white residences, where their identities were threatened.

Researchers first developed a comfort level between themselves and participants, who often invited them to attend fish fries, pow-wows, and art exhibits and repeatedly asked if they could come back. The following were the major findings of the study: (a) fewer than one third of participants found the Indian Child Welfare Act helpful; (b) parental issues, such as lack of day care, death, substance abuse, and teen pregnancy, necessitated the grandparents' involvement, which was further buttressed by cultural traditions; (c) parents still kept in contact with their children, though not on a day-to-day basis; (d) mistreatment at boarding schools was often discussed at length; and (e) some felt that grandparent support groups would be beneficial (Gross, 2005).

Many of these issues can easily be discussed within the context of human rights principles. First, there is a need for a just social and international order to realize human rights, as stated in the Universal Declaration (Article 28), like rights to work and education. If Native American communities have high unemployment rates, has government failed in establishing a just order? How is the educational system? Are there jobs for graduates? Second, documents following the Universal Declaration, like CEDAW, assert support groups, especially for rural women, as a human right, as well as quality day care. The ICCPR and CESCR address the right to self-determination in Article 1 in both conventions. Is the Indian community freely determining its political status and pursuing its economic, social, and cultural development? Based on the interviews, was genocide taking place, as defined in Article II of the Genocide Convention as "forcibly transferring children of one group to another group"? One could also look at the Draft Declaration on the Rights of Indigenous Peoples. Its principles, such as the "right to be educated . . . in a matter appropriate to cultural methods of teaching and learning" (Article 15), and government's responsibility for "special measures for immediate, effective and continuing improvement in economic conditions . . . in housing, sanitation, health, social security, and rights of indigenous elders, women, youth, children and disabled persons" (Article 22), support a persuasive argument that those in power have a duty to make available the necessary opportunities to realize the basic human rights of Indigenous Peoples, in this instance, Native Americans.

Student Projects Integrating Human Rights Into Qualitative Studies

Practice Illustration 5.3 shows how students have integrated human rights principles into their qualitative research projects.[5]

Practice Illustration 5.3
Examples Integrating Human Rights in Student Qualitative Projects

Interviewing four social workers and one psychiatrist, Diaz (2005), in his qualitative study of Views on Managed Care and Mental Health Productivity Standards, found "disempowerment encountered by practitioners" (p. 2) and that "billable productivity was not considered a factor that contributed to job satisfaction." Instead, aspects such as "the ability to establish an alliance, to increase coping skills, and to have the autonomy to make treatment recommendations were deemed more meaningful than billable units" (p. 12). He continues: "Human rights are relevant in social work practice. Senseless productivity standards that sacrifice the quality of care and silence the voices of practitioners do not assist in the development of a professional identity and self-esteem as social workers. . . . Article 22 of the UDHR affirms: Everyone, as a member of society, has the right to a social security and is entitled to realization, through national effort and international cooperation and in accordance with the organization and resources of each State, of the economic, social and cultural rights indispensable for his dignity and the free development of his personality" (p. 14). He concludes that "healers tend to measure their productivity by how many hearts they touch."

McQuillar (2005), in a qualitative study of the effects of schizophrenia on family relationships from the perspective of the person diagnosed with schizophrenia, cites that most of the literature on this topic was from the perspective of family members. Citing the Universal Declaration of Human Rights, that "all human beings are born and equal in dignity and rights. They are endowed with reason and conscience and should act toward one another in a spirit of brotherhood," she urges the need for more research in this area, concluding that, "because . . . individuals have developed a mental illness does not mean we take their dignity away by disregarding . . . their experience" (p. 13). Her coresearchers felt their families understood them better after they were given a diagnosis, but felt they and their families could still benefit from more education about their illness.

Foresta (2005) in examining the experience of child welfare workers, cited the Universal Declaration's Article 23, "the right to just and favorable conditions of work . . . [and] favorable remuneration"; Article 25, "Motherhood and childhood are entitled to special care and assistance"; and Article 28, "the right to a just social and international order," commenting that his coresearchers were all highly committed to helping children, but often felt overwhelmed by heavy caseloads and generally low pay. As Foresta states: "It is nothing short of miraculous that these coresearchers are able to assist children and families while operating in a context that consistently violates their human rights" (p. 18). Expressing the need for a human rights culture, which includes adequate health care, meaningful employment, and a standard of living worthy of "human dignity," all substantive to the Universal Declaration, he urges human rights advocacy for child welfare workers that would empower families, rather than the current system, which has "a series of punitive measures for 'faulty' parents" (p. 20).

Research Leading to Social Action

Human rights/social justice research that does not lead to action is meaningless. From the Latin *acts*, meaning "driving or moving," research that searches for truth must drive or move people to act. But acting doesn't necessarily have to be on a purely physical plane. Thinking is also acting, if changing one's thinking will eventually result especially in socially just actions. Recall Rev. Martin Niemoeller's (1892–1984) famous words inscribed on the New England Holocaust Memorial in Boston:

> They first came for the Communists, and I didn't speak up because I wasn't a Communist.
>
> Then they came for the Jews, and I didn't speak up because I wasn't a Jew.
>
> Then they came for the trade unionists, and I didn't speak up because I wasn't a trade unionist.
>
> Then they came for the Catholics, and I didn't speak up because I was a Protestant.
>
> Then they came for me, and by that time no one was left to speak up.

If people think it is all right to stay within their comfort zones, not to speak up, the action will most likely result in indifference. Similarly, if a person thinks that the United States is in the forefront in adherence to human rights principles, he or she may do nothing. But just knowing that research shows a lack of adherence can move someone to write on behalf of or speak up for those whose human rights are violated. The line between research and action is thin. This section discusses ways to get across information about human rights violations. There is no reason why evil must triumph because the good are silent.

Yet, when it comes to speaking, some cultures may find it egotistical, flamboyant, and genuinely downright rude to stand in front of an audience and lecture for an hour or two, a practice not that uncommon in academia. Such individuals may care about human rights and dignity, but unfortunately, the audience may not get that impression from the way they express themselves. There are also certain groups who may not have had adequate educational and other opportunities to learn to write well. Although it is important to acknowledge issues pertaining to diversity and opportunity, it is also necessary to acknowledge that the world may not be so sympathetic. It may not be a good idea to wait for the world to become compassionate about one's cultural background where opportunities to hone one's writing and speaking skills were severely limited. To do so would be like the vagabonds Estragon and Didi, in Samuel Beckett's *Waiting for Godot,* holding out for something to "give us the impression that we exist." The time to act is now to improve on writing and speaking skills, and be aware that the world in which we live may not be very accommodating. Whatever our reticence, there is an ethical obligation to share our understandings of the world through our experiences and research as a step to engage each other in dialogue. Individuals must come to these decisions in their meditative lives.

On Writing

When a person writes something, it is for the world to see. With the Internet, that it is literally true. The adage what comes around goes around is very pertinent when it comes to writing. If the writer cares enough to compose grammatically correct and flowing paragraphs, the reader will care enough to read them. Respecting the reader with diligent work will result in respect for the writer. Respect for the dignity of other persons is fundamental to human rights and social justice.

Practice Illustration 5.4 is from my home page. Although admitting much trepidation in writing something for the whole world to see, my overriding motivation was the need to get the word out about the importance of creating a human rights culture.

Practice Illustration 5.4
A Writing Example for a Home Page on the Internet

A human rights culture is a "lived awareness" of human rights principles among people throughout the world. By "lived awareness" I mean that the principles of such documents as the Universal Declaration of Human Rights are not known merely cognitively, that is, in the "head," but also on the feeling level, the "lived" level of the heart. It is not good enough for society to only "know," for example, that health care, shelter, and security in old age are human rights; it is important for a society to act on this knowledge in ways that can guarantee these rights for every person, everywhere. Issues, of course, are complicated. Every right does have a corresponding duty, according to the Universal Declaration, such that it can easily be said that what we are talking about is a culture of human duties. Thus, the right to health care requires the duty for each of us to keep healthy, eat correct foods or exercise, for instance. Yet we must remember that it is the duty of government to create a "social and international order," as stated also in the Universal Declaration, so that food is nutritious, accessible, culturally relevant at an affordable cost, and our towns and cities have ample opportunities for us to develop not only in body, but in mind and spirit as well.

Finally, as we shall see, such a culture will necessitate a "lived awareness" of the interdependency and indivisibility of rights. In other words, as organs of the human body function interdependently, so, too, do human rights. In brief, the right to health care, for example, is dependent on such rights as education (our health personnel must be educated), employment (they must receive a meaningful wage), and rest and leisure (they must have ample time to rest). What further complicates matters is what has become known as "cultural relativism." Thus, some cultures might believe that it is appropriate for a couple to be betrothed, rather than "choosing" each other, but choice of spouse is considered a human right according to the Universal Declaration. While we may also have a "knee jerk" response to condemn such cultures that engage in practices like female genital mutilation (FGM), we must recall the ancient injunction to examine the log in one's eye before plucking it from another's. Thus, some cultures condemning such practices may condone conditions resulting in deaths from anorexia nervosa or they may stockpiling weapons of mass destruction that threaten the basic human right to peace.

Creating a human rights culture, then, is a kind of paradox. On the one hand, we have the standards set out in major human rights documents drafted by the United Nations and to some extent regional organizations like the African Union, the Organization of American States, and the European Union. On the other hand, as Eleanor Roosevelt, Chairperson of the Drafting Committee of the Universal Declaration of Human Rights, said of the Universal Declaration of Human Rights, it was a "good document . . . not a perfect one," and human rights discussions cannot take place in a philosophic-historical vacuum. Perhaps it is our questioning together, acknowledging the importance of incorporating the voices of the oppressed in the policy debates, or what the philosopher Merleau-Ponty has called the "happiness of reflecting together," that may help us bring about such a culture where we treat one another with decency and human dignity.

There is no cookbook approach to writing. Famed author Aldous Huxley, whose wisdom the drafting committee of the Universal Declaration sought, wrote *Brave New World,* about an overly medicated and behaviorally manipulated society, and *Island,* about a land of sharing and caring, where the birds chirped, "Be here now." Huxley said that to write, one must get a pen and lots of paper and . . . well . . . write. Whereas there is a strong element of truth to Huxley's advice to just get on with it, commitments to human rights and social justice can take people beyond themselves. Writing, like any skill, must be practiced and honed, like learning a musical instrument. But if one loves what one is doing, it can just get better and better. The challenge is to choose what will be a labor of love. As Eric Fromm in his *Art of Loving* reminds us, love is willed. So, too, good writing is willed.

Some Suggestions

The first point is to only say something that must be said and use as few words as needed to express the point. In other words, **make every word count.** The sign "Buy your fresh fish here" bears that point. Obviously, they are selling fish. Would they sell stale fish? Is the fish being sold over there? No need for the sign at all, as one could smell the fish. Second, **it is important to do an inventory of rituals of procrastination** (Wolcott, 2001). When beginning to write, it is only too easy to start the laundry, pick up the remote, clean the house, or reach in the fridge for those final two scoops of Ben & Jerry's ice cream.

Third, **think display.** The reader shouldn't go fishing for the main points. Don't hide behind flamboyant language and long, involved sentences. They may give the impression of profundity, but your readers may not know what you're saying, but be afraid to admit their ignorance until one day, someone points out that the words are as naked as the emperor who had no clothes. Be forthright and easy to understand. Fourth, **write like you do math.** You must have good intrasentence, paragraph, and overall organization. Have subjects agree with the verb; all sentences support the paragraph's opening sentence, and good transitions from paragraph to paragraph. Everything must add up. Recall the five crucial notions in the Universal Declaration of Human Rights. They were listed one by one, with a brief discussion of the meaning of each.

Fifth, **integrate human voice with scholarship.** Writers are free to express their opinions, which should be based partly on experience, but also on scholarship, that is, the work of scholars in the field, preferably from peer review journals and those generally recognized as authorities. Then, it must all be put together with one's own personal style and in an interesting way. Sixth, **write so that the reader can take it in.** A case could easily be made that writing is an act of arrogance by an author, who expects the reader to plow through hundreds of pages of his or her wit, wisdom, and charm. But this attitude can be changed if the writers keep to the script, care about what they say, and write in ways that readers find reasonable. True, there may never be agreement on what is reasonable, but it is easy to spot an unreasonable person merely flouting opinions without context.

Seventh, **get feedback from others, but only after a near-final** copy. Otherwise, it suggests the writer wants someone else to do his or her work. Commit to rewrites, then, near the final copy, get feedback. Eight, **write something that stands the test of time.** It is here perhaps that integrating human rights into one's writing will make it eternal—yes, eternal, everlasting, timeless. Human rights and social justice often reflect millennia of social teachings of major spiritual systems regarding human dignity, nonviolence, duties to humanity, and getting out of one's comfort zone, a sine qua non of social action. Such issues are ancient and may very well be around till the end of time. The missions of major religious leaders, like Moses, Christ, Mohammad, and Buddha were all reflected, to varying degrees, in human rights principles. Ideally, one's writing, especially if it integrates human rights and social justice, shares this mission and sense of adventure. Finally, it is necessary to **care about one's writing,** which reflects caring about the world. It is a way to let your light shine, giving others the opportunity to shine theirs as well.

Practice Illustration 5.5 is an example of an editorial I wrote for a local paper, the *Amherst Bulletin,* about an Annual Reading of the Universal Declaration of Human Rights during human rights week in 2005.

Practice Illustration 5.5
Writing Example of an Editorial on
Human Rights for Every Person, Everywhere

Human Rights for Every Person, Everywhere

Soon, the Amherst Human Rights Commission will display its banner over South Pleasant which reads: "Human Rights for Every Person, Everywhere." The week of December 10th, the day that the Universal Declaration of Human Rights, the authoritative definition of human rights standards, was endorsed by the General Assembly in 1948 with no dissent, is globally recognized as human rights week. Although originally meant to be a hortatory document, urging governments to abide by its principles, today in this new millennium it is often referred to as *customary international law* not only in academic circles, but also a number of court cases, such as the case precedenting *Filartiga v. Pena-Irala* where U.S. federal judges ruled against a torturer for an act committed in Paraguay.

What are the principles of the Universal Declaration? Sadly, Eleanor Roosevelt's dream, that American school children will know about the Universal Declaration like they are aware of the American Bill of Rights, has not materialized. Thus, many Americans equate human rights with the Bill of Rights, a beautiful document indeed, but one that expresses only one facet of the entire body of what has become known as international human rights law, with the Universal Declaration at its core. In brief, the Universal Declaration consists of five crucial notions: (1) human dignity (Article 1); (2) non-discrimination (Article 2); (3) civil and political rights, like freedoms of speech, the press, religions, and peaceful assembly, and democracy in general (Articles 3–21); (4) economic, social, and cultural rights, like rights to health care, shelter, security in old age, meaningful and gainful employment, rest and leisure, and education (Articles 22–27); and (5) solidarity rights, the notion that every right has a corresponding duty and the right to a social and international order, from which rights to a clean environment, peace, humanitarian disaster relief, and international distributive justice get their sustenance (Articles 28–30).

What also needs emphasis is the fact that all rights are interdependent and indivisible. Thus, the third crucial notion, civil and political rights, which are largely consistent with the Bill of Rights and generally equated with human rights in this country, are ultimately meaningless without their "linkages" with the other sets of rights. Let me ask you: What is freedom of speech, to a person who is homeless, unable to provide for her or his family, and lives in a world at war? And, if rights are interdependent, can we rightfully speak of representative democracy, if it is an understatement that it often takes millions to run for major political offices, and that perhaps only the voices of the rich and powerful are heard?

Radical? Perhaps. After all, when asked if the Universal Declaration of Human Rights was dangerous to governments, Eleanor Roosevelt, who, it is often said, had "an FBI file larger than a stack of phone books," replied: "Yes. . . . Oh, yes"! But, if we are to truly get to the roots (and radical comes from the Latin *radix, radicis* meaning "root") of the matter, we need a cultural shift in values and the Universal Declaration of Human Rights may assist by expanding our awareness of what human rights truly are. So, our only criteria to have rights should not be based on whether a person is, for example, poor, rich, black, white, gay, lesbian, old or young to mention just a few ways that we tend to discriminate, or, for that matter, American, Iraqi, victims of a tsunami or earthquake, or the forty percent of the world who live on less than two dollars per day. The only criteria is that we are human, and every person, everywhere on this planet is a human, worthy of dignity, a notion that also mirrors millennia of teaching in most of the world's major spiritual belief systems.

We invite you to come to the reading of the Universal Declaration of Human Rights, followed by a candlelight vigil on the Amherst Common at 6 PM.

On Speaking

In human rights/social justice work, and particularly in the helping and health professions, it is often necessary to speak before groups. What good is it to keep one's thoughts to one's self? They must be communicated, a term that comes from the Latin, *communire,* meaning "to fortify, strengthen together." The human rights defender must communicate as a way of strengthening together. If a social activist is shy, time to get over it. But it may not be that simple. It might help to ask if being shy serves the aims to improve the human condition. It is always important to listen to one's inner muse.

Some Suggestions

After deciding on the importance of speaking in front of groups, reflecting on what it might mean culturally or ethically, it is important **first to have good diction,** enunciating words properly, slowly, loudly enough, and with a rhythm that is understandable to the audience. The Greek orator Demosthenes used to put pebbles in his mouth to improve his diction. That might have worked for him, but it might be better to just sit with a friend, share some words of a favorite text, and get feedback on the mechanics of your presentation.

But diction, proper volume, and cadence aren't everything. **Second, have a physical presence appropriate to your audience.** Dress respectfully for the occasion, establish eye contact, don't swing from side to side, and keep your hands out of your pockets. A good physical appearance is often important because when giving testimony, you may have only 2 or at most 15 minutes to get the point across. Many are loathe to admit, but literature consistently stresses that attractiveness, whatever that might entail in your specific culture, is very often a predictor of credibility. Don't ignore such findings. **Third, be interesting,** and funny if the occasion warrants. Nothing is worse than a boar! Yes, a play on words. A boar is a pig, but if someone is boring, he or she will literally muddle through a presentation at best. There is no need for that, especially nowadays when time is at a premium for almost everyone.

Putting aside for the moment that the Greeks had slaves and almost entirely excluded women from the democratic participation, their notions of *ethos* (ethics), *logos* (logic), and *pathos* (feeling) are seen as important to public speaking. But of those three, ethos, which simply means having an ethical character, was the most important. Therefore, **fourth, always be ethical.** It is obvious that no one will listen if the speaker is not considered trustworthy, fair, honest, and just. Over time, merely giving the appearance of possessing such attributes without having them will work against the public speaker. People will see the hypocrisy in the speaker's eyes and face. Eyes don't shine, wrote Emmanuel Levinas (2001), the philosopher of the face, "they speak." One needn't be perfect. But having a good ethical reputation might get the most points with the audience. If listeners see someone who puts needs of others before her or his own they are more likely to listen. Paradoxically, if one speaks with humility, people are more likely to listen. Such a speaker also knows that he or she can learn a lot from the audience. Paulo Freire, the educator/social activist, was good at sharing what he knew about philosophy or literature with the audience. But when speaking with farmers, he would ask what they knew about raising crops or agriculture. An honest give and take after a speech should further buttress one's sincerity and ethical reputation overall.

Fifth, the presentation must be logical (*logos*). Its argument must be sensibly and persuasively supported by facts. Both quantitative and qualitative data are persuasive in presenting a logical portrayal of facts. Research, for example, has demonstrated that low self-image and a poor high school experience are predictors of teenage pregnancy. Williams (1991), who administered a self-image scale to her coresearchers (30 in all) found the relationship between self-esteem and education to be statistically significant at the .0058 level. Those who were not enrolled or did not graduate high school (11) had a lower self-image than those who were enrolled or graduated high school (19). But she also integrated voices from coresearchers, with one remarking how poor her high school experience was. But the coresearcher said that in pregnancy school they treat you nice. Implications are the need for better schools, and taxes to pay for them, rather than malls, which outnumber high schools in the United States, and reasonable salaries for teachers. Recall that education, special protections for mothers and children, and reasonable wages are human rights.

Sixth, the presentation must have emotion (*pathos*). Putting one's heart into speaking might just create the fervor needed to light that spark in another's heart to work for human rights, dignity, and social justice for all. **Seventh, acknowledge your humanity.** Be mindful of Eleanor Roosevelt's words that the Universal Declaration was

> not a perfect document. . . . On the whole, however, it is a good document. We could never hope for perfection no matter how many times we revised the Declaration, for one could always see something a little better than one might do. (Department of Public Information, 1950, pp. 15–16)

In other words, the world could be on the verge of disaster, while the social activist is worrying whether the reader is going fishing or if sentences are grammatically correct. Defenders are human, like anyone else. When they feel they have done a good job, not a perfect one, it might be time to move on. Martin Luther King, Jr. had some wisdom to share on that point, as we will see at the end of Chapter 6.

Using the Media

The broadcast media also pose unique opportunities to relate to a broad spectrum of people. The key to speaking in the media is to establish a personal relationship with one person, the listener. Think of it as finding a way to read a telephone book and have the listener cry. As silly as that might sound, the kind of interaction characteristic of the broadcast media can be summed up in

Humphrey Bogart's classic words in the film *Casablanca,* "It's just me and you kid." The listener is in the living room or in the car, often alone with the speaker and engaging in a kind of inner personal dialogue with this one other person.

Don't kid yourself—the media can have tremendous influence. Going to and from work, it may be just you and the radio. Television personalities often have a subtle relationship with their viewers. The broadcasters during the holocaust in Rwanda, who referred to Tutsi as cockroaches, developed these personal relationships with their audience effectively. But they promulgated hate, leading to massacres of nearly 1 million in 3 months! The human rights defender will promulgate love, not hate. Speak in ways that are close-up and personal, not too fast, not too slow, but caringly and tenderly.

Examples of a Public Testimony and Presentation

In Practice Illustration 5.6, I would like to share an example of a testimony given in regard to the human rights bill discussed in Chapter 3. Note, it is important to always have contact information.

Practice Illustration 5.6
A Human Rights Testimony

Testimony for MA House Bill 706, June 7, 2005

Joseph Wronka, PhD, Board Member, Coalition for a Strong United Nations; Professor of Social Work, Springfield College; Principal Investigator of the Universal Declaration of Human Rights Project, Brandeis University, Heller School for Social Policy and Management
Contact Info: jwronka@spfldcol.edu
Home page: www.humanrightsculture.org

Good afternoon. I am Dr. Joseph Wronka. It was I who had originally contacted my representative Ms. Ellen Story in December 2000, asking her to sponsor a bill to incorporate international human rights law into Massachusetts laws and policies. After some discussion, we felt that it would be better to at least initially sponsor a bill that would establish a commission to examine how Massachusetts laws and policies compare with international human rights law, which consists in part of the Universal Declaration of Human Rights, as the former Pope John Paul II called a "milestone in the long and difficult struggle of the human race" and (to use his words again) the "long train of covenants and declarations following it," such as the Rights of the Child (ROC), Convention on the Elimination of Discrimination Against Women (CEDAW), and the Convention on the Elimination of Racial Discrimination (CERD). Our rationale for such a commission was in large measure because research has consistently demonstrated that only chosen values endure. No one can force international human rights on anyone. People must see for themselves how laws and policies measure up to such documents as the Universal Declaration and then make up their own mind, I think, whether they wish to incorporate such principles into their domestic laws and policies.

Cosponsors of then House Bill 850 were Anne Paulsen (Belmont) and Patricia Jehlen (Sommerville). Dr. David Gil of Brandeis, Chair of my dissertation which compared the Universal Declaration of Human Rights with the U.S. Constitution and all fifty state constitutions, was a strong supporter of the Bill, as well as the Massachusetts Chapter of the National Association of Social Work, the International Fourth World Movement, an organization dedicated to the eradication of extreme poverty, and, of course the Coalition for a Strong United Nations. It did not get out of committee, but two years later, we reintroduced it as House Bill 2840. Then, Benjamin Swan, Susan Fargo, and Kay Kahn were additional co sponsors. Other groups joined on, such as the Men's Resource Center in Amherst. During both hearings, no one gave testimony against the Bill. During that time, moreover, the Pennsylvania legislature had passed a similar bill, based on MA 850, with no dissent, 200 to 0!

Now there are roughly 40 organizations supporting the latest bill, HR 706, a few of the most notable being Physicians for Human Rights, the Northeast Regional Office of Amnesty International, and the Women's International League for Peace and Freedom.

Let me now briefly share with you some of my work in my dissertation which eventually became published as a book, *Human rights and social policy in the 21st century,* as an example of some of the things such a commission might do. Here is a copy of my book for the committee's consideration.

Briefly, the Federal Constitution has numerous correspondences with the Universal Declaration of Human Rights, but also, significant gaps. Using the method of content analysis and comparing relevant phrases that may not be total or precise, but agree in substance and sense, the U.S. Constitution is roughly similar to the Universal Declaration from Articles 1 through 21, which substantively deal with civil and political rights, such as freedoms of speech, the press, assembly, and from arbitrary interference with privacy. There are, however, no correspondences with notions of human dignity (in Article 1); the right to effective remedy (in Article 8); and protection of the family (in Article 16).

Furthermore, apart from protection of an author's interest, there are no correspondences between articles 22 and 30 of the Universal Declaration which deal substantively with economic, social, cultural, and solidarity rights, including, but not limited to, health care, food, adequate shelter, meaningful and gainful employment, rest and leisure, security in old age, and education.

States, which ought to act as "laboratories of democracy" according to former Supreme Court Justice Louis Brandeis and extend rights not found in the U.S. Constitution, have, indeed, extended such rights. Most states, for example, guarantee the right to education; the text of the Massachusetts Constitution does not. Whereas the U.S. Constitution does speak of "equal protection of the laws," it does not, however, distinctly assert the need for non discrimination based, for example, on race, gender, property, or political opinion as in the Universal Declaration. The State of Massachusetts, however, does assert non discrimination based on race, religion, color, sex, nation origin, and disability.

The State of Massachusetts, however, does not mention human dignity, right to an effective remedy, protection of the family or any of the other economic, social, cultural, and solidarity rights not found in the U.S. Constitution. Massachusetts, however, does mention the need for duties to the community, an essential notion also of the Universal Declaration (in Article 29).

I urge you to support House Bill 706.

Thank you for your attention.

I gave another talk on Human Rights and Sudan in Holyoke, Massachusetts, at the Talking Drum Café on June 3, 2005, as depicted in Practice Illustration 5.7. This talk also mentions some of the issues discussed in this book, such as the hypocrisy of governments and the importance of human rights reports.

Practice Illustration 5.7
A Presentation on the Darfur Situation

Presentation on Human Rights and Sudan

I must say that it is a pleasure being gathered here today with people concerned about those almost entirely strangers in a land thousands of miles away, Sudan, where since its independence from England in 1956 has seen all but 10 years since then caught up in a bloody civil war. We have come, thankfully, a long way from the Conference of Evian, called by the United States in 1938 urging members of the international community to stop the abuses of the Third Reich. The conference was a failure largely because many of the countries there did not want to bring attention to their own human rights abuses, such as lynchings in the United States, its sprawling urban ghettos, concentration camps in the Soviet Union and policies of apartheid, taxation without representation, and torture by some countries of Europe in Africa, of which I think the problem in Sudan, like Rwanda, is a legacy.

The conclusion of that conference, wrought by fear and hypocrisy, was that no one had the right to interfere with another's domestic affairs. What occurred was the killing of 10 million innocents, largely Jews, but also such groups as gays (lesbians were spared apparently), Roma, Jehovah's Witnesses, and one fourth of Poland. In order not to let this happen again the United Nations was formed in

1945 and soon thereafter under the able leadership of an American Ms. Eleanor Roosevelt. The Universal Declaration of Human Rights, was endorsed by the General Assembly with no dissenting vote in 1948 and was called a "Magna Carta" for humanity by Ms. Roosevelt. Today, however, no country would dare say it is against human rights. What goes on in one country, if it is an affront to human dignity, it is the world's business whether it is apartheid in South Africa, children living in extreme poverty in the United States, or in this case, Genocide in Sudan.

Genocide, from the Latin, *genus* meaning "tribe or loosely connected families" and *caedo* meaning "to cut or slay," adequately depicts some of the situation in Sudan. Select concerns, for example, of the Human Rights Monitoring Committees on the Convention on the Elimination against Racial Discrimination for Sudan are:

1. Concern over continuous reports of the abduction by armed militia of primarily, women, and children belonging to other ethnic groups. The Committee does not believe that these abductions are due to traditions deeply rooted in certain tribes as the State contends and it is the State's responsibility to bring this practice to an end.

2. Concern over the large number of internally displaced communities and in particular the forced relocation of civilians from the Nuer and Dinka ethnic groups in the upper Nile region. The Committee urges the state to uphold their fundamental rights to personal security, housing, food and to just compensation for property confiscated for public use.

Select concerns of the Human Rights Committee on the Convention on the Rights of the Child (which I must add the United States has not ratified and once ratified become law, as it is now the case in Sudan) are:

1. That structural adjustment policies are affecting the cost, quality, accessibility and effectiveness of services for children calling for a study in that regard

2. While praising Sudan for the establishment of the Sudan National Committee for the Eradication of Harmful Practices, including campaigns against female genital mutilation and the encouragement of child spacing, expresses concern that it has not ratified major human rights documents like the African Charter on the Rights and Welfare of the Child, The United Nations Convention against Torture, CEDAW and the Optional Protocol to the Rights of the Child on the involvement of children in armed conflict, child prostitution and child pornography

3. Concern that there are significant inequalities regarding access to basic health and education services between children, most especially between southern Sudan and the rest of the country and that discrimination against children, particularly discrimination based on religious beliefs must end

4. Concern that as much as 70% of children in parts of the country are not registered, leading among other things to sex trafficking

5. Concern that corporal punishment is widely practiced in the state, in the families, schools, and communities and by the police. Acts of torture, rape and other cruel

acts have been committed against children in the context of armed conflict calling for their immediate end and for the proper prosecution of perpetrators

6. The Committee urges that all child victims of violence and abuse have appropriate medical and psychological support, including recovery and social reintegration assistance for their families

7. Given that 40% of deaths of children under 5 are due to inadequate and unsafe drinking water calls for immediate action to have access to clean water

8. End the practice of recruiting child soldiers and give particular attention to the ending of the stigma of children with disabilities and also giving particular attention to ensuring the enrollment of girls, refugee children and children from nomadic groups in schools.

Well, I could go on and on. I see this as one of my jobs to tell people about these human rights reports, which must be submitted to human rights monitoring committees every few years or so, as a gauge to see how their country is doing. And, let me add that you may also wish to provide input into these reports as well, which many countries take seriously.

But in our zeal, for our concern to end racism or for the children of Sudan, let us be mindful of the words of Supreme Court Justice Louis Brandeis: "Men born to freedom are naturally alert to repel invasion of their liberty by evil-minded rulers. The greatest dangers to liberty lurk in insidious encroachment by men of zeal, well meaning, but without understanding." My point is that with a roughly 95% Muslim majority, and the fact that Sudan has only begun exporting oil in 1999, we must on guard to hidden agenda. Do we really care about those persecuted or is the government in a perverse kind of collusion with the media trying to whip up anger toward our Muslim brothers and sisters, because our economic and social system needs an enemy to survive and let us not forget oil. Let us also not forget that free market economics appears to have played a major factor in the fact that presently only 5% of the land in Sudan is arable. And, if the average age is roughly 18, Sudan like much of the world is undergoing what has been referred to as a "youth bulge" and globalization efforts to maximize profit at the expense of human need and development is leaving too much of our youth, the youth of Sudan or for that matter the United States (which in the industrialized world is the highest in terms of alienation) looking for identity in gangs, the military, and terrorist groups.

We must be concerned about Sudan certainly, but our rallying cry must be human rights for every person, everywhere. If you think this is impossible, who would have thought with the invention of gunpowder that the world would eventually be able to destroy every person, everywhere in a matter of days. But some people have had such nightmares which have become realities. Surely, Dr. Martin Luther King, Jr.'s dream of a Beloved Community can and should become our reality.

Finally, in Practice Illustration 5.8 is a presentation that I gave in Geneva, on September 24, 2007, before the Human Rights Council meetings urging further consideration of extreme poverty as a violation of human rights and the promotion of human rights education from the primary to professional levels.

Practice Illustration 5.8
Joint Statement on the Eradication of Extreme Poverty and the Need for Human Rights Education and Training

To: Human Rights Council as pertaining to Agenda Item 4, HR situations that require the HRC's attention

Fr: Joseph Wronka, (PhD), Affiliate for the International Association of Schools of Social Work (IASSW) and Ms. Ellen Mouravieff-Apostol, UN Geneva Representative for the International Federation of Social Workers (IFSW) to the 6th Human Rights Council Meeting, Geneva, September 10–28, 2007

Date of Delivery: September 24, 2007

Dear Esteemed Colleagues . . . May I say friends?
    The International Association of Schools of Social Work (IASSW) and the International Federation of Social Workers (IFSW), having consultative status with the UN, request further consideration of: (1) extreme poverty as a violation of fundamental human rights and dignity and (2) the incorporation of human rights education and training in our educational systems.
    The problem of extreme poverty is urgent and of increasing gravity. Nearly one billion people go to bed starving each night and even in wealthy countries like the USA, one out of three children go to bed hungry or are at risk of being hungry, according to the Children's Defense Fund. The ratio between the world's richest and poorest countries has grown in recent years and is now 1 to 103. Former President Jimmy Carter in his acceptance speech of the Nobel Peace Prize in 2002 said: "The citizens of the ten wealthiest countries are now seventy-five times richer than those who live in the ten poorest ones, and the separation is increasing every year, not only between nations, but also within them. The results of this disparity are root causes of most of the world's unresolved problems, including starvation, illiteracy, environmental degradation, violent conflict, and unnecessary illnesses that range from Guinea worm to HIV/AIDS."
    Please consider further debate on the *Draft Guiding Principles* on "Extreme poverty and human rights: Rights of the poor" (A/HRC/Sub.1/58/36, 11 September 2006) with an eye toward an internationally legally binding convention. This report echoes the Report on the Realization of Economic, Social, and

Cultural Rights (E/CN.4/Sub.2/1996/13, 28 June 1996) which referred to poverty as the world's most pitiless killer and viewed the eradication of poverty as one of the founding ideals of the UN system.

Mindful of this World Decade of Human Rights Education, we also urge our educational systems to incorporate human rights into their curricula from primary to professional levels. The helping and health professions, such as social work, psychology, nursing, and medicine, ought to include human rights principles in their training, which would include some lesser known, but equally important documents like the "Principles of Medical Ethics and the Protection of Persons with Mental Illness." Only chosen values endure. Research consistently demonstrates that once youth inculcate values, it is extremely difficult to change them. We will stop extreme poverty once we decide to and human rights education can play a pivotal role.

Recognizing the interdependence and indivisibility of human rights, let us work together developing proactive and reactive strategies to eradicate extreme poverty in a spirit of peace, tolerance, and friendship. In conclusion, we affirm the General Assembly's endorsement of the Draft Declaration on the Rights of Indigenous Peoples and we urge personal reflection on the wisdom of a major spiritual leader of the Sioux nation, Tashunkewitko, commonly known as Crazy Horse who said: "A very great vision is needed and the man [person] who has it must follow it as the eagle seeks the deepest blue of the sky."

Thank you for your attention to this urgent problem of extreme poverty.

Summary

This chapter examined the sixth level of intervention, which is research. Human rights documents are excellent means for defining the research problem. Given the power of this idea, such a framework can serve as a solid basis for socially just action projects, bearing witness to the violations of rights not generally considered human rights, for example, parental leave, support groups for rural women, and quality day care. Quantitative approaches comparing, for example, paid parental leaves in various countries, and qualitative approaches eliciting the voices of parents who had no paid leave are a couple of viable possibilities for such research. Such re-creations of the world through quantitative and qualitative lenses should pay particular attention to the ethical principles that arose, in large measure, out of the carnage of the Holocaust, and were enunciated at Nuremberg.

Examining executive, judicial, legislative, and public discourse movements toward compliance with human rights principles is another way to engage in human rights social action-research. One legislative example given was the paucity of economic, social, and cultural rights in U.S. federal and state constitutions. Human rights principles also place findings in context, such as viewing the historical legacies in some Native American communities from forcibly removing children to boarding schools as possible violations of the Genocide Convention.

Research is a worthless enterprise if this knowledge is not shared. Speaking, writing, and using the media are ways to get the message across. In brief, writing ought to be clear and easy for the reader to take in. Speaking ought to follow the basic principles of ethos, pathos, and logos, especially ethos, that is, having a strong ethical character. Working in the broadcast media requires, foremost, developing a personal relationship with the audience.

Finally, armed with this social justice framework, with human rights as its cornerstone, one must engage in social action and service. But is this "finning" actually the "beginning," to quote Norman O. Brown, a major figure of the counterculture movement in the 1960s, referencing James Joyce's *Finnegan's Wake*?[6] The end of this book is only the beginning in the reader's quest to heed Dr. King's call to implement the human rights principles that are on paper.

Questions for Discussion

1. What has helped you with your writing and speaking? What has not helped? Do a self-inventory. What were your experiences as a writer or speaker? Were they positive or negative? In other words, do you feel you are dealing with a little stress in the writing and speaking department? What do your experiences teach you about the educational system? What can you do to get out of your comfort zone? Should you get out of your comfort zone? What results would you like to see by leaving your comfort zone?

2. Does your profession follow basic precepts of the Nuremberg Code and ethical principles as discussed here? Give examples. Does your profession go beyond some of the ethical principles discussed? If so, how? If your profession does not follow basic ethical principles in your view, give examples of what it does and suggest ways to rectify the problem.

3. Are some forms of "Tuskegee-like" studies still going on? Is it necessary, for example, to study the effects of homelessness, when it is reasonable to assume that lack of adequate shelter leads to numerous psychological and physical illnesses? Can the same be said for studying where people go after they get off welfare or studying the effects of unemployment? Would time be better spent changing the social structures that lead to unemployment, rather than trying to understand its deleterious effects?

4. The challenge as always is to make research relevant, so it can be a catalyst for social change. How can this be done? Is Jean Paul Sartre (1993)

correct that a lot of research is merely about meaningless facts, rather than meaningful essences? Recall Hitler's assertion that if someone takes over a country, it would be necessary to keep intellectuals occupied by providing funding for research grants of dubious utility. Do you feel that is true? What can be done so research plays a major role in social change and social justice?

5. Retrieve a human rights document on the Internet and use it to define a research problem. For example, if the document asserts (as in CEDAW) "maternal leave with pay" is a human right, how could that principle serve as basis for your research? How would you construct a quantitative study? One could, for example, study other countries that offer paid maternity leave and come up with a "Maternity Paid Leave Grid." Given an increase in the number of men actively taking part in child rearing, should one also include paternity leave? How might one construct a qualitative study on paid maternity (and/or paternity) leave? One could, for instance, interview legislators about their perspectives on that notion of paid parental leave, write reports, and submit them to their constituencies. One could also interview mothers who had paid leave and those who didn't. Compare their stories with legislators' pronouncements and, while keeping to ethical guidelines, disseminate them to the community. Try to play with other human rights principles. Be creative.

6. Are certain instruments, like standardized tests, IQ tests, Scholastic Aptitude Inventories (SATs), Graduate Record Exams (GREs), personality inventories, and state achievement tests (like the MCAS) good indicators of intelligence, personality, and knowledge? Given the vast number of people needing placement in educational settings or therapeutic clinical groups, do they have good administrative utility? One wouldn't put slow students with gifted students, nor place someone diagnosed as paranoid schizophrenic in a group of people struggling with obsessive-compulsive issues. How can standardized tools be improved? Or should they be scrapped for other alternatives? What alternatives? Are there any experiences that you wish to share? How did you feel when PSAT scores were handed out in high school? Did it enhance your sense of human dignity or was it an affront to your human dignity? Did everyone start comparing one another, viewing each other as a number, rather than as John, Joan, Chris, or Carolyn with his or her own possibilities, rather than actualities, as a human person? What does all that have to do with human rights?

7. Do student evaluations of teachers with no qualitative feedback adequately reflect the experience of learning in the classroom? Do teacher evaluations of students adequately reflect their learning? What qualitative questions should be added to the evaluations so that professors and students can engage in true quality education? Given that every right has a corresponding duty, what duties do students and teachers have to adequately realize the right to

education? What duties do your professors have to students? Taking into consideration the levels of intervention discussed, how can students and professors fulfill their duties to realize the basic human right to education?

8. If you were to enact a bill similar to Massachusetts House Bill 760, An Act Relative to Integrating International Human Rights into Massachusetts Laws and Policies, how would you construct an adequate research methodology to monitor state compliance with international human rights principles? To what extent would you use quantitative and/or qualitative measures and procedures? Could you construct a grid? What would it look like? Whose voices would you include in monitoring your state's compliance with international human rights principles?

9. Do you feel that researchers are truly in search of truth, or are they hired guns for pharmaceuticals, hospitals, corporations, or places of employment, employed to make them look good? Are pharmaceutical companies, for example, more prone to tout the benefits of drugs that they trade on the stock exchange? Please try not to mystify or have an anticorporate animus. Just be a scholar and give examples. How about research by your professional organizations? Are they truly in search of truth, or do they tend to reinforce their own conceptual biases? Are the helping and health professions prone, for example, to study the efficacy of a therapeutic intervention, like psychoanalysis, behaviorism, rational-emotive, and/or client-centered therapies to combat depression? Why don't they study the therapeutic benefits of conversations with a grandparent on the porch on a hot summer day or the ongoing protection and wisdom of a sibling who consistently comforts a scapegoated family member? Given a trend toward strengths perspectives emanating from the humanistic psychologies of the 1970s and 1980s, like Maslow or Erwin Straus, or developments of earlier existential phenomenologists, like Sartre and Camus in Europe, do researchers study well-being as much as pathology? Although this trend acknowledges the importance of the strengths in one's environment and nontraditional healing interventions, do the helping and health professions subvert the notion that "the family is the fundamental unit of society" (Article 16 of the Universal Declaration) by basically looking at the effectiveness of only professional clinical interventions?

10. Imagine the following scenario: You have just received your professional degree. Now the expert, you want to implement universal human rights principles. One principle you are particularly concerned about is female genital mutilation. After researching this issue, and creating a well-written, structured, and targeted grant application, you receive funding to combat this procedure. You travel to Somalia, where roughly 90% of the female population undergoes this procedure. At a meeting you have arranged of key community leaders, you

read parts of the Rights of the Child, which in essence prohibits traditional and cultural practices inimical to the health of the child. People in the community respond that you come from a hypercritical culture that has ruthlessly attacked and ruined the beautiful land of Africa, citing, for example, King Leopold of Belgium's ruthless killings and the collusion of the Catholic Church with the Belgian government granting privileged positions to the Hutu, which eventually led to the Rwandan holocaust in the mid-1990s. Your country, America, they continue, spends roughly $400 billion on military arms annually. That money could be used to feed the millions starving in Africa. Besides, they say, their culture doesn't believe in experts and FGM is a way that a woman can find a husband. They add, angrily but sarcastically, that in American culture a woman has to be dead from anorexia nervosa to get a husband. How would you respond? Are they right, wrong, a little in between? What would you do, or should you do? Please comment on the following: According to Supreme Court Justice Louis Brandeis, government is our omnipresent teacher. In response to Michael Moore's film *Fahrenheit 9/11*, George H. W. Bush called him a "slimeball." What do you feel these government officials are teaching us?

Activities/Actions

1. Write an article integrating your human voice with scholarship, for a peer review journal. Send it in. Then write up an op-ed piece or letter to the editor and send it in. Make rewrites on rewrites if necessary, until your work is published. As you write, have your classmates act as peers for constructive feedback. How do you feel about giving and receiving feedback?

2. Try engaging in some activities where you must speak in public. For instance, write up and present a testimony on an issue of interest. Find a hearing where people have the power to make a difference. Follow up to see if your presentation and the presentations of others on the issue made a difference. If you are working on or have finished a research-action project, present it either as a work in progress or completed project at a conference of your choosing. Now try to get a spot on radio and/or television to talk about a particular issue. Get feedback from your friends, peers, and spouse/partner on your actions. Try to improve, do it again, and get feedback.

3. Develop a human rights survey and send it to professional organizations like the National Association of Social Workers, the Public Health Association, the American Nurses Association, the American Sociological Association, the American Medical Association, the American Psychiatric Association, the American Political Science Association, the American Anthropological Association, and the American Psychological

Association. Ultimately, the purpose of the survey is to determine if these organizations endorsed all of the rights in the Universal Declaration of Human Rights and whatever "select" rights you would like to include from other conventions. Perhaps you may wish to merely have them check off rights that they endorse. Come up with a report on each of the professional organization's endorsements of human rights principles. Send the report to each organization and other interested parties. Try engaging in coalition building by having professional organizations draft a letter to accrediting agencies, state, and/or federal governments urging them to include human rights principles in their laws and policies. But don't stop there. Work positively with organizations and governments with an eye toward implementation.

4. Do a content analysis of your state constitution in comparison with the Universal Declaration and/or any other human rights document of interest. How does the state constitution stand in relation to the human rights documents? Are there ways that the state constitution goes beyond the principles of the Universal Declaration? Write government leaders—the executive (governor), legislative (representatives and senators), and judicial (judges)—about any gaps that exist between the two documents and ask them if they could help to bridge this gap. Write a report on what they had to say, if they have responded to your communications. You may also wish to do comparisons with other state policy documents on, for example, the rights of the mentally ill with the UN's Protection for Persons With Mental Illness.

5. Using Article 24 of the Universal Declaration, which asserts the right to rest and leisure and reasonable limitations of working hours, ask colleagues how many jobs they have to support themselves and their families. Then ask them about some of their struggles in trying to juggle family life with work. Come up with a well-written report with both quantitative (e.g., number of people with two, three jobs, and/or whether they have benefits like health care and pensions) and qualitative (e.g., stories of their everyday struggles) data. Note if the data appear to violate CEDAW, which stresses government's duty to help families coordinate family responsibilities with the work of the world. Submit the report to the Department of State and ask if some of the data could be used in a report to the UN human rights monitoring committees.

Notes

1. Work can be defined as activities performed in formal settings, such as factories, mental health/substance abuse centers, hospitals, environmental, and academic settings. Also important is work in more or less informal settings, generally and

amazingly not considered work, like taking care of an ailing parent or relative, scrounging for food by a homeless person, or perhaps most important though often underestimated for human survival, taking care of one's own or another's children.

2. The MCAS is a standardized achievement test intended to measure a student's knowledge of various subjects. Failing this test could have major repercussions in a child's life, such as failure to graduate, extending perhaps over a lifetime.

3. Certainly, all human activities have their aims to fulfill human need, like hunger by eating, affiliation by providing for one's family, and protection from the elements by having adequate shelter. Nevertheless, it is important for coresearchers to understand that a study may be part of a requirement for a course or master's degree or PhD, that is, a means to an end, to get a job, put food on the table, or have adequate shelter.

4. Food insecurity is defined as lacking access to enough food at all times for active, healthy living (Children's Defense Fund, 2007). The percentage of 11.9% can be further broken down into food insecurity without hunger (8%); food insecurity with hunger (3.9%); and food insecurity with hunger among children (274,000 or 0.7%). (The Census Bureau does not include food insecurity among children without hunger.) Furthermore, tables can be constructed in a myriad of creative and persuasive ways. One could show how only 52% of eligible migrant children who are citizens get food stamps compared with 82% of eligible children overall. Even then, food stamps amount to $1.05 per meal, hardly enough to provide a nutritious, well-balanced meal ("Hunger and Food Stamps," 2007).

5. It is generally considered that at least eight participants are necessary before a redundancy of themes becomes apparent (McCracken, 1987). As a matter of expediency, students were required to interview five coresearchers. Results are suggestive, not definitive, yet could yield rich information to add to the implementation of effective social action strategies. To protect anonymity, projects are not available.

6. From lectures at Duquesne University, Pittsburgh, Pennsylvania, Fall 1971.

6

Ground Rules

When the power of love overcomes the love of power, the world will know peace.

—Jimi Hendrix

Toward the Paradoxical Commandments

There is an Arabic proverb that if a person does a good deed and announces it, it is as if he or she did nothing. In the final chapter of this work, that adage might come as a letdown. It may be human nature to want recognition for one's work. The question is whether the intellectual, helping, and health professions are nothing more than exercises in self-aggrandizement, the garnering of status by tending to the misfortune of another. But if one's accomplishments were never known and given rightful recognition, there could be no promotions, tenure, job security, or fair remuneration for a good day's work to provide for one's family or pay one's rent. Imagine all that could be accomplished if no one cared about who gets the credit.

Yet, a person must often report to those above them, who own the gold, about successes and regrettably failures, hopefully to learn from the latter. Without recognition of their work, would musicians, actors, and other artists perform the concerts or plays that thrill audiences, with their musical virtuosity or extraordinary skills in assuming the personae of characters totally divorced from their everyday lives? Likewise, emulating the wonderful ideals of such spiritual sages as Crazy Horse, noted for "his commitment to caring and constant humility, a man who dressed plainly, never display-ing symbols of achievement accruing to him because of his good deeds" (Marshall, 2006, p. 1), takes a lot of work.

Yet isn't hard work part of the human condition? Without it humans could not survive to participate in community building, or enjoy the arts for arts sake, *ars gratis artis*. Marcus Aurelius—philosopher committed to world citizenship, emperor, administrator, forerunner of the rational-emotive school of psychotherapy, and model coach (Jacobs, 2006)—may have been right when he wrote:

> Love your nature, and your nature's will. Crafts persons who love their trade will spend themselves to the utmost in laboring at it, even going unwashed and unfed. . . . These persons when their heart is in it are ready to sacrifice food and sleep to the advancement of their chosen pursuit. Is the service of the com-munity of less worth in your eyes, and does it merit less devotion? (Aurelius, 1984, p. 77)

Thousands if not millions of social activists combating social injustice may have secular versions of holier-than-thou attitudes, reciting Tartuffe-like incantations of their sacrifices to create a socially just world. Rather than wearing their hair shirt in public, perhaps their service is punctuated with incessant proclamations of "Oh, how I've suffered for social justice." As 1960s activist Abbie Hoffman said, the revolution is fun, and within such an atmosphere of joy in struggle it is certainly important to acknowledge the contributions not just of those already celebrated, but also the unsung heroes and heroines. Listen further to Emperor Aurelius:

> Fame is like the shifting of the sands in the desert. . . . [and] . . . Once you have done a person a service, what more would you have? . . . A man is born for deeds of kindness; and when he has done a kindly action, or otherwise served the common welfare, he has done what he was made for, and has received his quittance. (Aurelius, 1984, p. 149)

As helping and health professionals or just plain human beings in service to others, we should keep in mind Gandhi's eight blunders, which he saw as the cause of all the violence in the world: wealth without work; pleasure without conscience; knowledge without character; commerce without morality; science without humanity; worship without sacrifice; politics with-out principles; and rights without responsibilities. He was also aware of the intimate connection between the mind, heart, and body (1937). His vision, encompassing *satyagraha* (love for all humanity), risk taking, coalition

Figure 6.1   Gandhi, Believer and Practicer of *Satygraha*, Love for All, Disembarking From His Ship in England for Negotiations.

Source: Wikimedia Commons.

building, conflict resolution, refusal to mystify the enemy, and nonviolence, was reflected in his life and carried into his everyday actions. His way, the path of the social justice advocate, is clearly the road less traveled, to quote the poet Robert Frost. Such a road may be bumpy, and congested with weeds, overgrowth, and mud. The only certainty is that the outcome is uncertain, that our efforts may be in vain. But though we may be ignored or laughed at, we can continue down the path till social justice reigns.

On that journey, Kent Keith's "Paradoxical Commandments," written when he was a college student in the 1960s, may be useful. Found taped to the walls of Mother Teresa's children's home in Calcutta, they are worth quoting in their entirety:

People are illogical, unreasonable, and self-centered. Love them anyway.

If you do good, people will accuse you of selfish ulterior motives. Do good anyway.

If you are successful, you will win false friends and true enemies. Succeed anyway.

The good you do today will be forgotten tomorrow. Do good anyway.

Honesty and frankness make you vulnerable. Be honest and frank anyway.

The biggest men and women with the biggest ideas can be shot down by the smallest men and women with the smallest minds. Think big anyway.

People favor underdogs, but follow only top dogs. Fight for a few underdogs anyway.

What you spend years building may be destroyed overnight. Build anyway.

People really need help, but may attack you if you do help them. Help them anyway.

Give the world the best you have and you'll get kicked in the teeth. Give the world the best you have anyway. (Keith, 2001, cover jacket)

These words are not much different from those of Machiavelli in *The Prince:*

There is nothing more difficult to carry out, nor more doubtful of success, nor more dangerous to handle, than to initiate a new order of things. . . . The reformer has enemies in all those who profit by the old order, and only luke-warm defenders in all those who would profit by the new order. (as cited in Bornstein, 2004, p. 46)

Marcus Aurelius's, Mahatma Gandhi's, and Mother Teresa's ideas and actions illustrate almost all the levels of interventions mentioned throughout this book. Gandhi's symbolic March to the Sea, where he and his followers mined salt in violation of British law, was a direct macro-level nonviolent social action to win Indians their basic human right of self-determination by getting the British to leave India, to "leave as friends." He wanted to eliminate what he perceived as structural violence or, in the language of human rights, an unjust social order. Marcus Aurelius, a Roman Emperor, was a quintessential humanistic administrator, always mindful of the need for a community of compassion, eliciting public participation in the policy debates over the development of the Roman

Empire. Mother Teresa, on the other hand, dealt more with the symptoms of an unjust order, working relentlessly and indefatigably to provide care for the ill and injured of all religions, ages, castes, national origins, or any other status, as stated in the Universal Declaration. She cared for them simply because they were human. Each of these activists followed his or her own bliss. Social activists always need to search their own souls in their meditative lives, to reflect on while spontaneously tapping into their resources (Merleau-Ponty, 1967) as they engage in social action and service for every person, everywhere.

Some Ground Rules for Social Action and Service

This section lists some ground rules that social activists/human rights defenders might wish to consider as they engage in social action and service to others.[1] Some have already been mentioned, but are worth repeating. Before sharing them, consider these words of wisdom from Supreme Court Justice Louis Brandeis:

> Experience should teach us to be most on our guard to protect liberty when the government's purposes are beneficent. Men born to freedom are naturally alert to repel invasion of their liberty by evil-minded rulers. The greatest dangers to liberty lurk in insidious encroachment by men of zeal, well meaning but without understanding. (cited in Wronka, 1998b, p. ii)

Hell can be paved with good intentions, as Eleanor Roosevelt was fond of saying. Such a netherworld can easily be the outcome if helping and health professionals do not incorporate the voices of the oppressed in policy debates and treatment planning. Such professionals may be men or women of zeal, but it is important to work toward a human rights culture and beyond with constant caution, remaining vigilant to always seek understanding, tolerance, and friendship among people and nations. There is no set final time when a human rights culture will exist. Social justice, as defined in this book, requires constant struggle, like dieting, to maintain the results of your effort.

The rules listed here merely represent the most effective methods of getting people at least to listen to this idea of human rights, although the truth can be shocking to some. U.S. citizens, for example, might think their country is a leader in human rights, only to find that Article 25 of the Universal Declaration lists the right to health care and security in old age as basic human rights. Approximately 47 million people in the United States lack health insurance, and those covered must deal with managed (mangled?) care that is often inimical to the fulfillment of human need. Ever-higher copayments, exclusions, administrative bureaucracy, and voice-mail hell all produce an aggravation factor that's off the charts!

The term *rules* may be a misnomer. Rules must be consistent with a person's values, so they are followed from the heart. The rules presented here are only points for readers to ponder and come to their own conclusions about. Human rights defenders/social justice advocates must think for themselves. Yes, "the answer lies within" is a trite, yet meaningful phrase, going back to the Jungian notion of the need to uncover the 2-million-year-old sage within us, our source of wisdom, knowledge, and confidence. The following rules, therefore, summarize the major points made earlier with some additions.

First, the basic way to implement human rights is by not implementing human rights, that is, values must be chosen. To be the bedrock of social justice, ultimately, human rights must reflect one's values and cannot be forced on anyone. No person can impose this need for a lived awareness of human rights principles on others. Defenders/activists can teach about human rights; by example, they can demonstrate common human decency; and they can run human rights and social justice experiential workshops. But they cannot force others to create a human rights culture. They can only share what they know.

Second, helping and health professionals must refrain from elitist language as much as possible, adopting a nonelitist and nonhierarchical approach to human rights learning. True, the Universal Declaration and other human rights instruments do contain some legalese, with such phrases as "right to an effective remedy," "self-determination of peoples," and "refoulement." Yet, one must be mindful of the words of Eleanor Roosevelt, that the Universal Declaration is for the educated layperson, not the doctor of jurisprudence. These instruments exist for the people and consequently must be understood by the people. A basic challenge is to decipher some of that legalese and translate such phrases as "within the evolving capacities of the child" in the Rights of the Child into understandable terms that have implications for social justice. But we first must have a general consensus, that is, public sentiment that human rights values are worthy in their own right.

Third, one must not be afraid of tackling ambiguity. In social justice work, things aren't black and white; activists must learn to live in a world of ambiguity. Issues are not as simple as they appear, yet we need to make informed decisions for action, however difficult. Female genital mutilation is a serious issue, but the economic, social, and other forces that have led to such practices, though fraught with ambiguity, still need to be addressed. Engaging in dialogue is key, especially for Western cultures that may feel superior, but have dropped atom bombs, produced their share of concentration camps, and refused to acknowledge their role in global poverty let alone extreme poverty in their midst.

Fourth, one must adopt an attitude that thinking is doing and doing is thinking. It is an understatement to say that a person's thoughts make a person. Gil (1992) found this notion of symbolic consciousness to undergird many social policies. Symbols like the swastika or the cross can move people, not necessarily toward social justice, as evidenced by centuries of bloodshed from religious, ethnic, and class conflicts. The swastika, however, was originally a good-luck symbol, turned into a gruesome symbol of superiority and oppression, romanticized in Leni Riefenstahl's *Triumph of the Will,* Hitler's notorious propaganda film. Apart from the influence of such symbols, many regard the human species as basically selfish, in need of taming by a benign invisible hand. The economist-philosopher Adam Smith argued that, when people act selfishly, a benign helping hand prevents them from being too selfish. Such a view of the human condition may easily justify a political/economic system or social order that encourages accumulation, euphemistically labeled the free market. This market, not really a market at all but a highly persuasive metaphor, a guardian of liberty and free choice to exchange goods in the marketplace, has indeed become this millennium's great religion, leading to an ever-expanding global maldistribution of wealth (Wronka, 2007).

Another metaphor embedded in people's consciousness and in public discourse is pulling oneself up by one's bootstraps. Failures are those who have not carried their weight. Such symbols and metaphors carried into people's everyday lives can easily influence their thinking and actions, leading to policies of extermination, like concentration camps and the mass killings in Rwanda, or policies of exploitation, more subtle forms of annihilation through poverty and low wages with no benefits. The challenge is how to change thinking on a mass scale to get people to adopt symbols that create a culture of cooperation, an egalitarian order, such as Martin Luther King, Jr.'s Beloved Community or table of brotherhood.

Fifth, it is important to adopt a spirit of compassion for the other, and to be wary of creating evil images. Despite criticisms of governments who historically have shown a reluctance to implement human rights standards, activists must acknowledge many people in government are good people, trying their best to create a socially just world. Those in governments and other powerful entities, whether corporate, educational, or military, are also immersed in a system, often caught in the web of violence, structural or otherwise. They have their bosses, who have their bosses, who have their bosses, and so on. A little compassion never hurt a soul, so it is important to be sensitive to socioenvironmental context. Adopting such communities of compassion in work settings, with the spirit that everyone is in this together, wanting meaningful work, just wages, and proper benefits, will help demystify any evil images we may have of other people.

Sixth, we must constantly adhere to principles of direct nonviolence in advancing the cause of human rights. Despite what the media might present, that human rights can be promoted through violence, as in the justification for the Iraq conflict, for example, violence only begets violence. Even if one wins, the other side may only wait till it gains the strength to retaliate, and the damage done can be long lasting. The only choice is to attempt to solve the issue through peaceful means, as the Barons at Runnymede in 1215 did in drafting the Magna Carta. Having witnessed the horrors of the Crusades, most sat down with King John, though they could easily have slain him and his entourage, and drew up the Magna Carta, a document that remains a living testimony to the efficacy of nonviolence today.

Dr. King, in exemplary fashion, expressed his commitment to this ideal of nonviolence and its power:

> I've decided that I'm going to do battle for my philosophy. You ought to believe something in life, believe that thing so fervently that you will stand up with it till the end of your days. I can't make myself believe that God wants me to hate. I'm tired of violence. And I'm not going to let my oppressor dictate to me what method I must use. We have a power, power that cannot be found in Molotov cocktails, but we do have a power. . . . Somehow we must be able to stand before our opponents and say: "We shall match your capacity to inflict suffering by our capacity to endure suffering. We will meet your physical force with soul force. Do to us what you will and we will still love you. We cannot in all good conscience obey your unjust laws and abide by the unjust system, because noncooperation with evil is as much a moral obligation as is coopera-tion with good, and so throw us in jail and we will still love you. . . . Be assured that we'll wear you down by our capacity to suffer, and one day we will win our freedom. We will not only win freedom for ourselves, we will so appeal to your heart and conscience that we will win you in the process, and our victory will be a double victory." (King, 1987, pp. 71–72)

An international committee of 20 scholars at an International Colloquium on Brain and Aggression in Seville, Spain (1986), drew up what has become known as The Seville Statement on Violence, whose purpose was to do away with a widespread belief that human beings are inevitably disposed to war by biology that favors aggressive drives. Adopted by UNESCO and formally endorsed by numerous scientific and health and helping organizations, the statement con-cluded that "biology does not condemn humanity to war, and that humanity can be freed from the bondage of biological pessimism. . . . the same species who invented war is capable of inventing peace. The responsibility lies with each of us" (Seville Statement, 1990, p. 1168). Nonviolence is anything but passive. It is direct, active, and risk taking, and can have long-lasting effects.

Seventh, one must never give up. The Confucian dictum that "a wise person is someone who keeps on trying even though he [or she] knows it is futile" is most relevant to human rights/social justice work. There are successes, however. One example is Nobel Prize winner Jody Williams, who succeeded in getting nations, except her own, the United States, to ratify the International Ban on Land Mines Treaty. Painstakingly, she wrote thousands of letters to governments and secured a figurehead, Princess Diana, now deceased in a notorious car accident in Paris. Eventually, she won, but the United States, the world's largest producer of armaments, must sign on.

More often than not, however, this David versus Goliath scenario drags on indefinitely, with the added pressure of harassment of social justice advocates. It is an understatement that when someone sticks up for principles, especially those contrary to the prevailing order, ostracism can result. Some students, for example, have attempted to expand mandates of local human rights commissions to include not only monitoring unjust hiring and employment policies but also monitoring policies that have led to children living in extreme poverty. They were told that it would be impractical to include children living in poverty as part of their mandate because there are so many of them and it is not what human rights are about.

Recalling the Cyrano Effect, Milgram's famous study that revealed the prejudices of teachers, one of the most fundamental biases may be based on one's role in society, a failure to go beyond appearances. Still, many human rights defenders have been jailed, like King, Gandhi, and Nelson Mandela. Those were internationally publicized cases, but how about the many other defenders, sung and unsung, still languishing in prisons, such as Leonard Peltier, adopted as a prisoner of conscience by Amnesty International? And in a world where everyone looks out for number one, there are those out of prison, but imprisoned in their neighborhoods and their streets, afraid to venture out for fear of violence, or imprisoned in dead-end jobs, fearful of their families plummeting into extreme poverty if they leave. The victims of Katrina, violated by the failure of government to provide for humanitarian disaster relief, and denied the right to solidarity where so many have been left to fend for themselves, are other examples of the many forms of imprisonment that continue to exist. Caring about social justice means persistence— clear and simple.

Eighth, it is important to always be mindful of one's humanity, the frailty of the human condition. A self-righteous, holier-than-thou attitude is unproductive. It is important to be committed to a cause. But must one always be perfect, never failing, never making mistakes, and never wanting to slow down, have fun, or take a break? No. Being serious all the time is not only bad for one's health, it will inevitably turn off the very people one is trying to engage in dialogue. Perhaps this is a divisive issue, but one's motives needn't be pure all the time. Social activism is a wonderful use of one's time to make enduring friendships. But sometimes, for whatever personal reasons, it might be a good idea to leave the social action and service to others. There is just so much time in the day. Sometimes one's primary motives for getting involved in a social action may be to get out of the house, be with people, and have some fun. Why is anything wrong with that? After all, probably no one would be interested in the cause of social justice, if defenders were constantly serious. The only thing worse than a Mr. or Ms. Goody Two-Shoes is two Mr. or Ms. Goody Two-Shoes. A whole group of Goody Two-Shoes? Forget it! Who would listen? No one can be a Goody Two-Shoes all the time. It is okay to have some fun, to be "bad," just as long as you don't hurt anybody or anything. A person can make a positive contribution for a socially just world, yet still fulfill basic needs for affiliation.

Ninth, it is important to always keep an open mind. As obvious as that might sound, human rights/social justice work does not necessarily emanate from humanitarian concerns. For instance, in the 1980s the former Soviet Union and the United States clashed over the flaws of each other's systems. The latter lambasted the Soviet Union for its Gulag, a landmass nearly the size of France populated by criminals and reportedly thousands of political prisoners. The Soviets, in turn, criticized the United States for its racism, sprawling ghettos, and broken treaties with Native Americans. Both sides had valid points, but lacking a much-needed sense of humility, these confrontations amounted to little more than cheap shots. When discussing the abuses of Saddam Hussein such as his gassing of the Kurds, a worthy target for human rights action to be sure, one also needs to acknowledge abuses in the United States, where thousands of people are killed each year by handguns, a violation of the right to life addressed by the Human Rights Committee in its efforts to engage in creative dialogue at a recent hearing of compliance with the International Covenant on Civil and Political Rights.

Tenth, social activists must keep on smiling. This work can be lonely, considering that those who engage in such activism often question the status quo. They may be considered agitators in a pejorative sense. They demonstrate, in a scholarly and convincing way, that there are injustices in the world that people might perceive as socially just. For example, is it socially just to air ads on children's television that socialize these defenseless ones to give priority to "having," that is, the overaccumulation of material goods, over "being," that is, the quality of human and humane interpersonal relationships? Is that not a growing (and gnawing) problem the French existentialist,

Gabriel Marcel (1965), foresaw many years ago? Worse, this television advertising may be a tax write-off for wealthy corporate entities, approximately 30% of whose revenues come from public coffers. Activists may be told that such policy issues have nothing to do with human rights, that human rights issues involve only abuses occurring in faraway lands, like government killings of students in China's Tiananmen Square. To what extent would the world have heard of these killings, if China had already been a staunch advocate of the free market in 1989?

People must see that children are entitled to special care and assistance, and that everyone is entitled to a just social order as asserted in the Universal Declaration. It may be shocking to realize that nearly one in five children in this country goes to bed hungry or at risk of being hungry each night. Questioning the status quo and being willing to do something about it might result in loneliness, retaliation, and ostracism. "Smile," the theme song to Charlie Chaplin's *Modern Times,* might be worth singing to oneself (it is okay to sing to oneself): "Smile tho' your heart is aching, smile even tho' it's breaking, when there are clouds in the sky, you'll get by, if you smile through your fear and sorrow, smile and maybe tomorrow, you'll see the sun come shining through, for you." Chaplin was not allowed to return this country because of his political activism for some time. Anyway, the revolution is fun, as the 1960s activist Abbie Hoffman used to say. Smiling and laughter even have the power to strengthen the immune system and not only prolong one's life, but improve the quality of life for all, the ultimate aim of human rights and social justice work. Laughter is the best medicine (Cousins, 2005).

Eleventh, it is important to have a human rights/social justice support group. Granted, this work may, at times, become too serious. It is important to take human rights seriously, but there is also joy in struggle, and human rights work can and should be fun. Sharing with others who have similar concerns and can provide the social supports you need may be one way to appreciate this paradox. And, as I've argued and as my experiences working on an Amnesty International House at a county fair in Alaska have shown, human rights has the power to unite the left and the right. Radicals, liberals, and conservatives have all signed petitions to do away with torture, a major human rights violation worldwide. The challenge is to collectively demonstrate how torture is intimately related to other rights, such as peace, and meaningful and gainful employment, not to mention the dignity of the human person. However, this awareness will not come easily, as cultures are sometimes embedded in notions of superiority and correctness that hinder creative dialogue. The warmth of the herd, as Friedrich Nietzsche reminds us, should be helpful. The group solidarity of friends and colleagues searching for truth, in a spirit of humility, and trying to eke out a socially just world with human rights at its core should provide its own soulful healing mechanisms.

Twelfth, while working for social justice is serious business, it is important to have a playful attitude. It is no joke that nearly 40% of the world lives on less than two dollars per day, making each day a struggle for survival. To not burn out, one may need to have fun developing socially just action strategies. For instance, one of the social action activities suggested here was to show conservative, liberal, and radical groups a copy of the Universal Declaration (or other human rights document) and to try get them to agree to its principles as worthwhile goals. The human rights monitoring committees do not dictate how a country should go about meeting such principles, so, be playful. Take bets. Which group—conservative, liberal, or radical—will meet the goals of the Universal Declaration first? If privatization does it, so be it; if private/public partnerships do it, so be it; or if public initiatives do it, so be it. Imagine Democrats, Republicans, or Socialists buying their opponents dinner, for having met the goals of the Universal Declaration! A little silly? Perhaps. But play does have its place in this enterprise called humanity.

Thirteenth, build on strengths and work on weaknesses. People are good at some things and not so good at others. Find what you are good at, which almost certainly is something you like and enjoy. Be happy working for social justice. If the spirit moves you, work on your weaknesses. Some enjoy writing; others enjoy public speaking; others like playing a musical instrument or engaging in an artistic endeavor for peace and social justice; others enjoy joining demonstrations, marching, and picketing; others are good at resolving interpersonal conflict in groups or intrapersonal conflict in individuals; and still others aren't quite sure what they are good at yet. If you are not good at playing a musical instrument, but see its power for peace, maybe you could start learning to play one now. If you feel you are too old, too young, too experienced, or too inexperienced, don't discriminate against yourself. Anyone of any age can always make a contribution. Whatever your decisions, do some soul searching as to your strengths and weaknesses and act accordingly.

Fourteenth, and most controversial, human rights defenders/social justice advocates must be around. Some peacemakers, like King, Gandhi, and Mandela, have been imprisoned for their nonviolent actions. Their growing international notoriety aided their cause. King's *Letter from a Birmingham Jail* is a classic treatise in social action written in 1963, while King was serving a term for participating in demonstrations in Birmingham. He was responding to eight prominent white liberal clergymen, who wanted him to slow down, to leave the civil rights battle to the local and federal courts. One must take risks, but often the not-so-famous, everyday human rights defender can be locked up, and the key thrown away. Activists should not compromise their ethics; they should be bold and courageous like the eagle and foolish at times. Yet, being around is generally preferable to not being around. The famed late Beatle and peacemaker (aka walrus), John Lennon, was fond of saying that he and his beloved Yoko did not want to be called Mr. and Mrs. Dead Saint. Ultimately, however, this is a decision human rights defenders and social justice advocates can only make for themselves. Let history be the judge, provided it is not the lies written by the victors, as the poet Lawrence Ferlinghetti (1997) reminds us. One often hears about heroes dying for a cause. When it comes to human rights and social justice, why not live for a cause?

Fifteenth, make your own ground rules. Remember there is always a core of wisdom within each one of us, something akin to Carl Jung's notion of the 2-million-year-old person who exists deep within our souls. Listen to that core (from the French *coeur* meaning "heart"). What is your heart thinking, feeling, and saying? What does your inner being want you to do to create a socially just world? How are your inner musings similar and/or different from the material presented in this book? As the theologian Paul Tillich (2000) urged us, have the courage to be, to be yourself, come to your own conclusions, and take your own actions alone or in concert with others. Know the very simple secret that the fox told the little prince in Antoine Saint Exupery's (1971) classic tale: "It is only with the heart that one can see rightly; what is essential is invisible to the eye" (p. 87).

Finally, whatever our beliefs and despite setbacks, it is of absolute importance to keep a pathological belief in the impossible and the vision of hope that human rights/social justice work entails. This vision is necessary on all levels of intervention, from the meta-macro to the meta-micro. Social justice advocates can maintain allegiance to humanity, promote world citizenship, and work positively and creatively with global organizations like the WTO and the World Bank. They can promote health care and meaningful employment for all. They can, as administrators, develop communities of compassion in the workplace. In spite of an unjust social order, helping and health professionals can develop treatment modalities in accordance with internationally accepted standards of patient care and medical ethics. Research can incorporate human rights principles in ways that are persuasive and meaningful, adding to the policy debates in ways that can create massive social change. As helping and health professionals, or just human beings trying to live the best they know how, they may—with a smile, a kind word, or a concerned glance—make a difference in the life of a child, a homeless person, or those marginalized and barely visible to policy makers. Every right in the

Figure 6.2   A Mountain Sculpture of Crazy Horse. The great indigenous
spiritual leader called us to a life of peace, humility, and
everlasting love.

Source: Used with permission. © Crazy Horse Memorial Foundation.

Universal Declaration of Human Rights can be realized. We are socialized
into thinking this is not possible. But it is possible! And in social action and
service to humanity, we must ever be mindful of the spirit of Crazy Horse—
peace, humility, and everlasting love—who said: "A very great vision is
needed and the man [person] who has it must follow it as the eagle seeks the
deepest blue of the sky" (Indigenous Peoples' Literature, 2006, p. 1).

Conclusion

It was Voltaire who said, "The secret of being a bore . . . is to tell everything" (*Discours en vers sur l'homme*, cited in Partington, 1992, p. 716).
This book could not tell everything, but hopefully, it has kept your interest.
With the information provided, you should now have enough to go on, what
the professional literature refers to as minimal competency, to become independent scholar-practitioners and public-spirited world citizens moving
toward a human rights culture and a socially just world. The soil needs tilling with the tools that human rights provides so those engaged in social

action and service to every person, everywhere can, as Voltaire urged in his *Candide*, cultivate their garden.

Questions for Discussion

1. Comment critically on the following two responses to the question, How many human rights defenders, social justice advocates, and/or social activists does it take to screw in a light bulb?

Response 1: First, you need someone to create a persuasive argument that human rights should serve as a foundation for social justice. Screwing in a light bulb is a definite human right worth pursuing. Every person, everywhere, after all, needs a light bulb. An understanding of the philosophical and historical antecedents to the history of the idea of human rights would be necessary. Then, someone must draft a Declaration on the Human Right to Screw in a Light Bulb. Others must debate the extent to which the notion of duties ought to be part of the declaration, or whether a guiding principles document might be more appropriate. Another person is necessary to write a declaration; another to disseminate it for discussion to the appropriate bodies for signature and ratification. Then governments debate the declaration in the appropriate domestic legislative arena, and finally submit it for the advice and consent of appropriate policy makers. Others educate the populace about how to reach a general consensus on the fundamental freedom and corresponding duty to light bulb rotation. Some educate the judiciary, informing them of the Supremacy Clause of the U.S. Constitution that, should an International Convention on the Right to Screw in a Light Bulb (CRSLB) result, they would be "bound thereby." Should such a convention be successful, there would need to be an International Light Bulb Monitoring Committee to engage in a creative dialogue with the appropriate domestic body for each article of the convention. In turn, that domestic body would respond to the concluding comments of the Light Bulb Monitoring Committee. NGOs are necessary to ensure government accountability to their commitments to the CRSLB. After agreeing that, indeed, the right to screw in a light bulb is a fundamental human right and freedom, you then petition the government for money to buy a light bulb. However, the government responds that it has no funds, having allocated all monies to the drafting of light bulb documents, reports, and eliciting input from NGOs.

Response 2: It takes just one!

2. At the beginning of this journey, this book stressed dialogues between human rights principles and other value, spiritual, and belief systems focusing

on nonviolence, a thirst for social justice, care of the needy, and the Golden Rule, that is, to do unto others as you would have them do unto you. To what extent do you now find human rights principles consistent or inconsistent with such value systems? How would you now define social justice? How is your definition similar and/or different from principles presented in this work? How can continual creative dialogue be maintained with other perspectives and systems of belief and values to ensure socially just values are *chosen*, the only way that such principles can endure?

Now imagine the following scenario, which can be all too real. The scene begins with Khayrat, Palestinian Representative to the UN Human Rights Council in Geneva, and Simcha, Israeli Representative to the UN Human Rights Council, talking over a cup of coffee at *Bar Serpent*, an open informal gathering place at the UN, somewhat in the shape of a spiraling snake. (It is OK to be a little "bad" here, if you wish to imagine an accent, as long as you don't hurt anybody. But be certain to keep your musings to yourself.)

Khayrat (Palestinian Representative):	Simcha, they're building another wall again. My people can't find jobs, many are hungry, and drinkable water is at a premium.
Simcha (Israeli Representative):	I know, Khayrat. It's a terrible situation. I told them to stop, but they are not listening to me. They tell me there is violence there, and they need the wall to protect themselves.
Khayrat:	I know, Simcha. I told them to stop with the violence. But they are not listening to me. Whenever there is violence, there is a problem that is not being addressed.
Simcha:	I know, Khayrat. Centuries of religious and ethnic intolerance, nationalistic pride, and dogma. No one likes to see anyone suffer. When will it all end?
Khayrat:	I don't know, Simcha. Yes, centuries of intolerance, nationalist pride, and dogma. I think we need to be careful, Simcha. Maybe, if we continue to talk like this, we might be out of a job.
Simcha:	I know what you mean. Well, maybe. But sometimes I think those in power already know the truth, but for whatever reason, they don't say it.

Khayrat:	But things are complicated. Maybe dogma is OK. After all, human dignity, nonviolence, and duties to those less fortunate is fundamental to almost every spiritual belief system. Do unto others. And being decent to one another is essential to secular humanism and can be found in nearly every ethical code, professional or otherwise, and, of course, there is the Universal Declaration of Human Rights.
Simcha:	Ah, yes, the Universal Declaration, if we could only live it in thought and deed. Yes, Khayrat, very true, things are complicated.
Khayrat:	Or maybe they are just very simple. Do unto others! When will it all end? When will we learn to live together in peace?
Simcha:	Yes, when will we learn to live together in peace? We need what Martin Buber called an I-Thou relationship throughout the world where everyone, everywhere has human dignity and human rights. But we treat everyone as an I-It, as if merely a number . . .
Khayrat:	Or some kind of pawn in a game to be used, like a wage slave.

Both grimace and shake their heads back and forth.

Khayrat:	Verily, we honor every human being, says the Koran, not one or two or some, but everyone. (A long pause with an occasional sigh heard from both, as they continue to savor their coffee.) By the way, did your daughter decide what college she wants to go to?
Simcha:	She's not sure yet. But she wants to be a classical musician, another Beethoven I suppose. More power to her. I just hope she can make a living doing that. And your son?
Khayrat:	He's going into film. He wants to be another Steven Spielberg. Good for him. I hope he could make a living doing that, too.

Simcha:	Our kids always drive us crazy, don't they?
Khayrat:	You can say that again. But maybe crazy is OK.
Simcha:	Say, there's a really nice French restaurant that opened up down the street. Dinner's on me.
Khayrat:	No, I'll pay, you got it the last time.
Simcha:	No, I'll pay. I think you got it last time.
Khayrat:	I'll pay.
Simcha:	I'll pay.
Khayrat:	I'll pay.
Simcha:	I'll pay.

At an impasse, they agree to flip a coin.

Khayrat:	Well, I'm glad we were disagreeing about something. I felt we were degenerating into some kind of a mutual admiration society.
Simcha:	Me, too. Hmmm, we're doing it again. But I wish things were that simple.
Khayrat:	Me, too. There we go again.

At the beginning of dinner, both vow to keep to their diets, slowly giving in as the dinner progresses. After sharing a generous *Mille Feuilles* (called *Napoleon* in the United States), they chide each other for causing the other to go off the wagon, yet come up with an idea.

Simcha:	We have to do something next time to keep to our diets.
Khayrat:	Seems like I've heard that before. How about a socially conscious weight reduction group?
Simcha:	Great idea! After all, the less food we consume, the more there is to go around.
Khayrat:	Yes, we can eat simply so others can simply live, as corny as that saying is, and call it some kind of . . . hmmm.

Simcha:	How about something like a Gandhian Duties to the World Socially Conscious Weight Reduction Program?
Khayrat:	I think we will need to work on the title, but it's a good beginning, not bad, actually. Let's work on it.

They then both envision a support group of people of various religions, ethnicities, nationalities, occupations, and educational levels all sitting around a table united for the same cause. At the end of dinner, they say goodbye with the universal "Ciao" and ask to give regards to their respective significant other. After walking a few steps they spontaneously say in French *A demain,* meaning that they will see each other the next day.

Please comment before looking at the next questions.

Do you feel such a discussion is realistic or is it entirely imaginary? Could you imagine a similar scenario between other groups generally considered in conflict, such as in Northern Ireland or Kashmir? What would it look like? What other groups could you imagine? What do you think a second scene might look like for this scenario or for other groups? Would it turn out good or bad? How could there be a positive outcome?

What does the above dialogue have to say about the fact that working for human rights and social justice entails risk; that no one wants war; that everyone wants the best for their families; and that we are all plain, simple people trying to live the best we can? It would seem that sitting around a table discussing socially conscious weight reduction was not precisely the table of brotherhood that Martin Luther King, Jr. had in mind. What do you feel he envisioned? Does the above scenario have any "clues" as to how it can become a reality?

Do you feel that governments do respond to the will of the people, a phrase found in all 50 state constitutions in the United States? If not, how can governments fulfill the will of the people?

3. In Table 6.1, Gandhi's famous words, "First, they ignore you; then they laugh at you; then they fight you; then you win," are presented in a grid. Place x's at the stages at which you think the various entities listed across the top of the table are now in considering human rights/social justice in their policies and practices. Write down and/or discuss your reasoning in class. Consider breaking some entities into subcategories, for example, grammar school, high school, college, and postgraduate education, under Education. What other entities, organizations, or specific policies and practices should be listed? Should there

Table 6.1 A Gandhian Social Movement Assessment Grid of Compliance With Human Rights/Social Justice Principles

Gandhi's Words	Paraphrase	Legislation	President	Supreme Court Decisions	Corporate Practices	Professional Organizations	Educational Institutions	The Media	The General Consensus
First they ignore you	Ignored								
Then they laugh at you	Laughed at								
Then they fight you*	In the process of fighting								
Then you win*	Won								

*Fighting here means direct nonviolent action. Winning is the implementation of human rights/social justice principles based on profound mutual understandings of their importance and in the spirit of friendship and tolerance, as enunciated in the Universal Declaration and its progeny, rather than their superficial inclusion in policy and practice.

be different grids for civil and political; economic, social, and cultural; and solidarity rights? Be creative. Try to include the same organizations from the left and the right that you may have shown the Universal Declaration, as suggested in Chapter 1. Share your assessment with them as a springboard for creative dialogue. Considering that roughly one third of U.S. resources go to defense spending, should the military also be included? Why or why not?

4. Engage in a reflective meditation with some heavy-duty soul searching. Relax, close your eyes if you like, sit or lie comfortably, and think of all the commitments you have to yourself, your partner, friends, family, place of employment, education, and/or community. Now given your social and economic commitments, begin thinking about where you would like to direct your limited time and energies to make best use of your talents to create a socially just world. Now come back to the world and share whatever you would like about your meditations to whomever you would like. Think about doing similar meditations throughout your career as a human rights defender/social justice advocate.

5. Consider how you, as a world citizen, can create a socially just world, constructed from the foundation of a human rights culture, which is a lived awareness of human rights principles in mind, spirit, and body with patience, persistence, humility, courage, and creativity with vision and hope in the spirit of nonviolence for every person, everywhere, always seeking the voices and dignity of those you are trying to help while keeping in mind that, paradoxically, social justice is a joyful struggle. Be especially mindful of the wise words of Rev. Dr. Martin Luther King, Jr.:

> Everybody can be great because everybody can serve. You don't have to have a college degree to serve. You don't have to make your subject and your verb agree to serve. You don't have to know about Plato and Aristotle to serve. You don't have to know Einstein's theory of relativity to serve. You only need a heart full of grace. A soul generated by love. (King, 1987, p. 17)

Activity/Action

1. Create a socially just world constructed from a foundation of human rights principles with a heart full of grace and a soul generated by love!

Note

1. These ground rules, modified here, were initially given in a series of lectures in India, 2001: *The Dr. Ambedkar Lectures on the Theme of the Creation of a Human*

Rights Culture, published by the National Institute of Social Work and Social Sciences (NISWSS), Bhubaneswar, Orissa, India. Dr. Ambedkar, often called the Father of the Indian Constitution, is often credited with outlawing, at least in constitutional fiat, the caste system and untouchability.

Annotated Media Resources

Please note, especially in regard to R rated and, at times, NR (not rated) movies, viewer discretion is strongly advised.

A force more powerful (2000). [DVD]. Available from: www.aforce morepowerful.org. A PBS documentary illustrating the power of direct nonviolent action as a social change strategy to overcome oppression and promote social justice in the global community. Available with an accompanying book, games, and resources to understand and use nonviolence effectively. 180 min. NR.

Amnesty International. (1995). *Forsaken cries: The story of Rwanda—end genocide; educating for action* [Video]. New York: Author. Accompanied by an educational packet, this video, made on a small budget, examines historical antecedents to the massacre and questions why the world failed to respond to the anguished cries in this Rwandan holocaust. 35 min. NR.

Attenborough, R. (Director). (1982). *Gandhi* [Video]. Burbank, CA: Columbia Tristar Home Video. Winner of nine academy awards, this is about Mahatma Gandhi, who led a social movement to liberate India from England and achieve the right to self-determination of its people. 187 min. Rated G.

Barnen, R. (Society). (2003). *The sexual exploitation of children: Taking a stand* [DVD]. Princeton, NJ: Films for the Humanities and Sciences. Integrating articles from the Convention on the Rights of the Child, this film examines child sexual abuse within the context of globalization, calling for international adherence to human rights principles so that child molesters have no safe haven. 55 min. NR.

Board of Trustees of the University of Illinois. (1992). *The women of Hull House: A documentary* [Video]. Chicago: University of Illinois. Although a bit "status-conscious," this film examines some of the remarkable contributions of Jane Addams as a social entrepreneur and in regard to women's rights, international peace, and social justice. 28 min. NR.

Chaplin, C. (Director). (1940). *The great dictator* [DVD]. A kind of comic relief amid the tragedy of a major pogrom in human history, one of the world's most famous comedians, in his own inimitable style, attempted to bring attention to the Hitlerian threat, while Hollywood looked the other way. 120 min. NR.

Dannefer, R., & Haddon, H. (Directors). (2004). *Bloqueo: Looking at the US embargo against Cuba* [Video]. Available from: cinematicsisters@yahoo.com. Joining the Pastors for Peace Caravan and featuring voices from the streets of Havana, this video examines the impact of the U.S. embargo, including food and medical supplies, against Cuba. 45 min. NR.

Erman, J. (Director). (1982). *Eleanor: First lady of the world* [Video]. United States: Embassy Television. Starring Jean Stapleton, formerly the lovable wife of Archie Bunker, of the famed TV show *All in the Family,* this film recounts the competence and chutzpah of the former First Lady, Eleanor Roosevelt, Chairperson of the drafting committee of the Universal Declaration of Human Rights, as well as the story of some of the debates leading to its endorsement by the General Assembly with no dissent. 96 min. Rated G.

Forman, M. (Director). (1975). *One flew over the cuckoo's nest* [DVD]. Warner Brothers. An amusing, but perhaps poignant statement of how helping can hurt. This fictionalized account, however exaggerated, perhaps leads the viewer in dramatic sequencing to question how the helping and health professions adhere to fundamental principles of medical ethics and protection of persons with mental illness. 133 min. Rated R.

Frankenheimer, J. (Director). (1994). *The burning season: The Chico Mendes story* [Video]. Burbank, CA: Warner Home Video. Story of the nonviolent activist, union leader, political candidate, and socialist, which illustrates the interdependency of workers' rights with environmental sustainability. 125 min. Rated R.

George. T. (Director). (2004). *Hotel Rwanda* [DVD]. United Artists. A profile in courage, to borrow a term from President John F. Kennedy, this film highlights some necessary risks one must take to become a "true" human rights defender, in the face of odds that seem nearly impossible. It illustrates that one can achieve success, if one has a "pathological belief in the impossible." A learning packet is also available from Amnesty International. 120 min. Rated PG-13.

Greenwald, R. (Director). (2005). *Wal-mart: The high cost of low price* [DVD]. Culver City, CA: Brave New Films. A riveting documentary depicting what a major conglomerate can do to communities if left unchecked and how social activists intent on ensuring jobs with dignity and reasonable wages succeeded in curbing its influence. 97 min. with a condensed 20 min. version. NR.

Guggenheim, C. (Director). (1995). *The shadow of hate: A history of intolerance in America* [Video]. Montgomery, AL: Southern Poverty Law Center. With brief original footage of a KKK gathering in front of the country's Capitol, this film illustrates the oppressive power of hate speech. 40 min. NR.

Haggis, P. (Director). (2004). *Crash* [DVD]. Burbank, CA: Artisan Home Entertainment. Though concentrating primarily on race, this film poignantly demonstrates the insidious effects of racism in our everyday lives, but offers rays of hope, the possibility to transcend prejudice, and the need to place the highest priority on human life. 121 min. Rated R.

The honour of all: The story of Alkali Lake (1986). [Video]. Sante Fe, NM: Phil Lucas Productions. The story of a Native American community's struggle for self-determination, with particular attention to its successful attempt through community empowerment to combat alcoholism. Three parts. Part I is especially powerful. 56 min. (for Part I). NR.

Houston, B. (Director). (2002). *Mighty times: The legacy of Rosa Parks* [Video]. Montgomery, AL: Southern Poverty Law Center. A moving and inspirational account of Rosa Parks's courage, with a stirring speech from a younger Martin Luther King, Jr. 40 min. NR.

Hirsi, B., Abdallah, B., & Anthony, N. (Directors). (2002). *9/11 Through Saudi eyes* [DVD]. Princeton, NJ: Films for the Humanities and Sciences. Illustrating the importance of eliciting the voices of those often neglected, and calling for sustained international dialogue, this DVD poignantly depicts some of the events leading up to 9/11, including the anguish of the parents of the hijackers. 54 min. NR.

Katz, J. (Director). (2002). *Strange fruit* [DVD]. South Burlington, VT: California Newsreel/Resolution. About the song written by social activist Abel Meeropol and made popular by Billie Holiday, bringing viewers face to face with the terror of lynching, and also spotlighting the vision and courage of those who fought for social justice at the risk of one's livelihood if white and life if black. 57 min. NR.

Karezi, J., Kazakos, C, Negrepontis, Y., & Zervoulakos, G. (Directors). (1987). *Lysistrata* [Video]. Brooklyn: New York Film Annex. The play, put on at the beginning of the 2004 Olympics in Greece and read globally before the war in Afghanistan, thanks to WILPF; Aristophanes's classic comedy poignantly illustrates the power of one of the greatest community organizers of all time, Lysistrata, who persuaded women to go on a sex strike, to keep their men from going to war. Hilarious, but its message is indeed a terse statement on the human condition. In Greek with English subtitles. 101 min. NR.

Malcolm X: Death of a prophet (1972). [Video]. Fort Mill, SC: Sterling Entertainment Group. Story of the actual circumstances surrounding the death of Malcolm X, but most noteworthy for actual footage of the famed African American Islamic leader who asserted, for one, that the struggle is no longer a "matter of civil rights, but human rights." 60 min. NR.

Moore, M. (Director). (2007). *Sicko* [soon in DVD]. By the increasingly famous director of such movies as *Bowling for Columbine,* illustrating how "unlived life" can lead to destruction, and *Roger and Me,* about corporate policies of questionable ethics, this latest *tour de farce* is a humorous, yet paradoxically tragic look at the health system in the United States largely in comparison with other countries where medical care, a human right, is paid for by taxes. 113 min. Rated PG-13.

Peltier, M. (Director). (1994). *Break the silence: Kids against child abuse* [Video]. Sherman Oaks, CA: Arnold Shapiro Productions. The voices of children, speaking of their experiences of abuse and neglect, and providing insight, with a profound spirituality, into the bleak chasm of cruelty to children. 28 min. NR.

People's Decade for Human Rights Education. (2005). *Women hold up the sky* [Video]. Available from: www.pdhre.org. A number of short stories from various countries illustrating the struggle of women for empowerment. Approx. 120 min. NR.

Pontecorvo, G. (Director). (1965). *Battle of Algiers* [DVD]. A classic pseudodocumentary depicting a struggle for self-determination among the people of Algeria, while under alleged French protection. With stirring scenes of gross human rights violations, this picture is not for the fainthearted. 123 min. NR.

Riefenstahl, L. (Director). (1935). *Triumph of the will* [DVD]. Synapse. With stunning visual sequences and strategically crafted arguments by Adolf Hitler, the film is a distressing reminder of the power of the media to outrageously and blatantly violate the rights of millions. 110 min. NR.

Roberts, J. (Director). (1994). *The quiet revolution: Bangladesh* [Video]. One of the first films on the Grameen Bank, this story illustrates that "credit," in this case, the distribution of low-interest loans allowing recipients to live life becomingly and with dignity, can be a means of empowerment for families. 28 min. NR.

School of assassins (2001). [Video]. Maryknoll Productions. This video shows efforts of people from all walks of life protesting against the School of the Americas, in Fort Benning, Georgia, recently renamed the Western Hemisphere Institute for Security and Cooperation (WHISC), which protestors argue has served as an enforcer of Third World debt, structural adjustment policies, globalization, and the "war against the poor" in general. 30 min. NR.

September 11 (2002). [DVD]. Empire Pictures. Available from: www.empirepicturesusa.com. For the aspiring world citizen, a provocative and artistic international coproduction from 11 directors, 11 countries, each offering 11-minute vignettes responding to the events of 9/11 from unique cultural perspectives. 135 min. NR.

Singer, M. (Director). (2000). *Dark days* [DVD]. Available from: www.darkdays.com. A qualitative investigation with the homeless as "coresearchers" who share their struggles, hopes, and at times somber humor, while living in the subways of New York City. 84 min. NR.

Survivors fifty years after Hiroshima (1994). [Video]. Oakland, CA: Video Project. The actual voices of survivors of the atomic bombing of Hiroshima, with commentary by Robert Lifton, author of a qualitative study, *Death in life: Survivors of Hiroshima*. Approx. 50 min. NR.

Toledo, S. (Director). (1990). *One man's war* [Video]. Starring Anthony Hopkins, this is the story behind the federal case-precedenting *Filartiga v. Pena-Irala* (1980), which asserted the Universal Declaration of Human Rights as customary international law. Here Dr. Filartiga attempts to bring to justice in U.S. courts the torturers of his son, Joelita, for an horrific act committed in Paraguay. 91 min. Rated PG-13.

Williams, S. (Director). (2000). *Eleanor Roosevelt: The American experience* [PBS Video]. Burbank, CA: Time Warner. A documentary of the once most powerful woman in the United States, whose "FBI file was thicker than a stack of phone books." 150 min. NR.

Appendix A

The Universal Declaration of Human Rights

Whereas recognition of the inherent dignity and of the equal and inalienable rights of all members of the human family is the foundation of freedom, justice and peace in the world.

Whereas disregard and contempt for human rights have resulted in barbarous acts which have outraged the conscience of mankind, and the advent of a world in which human beings shall enjoy freedom of speech and belief and freedom from fear and want has been proclaimed as the highest aspiration of the common people.

Whereas it is essential, if man is not to be compelled to have recourse, as a last resort, to rebellion against tyranny and oppression, that human rights should be protected by the rule of law.

Whereas it is essential to promote the development of friendly relations between nations.

Whereas the peoples of the United Nations have in the Charter reaffirmed their faith in fundamental human rights, in the dignity and worth of the human person and in the equal rights of men and women and have determined to promote social progress and better standards of life in larger freedom.

Whereas Member States have pledged themselves to achieve, in co-operation with the United Nations, the promotion of universal respect for and observance of human rights and fundamental freedoms.

Whereas, a common understanding of these rights and freedoms is of the greatest importance for the full realization of this pledge.

Now, therefore, the General Assembly proclaims this Universal Declaration of Human Rights as a common standard of achievement for all peoples and all nations, to the end that every individual and every organ of society, keeping this Declaration constantly in mind, shall strive by teaching and education to promote respect for these rights and freedoms and by progressive measures, national and international, to secure their universal and effective recognition and observance, both among the peoples of Member States themselves and among the peoples of territories under their jurisdiction.

Article 1. All human beings are born free and equal in dignity and rights. They are endowed with reason and conscience and should act towards one another in a spirit of brotherhood.

Article 2. Everyone is entitled to all the rights and freedoms set forth in this Declaration, without distinction of any kind, such as race, color, sex, language, religion, political or other opinion, national or social origin, property, birth or other status.

Furthermore, no distinction shall be made on the basis of the political, jurisdictional or international status of the country or territory to which a person belongs, whether it be independent, trust, non-self governing or under any other limitation of sovereignty.

Article 3. Everyone has the right to life, liberty and security of person.

Article 4. No one shall be held in slavery or servitude; slavery and the slave trade shall be prohibited in all their forms.

Article 5. No one shall be subjected to torture or to cruel, inhuman or degrading treatment or punishment.

Article 6. Everyone has the right to recognition everywhere as a person before the law.

Article 7. All are equal before the law and are entitled without any discrimination to equal protection of the law. All are entitled to equal protection against any discrimination in violation of this Declaration and against any incitement to such discrimination.

Article 8. Everyone has the right to an effective remedy by the competent national tribunals for acts violating the fundamental rights granted him by the constitution or by law.

Article 9. No one shall be subjected to arbitrary arrest, detention or exile.

Article 10. Everyone is entitled in full equality to a fair and public hearing by an independent and impartial tribunal, in the determination of his rights and obligations and of any criminal charge against him.

Article 11. (1) Everyone charged with a penal offense has the right to be presumed innocent until proved guilty according to law in a public trial at which he has had all the guarantees necessary for his defense. (2) No one shall be held guilty of any penal offense on account of any act or omission which did not constitute a penal offense, under national or international law, at the time when it was committed. Nor shall a heavier penalty be imposed than the one that was applicable at the time the penal offense was committed.

Article 12. No one shall be subjected to arbitrary interference with his privacy, family, home or correspondence, nor to attacks upon his honor and reputation. Everyone has the right to the protection of the law against such interference or attacks.

Article 13. (1) Everyone has the right to freedom of movement and residence within the borders of each State. (2) Everyone has the right to leave any country, including his own, and to return to his country.

Article 14. (1) Everyone has the right to seek and to enjoy in other countries asylum from persecution. (2) This right may not be invoked in the case of prosecutions genuinely arising from non-political crimes or from acts contrary to the purposes and principles of the United Nations.

Article 15. (1) Everyone has the right to a nationality. (2) No one shall be arbitrarily deprived of his nationality nor denied the right to change his nationality.

Article 16. (1) Men and women of full age, without any limitation due to race, nationality or religion, have the right to marry and to found a family. They are entitled to equal rights as to marriage, during marriage and at its dissolution. (2) Marriage shall be entered into only with the free and full consent of the intending spouses. (3) The family is the natural and fundamental group unit of society and is entitled to protection by society and the State.

Article 17. (1) Everyone has the right to own property alone as well as in association with others. (2) No one shall be arbitrarily deprived of his property.

Article 18. Everyone has the right to freedom of thought, conscience and religion; this right includes freedom to change his religion or belief, and freedom, either alone or in community with others and in public or private, to manifest his religion or belief in teaching, practice, worship and observance.

Article 19. Everyone has the right to freedom of opinion and expression; this right includes freedom to hold opinions without interference and to seek, receive and impart information and ideas through any media and regardless of frontiers.

Article 20. (1) Everyone has the right to freedom of peaceful assembly and association. (2) No one may be compelled to belong to an association.

Article 21. (1) Everyone has the right to take part in the government of his country, directly or through freely chosen representatives. (2) Everyone has the right of equal access to public service in his country. (3) The will of the people shall be the basis of the authority of government; this will shall be expressed in periodic and genuine elections which shall be by universal and equal suffrage and shall be held by secret vote or by equivalent free voting procedures.

Article 22. Everyone, as a member of society, has the right to social security and is entitled to realization, through national effort and international co-operation and in accordance with the organization and resources of each State, of the economic, social and cultural rights indispensable for his dignity and the free development of his personality.

Article 23. (1) Everyone has the right to work, to free choice of employment, to just and favorable conditions of work and to protection against unemployment. (2) Everyone, without any discrimination, has the right to equal pay for equal work. (3) Everyone has the right to just and favorable remuneration ensuring for himself and his family an existence worthy of human dignity, and supplemented, if necessary, by other means of social protection. (4) Everyone has the right to form and to join trade unions for the protection of his interests.

Article 24. Everyone has the right to rest and leisure, including reasonable limitation of working hours and periodic holidays with pay.

Article 25. (1) Everyone has the right to a standard of living adequate for the health and well-being of himself and of his family, including food, clothing, housing and medical care and necessary social services, and the right to security in the event of unemployment, sickness, disability, widowhood, old age or other lack of livelihood in circumstances beyond his control. (2) Motherhood and childhood are entitled to special care and assistance. All children, whether born in or out of wedlock, shall enjoy the same social protection.

Article 26. (1) Everyone has the right to education. Education shall be free, at least in the elementary and fundamental stages. Elementary education shall be compulsory. Technical and professional education shall be made generally available and higher education shall be equally accessible to all on the basis of merit. (2) Education shall be directed to the full development of the human personality and to the strengthening of respect for human rights and fundamental freedoms. It shall promote understanding, tolerance and friendship among all nations, racial or religious groups, and shall further the activities of the United Nations for the maintenance of peace. (3) Parents have a prior right to choose the kind of education that shall be given to their children.

Article 27. (1) Everyone has the right to freely participate in the cultural life of the community, to enjoy the arts and to share in scientific advancement and its benefits. (2) Everyone has the right to the protection of the moral and material interests resulting from any scientific, literary or artistic production of which he is the author.

Article 28. Everyone is entitled to a social and international order in which the rights and freedoms set forth in this Declaration can be fully realized.

Article 29. (1) Everyone has duties to the community in which alone the free and full development of his personality is possible. (2) In the exercise of his rights and freedoms, everyone shall be subject only to such limitations as are determined by law solely for the purpose of securing due recognition and

respect for the rights and freedoms of others and of meeting the just requirements of morality, public order and the general welfare in a democratic
society. (3) These rights and freedoms may in no case be exercised contrary
to the purposes and principles of the United Nations.

Article 30. Nothing in this Declaration may be interpreted as implying for
any State, group or person any right to engage in any activity or to perform
any act aimed at the destruction of any of the rights and freedoms set forth
herein.

Appendix B

Portions of Select Articles
From Select Major International
Documents Following the Universal
Declaration of Human Rights[1]

The International Covenant on Civil and Political Rights (ICCPR)

Article 1. All people have the right of self-determination. By virtue of that right they freely determine their political status and freely pursue their economic, social and cultural development.

Article 6(5). Sentence of death shall not be imposed for crimes committed by persons below eighteen years of age and shall not be carried out on pregnant women.

Article 10(2). Accused juvenile persons shall be separated from adults and brought as speedily as possible for adjudication. (3). The penitentiary system shall comprise treatment of prisoners the essential aim of which shall be their reformation and social rehabilitation.

Article 14(6). When a person has by a final decision been convicted of a criminal offence and when subsequently his conviction has been reversed . . . the person who has suffered punishment as a result of such conviction shall be compensated . . .

Article 18(2). No one shall be subject to coercion which would impair his freedom to have or to adopt a religion or belief of his choice.

Article 20(1). Any propaganda for war should be prohibited by law.

Article 24(3). Every child shall be registered immediately after birth and shall have a name.

The International Covenant on Economic, Social and Cultural Rights (CESCR)

Article 7(1). State parties . . . recognize the right of everyone to the full enjoyment of just and favorable conditions of work which ensure in particular . . . fair wages and equal remuneration for work of equal value . . . safe and healthy working conditions . . . equal opportunity for everyone to be promoted in his employment to an appropriate higher level, subject to no considerations other than those of seniority and competence; rest, leisure and reasonable limitation of working hours and periodic holidays with pay, as well as remuneration for public holidays.

Article 10(2). Special protection should be accorded to mothers during a reasonable period before and after childbirth. During such period working mothers should be accorded paid leave or leave with adequate social security benefits.

Article 11(2). State parties . . . recognizing the fundamental right of everyone to be free from hunger shall take individually and through international co-operation, the measures, including specific programmes . . . to improve methods of production, conservation and distribution of food by making full use of technical and scientific knowledge, by disseminating knowledge of the principles of nutrition and by developing or reforming agrarian systems in such a way as to achieve the most efficient development and utilization of natural resources.

Article 12(1). State parties . . . recognize the right of everyone to the enjoyment of the highest attainable standard of physical and mental health. (2). Steps to be taken . . . to achieve the full realization of this right shall include . . . the provision of the reduction of the stillbirth-rate and of infant mortality and for the healthy development of the child; the improvement of all aspects of environmental and industrial hygiene; the prevention, treatment and control of epidemic, endemic, occupational and other diseases; the creation of conditions which would assure to all medical service and medical attention in the event of sickness.

The Convention on the Elimination of Discrimination Against Women (CEDAW)

Article 2(1). State parties condemn discrimination against women in all its forms, agree to pursue by all appropriate means and without delay a policy of eliminating discrimination against women . . . [and] undertake: to embody the principles of equality of men and women in their national constitutions . . . to take appropriate measures, including legislation, to modify or abolish existing laws, regulations, customs and practices which constitute discrimination against women.

Article 7(1). State parties shall . . . ensure to women, on equal terms with men, the right: to participate in the formulation of government policy and the implementation thereof and to hold public office and perform all public functions at all levels of government; to participate in non-governmental organizations and associations concerned with the public and political life of this country.

Article 10(1). State parties shall . . . eliminate discrimination against women . . . in the field of education . . . to ensure on the basis of equality of men and women the same conditions for career and vocational guidance, for access to studies . . . access to the same curricula, the same examinations . . . the elimination of any stereotyped concept of the roles of men and women at all levels . . . the same opportunities to benefit from scholarships and other study grants . . . the reduction of female student drop-out rates and the organization of programmes for girls and women who have left school prematurely . . . information and advice on family planning.

Article 11(1). State parties shall . . . eliminate discrimination against women . . . in the field of employment . . . to ensure on the basis of equality of men and women, the same right, in particular . . . the right to work as an inalienable right of all human beings; . . . the right to social security, particularly in cases of retirement, unemployment, sickness, invalidity and old age and other incapacity to work, as well as the right to paid leave; the right to protection of health and to safety in working conditions, including the safeguarding of the function of reproduction.

Article 11(2). State parties shall take appropriate measures to prohibit, subject to the imposition of sanctions, dismissal on the grounds of pregnancy or of maternity leave and discrimination in dismissals on the basis of marital status; to introduce maternity leave with pay or with comparable social benefits without loss of former employment, seniority or social allowances; to encourage the provision of the necessary supporting social services to enable parents to combine family obligations with work responsibilities and participation in public life, in particular through promoting the establishing and development of a network of child-care facilities.

Note

1. Caution is necessary so that articles are not viewed in isolation. Whereas core themes of major human rights documents are in the body of this text, they are here only for illustrative purposes depicting their exact wording as stated in portions of select articles. These and other major documents can be found on the Internet in their entirety at http://193.194.138.190/html/intlinst.htm

Glossary

Civil and Political Rights—Also referred to as first-generation or negative rights, they represent government's obligation to refrain from interfering with such rights as freedoms of speech, the press, and peaceful assembly.

Convention—Used interchangeably with the word *Covenant*, this generally refers to a legally binding document, often with the status of treaty, to which a government must adhere.

Cultural Relativism—An awareness that one culture is as good as another, necessitating noninterference with a particular culture even if there is evidence that it goes against fundamental human rights principles.

Customary International Law—Human rights principles by which the global community feels it must abide, irrespective of a state party's formal commitments.

Declaration—Often this is merely a hortatory statement of rights that a government and/or international body has agreed to, such as the *Declaration* of Independence and *Universal Declaration* of Human Rights.

Discrimination—Viewing the human person as an "actuality," rather than a "possibility," with the ability to transcend perceived characteristics divorced from a person's potential as a human being.

Economic, Social, and Cultural Rights—Also referred to as second-generation or positive rights, these represent governments' obligation to provide for such rights as health care, security in old age, and special protections for motherhood and the family.

Ethics Codes—Agreed-upon principles, most often by professional organizations, which tend to assert the importance of human rights and assist in the regulation of conduct of members of the organization or group.

Existential Phenomenology—A way of thinking that seeks to understand the experiencing person as a being in the world rather than a number or category fitting into a theoretic system divorced from the lived realities of being.

Final Comments of a Human Rights Committee—A summary of the analysis of a human rights monitoring committee's reports, which includes strengths of the report as well as areas of concern.

Grant Writing—A skill needing much practice and using cognitive and heartfelt emotional approaches to ultimately form shared partnerships working toward a culture of social justice, at least in the context of the helping and health professions.

Guiding Principles—Often these constitute the first step toward drafting a document legally binding on state parties, followed by a declaration, then a convention of an international body.

Helping and Health Professionals—Those who are authorities in and dedicated to the promotion and implementation of well-being and health of mind, heart, and body, and whose trust must not be abrogated.

Humanistic Administrator—A person acting as facilitator for workers to develop their human personalities for socially useful work and in a socially just work environment.

Human Needs—Elements of being that are necessary for survival of the species of *Homo sapiens*, including, but not limited to, spiritual quests, psychological well-being, biological fulfillment, creative participation, self-actualization, security, love, and self-esteem.

Human Rights—A term coined by the United Nations and recognized in international instruments; the legal mandate is often meaningless without general consensus that such rights are necessary to fulfill human need.

Human Rights Cabinet—A policy-making body envisioned on the federal level whose responsibility is to coordinate international human rights initiatives with domestic laws and policies.

Human Rights Culture—A "lived awareness" of human rights principles, which exist not only in one's mind, in a purely cognitive sense, but on the feeling level, the level of the heart, and dragged into one's everyday life.

Human Rights Defender—Often used interchangeably and at times together with social activist, social justice advocate, and social actionist; a person involved in helping others secure rights asserted in international human rights instruments.

Human Rights Monitoring Committee—Independent experts appointed by governments to monitor a country's compliance with human rights instruments that are legally binding on state parties.

Human Rights Reports—Reports that a country must file periodically with the human rights monitoring committees to assess compliance with international human rights standards.

Interdependency of Rights—Often used interchangeably with the notion of indivisibility, meaning that one cannot discuss rights without considering corresponding duties and the interrelationships among all human rights principles.

Interdisciplinary Cooperation—An awareness that, to ultimately deal with problems pertaining to the human condition, collaboration with other disciplines and professions is necessary.

Macro Level—Sometimes referred to as primary intervention, an area of practice requiring intervention that deals with whole populations, generally on the national level.

Meta-Macro Level—An area of practice requiring intervention on a global scale and possibly beyond, undercutting fundamental assumptions, such as the nation-state as a means of affiliation or a national currency as a means of exchange.

Meta-Micro Level—An area of practice requiring interventions often divorced from professionalism per se, that take place, by and large, in a person's everyday interactions with the world, broadly defined.

Mezzo Practice—Sometimes referred to as secondary intervention, an area of practice requiring professional involvement with at-risk populations and reflecting a failure of whole-population approaches.

Micro Practice—Sometimes referred to as tertiary intervention, an area of practice requiring professional involvement with clinical populations, whose symptoms often reflect shortcomings of previous levels of intervention.

Nongovernmental Organizations (NGOs)—With the proliferation of civil society, these are groups by and large accountable not to government, but rather to the people they often purport to represent.

Nonviolence—Essential to achieving human rights and social justice, the concept is often equated with peaceful resolution of conflict and is most effective when direct.

Pathological Belief in the Impossible—A belief, requiring persistence, that the entire world can live in peace and harmony and every person, everywhere can have hope and meaning in life.

Professional Encapsulation—An awareness that every discipline has limits and may not have all the answers to ameliorating individual and social malaise.

Psychotherapy—A mode of helping that is generally formalized, seeking to change the "self-as-object" to "self-as-subject" in the face of trauma and often difficult life circumstance.

Qualitative Research—A phenomenon-bound, rather than technique-bound, form of research that attempts to elicit meaning in human experience.

Quality of Life—The relation between people and their environment, which the helping and health professions aim to improve.

Quantitative Research—A form of research that uses mathematics and statistical analysis as a means of understanding.

Sanitization of Oppression—The use of euphemisms and flowery language in a seemingly humanistic intervention that can further oppression and violence.

Sisyphus—A mythical character, popularized by the existential writer Albert Camus as a prototype for the human rights defender/social justice advocate, who finds joy in the struggle, paradox, ambiguity, and imperfection of life.

Social Activist—A person committed to human dignity and rights for all, willing to take risks to implement socially just principles.

Social Justice—Literally, fair and equitable union among a group of friends, but defined here more specifically as adherence to the principles of the Universal Declaration of Human Rights in theory and in practice.

Social Order—In the Universal Declaration of Human Rights, often used with the word "international," this order consists of taken-for-granted assumptions and actions in a person's environment. When the environment is found deficient to satisfy human need, this is often referred to as structural violence.

Social Policy—Guiding principles to improve the quality of life and, if correctly implemented, to mirror a culture consistent with human rights principles.

Solidarity Rights—Also referred to as third-generation rights, these are indicative of the failure of domestic sovereignty to solve social ills on a global scale and include such fundamental freedoms as the rights to a clean environment, humanitarian disaster relief, the common and cultural heritages of humanity, peace, development, and international distributive justice.

Structural Violence—A social and international order inadequate to fulfill human need, dignity, and rights.

Supremacy Clause—Article VI of the U.S. Constitution, which asserts that all treaties, which would include international human rights conventions ratified by the United States, ought to be the "law of the land" and the "judges bound thereby."

World Citizenship—An allegiance to humanity, irrespective of state borders.

References

Abram, M. (1991, February 11). 47th session of the UN Commission on Human Rights by the United States Representative to the United Nations in Geneva on Item B, The Right to Development. Geneva: U.S. Mission Office of Public Affairs.

Addams, J. (1994). *On education.* New Brunswick, NJ: Transaction.

Albacete, L. (2006, February 3). For the love of God. *The New York Times,* p. A27.

Alinsky, S. (1989). *Rules for radicals.* New York: Vintage.

American Medical Association. (2007). Principles of medical ethics. Retrieved February 9, 2007, from www.ama-assn.org/ama/pub/category/2512.html

American Nurses Association Center for Ethics and Human Rights. (2007). Code of ethics for nurses with interpretive statements. Retrieved February 9, 2007, from http://nursingworld.org/ethics/code/protected_nwcoe303.htm#1.1

American Psychological Association. (2007). Ethical principles of psychologists and codes of conduct. Retrieved February 7, 2007, from www2.apa.org/ethics/code2002.doc

American Public Health Association. (2005). Human rights in the curricula for health professionals. Retrieved September 28, 2005, from www.apha.org/

American Sociological Association. (2005). Statement on human rights on the occasion of the American Sociological Association's centenary. Retrieved September 27, 2005, from www.asanet.org/page.ww?section=Issue+Statements&name=Statement+on+Human

Amnesty International. (2004). *The fourth R: Human rights education as basic as reading, writing, and arithmetic.* New York: Author.

Amnesty International. (2005, April 21). 2005 UN Commission on Human Rights: Amnesty International welcomes new UN mechanism on business and human rights (IOR 41/044/2005, News Service No. 104). New York: Author.

Anderson, R., & Cissna, K. (1997). *The Martin Buber-Carl Rogers dialogue: A new transcript with commentary.* Albany: State University of New York Press.

Anelauskas, V. (1999). *Discovering America as it is.* Atlanta, GA: Clarity.

Arendt, H. (1994). *Eichmann in Jerusalem: A report on the banality of evil.* New York: Penguin.

Aspel, J. (Ed.). (2005). *Teaching about human rights.* Washington, DC: American Sociological Association.

Aurelius, M. (1984) *Marcus Aurelius: Meditations.* (M. Staniforth, Trans.). New York: Penguin.

Axline, V. (1989). *Play therapy.* New York: Ballantine.

Ayer, A., & O'Grady, J. (1992). *A dictionary of philosophical quotations.* Malden, MA: Blackwell.

Beijing Women's Conference. (1997) The UN Role. Retrieved January 15, 2006, from www.un.org/geninfo/bp/women4.html

Bornstein, D. (2004). *How to change the world: Social entrepreneurs and the power of new ideas.* New York: Oxford University Press.

Boulding, E. (2000). *Cultures of peace: The hidden side of history.* Syracuse, NY: Syracuse University Press.

Boyle, F. (2004). *Destroying world order.* Atlanta, GA: Clarity.

Brown, L., Flavin, C., & French, H. (1999). *State of the world: Millennial edition.* New York: W. W. Norton.

Bruch, H. (1976) *Learning psychotherapy: Rationale and ground rules.* Cambridge, MA: Harvard University Press.

Buber, M. (1958). *I and thou.* (R. Smith, Trans.). New York: Scribner.

Buergenthal, T., Sheldon, D., & Stewart, D. (2002). *International human rights law in a nutshell.* St. Paul, MN: West.

Burnett, K. (2002). *Relationship fundraising: A donor-based approach to the business of raising money.* San Francisco: Jossey-Bass.

Burtman, B., & Williams, J. (2006, Summer). *Twelve ten.* Atlanta, GA: U.S. Human Rights Network.

Business and Human Rights Resource Center. (2005). *Tracking the positive and negative impact of over 3000 companies worldwide.* Retrieved December 17, 2005, from www.business-humanrights.org

Camus, A. (1991). *The myth of Sisyphus and other essays.* (J. O'Brien, Trans.). New York: Random House.

Carey, B. (2005, December 27). Psychotherapy on the road to . . . where? *The New York Times,* p. D1.

Carter, J. (2002). *The Nobel Peace Prize Lecture: Delivered in Oslo on the 10th of December 2002.* New York: Simon & Shuster.

Chafee, Z. (1952). *Documents on fundamental human rights.* Cambridge, MA: Harvard University Press.

Children's Defense Fund. (2007). Over 13 million children face food insecurity. Retrieved April 18, 2007, from www.childrensdefense.org/site/News2?page=NewsArticle&id=6642

Cho, E., Crooms, L., Dorow, H., Huff, A., Scott, E., & Thomas, D. (2006). *Something inside so strong: A resource guide on human rights in the United States.* Retrieved January 15, 2006, from www.ushrnetwork.org

Chomsky, N. (2002). *The umbrella of U.S. power: The Universal Declaration of Human Rights and contradictions of U.S. policy.* New York: Seven Stories Press.

Cisco Systems. (2005). *Human rights introduction.* Retrieved January 15, 2006, from http://www.cisco.com/web/about/ac227/about_cisco_corp_citi_human_rights.html

Claude, R., & Weston, B. (1992). *Human rights in the world community.* Philadelphia: University of Pennsylvania Press.

Colaizzi, P. (1978) Psychological research as the phenomenologist views it. In R. S. Valle & M. King (Eds.), *Existential phenomenological alternatives for psychology* (pp. 48–71). New York: Oxford University Press.

Committee on Economic, Social and Cultural Rights. (2003). *Concluding observations of the Committee: The Russian Federation.* (E/C.12/1/Add.94). New York: United Nations.

Committee on the Elimination of Racial Discrimination (CERD). (2000). *Report submitted by states parties under Article 9 of the Convention: The United States of America.* (CERD/C/351/Add.1). New York: United Nations.

Committee on the Elimination of Racial Discrimination (CERD). (2001). *Concluding observations: The United States of America.* (14/08/2001.A/56/18). New York: United Nations.

Committee on the Elimination of Racial Discrimination (CERD). (2007). *Concluding observations: The United States of America.* New York: United Nations.

Cooper, A. (2004). *Tests of global governance.* Tokyo: United Nations University Press. Retrieved January 15, 2006, from http://www.highbeam.com/doc/1G1-125947152.html

Cotterall, A. & Storm, R. (2003). *The ultimate encyclopedia of mythology.* London: Hermes House.

Cousins, N. (2005). *Anatomy of an illness as perceived by the patient.* New York: Bantam.

Cranston, M. (1961). *Locke.* London: Longmans and Green.

Curtis, M. (Ed.). (1981). *The great political theorists* (Vol. 2). New York: Avon Press.

Daes, E. (2001). Striving for self-determination for indigenous peoples. In Y. Kly & D. Kly (Eds.), *In pursuit of the right to self-determination* (pp. 50–62). Atlanta, GA: Clarity.

Danaher, K. (Ed.). (2004). *Corporations are gonna get your mama. Globalization and downsizing of the American dream.* Monroe, ME: Common Courage Press.

Davis, G. (1984). *My country is the world.* Burlington, VT: NWO Publishers.

D'Entreves, A. (1959). *The medieval contribution to political thought.* New York: Humanities Press.

Department of Public Information. (1950). These rights and freedoms, *The United Nations Weekly Bulletin,* November 1, 1948–January 15, 1949.

Despouy, L. (1996). *The realization of economic, social, and cultural rights: Final report on human rights and extreme poverty.* New York: United Nations Commission on Human Rights.

Diaz, T. (2005). *Views on managed care and mental health productivity standards.* Unpublished qualitative research project. Springfield, MA: Springfield College School of Social Work.

Dillow, A. (1986). Human rights and peace. In L. Pauling (Ed.), *World encyclopedia of peace* (pp. 423–427). New York: Pergamon.

Drinan, R. (1987). *Cry of the oppressed: The history and hope of the human rights revolution.* San Francisco: Harper & Row.

Ebenstein, W. (Ed.). (1960). *Great political thinkers* (3rd. ed.). New York: Holt, Rhinehart, and Winston.

Editorial. (2007, May 13). Hunger and food stamps. *The New York Times*, p. 11.

Eide, A. (1987). *Report on the right to food as a human right.* (E/CN.4/Sub.2/1987/23). New York: United Nations.

Ellul, J. (1967). *The technological society.* (J. Wilkinson, Trans.). New York: Vintage.

Falk, D. (1999, March). International policy on human rights. *NASW News, 44*(3), 17.

Farer, T. (1989). The United Nations and human rights: More than a whimper. In R. P. Claude & B. H. Weston (Eds.), *Human rights in the world community* (pp. 194–208). Philadelphia: University of Pennsylvania Press.

Fast, H. (1946). *The selected works of Tom Paine and citizen Tom Paine.* New York: Random House.

Fellman, G. (1998). *Rambo and the Dalai Lama: The compulsion to win and its threat to human survival.* Albany: State University of New York Press.

Fellmeth, R. (2002). *Civil rights and remedies: How the U.S. legal system affects children.* Atlanta, GA: Clarity.

Ferlinghetti, L. (1997). *A Far Rockaway of the heart.* New York: New Directions Books.

Fierman, L. (Ed.) (1965). *Effective psychotherapy. The contributions of Hellmuth Kaiser.* New York: Free Press.

Filartiga v. Pena-Irala, 630 F.2d 876 (2d Cir. 1980), 30 June 1980.

Fisher, E. & MacKay, L. (1996). *Gender justice: Women's rights are human rights,* Cambridge, MA: Unitarian Universalist Service Committee.

Foresta, D. (2005). *The experience of child welfare workers.* Unpublished qualitative research project. Springfield, MA: Springfield College School of Social Work.

Frankl, V. (1984). *Man's search for meaning.* New York: Washington Square Press.

Freire, P. (2004). *Pedagogy of the oppressed.* New York: Continuum.

Fromm-Reichmann, F. (1950). *Principles of intensive psychotherapy.* Chicago: University of Chicago Press.

Gandhi, M. (1937). Intellectual development. *Vyayam, 9*(1), 3.

Gardner, G., Assadourian, E., & Sarin, R. (2004). The state of consumption today. In L. Starke (Ed.), *State of the world: Special focus, the consumer society* (pp. 3–21). New York: W. W. Norton.

Gil, D. (1992). *Unraveling social policy* (rev. 5th ed.). Rochester, VT: Schenkman.

Gil, D. (1995) Preventing violence in a structurally violent society: Mission impossible. *American Journal of Orthopsychiatry, 44*(1), 77–84.

Gil, D. (1998). *Confronting social injustice: Concepts and strategies for social workers.* New York: Columbia University Press.

Gil, D. (2004). Perspectives on social justice. *Reflections, 10*(4), 32–39.

Gilmore, M. (1952). *The world of humanism.* New York: Harper.

Ginott, H. (2005). Pursuing human dignity: The legacies of Nuremberg for International Law, Human Rights, and Education, Conference, November 3–4. Cambridge, MA: Harvard Graduate School of Education.

Glélé-Ahanhanzo, M (1995). Report on contemporary forms of racism, racial discrimination, xenophobia and related intolerance in the USA. (E/CN.4/1995/78/Add.1). New York: Economic and Social Council, United Nations.

Goldmann, L. (1973). *The philosophy of the Enlightenment: The Christian burgess and the Enlightenment.* Cambridge, MA: MIT Press.

Gore, A. (2006). *An inconvenient truth: The planetary emergency of global warming and what we can do about it.* Emmaus, PA: Rodale.

Gross, S. (2005). *American Indian grandparents parenting their grandchildren in Michigan: A qualitative study report.* East Lansing: Michigan State University and Saginaw Inter-Tribal Center.

Hamilton, E. (1942). *Mythology: Timeless tales of gods and heroes.* New York: New American Library.

Hannah, B. (1981). *Encounters with the soul: Active imagination as developed by C.G. Jung.* Santa Monica, CA: Sigo.

Harrington, M. (1972). *Socialism.* New York: Saturday Review.

Harris, G., Carey, B., & Roberts, J. (2007, May 10). Psychiatrists, troubled children and drug industry's role. *The New York Times,* pp. A1, A20.

Hassan, R. (1982). On human rights and the Qur'anic perspective. In A. Swidler (Ed.), *Human rights in religious traditions* (pp. 51–65). New York: Pilgrim.

Healy, L. (2001). *International social work: Professional action in an interdependent world.* New York: Oxford University Press.

Heater, D. (1996). *World citizenship and government: Cosmopolitan ideas in the history of western political thought.* New York: St. Martin's.

Heidegger, M. (1959). *An introduction to metaphysics.* New Haven, CT: Yale University Press.

Higgenbotham, J. (1967). *Cicero: On moral obligation.* Berkeley: University of California Press.

Hoge, W. (2006, January 27). Rights groups fault U.S. vote in U.N on gays. *The New York Times,* p. A6.

Horne, C. (2006). The Avalon Project at Yale Law School: The Code of Hammurabi. Retrieved January 2, 2006, from www.yale.edu/lawweb/avalon/medieval/hammenu.htm

Hornstein, G. (2000). *To redeem one person is to redeem the world: The life of Freida Fromm-Reichmann.* New York: Free Press.

Human Rights Education Associates. (2007). International days. Retrieved February 11, 2007, from http://www.hrea.org/feature-events/index.html

In the Spirit of Crazy Horse. (nd). Retrieved July 18, 2006, from www.geocities.com/CapitolHill/2638/?200618

Indigenous Peoples' Literature. (2006). Crazy Horse/Tashunkewitko. Retrieved January 15, 2006, from www.indians.org/welker/crazyhor.htm

International Fourth World Movement. (2007). October 17, International Day to Eradicate Extreme Poverty. Retreived September 20, 2007, from http://www.atd-quartmonde.org/History.628.html

International Human Rights Internship Program and Asian Forum for Human Rights and Development. (2000). *Circle of rights: Economic, social, & cultural rights activism: A training resource.* Washington, DC: Author.

International Labor Organization (ILO). (2007). *Promoting decent work for all.* Retrieved September 28, 2007, from http://www.ilo.org/global/lang–en/index.htm

Iran, the Facts. (2007, March). Inside Iran. *New Internationalist,* p. 11.

Jacob Blaustein Institute. (1998). *Honoring the 50th anniversary of the Universal Declaration of Human Rights. In your hands: Community action guide for human rights year and beyond.* New York: Author.

Jacobs, A. (2006). *The spiritual wisdom of Marcus Aurelius: A poetic rendition of The Meditations.* New York: Barnes & Noble.

Jones, W. (1952). *A history of western philosophy.* New York: Harcourt Brace.

Kagan, D. (1965). *Sources in Greek political thought.* New York: Free Press.

Katz, R. (1982). *Boiling energy: Community healing among the Kalahari Kung.* Cambridge, MA: Harvard University Press.

Keen, E. (1972). *Psychology and the new consciousness.* Belmont, CA: Wadsworth.

Keith, K. (2001). *Anyway: The paradoxical commandments, finding meaning in a crazy world.* New York: G. P. Putnam.

King, C. (1987). *The words of Martin Luther King, Jr. (selected by Coretta Scott King).* New York: Newmarket Press.

Kivel, P. (2004). *You call this democracy? Who benefits, who pays, and who really decides.* New York: Apex.

Kolakowski, P. (1983). Marxism and human rights. *Daedalus, 112*(4), 81–92.

Kwitny, J. (1997). *Man of the century: Life and times of Pope John Paul II.* New York: Henry Holt.

Laing, R. D. (1962). Ontological insecurity. In H. Ruitenbeck (Ed.), *Psychoanalysis and existential philosophy* (pp. 41–69). New York: E. P. Dutton.

Laing, R. D. (1983). *Politics of experience.* New York: Pantheon.

Lappe, F., Collins, J., & Rosset, P. (1998). *World hunger: 12 myths* (2nd rev. ed.). New York: Grove.

Laqueur, W. & Rubin, B. (Eds.). (1990). *The human rights reader* (rev. ed.). New York: New American Library.

Larson, R. (2002). *Venture forth! The essential guide to starting a moneymaking business in your nonprofit organization.* Saint Paul, MN: Amherst H. Wilder Foundation.

Laski, H. (1925). *A defense of liberty against tyrants.* (J. Brutus, Trans.). New York: Harcourt Brace.

Lauffer, A. (1997). *Grants, etc.* (2nd ed.). Thousand Oaks, CA: Sage.

Lerner, M. (1991). *Surplus powerlessness: The psychodynamics of everyday life* (rev. ed.). Atlantic Highlands, NJ: Humanities Press.

Levinas, E. (2001). *Totality and infinity* (4th ed., A. Lingis, Trans.). New York: Springer.

Lifton, R. (1967). *Death in life: Survivors of Hiroshima.* New York: Simon & Schuster.

Lifton, R. (2000). *Nazi doctors: Medical killing and the psychology of genocide.* New York: Basic Books.

Link, R., & Healy, L. (2005). *Teaching international content: Curriculum resources for social work education.* Alexandria, VA: Council on Social Work Education.

Lloyd-Jones, H. (1971). *The justice of Zeus.* Berkeley: University of California Press.

Lorenz, W. (1994). *Social work in a changing Europe.* London: Routledge.

Machiavelli, N. (1975). *Machiavelli: The prince.* (G. Bull, Trans.). Baltimore: Penguin.

Mann, J., & Tarantola, D. (1998). Responding to HIV/AIDS: A historical perspective. *Health and Human Rights, 2*(4), 5–8.

Marcel. G. (1965). *Being and having.* (K. Farrer, Trans.). New York: Collins.

Marcel, G. (1967). *Homo viator: Introduction to a metaphysic of hope*, (E. Crawford, Trans.). Magnolia, MA: Peter Smith.

Marshall, C., & Rossman, G. (1999). *Designing qualitative research* (3rd ed.). Thousand Oaks, CA: Sage.

Marshall, J. (2006). Crazy Horse (Tasunke Witko). In *Encyclopedia of North American Indians*. Retrieved February 8, 2006, from www.college.hmco.com/history/readers comp/naind/html/na_08900_crazyhorse.htm

Maslow, A. (1987). *Motivation and personality* (3rd ed.). New York: HarperCollins.

Mawn, B. (1998). Integrating women's perspectives on prenatal HIV screening: Toward a socially just policy. *Research, Nursing & Health, 21,* 499–509.

McCartney, I. (2007, March 13). *Statement by the United Kingdom of Great Britain and Northern Ireland by the Minister of the Foreign and Commonwealth Office.* Geneva: United Nations Human Rights Council.

McCracken, G. (1987). *The long interview.* Newbury Park, CA: Sage.

McQuillar, D. (2005). *The effects of schizophrenia on family relationships from the perspective of the person diagnosed with schizophrenia.* Unpublished qualitative research project. Springfield, MA: Springfield College School of Social Work.

Merleau-Ponty, M. (1964). *Signs,* (R. McCleary, Trans.). Evanston, IL: Northwestern University Press.

Merleau-Ponty, M. (1967). *The phenomenology of perception.* (C. Smith, Trans.) New York: Routledge and Kegan Paul.

Mihesuah, D. (1996). *Native American myths and realities.* Atlanta, GA: Clarity.

Milgram, S., Sabini, J., & Silver, M. (1992). *The individual in a social world: Essays and experiments* (2nd ed.). New York: McGraw-Hill.

Minkowitz, T., Galves, A., Brown, C., Kovary, M., & Remba, E. (2006). Alternative Report on Forced Drugging, Forced Electroshock, and Mental Health Screen of Children in Violation of Article 7. Retrieved September 21, 2006, from www .ushrnetwork.org/pubs/

Montanari, S. (2005, September/October). Global climate change linked to increasing world hunger. *Worldwatch: Vision for a sustainable world, 18*(5), 6.

Morgenson, G. (2004, January 25). Explaining (or not) why the boss is paid so much. *The New York Times,* sec. 3, p. 1.

Moss, D. (2001). The roots and genealogy of humanistic psychology. In K. Schneider, J. Bugental, & J. Pierson (Eds.), *The handbook of humanistic psychology* (pp. 5–20). Newbury Park, CA: Sage.

Moustakas, C. (1990). *Heuristic research: Design, methodology, and applications.* Newbury Park, CA: Sage.

Moustakas, C. (1994). *Phenomenological research.* Newbury Park, CA: Sage.

Moustakas, C. (1997). *Relationship play therapy.* Northvale, NJ: Jason Aronson.

Northeastern University Program on Human Rights and the Global Economy, Law School and Suffolk University Law School. (2007). *Human rights for all: A training resource on the local implementation of International Human Rights to Protect Human Dignity and Freedom.* Boston: Author.

Numbers. (2007, July 2). *Time Magazine,* p. 18.

Palumbo, M. (1982). *Human rights: Meaning and history.* Malabar, FL: Krieger.

Partington, A. (1992). *The Oxford dictionary of quotations* (4th ed.). New York: Oxford University Press.

Peace Pilgrim. (1991). *Peace pilgrim: Her life and work in her own words.* Sante Fe, NM: Ocean Tree.

Poor People's Economic Human Rights Campaign. (2006). Report from the National Truth Commission. Retrieved September 5, 2006, from www.economichumanrights .org/ntc_report1.shtml

Prokosch, M., & Raymond, L. (2002). *The global activist's manual: Local ways to change the world.* New York: Thunder's Mouth Press.

Public Broadcasting System. (2000). *Eleanor Roosevelt* (Home Video). Burbank, CA: Time Warner Entertainment.

Real, T. (1997). *I don't want to talk about it: Overcoming men's depression.* New York: Scribner.

Reardon, B. (1995). *Educating for human dignity: Learning about rights and responsibilities, a K-12 teaching resource.* Philadelphia: University of Pennsylvania Press.

Reichert, E. (2006). *Understanding human rights: An exercise book.* Newbury Park, CA: Sage.

Reinharz, S. (1992). *Feminist methods in social research.* New York: Oxford University Press.

Resnais, A. (1955). *Night and fog.* Film available at: www.amazon.com

Renner, M. (2005, September/October). Military spending near record high. *Worldwatch: Vision for a sustainable world, 18*(5), 7.

Riak, J. (5 May, 2001). Letter to the editor. *The New York Times,* p. A23.

Ricoeur, P. (1967). *The symbolism of evil.* Boston: Beacon Press (under the auspices of the Unitarian Universalist Association).

Robinson, A. (2001). *Selling social change (without selling out).* San Francisco: Jossey-Bass.

Rogers, C. (1995). *On becoming a person: A therapist's view of psychotherapy.* Boston: Houghton Mifflin.

Roosevelt, F. (1941). "Four Freedoms" Speech, 87-I Cong. Rec. 4, 46–47.

Roque, F. P. (2007, March 13). Statement of the Republic of Cuba at the 4th Session of the Human Rights Council. Geneva: United Nations Human Rights Council.

Rosenstock-Huessy, E. (1969). *Out of revolution: Autobiography of western man.* Norwich, VT: Argo.

Sachs, J. (2005). *The end of poverty: Economic possibilities for our time.* New York: Penguin.

Safransky, S. (Ed.). 1990. *Sunbeams: A book of quotations.* Berkeley, CA: North Atlantic Books.

Saint Exupery, A. (1971). *The little prince.* (K. Woods, Trans.). New York: Harcourt, Brace Jovanovich.

Sartre, J. (1957). *The transcendence of the ego: An existentialist theory of consciousness,* (A. Brown, Trans.). New York: Noonday.

Sartre, J. (1993). *The emotions: Outline of a theory,* (B. Frechtman, Trans.). New York: Philosophical Library.

Sartre, J. (1995). *Anti-Semite and Jew: An exploration of the etiology of hate.* (M. Walzer Trans. & Ed.). New York: Schocken.

Sebring, H., Beals, W., & Crawford, J. (1999). The judgment, Aug. 20, 1947. In J. Mann, S. Gruskin, M. Grodin, & G. Annas (Eds.), *Health and human rights* (pp. 292–300). London: Routledge.

Selye, H. (1978). *The stress of life.* New York: McGraw-Hill.

Seville Statement on Violence. (1990). *American Psychologist, 45*(10), 1167–1168.

Sharp, G. (2005). *Waging nonviolent struggle: 20th century practice and 21st century potential.* Boston: Porter Sargent.

Skoll Foundation. (2005). About social entrepreneurship. Retrieved January 2, 2006, from www.skollfoundation.org/aboutsocialentrepreneurship/index.asp

Social Responsibility Report for GAP. (2005). Retrieved December 17, 2005, from www.business-humanrights.org

Southern Poverty Law Center. (2005, December). Monitoring hate, teaching tolerance, seeking justice. *Southern Poverty Law Center Report. 35*(4), 4.

Spirer, H. & Spirer, L. (1993). *Data analysis for monitoring human rights.* Washington, DC: American Association for the Advancement of Science.

Steiner, H., & Alston, P. (2000). *International human rights in context: Laws, politics, morals.* (2nd ed.). New York: Oxford University Press.

Sterling Entertainment Group. (1992). *Malcolm X: Death of a prophet.* Available from: Sterling Entertainment Group, Fort Mill, SC 29708.

Stone, D. (2001). *Policy paradox: The art of political decision making* (3rd ed.). New York: W. W. Norton.

Stubbe, D. W., & Thomas, W. J. (2002). A survey of early-career child and adolescent psychiatrists: Professional activities and perceptions. *Journal of the American Academy of Child and Adolescent Psychiatry, 41,* 123–130.

Szabo, I. (1982). Historical foundations of human rights and subsequent developments. In K. Vasak (Ed.), *The international dimensions of human rights.* (Vol. 1, pp.11–41). Westport, CT: Greenwood.

Tillich, P. (2000). *The courage to be.* New Haven, CT: Yale University Press.

Tomasevski, K. (1993). *Women and human rights.* Atlantic Highlands, NJ: Zed Books.

Tucker, R. (1978). *The Marx-Engels Reader* (2nd ed.). New York: W. W. Norton.

UNESCO. (2006). *Plan of action: World program for human rights education.* New York: Author.

United Nations. (1948–1949). *Yearbook of the United Nations.* Lake Success, NY: UN Department of Public Information.

United Nations. (1986). *ABC, teaching human rights.* New York: UNESCO.

United Nations. (1994). *Human rights and social work: A manual for schools of social work and the social work profession.* New York: Author.

United Nations. (2000). *International Convention on the Elimination of all Forms of Racial Discrimination: Report submitted by the United States of America.* (CERD/C/351/Add.1). New York: Author.

United Nations. (2001). *Concluding observations on the Committee on the Elimination of Racial Discrimination.* (A/56/18. paras. 380–407). New York: Author.

United Nations. (2006). United Nations conferences: What have they accomplished? Retrieved January 15, 2006, from http://www.un.org/News/facts/confercs.htm

United Nations. (2007). Periodic report of the U.S. to the U.N. Committee on the Elimination of Racial Discrimination. Retrieved from April 28, 2007, from http://www.state.gov/documents/organization/83517.pdf

UN Development Program. (2005). *Human development report. International cooperation at a crossroads: Aid, trade and security in an unequal world.* New York: Author.

UN Human Rights Expert. (2006, September 27). *International Herald Tribune,* pp. 1–2.

U.S. Census Bureau. (2007). Statistical tables. Retrieved April 18, 2007, from www.census.gov/statab/

U.S. Department of State. (1995). *Response to the UN Special Rapporteur's Report on Racism and Other Forms of Intolerance in the United States of America.* Washington, DC: Author.

U.S. Department of State. (2003). Human Rights Day, Bill of Rights Day, and Human Rights Week: A proclamation by the President of the USA. Retrieved March 16, 2003, from www.state.gov/g/drl/rls/rm/15808.htm

U.S. Department of State Report on Country's Human Rights Practices. (1993). Washington, DC: Government Printing Office.

Van Wormer, K. (1997). *Social welfare: A world view.* Chicago: Nelson-Hall.

Vos van Steenwijk, A. (1996). *Father Joseph Wresinski: Voice of the poorest.* Santa Barbara, CA: Queenship.

Warwick, M., Hart, T., & Allen, N. (2002). *Fundraising on the Internet.* San Francisco: Jossey-Bass.

Washington, J. (Ed.) 1986. *A testament of hope: The essential writings and speeches of Martin Luther King, Jr.* San Francisco: HarperCollins.

Weissbrodt, D., Fitzpatrick, J., & Newman, F. (2001). *International human rights: Law, policy, and process.* Cincinnati, OH: Anderson.

Weissbrodt, D., Fitzpatrick, J., Newman, F., Hoffman, M., & Rumsey, M. (2001). *Selected international human rights instruments and bibliography for research on international human rights law.* (3rd ed.). Cincinnati, OH: Anderson.

Weston, B. (1989). Human rights. In R. Claude & B. Weston (Eds.), *Human rights in the world community* (pp. 208–220). Philadelphia: University of Pennsylvania Press.

Wiesel, E. (2006). *Night.* New York: Hill and Wang.

Williams, C. (1991). *Black teenage mothers: Pregnancy and childrearing from their perspective.* Cambridge, MA: Lexington.

Wilson, T. (2005, December 29). Don't think twice, it's all right. *The New York Times,* p. A27.

Wolcott, H. (2001). *Writing up qualitative research.* Newbury Park, CA: Sage.

Workshop on Data Collection and Disaggregation for Indigenous Peoples. (2004). *The concept of Indigenous Peoples* (PFII/2004/WS.1/3). Geneva: United Nations Department of Economic and Social Affairs.

World Almanac and Book of Facts. (2005). New York: World Almanac Books.

Wronka, J. (1993). Science and Indigenous cultures. *Humanistic Psychologist, 21,* 341–353.

Wronka, J. (1995a). Human rights. In R. Edwards (Ed.), *Encyclopedia of social work* (pp. 1404–1418). Washington, DC: National Association of Social Work.

Wronka, J. (1995b). On the human rights committee's consideration of the initial report of the USA on the International Covenant on Civil and Political Rights. *Human rights interest group newsletter of the American Society of International Law,* (5)3, 14–16.

Wronka, J. (1998a, Summer). A little humility, please: Human rights and social policy in the United States. *Harvard International Review, 20*(3), 72–75.

Wronka, J. (1998b). *Human rights and social policy in the 21st century: A history of the idea of human rights and comparison of the United Nations Universal Declaration of Human Rights with United States federal and state constitutions* (rev. ed). Lanham, MD: University Press of America.

Wronka, J. (2001a). Eradicating the legacy of slavery in US research and policy. In Y. Kly & D. Kly (Eds)., *In pursuit of the right to self-determination: Collected papers and proceedings of the First International Conference on the Right to Self-determination and the United Nations, Geneva 2000* (pp. 201–203) Atlanta, GA: Clarity.

Wronka, J. (2001b, July). Human Rights House Bill No. 850: A request for support. *NASW News, 46*(7), 4.

Wronka, J. (2004). Human rights and advanced generalist practice. In A. Roy & F. Vecchiolla (Eds.). *Thoughts on advanced generalist education: Models, readings, and essays* (pp. 223–242). Peosta, IA: Eddie Bowers.

Wronka, J. (2007). Global distributive justice as a human right: Implications for the creation of a human rights culture. In E. Reichert (Ed.). *Challenges in human rights: A social work perspective.* (pp. 44–75). New York: Columbia University Press.

Zinn, H. (1990). *A people's history of the United States.* New York: Harper & Row.

Zola, I. (1983). *Socio-medical inquiries.* Philadelphia: Temple University Press.

Index

About the Author

Dr. Joseph Wronka is Professor of Social Work at Springfield College, Springfield, Massachusetts, and Principal Investigator of the Universal Declaration of Human Rights Project, originating in the Center for Social Change at the Heller School for Social Policy and Management, Brandeis University. His PhD in social policy is from the Heller School's Center for Social Change. His Master's is in existential-phenomenological psychology with a clinical-community concentration from Duquesne University. He has also studied the phenomenology of the performing musician at the University of Nice, France. Select academic appointments have included West Georgia College, St. Francis College, New York University, Ramapo College, College of the Holy Cross, Simmons, Chukchi Community College, the University of Alaska, Fairbanks, Boston College, and schools of social work at Berne, Switzerland, and Sankt-Poelton and Vienna, Austria. He was also a counselor at alcoholism and methadone maintenance treatment centers, a clinician in private practice and community mental health centers, a director of a mental health/substance abuse center, a human rights commissioner, and Vice President of the World Citizen Foundation. Currently, he is an advisory board member for the Coalition for a Strong United Nations, Boston, MA, president of Human Rights Action International, Amherst, MA, and honorary advisory board member for the International Center for Human Rights, Brussels, Belgium. He recently represented the International Association of Schools of Social Work at the sixth session of the UN Human Rights Council in Geneva, Switzerland. Published widely in popular and scholarly forums, he has presented his work in roughly 14 countries. His interest is primarily in the development of social change strategies to implement human rights standards, which mirror substantively millennia of the teaching of various spiritual and ethical belief systems, so that every person, everywhere can live with human dignity and achieving their potential, without discrimination. He likes to swim laps, bike ride, play classical music on the piano and concert and international pieces on the accordion, and fish from his kayak.